Y0-DYG-718

ESSAYS AND SKETCHES

Volume III

John Henry Cardinal Newman

ESSAYS AND SKETCHES

Volume III

GREENWOOD PRESS, PUBLISHERS
WESTPORT, CONNECTICUT

First Greenwood Reprinting 1970

SBN 8371-2842-0 (SET)
SBN 8371-2841-2 (VOL. 3)

PRINTED IN UNITED STATES OF AMERICA

PREFACE

ALL OF THE MATERIALS in this volume, except the final essay, are from the second volume of Newman's *Historical Sketches* (1872–73); the last essay is from *Discussions and Arguments* (1872). None of the texts have been altered or abridged. There have been, however, certain omissions: from "The Church of the Fathers," I have omitted the chapters devoted to Demetrias and to Martin and Maximus. Also omitted from the *Historical Sketches* is the paper on the "Trials of Theodoret." These omissions were unavoidable if the texts in the rest of volume two of the *Sketches* were to remain intact.

Of the essays here reprinted only those entitled "The Church of the Fathers" saw independent publication before the 1870's. After its appearance in the *British Magazine* in 1833, it was published anonymously as a volume in 1840, and saw four editions by 1868. Between 1871 and 1874 Newman gathered his uncollected essays, as they had appeared in the *British Critic*, the *British Magazine*, the *Month*, the *Rambler*, and *Atlantis*, and republished them under the titles we have already had occasion to note. Thus not only "The Church of the Fathers" but also "St. Chrysostom," and the "Benedictine Schools," came out in the second volume of *Historical Sketches* in 1873. Since that date the text has remained unchanged.

We may note in conclusion that from the third volume of *Historical Sketches*, the following have been omitted from these present volumes: "The Northmen and Normans in

England and Ireland," "Medieval Oxford," and "The Convocation of the Province of Canterbury." Even with these omissions—which comparatively inferior quality would seem to justify—the present volume gives the reader a broad view of Newman's interests and writings, from the early years of the Tractarian Movement to the years immediately following the publication of the *Apologia.*

Charles Frederick Harrold

The Ohio State University
Columbus, Ohio
April 25, 1947

CONTENTS

INTRODUCTION

AMONG THE RESULTS of Newman's decision in 1828 to engage in a chronological reading of the early Fathers of the Church was not merely his *Arians of the Fourth Century* (1833), but also a much more "popular" work which appeared in the *British Magazine*, in 1833 and the following years, under the title of *The Church of the Fathers*. In the Advertisement with which he prefaces its reprinting in the second volume of *Historical Sketches*, he tells us that he aims merely "to illustrate . . . the tone and modes of thought, the habits and manners of the early times of the Church, . . . bringing out or recommending one or two of the characteristics of primitive Christianity." Though principally historical, these sketches are, he adds, "in their form and character polemical, as being directed against certain Protestant ideas and opinions." Newman is writing as a high Anglican, from a point of view which is Catholic while not being Roman, addressing himself to Anglicans, and presenting to them the ideals of fourth and fifth century Christianity. He is profuse in his quotations from the letters of Basil and Gregory, from biographical materials relative to St. Anthony and St. Augustine. His translations of these documents, he assures the reader, will "express in English the *sense* of the original, the actual words of the latter being viewed mainly as *directions into* its sense." He admits to omissions of passages and to condensations of sentences, "a studious endeavour being all along made to preserve the sense from injury." Manifesting here, once more, how often his works are of an "occasional," even an amateurish, character, he says that "where something must be sacrificed, precision or intelligibility, it is better in a popular work to be understood by those who are not critics, than to be applauded by those who are."

The Church of the Fathers has long had many admirers. The Abbé Bremond, commenting especially on the Introduction to "St. Chrysostom," declares that "kindred masters in opposite camps, a Sainte-Beuve, a Renan, would have gladly put their names to this lively, joyous, and confident preface; and if they had read the 'Chrysostom' . . . they would have saluted in Newman one of their equals." And of course, such a writer as Denys Gorce, in his *Newman et les pères,* will naturally grow enthusiastic as he notes the degree in which Newman "naturalizes" himself in the realm of the early Fathers of the fourth century, as he more and more speaks their language, adopts their imagery, and enters into their ideals of the monastic life. Though the literary quality of *The Church of the Fathers* is extremely uneven, there are enough distinguished passages in it to keep it alive as literature, and enough autobiographical intimations in it to preserve its value for any student of Newman's life and thought. One notes his evident feeling of kinship between himself and Basil and Gregory. These early saints had, like Newman, a background of Christian humanism; both had a Newman-like conception of "the gentleman," even as monk. In the other chapters of *The Church of the Fathers,* one discerns the common ground of bitterness of misunderstanding experienced by such diverse personalities as Basil and Augustine, Gregory and Chrysostom and Anthony. In their sufferings Newman saw, as it were, a reflection of his own. Like him, they had all been forced to fight for their integrity in an age, like his own, given up to unbelief and disintegration. Their dreams, their symbolism, their very superstitions (in so far as they were such), their thought-patterns enter deeply into Newman's mind, and make him feel at home in their almost Apostolic, certainly (to him) un-Protestant world. The reader of *The*

Church of the Fathers is struck with the frequency with which Newman turns from his fourth century subject-matters and delivers brief thrusts at "Wesleyanism," Calvin, or the Evangelical liberalism of his own Church. His work on the Fathers is, of course, just as much a part of the Tractarian Movement as the Tracts themselves. Here we see how early Newman had placed himself, spiritually and intellectually, in the world of early Monachism, of "austerities, prayers, retirement, and obedience." Long before he became an "Anglo-Catholic" he had already felt with St. Basil "a profound sense of the world's nothingness and the world's defilement." But he was still sure that the Anglican Church had within her the fundamentals of a truly Catholic institution. She needed but to be shown her primitive roots in the early Fathers for her to throw off whatever was Protestant in her and take up again her rightful place in the great Catholic tradition of Christianity. To show her the way was, in some degree, the aim of Newman's *Church of the Fathers.*

"The Last Years of St. Chrysostom" first appeared in the pages of the *Rambler,* 1859–60. It was an attempt to bring before the reader's mind St. John Chrysostom in both his personal and his ethical aspects. Originally it was planned as part of a projected volume, to be entitled *Ancient Saints,* and to include such other figures as St. Ambrose, St. Jerome, and perhaps St. Athanasius. With the publication of the chapters on St. Chrysostom and on the trials of Theodoret, Newman reluctantly gave up the hope of completing the series of historical studies. This was the period in Newman's life when his fortunes were at their lowest. In Wilfrid Ward's *Life of Newman,* the chapter covering 1859–64 is entitled "Sad Days." Almost every work he had undertaken as a Catholic had failed. He had no premonition of how the year 1864 was to bring him his great opportunity to vindicate himself, and to make himself once more a power in the land For the present he clung to his humble duties. And we can fancy him turning, in his leisure hours, to the writing of his volume on *Ancient Saints*. Certainly the Introduction to "St. Chrysostom" gives us an almost intimate glimpse of Newman's enthusiasm in the privacy of his study, where he could withdraw from the harshness of nineteenth-century Birmingham and commune with one of the great saints, through the 240 letters which the world had inherited. Here he could luxuriate in tracing "the real, hidden but human, life, or the *interior*" of St. John Chrysostom. That saint's real life, as seen in his letters, impressed him with "the idea of moral unity, identity, growth, continuity, personality." He could say of Chrysostom what he also says of Augustine and Basil, that in reading his letters, one "holds converse with a beautiful, grace-illumined soul, looking out into this world of sense, and leavening it with itself." On the other hand, Newman wishes to remember that the saints were human and had their weaknesses; and he expects to write of them without too much regard for "the endemic perennial fidget which possesses us about giving scandal."

The chapters which follow the Introduction are leisurely, loosely contrived, burdened with lengthy and often tedious quotations from Chrysostom's letters. But one does not soon forget the famous passage on "The Euxine! that strange mysterious sea . . . " or the splendid account, at the beginning of Chapter V, of St. Chrysostom's peculiar charm. At times we find Newman at his most concrete and idiomatic: after saying that the saint is to undergo "cold and heat, wind and rain, night-air, bad lodging, unwholesome water, long footmarches, rough-paced mules," Newman adds quietly, "He was to die by inches; want of sleep, want of rest, want of food and medicine . . . were to extinguish the brave spirit which hitherto had risen superior to all sorrows." Thus there is throughout the whole account of Chrysostom that realism and concreteness which, in spite of frequent *longueurs*, keeps Chrysostom the man steadily before our mind. We may lament Newman's failure to keep his chronology straight; we may admire his geographical accuracy in following Chrysostom's tragic itinerary; in any case, we realize that Newman, in the privacy of his reading, truly experienced a living communion with St. John the "Golden-mouthed."

The papers on St. Benedict and the Benedictine schools were originally entitled "The Benedictine Centuries," and appeared in the *Atlantis* magazine (which Newman helped to found) in 1858–59. They were in fact part of Newman's general effort to inform Victorian Catholics, to orient them in the intellectual situation of their time. The *Atlantis* had been planned as a solid uncontroversial magazine devoted to literature and science. It was indeed a part of the Catholic university scheme on which Newman had worked for so many years; and its object was to keep Catholics abreast of the times, especially in relation to science, history, literature, and research.

In "The Benedictine Centuries"—later to be re-titled "Benedictine Schools"—Newman set forth the conservative habit of the Benedictines of the eighth and ninth centuries, those centuries which fall between the Patristic and the Scholastic ages, centuries popularly known as the "Dark Ages." In both the Patristic and the Scholastic periods theologians and men of learning were compelled to place Christianity in relation to the intellectual life of their time; the rise of heresy and the growth of theology alone demanded such an effort. Newman recognized that nineteenth-century England offered just such an opportunity as the thirteenth century for creative thinking in religion. His age had more affinity with the age of Origen and the great times of St. Thomas than with the Benedictine monasteries of the eighth century. But not many of Newman's Catholic contemporaries seemed to be aware of this fact; they took their stand on an uncreative opposition to all the vital thought of the day. Newman realized that there is a time for conservatism and a time for advance. So he wrote "The Benedictine Centuries" to show, historically, how a justly conservative spirit could, and should, flourish under the proper circumstances. The Patristic era had been succeeded by a period of theological conservatism because the world was "old, decayed, and moribund. . . . Society was in the slow fever of consumption, [but] it was powerful to seduce and deprave." The one, natural idea of the Benedictines was flight from this world and this society, which was so troubled, jaded, stricken, and corrupt that only by negative measures could the religious mind come to terms with it. It was an age in which the one thing needful was a pause, and the preservation of the theological treasures of antiquity, rather than creative additions which would probably be misunderstood and misused. Thus the age brought out the true Benedictine genius, that of peace and prayer and seclusion, of faithful conservatism, not of bold speculation. The Benedictines' object, says Newman, "was rest and peace; their state was retirement; their occupation was some work that was simple, as opposed to intellectual, viz., prayer, fasting, meditation, study, transcription, manual labor. . . ." The Benedictines were the stewards of a great treasure. But when the speculative intellect again was stirred to life, when the mind of Abelard disturbed the ancient peace of the Church, and Arabian pantheism and Aristotelianism and Jewish speculation later invaded the Christian Schools, the challenge was one for which the Benedictine mentality was not prepared. The Benedictine schools had been admirable institutions for educating the young, excellent defenses and retreats in an age of barbarism. But with the rise of universities and the growth of heresies, bolder intellects came to the front. In the very title of St. Thomas Aquinas' *Summa contra Gentiles,* we see something of the nature and scope of the new problems. As Aquinas developed his synthetic philosophy and theology, turning Aristotle into a hewer of wood and a drawer of water for the Church, and uniting the resources of ancient thought with his own, the Benedictine age, historically speaking, saw its twilight, and gave way to the Dominican.

Though "The Benedictine Centuries" may have been a negative way of calling for a *Novum Organum* in nineteenth-century theology, there is much evidence in the work that Newman was as thoroughly at home with the Benedictines as he was with St. John Chrysostom. The style of the two papers, "The Mission of St. Benedict" and "The Benedictine Schools," has a notable unity of effect, a quiet and almost soliloquizing tone, as if Newman had found just the subject suited to his mood. These papers have a slow, majestic beginning; they proceed in the leisurely fashion of a man at one with his subject, and in no hurry to reach the end. Nowhere has Newman better stated the nature of Monachism than in section three of "The Mission of St. Benedict"; nowhere has he more poetically described a region than in his account of the location of Benedictine abbeys, in section eight. "The Benedictine Schools" has perhaps less vigor and interest than the first paper, but it does have its excellent passages, as in section two: "The lonely Benedictine rose from his knees and found himself a city. . . ." Slowly and gravely Newman follows the Benedictines as they gradually emerge from their cloisters and take up some of the burdens of the world—in education, in politics, in the administration of property. We see them become involved in the tremendous revolutions consequent on the rule of Charlemagne, so that eventually the monks who had once been so withdrawn from the world now found themselves "grown into large communities, into abbeys, into corporations with civil privileges, into land-holders with tenants, serfs, and baronial neighbors." It is all told in a calm, clear voice, as if Newman were conversing with us quietly among his books.

The final essay in the present volume is a review of J. R. Seeley's *Ecce Homo* (1865), published in the *Month* magazine of June, 1866. Like the review of Milman's *History of Christianity,* in volume two, it is a good example of Newman's religious journalism. It shows him characteristically entering into Seeley's point of view, doing the writer full justice, then turning about and letting his mind play devastatingly on Seeley's shortcomings. *Ecce Homo* had been the sensation of the season. It had appealed especially to one class of Anglicans, those brilliantly described in section three of the review—those "who love the conclusions of Catholic theology better than the proofs, and the methods of modern thought better than its results." Newman's review is important in that it not only reflects the religious situation of the 1860's in England but also expresses the continuing conflict between the Liberal tendency to be eclectic and the Catholic staunchness in holding an organic view of Christianity. Thus Newman is appalled not simply by the author's "bad logic," "rash and gratuitous assumptions," and "half-digested thought," but even more by his arbitrary selections of those portions of Christianity which happen to appeal to his mind. A comparison of this review with that of Milman's volume will show how little Newman's standpoint has changed between 1841 and 1866. Four years before his conversion to Rome, he had written with as Catholic a touch as he was to display twenty-five years later.

—C.F.H.

I

THE CHURCH OF THE FATHERS

Quæ est ista, quæ progreditur quasi aurora consurgens, terribilis ut castrorum acies ordinata?

TO MY DEAR AND MUCH-ADMIRED

ISAAC WILLIAMS, B.D.

FELLOW OF TRINITY COLLEGE, OXFORD;

THE SIGHT OF WHOM

CARRIES BACK HIS FRIENDS

TO ANCIENT, HOLY, AND HAPPY TIMES.

Feb. 21, 1840.

INTRODUCTION

THIS IS A WORLD of conflict, and of vicissitude amid the conflict. The Church is ever militant; sometimes she gains, sometimes she loses; and more often she is at once gaining and losing in different parts of her territory. What is ecclesiastical history but a record of the ever-doubtful fortune of the battle, though its issue is not doubtful? Scarcely are we singing *Te Deum*, when we have to turn to our *Miserere*s: scarcely are we in peace, when we are in persecution: scarcely have we gained a triumph, when we are visited by a scandal. Nay, we make progress by means of reverses; our griefs are our consolations; we lose Stephen, to gain Paul, and Matthias replaces the traitor Judas.

It is so in every age; it is so in the nineteenth century; it was so in the fourth; and about the fourth I am proposing to write. An eventful century, a drama in three acts, each marvellous in itself, each different from the other two! The first is the history of the Roman Empire becoming Christian; the second, that of the indefectible Church of God seeming to succumb to Arianism; the third, that of countless barbarians pouring in upon both Empire and Christendom together. And, as the great convulsions of the earth involve innumerable commotions in detail and local revolutions, and each district and neighbourhood has its own story of distress and confusion, so, in the events of the social world, what is done in the camp or synod vibrates in every town and in every bishopric. From one end of the century to the other, the most momentous changes and the most startling vicissitudes took place; and the threshold of the Apostles was now darkened by messengers of ill, and now lit up with hope and thanksgiving.

So was it in the fourth century; so will it be to the end:

Thus bad and good their several warnings give
Of His approach, whom none may see and live.
  Faith's ear, with awful still delight,
  Counts them like minute bells by night,
Keeping the heart awake till dawn of morn,
While to her funeral pile this aged world is borne.

However, I am attempting here, neither the grand outlines, nor the living details of the century, but some scenes or passages which chronologically or morally belong to it. And I preface them with this allusion to the century itself, because they are thereby duly located, and receive their proper colour. And now, without more words, I shall begin my course, travelling after the sun from East to West: beginning with Greece and Asia Minor, and then visiting, in succession, Egypt, Africa, Spain, and Gaul, where I shall come to an end.

CHAPTER I

TRIALS OF BASIL

"As a servant longeth for the shade, as the hireling looketh for the end of his work, so I also have had empty months, and wearisome nights have I numbered unto me."

I

AS ATHANASIUS WAS the great champion of the Catholic Faith, while the Arians were in the ascendant, so Basil and Gregory in the East, and Ambrose in the West, were the chief instruments of Providence in repairing and strengthening its bulwarks, by word, writing, and deed, when the fury of their assaults was spent. I am not concerned just now with the great Western luminary, Ambrose, but with Basil and Gregory. Of these two saints, one had to contend with an Arian sovereign, the other with an Arian populace; and they gained the victory, each on his own field of battle, the one with the loss of his see, the other at the sacrifice of his life. Premature death, a solitary old age, were the contrary destinies of two great saints and dear friends; the labours of Basil were cut short, and the penances of Gregory were lengthened out. The scene of Gregory's struggle was the imperial city of Constantinople; of Basil's, the length and breadth of Asia Minor and the adjoining provinces. These countries had from the first been overrun by the heretics, and, as far as religion was concerned, were, in the middle of the fourth century, in a deplorable state of confusion. Basil's care of the churches, in that time of trouble, as that of a Missionary or Preacher, extended far beyond the limits of his own jurisdiction; for by ecclesiastical right he was only priest first, and afterwards bishop, of the church of Cæsarea, and exarch of the remote and barbarous Cappadocia, from A.D. 358 to A.D. 379.

At the former of these dates, Dianius was in possession of the see. He seems to have baptized Basil, who speaks warmly in his praise, expressing the affection and respect he felt for him, and the pleasure he took in his society; and describing him as a man remarkable for his virtue, as frank, generous, and venerable, while he was amiable and agreeable in his manners. However, he fell in with the fashion of the age, and had for nearly twenty years sided with the court faction against Athanasius and his holy cause. Accordingly, he signed without scruple the heretical formulary of the council of Ariminum, which was presented to him A.D. 360, and in which the test of the Homoüsion, or Consubstantial, contained in the Nicene Creed, was abandoned, and the Catholic doctrine evaded under the pretence of expressing it only in terms of Scripture. Basil felt bitterly this weakness, to give it its mildest name, on the part of one he so much loved; and though he did not consider that there was a call on him for any public protest, he ceased to hold intercourse with him, nor did he come near him till two years afterwards, when Dianius sent for him to attend his death-bed, and professed solemnly his adherence to the faith of the Church.

Eusebius, the successor of Dianius, was a bishop of orthodox profession, but had little of the theological knowledge or force of character necessary for coping with the formidable heresy by which the Church was assailed. For some reason or other, perhaps from a feeling of jealousy, he manifested a coldness towards the rising theologian, who is to be the subject of this chapter; and Basil, who was now a priest, unwilling to excite the people, or create parties in the Church, retired from the metropolitan city.

2

HIS RETREAT, BOTH NOW and in the lifetime of Dianius, was the wild region of Pontus, where he had founded a number of monasteries, over one of which he presided. He had retired thither first about A.D. 355 (the year in which the Egyptian St. Antony, the first Solitary, died), for the purposes of study and mortification; and to a mind ardent and sensitive, such as his, nothing was more welcome than such a temporary retreat from the turbulence of ecclesiastical politics. Nor was his life at this time one of inaction or solitude. On occasion of a famine in the neighbouring town and country, he converted his lands into money, to supply the wants of the people; taking upon himself particularly the charge of their children, besides relieving all who applied to him, among whom the Jews are mentioned as receiving a share in his liberality. His monasteries became, in a short time, schools of that holy teaching which had been almost banished from the sees of Asia; and it is said that he was in the practice of making a circuit of the neighbouring towns, from time to time, to preach to them the Nicene doctrine. This indeed was a benefit which was not unfrequently rendered to the Church, in that day of apostasy, by the ascetics, according to the promise that they who have a clean heart shall see God.

The reason, [says Sozomen] why the doctrines [of the heretics Eunomius and Apollinaris] had not any extensive success, in addition to the causes above mentioned, is, that the Solitaries of the day took part against them. For those of Syria and Cappadocia, and the neighbouring districts, firmly adhered to the creed of Nicæa. At one time, the oriental provinces, from Cilicia to Phœnicia, were near becoming Apollinarian, while those from Cilicia and the Taurus to the Hellespont and Constantinople were exposed to the heresy of Eunomius; each heresiarch having success in his own neighbourhood. And then the history of Arianism was acted over again; for the populace in those parts had that reverence for the characters and the works of the Solitaries, as to trust their doctrine as orthodox; and they shrank from those who held otherwise, as impure, for their adulterate doctrine; just as the Egyptians followed the Solitaries of Egypt and opposed the Arians.—*Hist*. vi. 27.

Basil had lived in his second retirement about three years, when the attack of the Arians upon the Church of Cæsarea, under the emperor Valens, made his loss felt, and his friend, Gregory of Nazianzus, successfully interposed his mediation between him and Eusebius. Gregory's letters are extant, and I here present them to the reader.

GREGORY TO BASIL

This is a time for good counsel and fortitude. We must surpass others in courage, nor suffer all our past toil and labour to be undone in a moment. Why do I write thus? Because our most gracious bishop (for such we ought to think and call Eusebius henceforth) has most amicable and kind feelings towards us, and like steel in the fire, is softened by time. I even expect that you will receive a communication from him, with pleasant words, and a summons, as he himself hinted to me, and many of his confidential friends assure me. Let us then anticipate his advances, either by our presence or by writing, or what would be better still, by first writing and then making our appearance, lest we be hereafter worsted with disgrace, when we might have conquered by a worsting which was honourable and dignified; which, indeed, most men expect of us. Come, then, according to my entreaty, both on this account, and for the times' sake. In truth, the heretical faction is trampling the Church under foot; some of them are already among us and are at work; others, it is said, will follow soon. Surely there is danger of their sweeping away the word of truth, unless the spirit of our Bezaleel speedily awake, that cunning master-builder of argument and doctrine. If you wish me to be present and to assist in this business, or to be the companion of your journey, I am at your service."—*Ep*. 19.

It is impossible not to be struck with Gregory's delicacy in this letter, in which he speaks as if he himself were estranged from Eusebius, as well as Basil, though he stood at the time high in his favour. His next letter is to the bishop himself, whose intentions he anticipates with equal delicacy.

GREGORY TO EUSEBIUS, BISHOP OF CÆSAREA

I know I am addressing one who hates insincerity himself, and is especially keen in detecting it in another, though cloaked in ever so artful and subtle a disguise; and indeed, I may say, if you will pardon the impertinence, I am myself averse to it, both by natural disposition and from Christian education. So I write what is uppermost on my mind, and beg you to excuse my freedom. Indeed it would be an injury to me to restrain me and bid me keep my pain to myself, as a sore festering in my heart. Proud as I am of your notice (for I am a man, as some one says before me), and of your invitations to religious consultations and meetings, yet I cannot bear your holiness's past and present slight of my most honoured brother Basil, whom I selected from the first and still possess as my friend, to live with me and study with me, and search with me into the deepest wisdom. I have no need to be dissatisfied with the opinion I have formed of him, and if I do not say more to his praise, it is lest, in enlarging on his admirable qualities, I should seem to be praising myself. Now, your favour towards me, and discountenance of him, is as if a man should stroke one's head with one hand, and with the other strike one's cheek; or decorate a house with paintings and beautify the outside, while he was undermining its foundations. If there is any thing you will grant me, let it be this; and I trust you will, for really it is equitable. He will certainly defer to you, if you do but pay a reasonable deference to him. For myself, I shall come after him as shadows follow bodies, being small, and a lover of quiet. Miserable indeed should we be, if, while we were desirous of wisdom in other matters, and of choosing the better part, we yet thought little of that grace, which is the end of all our doctrine—charity; especially in the case of one who is our bishop, and so eminent, as we well know, in life, in doctrine, and in the government of his diocese; for the truth must be spoken, whatever be our private feelings.—*Ep.* 20.

Great men love to be courted, and little men must not mind rebuffs. Gregory did not succeed in this first attempt with

Eusebius, who seems to have been offended at his freedom; and he himself was disgusted in turn, at the Bishop's stiffness. However, the danger of the Church was too great to allow of the continuance of such feelings on either side, and Gregory had, in a little while, the satisfaction of seeing Basil at Cæsarea.

3

THE VIGOROUS TALENTS OF BASIL soon put to rights the disorders and variances which had been the scandal of the Church of Cæsarea; and with the assistance of Gregory, he completely vanquished the Eunomian disputants, from whose subtlety the peace of the Church had principally suffered. What was of more consequence to its permanent welfare, he was successful in obliterating all the suspicions which his bishop had entertained of him, and at length gained such influence over him, that he had really the government of the see in his own hands. This was the more desirable, as Eusebius had not been regularly educated for the ministerial office, but had been called by the sudden voice of the people, as sometimes happened, to fill the episcopal chair. At length (A.D. 370) Eusebius died; and Basil, as might be expected, though not without a strong opposition, was elected, at the age of forty, to supply his place. This opposition was excited by the governing powers of the country, who might naturally be supposed to fear a man of Basil's commanding character, and who were joined by some of the bishops of the exarchate, and by an irreligious party in the city itself.

He had not been long in his see when he was brought into open collision with the civil power. The Arian Emperor, Valens, made a progress through the East, from Constantinople to Antioch, in A.D. 371, 372, with the determination of deposing the Catholic bishops in the countries which he traversed; and about the end of the former year he came to Cæsarea. The Prætorian Prefect, Modestus, travelled before him, proposing to the bishops of the cities, which lay on his road, the alternative of communicating with the Arians, or losing their sees. He summoned Basil into his presence, in his turn, and set before him the arguments which had been already found successful with others,—that it was foolish to resist the times, and to trouble the Church about inconsiderable questions; and he promised him the prince's favour for him and his friends, if he complied. Failing by soft language, he adopted a higher tone; but he found his match. Gregory has preserved the dialogue which passed between them.

What is the meaning of this, you Basil [said the Prefect, a bitter Arian, not deigning to style him bishop], that you stand out against so great a prince, and are self-willed when others yield?

BASIL: What would you? and what is my extravagance? I have not yet learned it.

MODESTUS: Your not worshipping after the emperor's manner, when the rest of your party have given way and been overcome.

BASIL: I have a Sovereign whose will is otherwise, nor can I bring myself to worship any creature—I a creature of God, and commanded to be a god.

MODESTUS: For whom do you take me?

BASIL: For a thing of nought, while such are your commands.

MODESTUS: Is it, then, a mere nothing for one like you to have rank like myself, and to have my fellowship?

BASIL: You are Prefect, and in noble place: I own it. Yet God's majesty is greater; and it is much for me to have your fellowship, for we are both God's creatures. But it is as great a thing to be fellow to any other of my flock, for Christianity lies not in distinction of persons, but in faith.

The Prefect was angered at this, and rose from his chair, and abruptly asked Basil if he did not fear his power.

BASIL: Fear what consequences? what sufferings?

MODESTUS: One of those many pains which a Prefect can inflict.

BASIL: Let me know them.

MODESTUS: Confiscation, exile, tortures, death.

BASIL: Think of some other threat. These have no influence upon me. He runs no risk of confiscation, who has nothing to lose, except these mean garments and a few books. Nor does he care for exile, who is not circumscribed by place, who does not make a home of the spot he dwells in, but everywhere a home whithersoever he be cast, or rather everywhere God's home, whose pilgrim he is and wanderer. Nor can tortures harm a frame so frail as to break under the first blow. You could but strike once, and death would be gain. It would but send me the sooner to Him for whom I live and labour, for whom I am dead rather than alive, to whom I have long been journeying.

MODESTUS: No one yet ever spoke to Modestus with such freedom.

BASIL: Peradventure Modestus never yet fell in with a bishop; or surely in a like trial you would have heard like language. O Prefect, in other things, we are gentle, and more humble than all men living, for such is the commandment; so as not to raise our brow, I say not against "so great a prince," but even against one of least account. But when God's honour is at stake, we think of nothing else, looking simply to Him. Fire and the sword, beasts of prey, irons to rend the flesh, are an indulgence rather than a terror to a Christian. Therefore insult, threaten, do your worst, make the most of your power. Let the emperor be informed of my purpose. Me you gain not, you persuade not, to an impious creed, by menaces even more frightful.—*Greg.* Orat. 43.

Modestus parted with him with the respect which firmness necessarily inspires in those who witness it; and, going to the emperor, repeated the failure of his attempt. A second conversation between the bishop and the great officers of the court took place in the presence, as some suppose, of Valens himself, who had generosity enough to admire his high spirit, and to dismiss him without punishment. Indeed, his admiration of Basil occasioned a fresh trial of the archbishop's constancy, more distressing, perhaps, than any which he had hitherto undergone. On the feast of the Epiphany, he attended, with all his court, the church where Basil offered the Holy Sacrifice, and heard his sermon. The collected air of the Bishop, the devotion of the clergy, the numbers and the attention of the congregation, and the power of their voices, fairly overcame him, and he almost fainted away. At the Offertory he made an effort to approach the altar to present his oblation; but none of the ministers of the church presenting themselves to receive it from him, his limbs again gave way, and it was only by the assistance of one of them that he was kept from falling.

It would be a satisfaction to be able to indulge a hope that the good feelings of the emperor were more than the excitement of the moment; but his persevering persecution of the Catholics for years afterwards forbids the favourable supposition. However, for the time Basil gained him. Modestus even became the saint's friend; Cappadocia was secured, in great measure, from the sufferings with which the Catholics elsewhere were visited, and some of the best of the imperial lands in the neighbourhood were made over for the endowment of an hospital which Basil had founded for lepers. He seems in the event to have succeeded in introducing such institutions throughout his province.

4

BASIL, FROM HIS MULTIPLIED TRIALS, may be called the Jeremiah or Job of the fourth century, though occupying the honoured place of a ruler in the Church at a time when heathen violence was over. He had a sickly constitution, to which he added the rigour of an ascetic life. He was surrounded by jealousies and dissensions at home; he was accused of heterodoxy abroad; he was insulted and roughly treated by great men; and he laboured, apparently without fruit, in the endeavour to restore unity to Christendom and stability to its Churches. If temporal afflictions work out for the saints "an exceeding weight of glory," who is higher in the kingdom of heaven than Basil?

As to his austerities, we know something of them from his own picture what a monk's life should be, and from Gregory's description of them. In a letter to the latter (*Ep.* 2), Basil limits the food of his recluses to bread, water, herbs, with but one meal a day, and allows of sleep only till midnight, when they were to rise for prayer. And he says to the emperor Julian, "Cookery with us is idle; no knife is familiar with blood; our daintiest meal is vegetables with coarsest bread and vapid wine."—*Ep.* 41. Gregory, in like manner, when expecting a visit from Basil, writes to Amphilochius to send him "some fine pot-herbs, if he did not wish to find Basil hungry and cross."—*Ep.* 12. And in his account of him, after his death, he says, that "he had but one inner and one outer garment; his bed was the ground; little sleep, no bath; his food bread and salt, his drink the running stream."—*Orat.* 20. He slept in a hair-shirt, or other rough garment; the sun was his fire; and he braved the severest frosts in the severe climate of Cappadocia. Even when Bishop he was supported by the continual charity of his friends. He kept nothing.

His constitution was naturally weak, or rather sickly. What his principal malady was, is told us in the following passage of his history, which furnishes at the same time another instance of the collisions in which he was involved with the civil power. A widow of rank being importuned with a proposal of marriage from a powerful quarter, fled for refuge to the altar. St. Basil received her. This brought him into trouble with the Vicar of Pontus, whose jurisdiction extended over Cappadocia, and who in extreme indignation summoned him. When he presented himself, the magistrate gave orders to pull off his outer garment. His inner garment, which remained, did not conceal his emaciated body. The brutal persecutor threatened to tear out his liver. Basil smiled and answered, "Thanks for your intention: where it is at present, it has been no slight annoyance." However, though it is hardly to the point here to mention it, the Vicar got the worst of it. The city rose,—Cæsarea, I suppose; the people swarmed about the Court, says Gregory, as bees smoked out of their home. The armourers, for whom the place was famous, the weavers, nay the women, with any weapon which came to hand, with clubs, stones, firebrands, spindles, besieged the Vicar, who was only saved from immediate death by the interposition of his prisoner.

But to return: on one occasion he gives the following account of his maladies to Eusebius, Bishop of Samosata.

What was my state of mind, think you, when I received your piety's letter? When I thought of the feelings which its language expressed, I was eager to fly straight to Syria; but when I thought of the bodily illness, under which I lay bound, I saw myself unequal, not only to flying, but to turning even on my bed. This is the fiftieth day of my illness, on which our beloved and excellent brother and deacon Elpidius has arrived. I am much reduced by the fever, which, failing what it might feed on, lingers in this dry flesh as in an expiring wick, and so has brought on a wasting and tedious illness. Next, my old plague, the liver, coming upon it, has kept me from taking nourishment, prevented sleep, and held me on the confines of life and death, granting just life enough to feel its inflictions. In consequence I have had recourse to the hot springs, and have availed myself of aid from medical men.—*Ep.* 138.

The fever here mentioned seems to have been an epidemic, and so far unusual; but his ordinary state of health will be understood from the following letter, written to the same friend in the beginning of his illness, in which he describes the fever as almost a change for the better.

In what state the good Isaaces has found me, he himself will best explain to you; though his tongue cannot be tragic enough to describe my sufferings, so great was my illness. Yet any one who knows me ever so little, will be able to conjecture what it was. For, if when I am called well, I am weaker even than persons who are given over, you may fancy what I was when I was thus ill. However, since disease is my natural state, it would follow (let a fever have its jest) that in this change of habit, my health became especially flourishing. But it is the scourge of the Lord which goes on increasing my pain according to my deserts; therefore I have received illness upon illness, so that now even a child may see that this shell of mine must for certain fail, unless perchance God's mercy, vouchsafing to me in His long-suffering time for repentance, now, as often before, extricate me from evils beyond human cure. This shall be as it is pleasing to Him and good for myself.—*Ep.* 136.

Eusebius seems to have been especially the confidant of his bodily sufferings. Five years before, he writes to him a similar description in answer to a similar call. "When," he says, "by God's grace and the aid of your prayers, I seemed to be somewhat recovering from my illness, and had rallied my strength, then the winter came upon me, keeping me in-doors and confining me where I was. It was, indeed, much milder than usual, yet enough to prevent, not only my travelling during it, but even my putting out my head even a little from my room."—*Ep.* 27. And nine years later than this, and three years before his death, he says, that for a time "all remaining hope of life had left him." "I cannot number," he adds, "the various afflictions which have befallen me, my weakness, the violence of the fever, and the bad state of my constitution."—*Ep.* 198. One especial effect of his complaints was to hinder his travelling, which, as his presence was continually needed, accounts for his frequently insisting on them. To Amphilochius, bishop of Iconium, he writes in the same year: "The remains of my illness are sufficient to keep me from the least motion. I went in a carriage as far as the Martyrs, and had very nearly a relapse; so I am obliged to beg you to excuse me. If the matter could be put off for a few days, then, by God's grace, I will be with you, and share your counsels."—*Ep.* 202. To a friend, whom at an earlier date he was urging to visit him in his retreat, he says, "You must not answer with Diogenes to Alexander, It is no farther from you to me, than from me to you. For my sickness almost makes me like a plant, confined ever to one spot; besides, to pass life in hiding I account among the first of goods."—

Ep. 9. He elsewhere speaks of his state of health as "bodily weakness, natural to him from childhood to age, and chastening him according to the just judgment of an Allwise Governor."—*Ep.* 203. At forty-five he calls himself an old man; and by the next year he had lost his teeth. He died at the age of fifty.

Yet, in spite of his infirmities, he does not seem at all to have spared himself the fatigue of travelling. He writes to Meletius, bishop of Antioch,—

> Many other journeys from my own country have engaged me. I crossed over to Pisidia, to arrange, in conjunction with the bishops there, the affairs of our Isaurian brethren. The journey to Pontus followed, Eustathius having put Dazimon into sufficient confusion, and persuaded many there to separate from my church. I went as far as my brother Peter's cottage near Neocæsarea. On my return, when I was very ill from the rains and from despondency, letters arrived forthwith from the East, [etc.].—*Ep.* 216.

5

SOMETHING OF ST. BASIL'S tone of mind is seen in the above extracts; it will be seen more fully in three letters of expostulation to friends, written under very different circumstances.

The first is a familiar letter to one who, having congratulated him on his elevation to the see of Cæsarea, was disappointed at not receiving a reply.

BASIL TO PERGAMIUS

I am naturally forgetful, and have had a multitude of engagements, which has increased my infirmity. If I do not remember receiving a letter from your nobleness, I still believe you sent it to me; it is impossible you should be incorrect. Yet it is not I that am in fault, but he who did not ask for an answer. However, you now receive from me what will at once account for what is past, and have a claim on you for a reply. So, when you next write, you must not think that you are making a second beginning of our correspondence, but merely paying your debt for my present letter. For though it be an acknowledgment of what has gone before, yet being more than twice as long, it will answer the other office too. Do you observe how sharp leisure makes me? My good friend, let me beg of you not to turn, as you have done, what is a small matter, into a charge so great, that perhaps no greater baseness could be imputed to me. For a forgetfulness of friendships, and insolence engendered by power, contain in them all that is wretched. Whether it is that we do not love, as the Lord has bid us, then we have lost His image; or whether we are puffed up and gorged with vain glory and boasting, we fall into the sure condemnation of the devil. Therefore, if you have accused me advisedly, pray for my escape from the sin which you discern in my conduct; if, on the other hand, from a habit I do not understand, your tongue has fallen into those words, I shall take comfort and shall tax your goodness to adduce facts in proof of it. Be sure of this, that my present annoyance has been the means of humbling me. I am not likely to forget you till I forget myself; so, for the future, do not let my engagements be considered as a proof of a bad disposition.—*Ep.* 56.

Basil's election had been very distasteful to a certain number of bishops of his province; who, finding they could not prevent it, refused to be present at his consecration, or to hold intercourse with him. Among these was Basil's uncle, Gregory. This was more than usually distressing, inasmuch as Gregory had been more than an ordinary uncle to him. He had been closely connected with Basil's family circle, which was a sort of nursery of bishops and saints. His father, whose name also was Basil, and whose profession was that of rhetoric, was a man of landed property in Pontus and Cappadocia, and of good family, as was his wife Emmelia, Basil's mother. He numbered on the line of both his parents, high functionaries, military and civil. Nor was his descent less illustrious in a Christian aspect. His maternal grandfather was a martyr; his father's parents had been driven to live seven years in the woods and mountains of Pontus, during the Diocletian persecution. Basil was one of ten children; three of them lived to be bishops; four of them are saints, St. Basil himself, St. Gregory Nyssen, St. Peter, and St. Macrina, besides his mother, St. Emmelia. Another brother, Naucratius, embraced the life of a solitary, and was drowned while engaged in works of mercy. Such being the character of Basil's paternal home, a difference with Gregory, his paternal uncle, would, under any circumstances, have been painful; but it so happened that the latter had been called to take on him a father's duties towards Basil and his brothers. Their father had died when they were young, and Gregory, who was one of the bishops of Cappadocia, had superintended what remained of Basil's education. As to his mind, it had already been formed by three women, his grandmother Macrina, his mother Emmelia, and another Macrina, his elder sister.

Basil had conceived that his uncle's estrangement from him was removed; but on his saying so, his uncle wrote to him to deny the fact. On this he wrote the following letter, which happily had the desired effect.

BASIL TO HIS UNCLE GREGORY

I have kept silence; must there be no end of it? Shall I bear any longer to enforce this most heavy penalty of silence against myself—neither writing nor conversing with you? Indeed, in persisting hitherto in this melancholy determination, I seem to have a right to use the Prophet's words—"I have been still, and refrained myself as a woman in travail"—always anxious to see or hear from you, always for my sins disappointed. No other cause can be assigned for the present state of things, except that my estrangement from your love is certainly an infliction on me for old transgressions. Yet, even though the very naming of estrangement were not a sin, if shown towards you by whomsoever, yet certainly it were, if shown by me, to whom you have been from the first in place of a father. However, the time of my punishment has been long indeed. So I can hold no longer, and am the first to speak; beseeching you to remember both me and yourself, who have treated me, all through my life, with a greater tenderness than relationship could claim, and to love the city which I govern for my sake, instead of alienating yourself from it on my account.

If, therefore, there is any consolation in Christ, if there is any fellowship of the Spirit, if any bowels of commiseration, fulfil my prayer; put an end at once to this gloom, making a beginning of a more cheerful state of things for the future, becoming yourself the guide of the others towards right, not following another towards wrong. No one's features were ever more strongly marked, than your soul is characterized with peaceableness and mildness. It becomes such an one to draw others to him, and to supply all who approach him, as it were, with the fragrant oil of his own amiableness. There may be obstacles just now; but, in a short time the blessedness of peace will be recognized. But while our dissension gives opportunity to tale-bearers, our complaints of each other must necessarily be increasing. It is unbecoming in other parties to neglect me, but more than any, in your venerableness. Tell me if I am any where wrong, and I shall be the better in future. But it is impossible to do so without intercourse. If, on the other hand, I have committed no offence, why am I hated? This I say by way of self-defence.

What those churches will say for themselves, which with so little honour are partners in our dispute, I will not ask, for I have no wish to give offence by this letter, but to remove it. You are too clear-sighted for anything of this kind to escape you; and will take, and lay before others, a much more accurate view than mine can be. Indeed, you were sensible of the existing evils in the churches before I was, and have felt them more keenly, having long ago learnt of the Lord not to despise any of the least of His matters. At present, however, the mischief is not confined to one or two individuals, but whole cities and communities are partners in our misfortune. Comfort me then, either by coming to see me, or by writing, or by sending for me, or in any way you will. My own earnest wish is, that you would make your appearance in my church, so that both I and my people might be benefited by the sight and the words of your grace. This will be best, if possible; but I shall welcome any proposition which you will make. Only, let me beg of you to give me some sure intelligence of your intention.—*Ep.* 59.

6

THIS MISUNDERSTANDING HE SURMOUNTED: but the following was on a far more painful matter, being not so much a misunderstanding between friends, as a real difference of religious creed, which did not admit of removal.

Eustathius had been one of the pupils of Arius at Alexandria, and was admitted into orders at Antioch by the Arians. After a time, he joined the Semi-Arian, or middle, party in Asia Minor, with whom he continued some years. On the death of the Emperor Constantius this party lost the patronage of the court; and during the reign of Valens, a purely Arian prince, Eustathius deserted them, and, after a time, professed himself of the new Emperor's religion. Up to this date he had the friendship of Basil, as bearing about him all the marks of a zealous and honest, though erring man. He was austere in his manner of life, professed a most strict adherence to truth, and seemed not destitute of the spirit of Christian love. On occasion of his first lapsing after the death of Constantius, he carried the appearance of sincerity so far as even to betake himself to Rome for the purpose of subscribing the Catholic creed, and to acknowledge publicly his offence. Afterwards he became a bitter enemy of Basil. The following letter was written A.D. 375, about the time of the first rupture between him and Basil, and is interesting as disclosing some particulars of the early life of the latter.

BASIL IN ANSWER TO EUSTATHIUS, BISHOP OF SEBASTE

There is a time for silence, and a time for speaking, as the preacher says; so now, after keeping silence a sufficient time, it is seasonable to open my mouth in order to explain what is unknown. For great Job himself endured his afflictions silently a long while, manifesting his fortitude by bearing up against the heaviest afflictions. But after fulfilling that silent conflict, that continued confinement of his grief in the depth of his heart, then he opened his mouth and uttered what all know, and spoke aloud what is told us in Scripture. I too have been near three years silent, and may aspire to the prophet's boast, being as one who heard not, and in whose mouth are no reproofs. Thus I shut up within me the pain that I felt from the calumnies heaped upon me. I expected the evil would cure itself; for I supposed that things were said against me, not from any bad feeling, but from ignorance. Now, however, that I perceive the enmity against me continues, and that the parties who manifest it show no sorrow for what they have said, nor are anxious to heal what is past, but increase their united efforts towards the same end which they originally proposed, to annoy me and injure my reputation with the brethren, silence is no longer safe.

After long time spent in vanity, and almost the whole of my youth vanishing in the idle toil of studying that wisdom which God has made folly, when at length, roused as from a deep sleep, I gazed upon the marvellous light of Gospel truth, and discerned the unprofitableness of the wisdom taught by the perishing authorities of this world, much did I bewail my wretched life, and pray that guidance would be vouchsafed to me for an entrance into the doctrines of godliness. And above all was it a care to me to reform my heart, which the long society of the corrupt had perverted. So when I read the Gospel, and perceived thence that the best start towards perfection was to sell my goods and share them with my indigent brethren, and altogether to be reckless of this life, and to rid my soul of all sympathy with things on earth, I earnestly desired to find some brother who had made the same choice, and who might make the passage with me over the brief waves of this life. Many did I find in Alexandria, many in the rest of Egypt, and in Palestine, in Cœle-Syria and Mesopotamia, whose abstinence and endurance I admired, and whose constancy in prayer I was amazed at; how they overcame sleep, in spite of the necessity of nature, bearing ever a high and free spirit in hunger and thirst, in cold and nakedness, not regarding the body, nor enduring to spend any thought upon it, but living as if in flesh not their own; how they showed in deed what it is to be sojourners in this world, what it is to have our conversation in heaven. Admiring and extolling the life of these men, who could so in deed carry about with them the dying of the Lord Jesus, I desired that I myself, as far as I could attain, might be an imitator of them.

This expedition was in the year 357, when Basil was twenty-eight, some years after his stay at Athens, and immediately upon the loss of his brother, Naucratius. He proceeds:

With this object, finding that there were persons in my own country attempting to rival them, I deemed I had found some aid towards my own salvation, and I made what was seen the token of what was hidden. And since it is difficult to get at the secret heart of a man, I reckoned it was argument enough of humbleness to have an humble clothing; and I gave my faith to the coarse garment, and the girdle, and the untanned sandals. And when many would have dissuaded me from their converse, I would not hear of it, seeing that these men preferred an hardness of living to self-indulgence; and being taken with their extraordinary life, I was zealous in my defence of them. It followed that I would not suffer any attack upon their doctrines, though many contended that they were unsound in creed, and secretly disseminated the doctrines of their master, the founder of the now prevailing heresy. Having never myself heard such from them, I thought the report calumnious. Afterwards, when called to the government of the church, what these chosen guardians and keepers of my life turned out to be, with their pretences to loving aid and intercourse, I say not, lest its seeming incredibility should reflect upon myself, or the belief of it should infect the hearer with misanthropy. And this, indeed, was almost my calamity, had not God's mercies quickly prevented me; for I well nigh fell into a suspicion of every one, thinking truth was nowhere to be found, being wounded in my mind by their deceitful blows. Yet for a while I kept up some sort of intercourse with them; and we had several discussions about points of dogma, and it appeared as if we really agreed. They found in me the same faith which they had heard from me before, for though I have done many things worthy of groans, yet so much I may boast in the Lord, that I never held erroneous doctrine concerning God, nor have had to change my profession. The idea of God which I had from my blessed mother, and her mother Macrina, that has ever grown within me. I did not change about, as reason unfolded, but perfected the rudiments of faith by them delivered to me.

I am charged of blasphemy towards God, though neither former writing of mine on matters of faith, nor word of mouth uttered publicly by me without book, as usual in the churches of God, can be brought against me. Ask yourself. How often have you visited me at my monastery on the Iris, when my most religious brother, Gregory, was with me, following the same rule of life as myself! Did you then hear from me any such thing? or catch any hint of it, strong or slight? How many days did we pass together as friends, in the village opposite with my mother, and discussed subjects night and day, in which we found each other sympathize?

A man ought to take much thought—nay, pass many sleepless nights, and seek his duty from God with many tears, ere he ventures to break up a friendship. They ground their conduct altogether on one letter, and that a doubtful one. But in reality this letter is not the cause of their separation. I am ashamed to mention the real reason; and I should not tell it now, nor indeed ever, had not their present behaviour made it necessary for the general good to publish an account of their whole design. These honest persons considered that intimacy with me would stand in the way of their promotion; so, since they had committed themselves by subscription to a creed which I imposed on them (not that I at that time distrusted their views, I own it, but from a wish to obviate the suspicions which most of my brethren who felt with me entertained against them), to prevent their rejection on the part of the now ascendant party, on account of this confession, they then renounced my communion: and this letter was pitched upon as a pretext for the rupture. There cannot be a clearer proof of this than the fact, that, on their disowning me, they circulated their accusations on every side, before acquainting me with them. Their charge was in the hands of others seven days before it reached me: and these persons had received it from others, and intended to send it on. I knew this at the time, from friends who sent me certain intelligence of their measures; but I determined to keep silence, till He, who brings to light the deep secrets, should make manifest their plans by the clearest and most cogent evidence.—*Ep.* 223.

7

SENSITIVE, ANXIOUS, AND AFFECTIONATE as Basil appears in his letters, he had a reserve and sedateness of manner which his contemporaries sometimes attributed to pride, sometimes to timidity. Gregory Nazianzen notices the former charge, and exclaims:—

Is it possible for a man to embrace lepers, abasing himself so far, and yet to be supercilious towards those who are in health? to waste his flesh with mortification, yet be swollen in soul with empty elation? to condemn the Pharisee, and to enlarge on his fall through pride, and to know that Christ descended even to a servant's form, and ate with publicans, and washed the disciples' feet, and disdained not the Cross, that He might nail to it *my* sin, and yet to soar beyond the clouds, and count no one his equal; as appears to them who are jealous of him? But I suppose it was the self-possession of his character, and composure and polish, which they named pride.—*Orat.* 43.

This testimony is the stronger, as coming from one whom on one occasion, as we shall see by-and-by, Basil did offend, by behaviour which on the part of some moderns is alleged as the great specimen of his arrogant temper. It is certain, however, from what Gregory says, that the imputation was fastened on him in his day, and the report of it was heard, perhaps believed, by Jerome in his cave at Bethlehem. Words are no safe test of actions; yet most persons, I think, will allow that the following sentences from his *Homily on Humility*, corroborate what Gregory says in his defence:—

How [he asks,] shall we attain to saving humility, abandoning the deadly elevation of pride? by practising some act of humility in everything that we do, and by overlooking nothing, from an idea that we shall gain no harm from the neglect. For the soul is influenced by outward observances, and is shaped and fashioned according to its actions. Let, then, thy appearance, and garment, and gait, and sitting, and table, and bedroom, and house, and its furniture, all be directed according to lowliness. And thy speech and singing and conversation, in like manner, look towards meanness and not exaltation. But perhaps thou art awarded the highest seat, and men observe and honour thee? Become equal to those who are in subjection; "not lording it over the clergy," said Scripture; be not like to rulers of this world. For whoso would be first, him our Lord bids be servant of all. In a word, follow after humility, as one enamoured of it. Be in love with it, and it shall glorify thee. So shalt thou nobly journey on to true glory, which is among the Angels; which is with God; and Christ will acknowledge thee as His own disciple, before the Angels, and will glorify thee, if thou learn to copy His humility.—*Hom. de Humil.*

The opposite charge to which his reserve gave rise was that of timidity. It is remarkable that he himself, writing to a friend, playfully notices "the want of spirit" and "the sluggishness" of the Cappadocians, and attributes these qualities to himself.—*Ep.* 48. Accordingly, after his death, the heretic Eunomius accuses the opponent of Valens and Modestus of being "a coward and craven, and skulking from the heavier labours," speaking contemptuously of his "retired cottage and his closely-fastened door, and his fluttered manner on persons entering, and his voice, and look, and expression of countenance, and the other symptoms of fear."—*Greg. Nyss., App.* p. 46. This malicious account may be just so far founded on truth, as to make it worth while noticing a curious difference in a little matter which it brings out between Basil and the great Ambrose of Milan, who was a man of the world; for while the former is here represented as fastening his door, it was the peculiarity of Ambrose never to shut himself into his house, but to be accessible at all times. Philostorgius, the Arian historian, in like manner, speaks of Basil, as "superior to many in the power of discussion; but, from timidity of mind, withdrawing from public disputations." And Gregory makes several remarks on his friend, which serve to illustrate the shyness or refinement of mind complained of by these writers. The following is curious, as bringing Basil before our eyes.

Such were the virtues of the man, such the fulness of his celebrity, that others, in order to gain reputation, copied many even of his peculiarities, nay, his bodily imperfections; I mean, for instance, his paleness, his beard, the character of his gait, his deliberateness in speaking, as being generally deep in thought, and intent on his subject; which things most of them copying ill, and indeed not understanding, turned into gloom;—moreover, the quality of his garment, and the shape of his bed, and his mode of eating, nothing of which in him was studied, but natural and spontaneous. And you may fall in with many Basils as far as outside goes, figures in shadow; it is too much to say echoes. For echo, at least, repeats the last syllables even more clearly; but these are much farther off from Basil than they desire to be near him. Moreover, it is no longer a common, but the greatest of honours, and with reason, to have ever happened to have been in his company, or to have shown attentions to him, or to carry with one the memory of anything said or done by him, playfully or in earnest, since the by-doings of this man are more precious and illustrious than what others do with labour.—*Orat.* 43.

Reference is made in these last words to Basil's playfulness. This quality his letters abundantly vindicate to him, though it is of a pensive sort. Lest the reader should go away with a more austere notion of him than truth warrants, I will add the following passage from St. Gregory.

Who made himself more amiable than he to the well-conducted? or more severe when men were in sin? whose very smile was many a time praise, whose silence a reproof, punishing the evil in a man's own conscience. If he was not full of talk, nor a jester, nor a holder forth, nor generally acceptable from being all things to all men, and showing good-nature; what then? Is not this to his praise, not his blame, among sensible men? Yet, if we ask for this, who so pleasant as he in social intercourse, as I know who have had such experience of him? Who could tell a story with more wit? who could jest so playfully? who could give a hint more delicately, so as neither to be overstrong in his rebuke, nor remiss through his gentleness?—*Orat.* 43.

Basil died on the first of January, A.D. 379, having been born in 329. He rallied before his death, and his last discourses were delivered with more strength than usual. His closing act was to ordain some of his immediate disciples. He died with the words upon his tongue, "Into Thy hands I commend my spirit."

CHAPTER II

LABOURS OF BASIL

"And I said, I have laboured in vain; I have spent my strength without cause, and in vain: therefore my judgment is with the Lord, and my work with my God."

I

THE INSTRUMENTS RAISED up by Almighty God for the accomplishment of His purposes are of two kinds, equally gifted with faith and piety, but from natural temper and talent, education, or other circumstances, differing in the means by which they promote their sacred cause. The first of these are men of acute and ready mind, with accurate knowledge of human nature, and large plans, and persuasive and attractive bearing, genial, sociable, and popular, endued with prudence, patience, instinctive tact and decision in conducting matters, as well as boldness and zeal. Such in a measure we may imagine the single-minded, the intrepid, the much-enduring Hildebrand, who, at a time when society was forming itself anew, was the saviour, humanly speaking, of the City of God. Such, in an earlier age, was the majestic Ambrose; such the never-wearied Athanasius. These last-named luminaries of the Church came into public life early, and thus learned how to cope with the various tempers, views, and measures of the men they encountered there. Athanasius was but twenty-seven when he went with Alexander to the Nicene Council, and the year after he was Bishop of Alexandria. Ambrose was consecrated soon after the age of thirty.

Again, there is an instrument in the hand of Providence, of less elaborate and splendid workmanship, less rich in its political endowments, so to call them, yet not less beautiful in its texture, nor less precious in its material. Such is the retired and thoughtful student, who remains years and years in the solitude of a college or a monastery, chastening his soul in secret, raising it to high thought and single-minded purpose, and when at length called into active life conducting himself with firmness, guilelessness, zeal like a flaming fire, and all the sweetness of purity and integrity. Such an one is often unsuccessful in his own day; he is too artless to persuade, too severe to please; unskilled in the weaknesses of human nature, unfurnished in the resources of ready wit, negligent of men's applause, unsuspicious, open-hearted, he does his work, and so leaves it; and it seems to die; but in the generation after him it lives again, and on the long run it is difficult to say, which of the two classes of men has served the cause of truth the more effectually. Such, perhaps, was Basil, who issued from the solitudes of Pontus to rule like a king, and minister like the lowest in the kingdom; yet to meet little but disappointment, and to quit life prematurely in pain and sorrow. Such was his friend, the accomplished Gregory, however different in other respects from him, who left his father's roof for an heretical city, raised a church there, and was driven back into retirement by his own people, as soon as his triumph over the false creed was secured. Such, perhaps, St. Peter Damiani in the middle age; such St. Anselm, such St. Edmund. No comparison is, of course, attempted here between the religious excellence of the two descriptions of men; each of them serves God according to the peculiar gifts given to him. If we might continue our instances by way of comparison, we should say that St. Paul reminds us of the former, and Jeremiah of the latter.

These remarks are intended as introductory to portions of Basil's letters, on various subjects indeed, but all illustrative of the then distracted state of the Church in his part of

Christendom, and of his labours, apparently fruitless at the time, in restoring to it truth and peace.

2

THE DISORDERS OF CHRISTENDOM, and especially of the East, and still more of Asia Minor, were so great in Basil's day, that a heathen spectator might have foretold the total overthrow of the Church. So violent a convulsion never has been experienced in Christendom since, not even in the times of St. Gregory the Seventh and St. Pius the Fifth; it would almost seem as if the powers of evil, foreseeing what the Kingdom of the Saints would be, when once heathen persecutions ceased, were making a final effort to destroy it. In Asia Minor the Church was almost without form, "and void and empty"; religious interests were reduced, as it were, to a state of chaos, and Basil seems to have been the principle of truth and order, divinely formed, divinely raised up, for harmonising the discordant elements, and bringing them to the unity of faith and love. However, the destined result did not show itself in his day. Valens persecuted in behalf of Arianism till the year before the saint's death; the Semi-Arians continued their schism after it: and, trying to lead them towards the truth, Basil exposed himself to calumnies both on the part of his brethren, as if favouring the prevailing heresy, and of the heretics, as if maintaining an opposite one. There were dissensions, too, existing within the Church, as well as without. I have already spoken of Basil's difference with his predecessor Eusebius, and of a party which his uncle joined, which was formed against him on his succeeding to the see. Jealousies or suspicions, of which he was the subject, extended throughout his exarchate. He seems to have had authority, more or less defined, over the whole of the country which the Romans called Pontus, which was more than half of Asia Minor, and comprised in it eleven provinces. Ancyra, Neocæsarea, Tyana, among other principal sees, acknowledged him more or less as their ecclesiastical superior. Now we have records of his being opposed by the bishops of each of these cities. When he passed out of his own district into the neighbouring jurisdiction of Antioch, he found that metropolis distracted by schism; four bishops in the see at once, two heretical, a third acknowledged by Rome and the Alexandrians, a fourth in communion with himself. When he went on to the South and West, and negotiated with Alexandria and Rome for the settlement of these disorders, he met with nothing but disappointment, though saints were upon the ecclesiastical thrones of either city. Such is the history of his episcopate,—for which he exchanged his sweet monastic life.

As to the party of bishops who withstood his election, he overcame most of them in the course of a few years, as he did his uncle, by firmness and kindness, though for a time they gave him trouble. "Our friends," he says to Eusebius of Samosata, shortly after his elevation, "have not shown themselves at all better than we expected. They made their appearance immediately you were gone, and said and did many disagreeable things; and at length departed, confirming their schism with us."—*Ep.* 20. Three years afterwards he complains to the same friend of the impediments which their conduct threw in the way of his exertions for the Church.

That you may not suppose, [he says,] that the interests of the Churches are betrayed to our enemies by my negligence, I would have your reverence know, that the bishops in communion with me, whether from disinclination, or from continued suspicion of me and want of frankness, or from that opposition to right measures, which the devil engenders, refuse to act with me. In profession, indeed, the greater number of us are all together, including the excellent Bosporius; but in truth in not one even of the most important matters do they act with me. The despondency which this occasions is the principal cause why I do not get well, indisposition returning to me continually from excessive grief. What can I do by myself? the canons, as you yourself know, do not permit one man to put them in force. Yet what remedy have I not tried? What rule is there to which I have not called their attention, by letter or in conversation? For they came up into town on the news of my death; and, when it pleased God that they found me alive, I represented to them what was reasonable. And they defer to me when present, and promise all that is reasonable; but when they have gone away, they recur to their own opinion.—*Ep.* 141.

Among the injuries which Eustathius inflicted upon Basil, was his spreading a report that Basil was a follower of the heresiarch Apollinaris. This calumny, which is alluded to in the letter written in his own defence in answer to Eustathius, which I have quoted in the foregoing chapter, seems to have reached and been believed by the bishop of Ancyra, by name Athanasius; who, having been once an Arian, had since conformed, and shown a good deal of zeal for the true faith. This bishop said some very harsh things of Basil in consequence; which led the latter, who had an esteem for him, to write him the following letter:—

BASIL TO ATHANASIUS, BISHOP OF ANCYRA

I am told by persons who come to me from Ancyra, and that by many more than I can number, and all saying the same thing, that you, dear friend (how may I use mild terms?) have not the kindest recollections of me, nor feel in the way natural to you. For myself, nothing that can happen astonishes me, be sure of that; there is no one at all whose change would contradict my expectation, since I have long learned the weakness of human nature and its proneness to turn right round. Hence I think it no great matter, though my cause has fallen back, and for the honour which I had, calumny and slight are my present portion. But this is what seems to me so very strange and preternatural, that you should be the man to be angry or incensed with me; nay, and to use threats against me, as those say who heard them. Now, as to the threats, I must speak frankly, I plainly laughed at them. Indeed, I should be a very child to fear such bugbears. But what is a real cause of apprehension to me, and of much anxiety, is, that an accurate judgment, such as yours,—which I believed was preserved for the comfort of the Churches, both as a rare foundation of orthodoxy and a seed of ancient and genuine love,—that it should so far yield to the existing state of things, as to trust the calumnies of chance-comers more than your long experience of myself, and to be carried away without evidence, to such extravagant suspicions. Yet why do I say suspicions? for a person who was indignant, and who threatened, as they report of you, seems to have manifested the anger, not of suspicion, but of clear and unanswerable conviction.

But as I have said, I ascribe it all to the times; for what was the trouble, excellent man, in your (as it were) talking with me confidentially in a short letter, on the matters you wished to speak about? or, if you did not like to trust such things to writing, why not send for me? But if it was altogether necessary to speak out, and the impetuosity of anger left no time for delay, at any rate you might have made use of some intimate friend, who could keep a secret, to convey your message to us. But, as the case stands, who has come to you on any business, whose ears have not been filled with the charge, that I am writing and putting together certain mischievous things? For this was your very word, as accurate reporters say. I have thought a good deal on the subject, but am in as great difficulty as ever. It has come into my mind to think whether some heretic, maliciously giving my name to his own writing, has not distressed your orthodoxy, and led you to utter that speech. You yourself may free me from my perplexity, if you would kindly state, without reserve, what has induced you to take such offence at me.—*Ep.* 25.

3

ANOTHER ACHIEVEMENT of the same Eustathius was the separation of a portion of the coast of Pontus from the Church of Cæsarea, on the pretence that its bishops were in heresy, which for a time caused Basil great despondency, as if he were being left solitary in all Christendom, without communion with other places. With the advice of the bishops of Cappadocia, he addressed an expostulation to these separatists; a portion of which runs as follows:—

Up to this day I live in much affliction and grief, having the feeling present before me, that you are wanting to me. For when God tells me—who took on Him His sojourn in the flesh for the very purpose that, by patterns of duty, He might regulate our life, and might by His own voice announce to us the Gospel of the kingdom—when He says, "By this shall all men know that you are My disciples, if you love one another," and whereas the Lord left His own peace to His disciples as a farewell gift, when about to complete the dispensation in the flesh, saying, "Peace I leave with you, My peace I give you," I cannot persuade myself that without love to others, and without, as far as rests with me, peaceableness towards all, I can be called a worthy servant of Jesus Christ. I have waited a long while for the chance of your love paying us a visit. For ye are not ignorant that we, being exposed on all sides, as rocks running out into the sea, sustain the fury of the heretical waves, which, because they break around us, fail to cover the district behind us. I say "we," in order to refer it, not to human power, but to the grace of God, who, by the weakness of men shows His power, as says the prophet, in the person of the Lord, "Will ye not fear me, who have placed the sand as a boundary to the sea?"—for by the weakest and most contemptible of all things, the sand, the Mighty One has bounded the great and full sea. Since, then, this is our position, it became your love to be frequent in sending true brothers to visit us who labour with the storm, and more frequently letters of love, partly to confirm our courage, partly to correct any mistake of ours. For we confess that we are liable to numberless mistakes, being men, and living in the flesh.

Let not this consideration influence you—"We dwell on the sea, we are exempt from the sufferings of the generality, we need no succour from others; so what is the good to us of foreign communion?" For the same Lord who divided the islands from the continent by the sea, bound the island Christians to the continental by love. Nothing, brethren, separates us from each other, but deliberate estrangement. We have one Lord, one faith, the same hope. The hands need each other; the feet steady each other.

The eyes possess their clear apprehension from agreement. We, for our part, confess our own weakness, and we seek your fellow-feeling. For we are assured, that though ye are not present in body, yet by the aid of prayer, ye will do us much benefit in these most critical times. It is neither decorous before men, nor pleasing to God, that you should make avowals which not even the Gentiles adopt, which know not God. Even they, as we hear though the country they live in be sufficient for all things, yet, on account of the uncertainty of the future, make much of alliances with each other, and seek mutual intercourse as being advantageous to them. Yet we,—the sons of fathers, who have decreed, that by brief notes the proofs of communion should be carried about from one end of the earth to the other, and that all should be citizens and familiars with all,—we now sever ourselves from the whole world, and are neither ashamed at our solitariness, nor shudder that on us is fallen the fearful prophecy of the Lord, "Because of lawlessness abounding, the love of the many shall wax cold."—*Ep.* 203.

It does not appear what success attended this appeal; difficulties of a similar but more painful nature, which occurred at the same time, hide from us the sequel of the history. I allude to the alienation from him of the Church of Neocæsarea, a place dear to Basil, as having been his residence in youth, the home of many of his relations, and the see of St. Gregory, the Wonder-worker, in the third century, from whom, through his father's family, Basil had especially received his traditions of Christian truth. There seems to have been in high quarters there a lurking attachment to Sabellian doctrine. Sabellianism is the opposite extreme to Arianism; and its upholders would call Basil Arian, first because he was Catholic, and not Sabellian, as is the way with the partisans of extremes; and next, because he had Semi-Arian friends. This was one chief cause of the opposition shown to him; but there were other causes unknown. It is remarkable that the coolness began in the episcopate of Musonius, though he was a man whom Basil mentions with much respect and gratitude. He thus speaks of him, on his death, in a letter of condolement addressed to the Neocæsareans. This was before Basil's elevation to the episcopate.

A man is gone, undeniably preëminent among his contemporaries for all earthly endowments, the bulwark of his country, the ornament of the Churches, a pillar and ground of the truth, the firm stay of faith in Christ, a protection to his friends, invincible by his adversaries, a guardian of the rules of the Fathers, a foe to innovation; exemplifying in himself the Church's primitive fashion, moulding the form of the Church, committed to him, after its ancient constitution, as after some sacred image, so that those who lived with him seemed to have lived with those who have been luminaries in it for two hundred years and more. [He adds,] I would have you aware, that if this blessed man did not concur with me in the pacification of the Churches, on account of certain previous views, as he avowed to me, yet (as God knows, and men know who have had experience of me) at least I omitted no opportunity of fellowship of sentiment with him, and of inviting his assistance in the struggle against heretics.—*Ep* 28.

4

BUT TO RETURN: if Basil's Semi-Arian acquaintances brought suspicion upon himself in the eyes of Catholic believers, much more, I say, would they be obnoxious to persons attached, as certain Neocæsareans were, to the Sabellian party, who were in the opposite extreme to the Semi-Arians, and their especial enemies in those times. It is not wonderful, then, that, some years after, he had to write to the Church in question in a strain like the following:—

There has been a long silence on both sides, revered and well-beloved brethren, just as if there were angry feelings between us. Yet who is there so sullen and implacable towards the party which has injured him, as to lengthen out the resentment which has begun in disgust, through almost a whole life of man? This is happening in our case, though no just occasion of estrangement exists, as far as I myself know, but on the contrary, there being, from the first, many strong reasons for the closest friendship and unity.

The greatest and first is this, our Lord's command, who pointedly says: "By this shall all men know that ye are My disciples, if ye have love one to another." Next, if it tend much towards intimacy to have the same teachers, there are to you and to me the same teachers of God's mysteries and spiritual Fathers, who from the beginning were the founders of your Church. I mean the great Gregory, and all who, succeeding in order to the throne of your episcopate, like stars rising one after another, have tracked the same course, so as to leave the tokens of the heavenly polity most clear to all who have desire for them. Why is it, then, O venerable among cities, for through you I address the whole city, that no courteous writing comes from you, no welcome voice, but your ears are open to those who aim at slander? What say I, brethren? not that I am a sinless man; not that my life is not full of numberless faults. I know myself; and indeed I cease not my tears by reason of my sins, if by any means I may be able to appease my God, and to escape the punishment threatened against them. But this I say: let him who judges me, search for motes in my eye, if he can say that his own is clear. And in a word, brethren, if my offences admit of cure, why does not such a one obey the Doctor of the Churches, saying, "Reprove, rebuke, exhort?" If, on the other hand, my iniquity be past cure, why does he not withstand me to the face, and by publishing my transgressions, deliver the Churches from the mischief which I bring on them? There are bishops; let appeal be made to them. There is a clergy in each of God's dioceses; let the most eminent be assembled. Let whoso will, speak freely, that I may have to deal with a charge, not a slander. If the fault be in a point of faith, let the document be pointed out to me. Again let a fair and impartial inquiry be appointed. Let the accusation be read; let it be brought to the test, whether it does not arise from ignorance in the accuser, not from blame in the matter of the writing. For right things often seem otherwise to those who are deficient in accurate judgment. Equal weights seem unequal, when the arms of the balance are of different sizes.

I interrupt the thread of his self-defence to call attention to this happy illustration. The weights in a balance are the antagonist arguments for and against a point; and its arms represent the opposing assumptions and presumptions on either side, which, varying with each individual judging, modify and alter the motive force of the weights. He continues:—

Let no one suppose I am making excuses to evade the charge. It is put into your hands, dearest brethren, to investigate for yourselves the points alleged against me. If there be anything you do not understand, put questions to me through persons of your appointment, who will do justice to me; or ask of me explanations in writing. And take all kinds of pains, that nothing may be left unsifted.

What clearer evidence can there be of my faith, than that I was brought up by my grandmother, blessed woman! who came from you? I mean the celebrated Macrina, who taught me the words of the most blessed Gregory; which, as far as memory had preserved down to her day, she cherished herself, while she fashioned and formed me, while yet a child, upon the doctrines of piety. And when I gained the capacity of thought, my reason being matured by full age, I travelled over much sea and land, and whomever I found walking in the rule of religious faith as delivered to us, those I set down as fathers.

The fair thing would be to judge of me, not from one or two who do not walk uprightly in the truth, but from the multitude of bishops throughout the world, united with me through the grace of the Lord. Make inquiry of Pisidians, Lycaonians, Isaurians, Phrygians of both provinces, Armenians your neighbours, Macedonians, Achæans, Illyrians, Gauls, Spaniards, the whole of Italy, Sicilians, Africans, the healthy part of Egypt, whatever is left of Syria; all of whom send letters to me, and in turn receive them from me. Whoso shuns communion with me, he, it cannot escape your accuracy, cuts himself off from the whole Church. Look round about, brethren, with whom do *you* hold communion? if you will not receive it from me, who remains to acknowledge you? Do not reduce me to the necessity of counselling anything unpleasant concerning a Church so dear to me. Ask your fathers, and they will tell you that, though our districts were divided in position, yet in mind they were one, and were governed by one sentiment. Intercourse of the people was frequent; frequent the visits of the clergy; the pastors, too, had such mutual affection, that each used the other as teacher and guide in things pertaining to the Lord.—*Ep.* 204.

5

No good could come of these expostulations, however sincere and affectionate, when there was an heretical spirit at work at bottom. But now let us turn from the North to the South, from Basil's own neighbourhood to foreign Churches, from the small Sabellian party at home, to the extended Arian confederation abroad. We shall find fresh trials befalling Basil. Arianism, indeed, itself, in spite of the patronage of Valens, languished and gave tokens of dying a natural death; but its disputants had raised questions which perplexed numbers whom they did not draw over; till at length the sacred subject in controversy was so clouded and confused by explanations, refinements, and distinctions, that there seemed no chance of Christians ever becoming unanimous in the orthodox creed. The particular party labouring under this mistiness of theological opinions at that day were called Semi-Arians, or Macedonians, for reasons it is not necessary here to detail. They were zealous opponents of the Arians, though originating from among them; and, after the death of Constantius (A.D. 361), they showed a disposition to come back to the Catholics. A union was partially effected, but matters were still in an unsatisfactory state on Basil's elevation (A.D. 371), when he wrote the following letter concerning them to the great Athanasius, then on the point of removal from the Church below:—

BASIL TO ATHANASIUS, BISHOP OF ALEXANDRIA

I suppose there is no one feels such pain at the present condition, or rather want of condition of the Churches, as your Grace; comparing, as you naturally must, the present with the past, and considering the difference between the two, and the certainty there is, if the evil proceeds at its present pace, that in a short time the

Churches will altogether lose their existing constitution. I have often thought with myself, if the corruption of the Churches seems so sad to me, what must be the feelings of one who has witnessed their former stability and unanimity in the faith. And as your Perfectness has more abundant grief, so one must suppose you have greater anxiety for their welfare. For myself, I have been long of opinion, according to my imperfect understanding of ecclesiastical matters, that there was one way of succouring our Churches—viz., the coöperation of the bishops of the West. If they would but show, as regards our part of Christendom, the zeal which they manifested in the case of one or two heretics among themselves, there would be some chance of benefit to our common interests; the civil power would be persuaded by the argument derived from numbers, and the people in each place would follow their lead without hesitation. Now there is no one more able to accomplish this than yourself, from sagacity in counsel, and energy in action, and sympathy for the troubles of the brethren, and the reverence felt by the West for your hoary head. Most Reverend Father, leave the world some memorial worthy of your former deeds. Crown your former numberless combats for religion with this one additional achievement. Send to the bishops of the West, from your Holy Church, men powerful in sound doctrine: relate to them our present calamities; suggest to them the mode of relieving us. Be a Samuel to the Churches; condole with flocks harassed by war; offer prayers of peace; ask grace of the Lord, that He may give some token of peace to the Churches. I know letters are but feeble instruments to persuade so great a thing; but while you have no need to be urged on by others, any more than generous combatants by the acclamation of boys, I, on the other hand, am not as if lecturing the ignorant, but adding speed to the earnest.

As to the remaining matters of the East, you will perhaps wish the assistance of others, and think it necessary to wait for the arrival of the Western bishops. However, there is one Church, the prosperity of which depends entirely on yourself—Antioch. It is in your power so to manage the one party, and to moderate the other, as at length to restore strength to the Church by their union. You know, better than anyone can tell you, that, as is seen in the prescriptions of wise physicians, it is necessary to begin with treating the more vital matters. Now what can be more vital to Christendom than the welfare of Antioch? If we could but settle the differences there, the head being restored, the whole body would regain health.—*Ep.* 66.

I have already observed, that there were two orthodox bishops at Antioch, one of the original succession, the other of the Arian, who had conformed. At the period under review, the Eastern bishops, and Basil among them, had bound themselves in communion with the bishop of the Arian stock; whereas Athanasius, as well as the Western Churches, were, from the very first, on terms of friendship and intercourse with the representative of the original line. In this letter, then, Basil invites Athanasius to what was, in fact, impossible, even to the influence and talents of the great primate of Egypt; for, having recognised one side in dispute, he could not mediate between them. Nothing, then, came of the application.

6

BASIL NEXT ADDRESSED himself to the Western Churches. A letter is extant, which is seemingly written to the then Pope, Damasus, on the affairs of the East.

What, [he says,] can be more pleasant than to see persons who are so far disjoined by place, yet, by the union of love, connected into harmony of membership in the body of Christ? Nearly the whole East, most reverend Father, by which I mean the country from Illyricum to Egypt, labours under a heavy storm and surge. We have been in expectation of a visitation from your tender compassion, as the one remedy of these evils. Your extraordinary love has in past time ever charmed our souls, and they were encouraged for a while by the glad report that we were to have some visitation on your part. Send persons like-minded with us, either to reconcile the parties at variance, or to bring the Churches of God to unity, or at least to give you a clearer understanding of the authors of the confusion: so that you may be clear in future with whom it is fitting to hold communion. We are pressing for nothing at all new, but what was customary with the other blessed and divinely-favoured men of old time, and especially with you. We know, from the memory of former times, as we learn on questioning our fathers, and from documents which we still preserve, that Dionysius,[1] that most blessed bishop, who was eminent with you for orthodoxy and other virtues, visited by letter our Church of Cæsarea, and consoled by letter our fathers, and sent persons to ransom the brotherhood from captivity.—*Ep.* 70.

He next addressed the Western bishops generally, in two letters, which give a most painful account of the state of the East.

BASIL TO HIS HOLY BRETHREN, THE BISHOPS OF THE WEST.

The merciful God, who ever joins comfort to affliction, has lately given me some consolation amid my sorrows, in the letters which our most reverend Father, Athanasius, has transmitted to us from your Holinesses. Our afflictions are well known without my telling; the sound of them has now gone forth over all Christendom. The dogmas of the fathers are despised; apostolical traditions are set at nought; the discoveries of innovators hold sway in the Churches. Men have learned to be speculatists instead of theologians. The wisdom of the world has the place of honour, having dispossessed the glorying in the Cross. The pastors are driven away, grievous wolves are brought in instead, and plunder the flock of Christ. Houses of prayer are destitute of preachers; the deserts are full of mourners; the aged sorrow, comparing what is with what was; more pitiable the young, as not knowing what they are deprived of. What has been said is sufficient to kindle the sympathy of those who are taught in the love of Christ, yet, compared with the facts, it is far from reaching their gravity.—*Ep.* 90.

In the second letter, addressed to the bishops of Italy and Gaul, he says:—

The danger is not confined to one Church; not two or three only have fallen in with this heavy tempest. Almost from the borders of Illyricum down to the Thebais, this evil of heresy spreads itself. The doctrines of godliness are overturned; the rules of the

[1] Pope, about A.D. 260.

Church are in confusion; the ambition of the unprincipled seizes upon places of authority; and the chief seat is now openly proposed as a reward for impiety; so that he whose blasphemies are the more shocking, is more eligible for the oversight of the people. Priestly gravity has perished; there are none left to feed the Lord's flock with knowledge; ambitious men are ever spending, in purposes of self-indulgence and bribery, possessions which they hold in trust for the poor. The accurate observance of the canons is no more; there is no restraint upon sin. Unbelievers laugh at what they see, and the weak are unsettled; faith is doubtful, ignorance is poured over their souls, because the adulterators of the word in wickedness imitate the truth. Religious people keep silence; but every blaspheming tongue is let loose. Sacred things are profaned; those of the laity who are sound in faith avoid the places of worship, as schools of impiety, and raise their hands in solitude with groans and tears to the Lord in heaven.

While, then, any Christians seem yet to be standing, hasten to us; hasten then to us, our own brothers; yea, we beseech you. Stretch out your hands, and raise us from our knees, suffer not the half of the world to be swallowed up by error; nor faith to be extinguished in the countries whence it first shone forth. What is most melancholy of all, even the portion among us which seems to be sound, is divided in itself, so that calamities beset us like those which came upon Jerusalem when it was besieged.—*Ep.* 92.

Elsewhere Basil says: "The name of the episcopate has at length belonged to wretched men, the slaves of slaves, none of the servants of God choosing to make himself their rivals, none but the abandoned."—*Ep.* 239. His friend Gregory gives us, in various parts of his works, the very same account of the Eastern Church in his day.

At this time, [he says,] the most holy Order is like to become the most contemptible portion of all that is ours. For the chief seat is gained by evil-doing more than by virtue; and the sees belong not to the more worthy, but to the more powerful. A ruler is easily found, without effort, who is but recent in point of reputation, sown and sprung up all at once, as fable speaks of giants. We make saints in a day, and we bid men have wisdom who have not learned it, nor have brought beforehand anything to their Order, over and above the will to rise to it.—*Orat.* 43.

7

THE LETTERS ADDRESSED to the bishops of the West, which have already been reviewed, were written in 372. In the course of three years, Basil's tone changes about his brethren there: he had cause to be dissatisfied with them, and above all with Pope Damasus, who, as he thought, showed little zeal for the welfare of the East. Basil's discontent is expressed in various letters. For instance, a fresh envoy was needed for the Roman mission; and he had thoughts of engaging in it his brother Gregory, bishop of Nyssa.

But, [he says,] I see no persons who can go with him, and I feel that he is altogether inexperienced in ecclesiastical matters; and that, though a candid person would both value and improve his acquaintance, yet when a man is high and haughty, and sits aloft, and is, in consequence, unable to hear such as speak truth to him from the earth, what good can come for the common weal, from his intercourse with one who is not of the temper to give in to low flattery?—*Ep.* 215.

It is observable and curious, that he who was unjustly accused by saints of pride, falls into a like injustice of accusing another saint of pride himself. In another letter, he says to his friend Eusebius:—

The saying of Diomede suggests itself as applicable, "I would thou hadst not begged, for haughty is that man." For, in truth, an elated mind, if courted, is sure to become only still more contemptuous. Besides, if the Lord be entreated, what need we more? but if God's wrath remain, what succour lies for us in Western superciliousness? [1] They neither know nor bear to learn the true state of things, but, preoccupied by false suspicions, they are now doing just what they did before in the case of Marcellus, when they quarrelled with those who told them the truth, and by their

[1] τῆς δυτικῆς ὀφρύος.

measures strengthened the heresy. As to myself, I had in mind to write to their chief, putting aside form—nothing, indeed, ecclesiastical, but just so much as to insinuate, that they do not know our real state, nor go the way to learn it; and to write generally, concerning the impropriety of pressing hard upon those who are humbled by temptations, or of considering haughtiness as dignity, a sin which is, by itself, sufficient to make God our enemy.—*Ep.* 239.

Though he began to despair of aid from the West, he did not less need it. By the year 376 matters had got worse in the East, and, in spite of his dissatisfaction, he was induced to make a fresh application to his distant brethren. His main object was to reconcile the East and West together, whereas the latter, so far from supporting the Catholics of Asia against the Arians, had been led to acknowledge a separate communion at Antioch,—almost to introduce a fresh succession,—and had thereby indirectly thrown suspicion upon the orthodoxy of Basil and his friends.

Why, [he expostulates,] has no writing of consolation been sent to us, no invitation of the brethren, nor any other of those attentions which are due to us from the law of love? This is the thirteenth year since the heretical war arose against us, during which more afflictions have come on the Churches than are remembered since Christ's Gospel was preached. Matters have come to this:—the people have left their houses of prayer, and assemble in deserts; a pitiable sight, women and children, old men and others infirm, wretchedly faring in the open air amid the most profuse rains, and snow-storms, and winds, and frost of winter; and again in summer under a scorching sun. To this they submit, because they will not have part in the wicked Arian leaven.—*Ep.* 342.

He repeats this miserable description in another letter, addressed about the same time specially to the bishops of Italy and Gaul.

Only one offence is now vigorously punished, an accurate observance of our fathers' traditions. For this cause the pious are driven from their countries and transported into the deserts. The iniquitous judges have no reverence for the hoary head, nor for pious abstinence, nor for a Gospel life continued from youth to age. The people are in lamentation; in continual tears at home and abroad; condoling in each other's sufferings. Not a heart so stony but at a father's loss must feel bereavement. There is a cry in the city, a cry in the country, in the roads, in the deserts; one pitiable voice of all, uttering melancholy things. Joy and spiritual cheerfulness are no more; our feasts are turned into mourning; our houses of prayer are shut up; our altars deprived of the spiritual worship. No longer are there Christians assembling, teachers presiding, saving instructions, celebrations, hymns by night, or that blessed exultation of souls, which arises from communion and fellowship of spiritual gifts. Lament for us; that the Only-begotten is blasphemed, and there is no one to protest; the Holy Spirit is set at nought, and he who could refute, is an exile. Polytheism has got possession. They have among them a great God and a lesser; "Son" is considered not to denote nature, but to be a title of honour. The Holy Spirit does not complete the Trinity, nor partake in the Divine and Blessed Nature, but, as if one among creatures, is carelessly and idly added to Father and Son. The ears of the simple are led astray, and have become accustomed to heretical profaneness. The infants of the Church are fed on the words of impiety. For what can they do? Baptisms are in Arian hands; the care of travellers; visitation of the sick; consolation of mourners; succour of the distressed; helps of all sorts; administration of the mysteries; which all, being performed by them, become a bond to the people to be on a good understanding with them; so that in a little while, even though liberty be granted to us, no hope will remain that they, who are encompassed by so lasting a deceit, should be brought back again to the acknowledgment of the truth.—*Ep.* 243.

8

I WILL ADD ONE LETTER MORE; written several years before these last; and addressed to Evagrius, a priest of Antioch, who had taken part in Basil's negotiations with Rome, and had expressed an intention, which he did not fulfil, of communicating with Meletius, the bishop of Antioch, whom Basil and the East acknowledged. The letter insinuates the same charges against the Western bishops, which we have seen him afterwards expressing with freedom.

BASIL TO EVAGRIUS, PRESBYTER

So far from being impatient at the length of your letter, I assure you I thought it even short, from the pleasure it gave me in reading it. For is there anything more pleasing than the idea of peace? Or, is anything more suitable to the sacred office, or more acceptable to the Lord, than to take measures for effecting it? May you have the reward of the peacemaker, since so blessed an office has been the object of your good desires and efforts. At the same time, believe me, my revered friend, I will yield to none in my earnest wish and prayer to see the day when those who are one in sentiment shall all fill the same assembly. Indeed, it would be monstrous to feel pleasure in the schisms and divisions of the Churches, and not to consider that the greatest of goods consists in the knitting together the members of Christ's body. But, alas! my inability is as real as my desire. No one knows better than yourself, that time alone is the remedy of ills that time has matured. Besides, a strong and vigorous treatment is necessary to get at the root of the complaint. You will understand this hint, though there is no reason why I should not speak out.

Self-importance, when rooted by habit in the mind, yields to the exertions of no one man, nor one letter, nor a short time; unless there be some arbiter in whom all parties have confidence, suspicions and collisions will never altogether cease. If indeed the influence of divine grace were shed upon me, and gave me power in word and deed and spiritual gifts to prevail with these rival parties, then this daring experiment might be demanded of me; though, perhaps, even then you would not advise me to attempt this adjustment of things by myself, without the coöperation of the bishop [Meletius of Antioch] on whom principally falls the care of the church. But he cannot come hither, nor can I easily undertake a long journey while the winter lasts, or rather I cannot any how, for the Armenian mountains will be soon impassable even to the young and vigorous, to say nothing of my continued bodily ailments. I have no objection to write to tell him all this; but I have no expectation that writing will lead to anything, for I know his cautious character, and after all, written words have little power to convince the mind. There are so many things to urge, and to hear, and to answer, and to object, and to all this a letter is unequal, as having no soul, and being in fact only so much waste paper. However, as I have said, I will write. Only give me credit, most religious and dear brother, for having no private feeling in the matter. Thank God, I have such towards no one. I have not busied myself in the investigation of the supposed or real complaints which are brought against this or that man; so my opinion has a claim on your attention as that of one who really cannot act from partiality or prejudice. I only desire, through the Lord's good-will, that all things may be done with ecclesiastical propriety.

I was vexed to find from my dear son, Dorotheus, our associate in the ministry, that you had been unwilling to communicate with him. This was not the kind of conversation which you had with me, as well as I recollect. As to my sending to the West, it is quite out of the question. I have no one fit for the service. Indeed, when I look round, I seem to have no one on my side. I can but pray I may be found in the number of those seven thousand who have not bent the knee to Baal. I know the present persecutors of all of us seek my life; yet that shall not diminish aught of the zeal which I owe to the Churches of God.—*Ep.* 156.

The reader cannot have failed to remark the studiously courteous tone in which the foregoing letters are written. The truth is, Basil had to deal on all hands with most untoward materials, which one single harsh or heedless word addressed to his correspondents would have served to set in a blaze. Thus he, the Exarch of Cæsarea, made himself the servant of all.

My brother Dorotheus, [he writes to Peter of Alexandria, the successor of Athanasius, in 337,] distressed me by failing, as you report, in gentleness and mildness in his conversations with your excellency. I attribute this to the times. For I seem, for my sins, to prosper in nothing, since the worthiest brethren are found deficient in gentleness and fitness for their office, from not acting according to my wishes.—*Ep.* 266.

Basil did not live to see the Churches, for which he laboured, in a more Catholic condition. The notes of the Church were impaired and obscured in his part of Christendom, and he had to fare on as he best might,—admiring, courting, yet coldly treated by the Latin world, desiring the friendship of Rome, yet wounded by her reserve,—suspected of heresy by Damasus, and accused by Jerome of pride.

CHAPTER III

BASIL AND GREGORY

"What are these discourses that you hold one with another, as you walk and are sad?"

1

IT OFTEN HAPPENS that men of very dissimilar talents and tastes are attracted together by their very dissimilitude. They live in intimacy for a time, perhaps a long time, till their circumstances alter, or some sudden event comes to try them. Then the peculiarities of their respective minds are brought out into action; and quarrels ensue, which end in coolness or separation. It would not be right or true to say that this is exemplified in the instance of the two blessed Apostles, whose "sharp contention" is related in the Book of Acts; for they had been united in spirit once for all by a divine gift; and yet their strife reminds us of what takes place in life continually. And it so far resembled the everyday quarrels of friends, in that it arose from difference of temper and character in those favoured servants of God. The zealous heart of the Apostle of the Gentiles endured not the presence of one who had swerved in his course; the indulgent spirit of Barnabas felt that a first fault ought not to be a last trial. Such are the two main characters which are found in the Church,—high energy, and sweetness of temper; far from incompatible, of course, united in Apostles, though in different relative proportions, yet only partially combined in ordinary Christians, and often altogether parted from each other.

This contrast of character, leading, first, to intimacy, then to differences, is interestingly displayed, though painfully, in one passage of the history of Basil and Gregory;—Gregory the affectionate, the tender-hearted, the man of quick feelings, the accomplished, the eloquent preacher,—and Basil, the man of firm resolve and hard deeds, the high-minded ruler of Christ's flock, the diligent labourer in the field of ecclesiastical politics. Thus they differed; yet not as if they had not much in common still; both had the blessing and the discomfort of a sensitive mind; both were devoted to an ascetic life; both were men of classical tastes; both were special champions of the Catholic creed; both were skilled in argument, and successful in their use of it; both were in highest place in the Church, the one Exarch of Cæsarea, the other Patriarch of Constantinople. I will now attempt to sketch the history of their intimacy.

2

BASIL AND GREGORY were both natives of Cappadocia, but here, again, under different circumstances; Basil was born of a good family, and with Christian ancestors: Gregory was the son of the bishop of Nazianzus, who had been brought up an idolater, or rather an Hypsistarian, a mongrel sort of religionist, part Jew, part Pagan. He was brought over to Christianity by the efforts of his wife Nonna, and at Nazianzus admitted by baptism into the Church. In process of time he was made bishop of that city; but not having a very firm hold of the faith, he was betrayed in 360 into signing the Ariminian creed, which caused him much trouble, and from which at length his son recovered him. Cæsarea being at no unsurmountable distance from Nazianzus, the two friends had known each other in their own country; but their intimacy began at Athens, whither they separately repaired for the purposes of education. This was about A.D. 350, when each of them was twenty-one years of age. Gregory came to the seat of learning shortly before Basil, and thus was able to be his host and guide on his arrival; but fame had reported Basil's merits before he came, and he seems to have made his way, in a place of all others most difficult to a stranger, with a facility peculiar to himself. He soon found himself admired and respected by his fellow-students; but Gregory was his only friend, and shared with him the reputation of talents and attainments. They remained at Athens four or five years; and, at the end of the time, made the acquaintance of Julian, since of evil name in history as the Apostate. Gregory thus describes in after life his early intimacy with Basil:—

Athens and letters followed on my stage;
Others may tell how I encountered them;—
How in the fear of God, and foremost found
Of those who knew a more than mortal lore;—
And how, amid the venture and the rush
Of maddened youth with youth in rivalry,
My tranquil course ran like some fabled spring,
Which bubbles fresh beneath the turbid brine;
Not drawn away by those who lure to ill,
But drawing dear ones to the better part.
There, too, I gained a further gift of God,
Who made me friends with one of wisdom high,
Without compeer in learning and in life.
Ask ye his name?—in sooth, 'twas Basil, since
My life's great gain,—and then my fellow dear
In home, and studious search, and knowledge earned.
May I not boast how in our day we moved
A truest pair, not without name in Greece;
Had all things common, and one only soul
In lodgment of a double outward frame?
Our special bond, the thought of God above,
And the high longing after holy things.
And each of us was bold to trust in each,
Unto the emptying of our deepest hearts;
And then we loved the more, for sympathy
Pleaded in each, and knit the twain in one.

The friends had been educated for rhetoricians, and their oratorical powers were such, that they seemed to have every prize in prospect which a secular ambition could desire. Their names were known far and wide, their attainments acknowledged by enemies, and they themselves personally popular in their circle of acquaintance. It was under these circumstances that they took the extraordinary resolution of quitting the world together,—extraordinary the world calls it, utterly perplexed to find that any conceivable objects can, by any sane person, be accounted better than its own gifts and favours. They resolved to seek baptism of the Church, and to consecrate their gifts to the service of the Giver. With characters of mind very different,—the one grave, the other lively; the one desponding, the other sanguine; the one with deep feelings, the other with feelings acute and warm;—they agreed together in holding, that the things that are seen are not to be compared to the things that are not seen. They quitted the world, while it entreated them to stay.

What passed when they were about to leave Athens represents as in a figure the parting which they and the world took of each other. When the day of valediction arrived, their companions and equals, nay, some of their tutors, came about them, and resisted their departure by entreaties, arguments, and even by violence. This occasion showed, also, their respective dispositions; for the firm Basil persevered, and went; the tender-hearted Gregory was softened, and stayed a while longer. Basil, indeed, in spite of the reputation which attended him, had, from the first, felt disappointment with the celebrated abode of philosophy and literature; and seems to have given up the world from a simple conviction of its emptiness.

> He, [says Gregory,] according to the way of human nature, when, on suddenly falling in with what we hoped to be greater, we find it short of its fame, experienced some such feeling, began to be sad, grew impatient, and could not congratulate himself on his place of residence. He sought an object which hope had drawn for him; and he called Athens "hollow blessedness."

Gregory himself, on the contrary, looked at things more cheerfully; as the succeeding sentences show.

Thus Basil; but I removed the greater part of his sorrow, meeting it with reason, and smoothing it with reflections, and saying (what was most true) that character is not at once understood, nor except by long time and perfect intimacy; nor are studies estimated, by those who are submitted to them, on a brief trial and by slight evidence. Thus I reassured him, and by continual trials of each other, I bound myself to him.—*Orat.* 43.

3

YET GREGORY HAD INDUCEMENTS of his own to leave the world, not to insist on his love of Basil's company. His mother had devoted him to God, both before and after his birth; and when he was a child he had a remarkable dream, which made a great impression upon him.

While I was asleep, [he says in one of his poems, which runs thus in prose,] a dream came to me, which drew me readily to the desire of chastity. Two virgin forms, in white garments, seemed to shine close to me. Both were fair and of one age, and their ornament lay in their want of ornament, which is a woman's beauty. No gold adorned their neck, nor jacinth; nor had they the delicate spinning of the silkworm. Their fair robe was bound with a girdle, and it reached down to their ankles. Their head and face were concealed by a veil, and their eyes were fixed on the ground. The fair glow of modesty was on both of them, as far as could be seen under their thick covering. Their lips were closed in silence, as the rose in its dewy leaves. When I saw them, I rejoiced much; for I said that they were far more than mortals. And they in turn kept kissing me, while I drew light from their lips, fondling me as a dear son. And when I asked who and whence the women were, the one answered, "Purity," the other, "Sobriety"; "We stand by Christ, the King, and delight in the beauty of the celestial virgins. Come, then, child, unite thy mind to our mind, thy light to our light; so shall we carry thee aloft in all brightness through the air, and place thee by the radiance of the immortal Trinity."—*Carm.* p. 930.

He goes on to say, that he never lost the impression this made upon him, as "a spark of heavenly fire," or "a taste of divine milk and honey."

As far, then, as these descriptions go, one might say that Gregory's abandonment of the world arose from an early passion, as it may be called, for a purity higher than his own nature; and Basil's, from a profound sense of the world's nothingness and the world's defilements. Both seem to have viewed it as a sort of penitential exercise, as well as a means towards perfection.

When they had once resolved to devote themselves to the service of religion, the question arose, how they might best improve and employ the talents committed to them. Somehow, the idea of marrying and taking orders, or taking orders and marrying, building or improving their parsonages, and showing forth the charities, the humanities, and the gentilities of a family man, did not suggest itself to their minds. They fancied that they must give up wife, children, property, if they would be perfect; and, this being taken for granted, that their choice lay between two modes of life, both of which they regarded as extremes. Here, then, for a time, they were in some perplexity. Gregory speaks of two ascetic disciplines, that of the solitary or hermit, and that of the secular; [1] one of which, he says, profits a man's self, the other his neighbour. Midway, however, between these lay the Cœnobite, or what we commonly call the monastic; removed from the world, yet acting in a certain select circle. And this was the rule which the friends at length determined to adopt, withdrawing from mixed society in order to be of the greater service to it.

The following is the passage in which Gregory describes the life which was the common choice of both of them:—

> Fierce was the whirlwind of my storm-toss'd mind,
> Searching, 'mid holiest ways, a holier still.
> Long had I nerved me, in the depths to sink
> Thoughts of the flesh, and then more strenuously.

[1] *ἄζυγες* and *μιγάδες*

Yet, while I gazed upon diviner aims,
I had not wit to single out the best:
For, as is aye the wont in things of earth,
Each had its evil, each its nobleness.
I was the pilgrim of a toilsome course,
Who had o'erpast the waves, and now look'd round,
With anxious eye, to track his road by land.
Then did the awful Thesbite's image rise,
His highest Carmel, and his food uncouth;
The Baptist wealthy in his solitude;
And the unencumbered sons of Jonadab.
But soon I felt the love of holy books,
The spirit beaming bright in learned lore,
Which deserts could not hear, nor silence tell.
Long was the inward strife, till ended thus:—
I saw, when men lived in the fretful world,
They vantaged other men, but risked the while
The calmness and the pureness of their hearts.
They who retired held an uprighter port,
And raised their eyes with quiet strength towards heaven;
Yet served self only, unfraternally.
And so, 'twixt these and those, I struck my path,
To meditate with the free solitary,
Yet to live secular, and serve mankind.

4

NOT MANY YEARS PASSED after their leaving Athens, when Basil put his resolution into practice; and, having fixed upon Pontus for his retirement, wrote Gregory to remind him of his promise. On Gregory's hesitating, he wrote to expostulate with him. Gregory's answer was as follows:—

I have not stood to my word, I own it; having protested, ever since Athens and our friendship and union of heart there, that I would be your companion, and follow a strict life with you. Yet I act against my wish, duty annulled by duty, the duty of friendship by the duty of filial reverence. . . . However, I still shall be able to perform my promise in a measure, if you will accept thus much.

I will come to you for a time, if, in turn, you will give me your company here: thus we shall be quits in friendly service, while we have all things common. And thus I shall avoid distressing my parents, without losing you.—*Ep.* 1.

When we bear in mind what has been already mentioned about Gregory's father, we may well believe that there really were very urgent reasons against the son's leaving him, when it came to the point, over and above the ties which would keep him with a father and mother both advanced in years. Basil, however, was disappointed; and instead of retiring to Pontus, devoted a year to visiting the monastic institutions of Syria and Egypt. On his return, his thoughts again settled on his friend Gregory; and he attempted to overcome the obstacle in the way of their old project, by placing himself in a district called Tiberina, near Gregory's own home. Finding, however, the spot cold and damp, he gave up the idea of it. On one occasion, while he was yet living in Cæsarea, where for a time he had taught rhetoric, Gregory wrote to him the following familiar letter, as from a countryman to an inhabitant of a town, not without a glance at Basil's peculiarities:—

You shall not charge Tiberina upon me, with its ice and bad weather, O clean-footed, tip-toeing, capering man! O feathered, flighty man, mounted on Abaris's arrow, who, Cappadocian though you be, shun Cappadocia! A vast injury it is, when you townspeople are sallow, and have not your breath full, and dole out the sun; and we are plump and in plenty, and have elbow-room! However, such is your condition; you are gentlemanlike, and wealthy, and a man of the world; I cannot praise it. Say not a word more, then, against our mud (you did not make the town, nor I the winter); if you do, I will match our wading with your trading,[1] and all the wretched things which are found in cities.—*Ep.* 2.

Meanwhile Basil had chosen for his retreat a spot near Neocæsarea, in Pontus, close by the village where lay his

[1] ἀντὶ πηλῶγ τοὺς καπήλους.

father's property, where he had been brought up in childhood by his grandmother, Macrina, and whither his mother and sister had retired for a monastic life after his father's death. The river Iris ran between the two places. Within a mile of their monastery was the Church of the Forty Martyrs, where father, mother, and sister were successively buried. These Martyrs were a number of the victims of the persecution of Licinius, at Sebaste; Emmelia, Basil's mother, had collected their relics, and he himself and his brother Gregory of Nyssa have left us homilies in celebration of them. Here, then, it was that St. Basil dwelt in holy retirement for five or six years. On settling there, he again wrote to Gregory:—

My brother Gregory writes me word that he has long been wishing to be with me, and adds, that you are of the same mind; however, I could not wait, partly as being hard of belief, considering I have been so often disappointed, and partly because I find myself pulled all ways with business. I must at once make for Pontus, where, perhaps, God willing, I may make an end of wandering. After renouncing, with trouble, the idle hopes which I once had, or rather the dreams (for it is well said, that hopes are waking dreams), I departed into Pontus in quest of a place to live in. There God has opened on me a spot exactly answering to my taste, so that I actually see before my eyes what I have often pictured to my mind in idle fancy.

There is a lofty mountain, covered with thick woods, watered towards the north with cool and transparent streams. A plain lies beneath, enriched by the waters which are ever draining off upon it; and skirted by a spontaneous profusion of trees almost thick enough to be a fence; so as even to surpass Calypso's Island, which Homer seems to have considered the most beautiful spot on earth. Indeed, it is like an island, enclosed as it is on all sides; for deep hollows cut it off in two directions; the river, which has lately fallen down a precipice, runs all along one side, and is impassable as a wall; while the mountain, extending itself behind, and meeting the hollows in a crescent, stops up the path at its roots. There is but one pass, and I am master of it. Behind my abode there is another gorge, rising to a ledge up above, so as to command the extent of the plain and the stream which bounds it, which is not less beautiful to my taste than the Strymon, as seen from Amphipolis. For while the latter flows leisurely, and swells into a lake almost, and is too still to be a river, the former is the most rapid stream I know, and somewhat turbid, too, by reason of the rock which closes on it above; from which, shooting down, and eddying in a deep pool, it forms a most pleasant scene for myself or anyone else; and is an inexhaustible resource to the country people, in the countless fish which its depths contain. What need to tell of the exhalations from the earth, or the breezes from the river? Another might admire the multitude of flowers, and singing-birds; but leisure I have none for such thoughts. However, the chief praise of the place is, that being happily disposed for produce of every kind, it nurtures what to me is the sweetest produce of all, quietness; indeed, it is not only rid of the bustle of the city, but is even unfrequented by travellers, except a chance hunter. It abounds indeed in game, as well as other things, but not, I am glad to say, in bears or wolves, such as you have, but in deer, and wild goats, and hares, and the like. Does it not strike you what a foolish mistake I was near making when I was eager to change this spot for your Tiberina, the very pit of the whole earth? Pardon me, then, if I am now set upon it; for not Alcmæon himself, I suppose, would endure to wander further when he had found the Echinades.—*Ep*. 14.

Gregory answered this letter by one which is still extant, in which he satirises, point by point, the picture of the Pontic solitude which Basil had drawn to allure him, perhaps from distaste for it, perhaps in the temper of one who studiously disparages what, if he had admitted the thought, might prove too great a temptation to him. He ends thus:—

This is longer perhaps than a letter, but shorter than a comedy. For yourself, it will be good of you to take this castigation well; but if you do not, I will give you some more of it.—*Ep*. 7.

5

Basil *did* take it well; but this did not save him from the infliction of the concluding threat; for Gregory, after paying him a visit, continues in the same bantering strain in a later epistle.

GREGORY TO BASIL

Since you take my castigation in good part, I will now give you some more of it; and, to set off with Homer, let us

"Pass on, and sing thy garniture within,"

to wit, the dwelling without roof and without door,—the hearth without fire and smoke,—walls, however, baked enough, lest the mud should trickle on us, while we suffer Tantalus's penalty, thirst in the midst of wet;—that sad and hungry banquet, for which you called me from Cappadocia, not as for the frugal fare of the Lotophagi, but as if for Alcinous's board for one lately shipwrecked and wretched. I have remembrance of the bread and of the broth —so they were named—and shall remember them: how my teeth got stuck in your hunches, and next lifted and heaved themselves as out of paste. You, indeed, will set it out in tragic style yourself, taking a sublime tone from your own sufferings. But for me, unless that true Lady Bountiful, your mother, had rescued me quickly, showing herself in need, like a haven to the tempest-tossed, I had been dead long ago, getting myself little honour, though much pity, from Pontic hospitality. How shall I omit those ungardenlike gardens, void of pot-herbs? or the Augean store, which we cleared out and spread over them; what time we worked the hillside plough, vine-dresser I, and dainty you, with this neck and hands, which still bear the marks of the toil (O earth and sun, air and virtue! for I will rant a bit), not the Hellespont to yoke, but to level the steep. If you are not annoyed at this description, nor am I; but if you are, much more I at the reality. Yet I pass over the greater part, from tender remembrance of those other many things which I have shared with you.—*Ep.* 5.

This certainly is not a picture of comfort; and curiously contrasts with Basil's romantic view of the same things. But for the following letter, one could fancy that it was too much even for Gregory; but on Basil seeming to be hurt, he wrote thus:—

GREGORY TO BASIL

What I wrote before, concerning your Pontic abode, was in jest, not in earnest; but now I write very much in earnest. "Who shall make me as in months past, as in the days" when I had the luxury of suffering hardship with you? since voluntary pain is a higher thing than involuntary comfort. Who shall restore me to those psalmodies, and vigils, and departures to God through prayer, and that (as it were) immaterial and incorporeal life? or to that union of brethren, in nature and soul, who are made gods by you, and carried on high? or to that rivalry in virtue and sharpening of heart, which we consigned to written decrees and canons? or to that loving study of divine oracles, and the light we found in them, with the guidance of the Spirit? or, to speak of lesser and lower things, to the bodily labours of the day, the wood-drawing and the stone-hewing, the planting and the draining? or to that golden plane, more honourable than that of Xerxes, under which, not a jaded king, but a weary monk did sit?—planted by me, watered by Apollos (that is, your honourable self), increased by God, unto my honour; that there should be preserved with you a memorial of my loving toil, as Aaron's rod that budded (as Scripture says and we believe) was kept in the ark. It is very easy to wish all this, not easy to gain it. Do you, however, come to me, and revive my virtue, and work with me; and whatever benefit we once gained together, preserve for me by your prayers, lest otherwise I fade away by little and little, as a shadow, while the day declines. For you are my breath, more than the air, and so far only do I live, as I am in your company, either present, or, if absent, by your image. —*Ep.* 6.

From this letter it appears that Basil had made up for Gregory's absence by collecting a brotherhood around him; in which indeed he had such success that he is considered the founder of the monastic or cœnobitic discipline in Pontus, —a discipline to which the Church gave her sanction, as soon as her establishment by the temporal power had increased the reasons for asceticism, and, increasing its professors, had created the necessity of order and method among them. The following letter, written by Basil at the time of the foregoing letters of Gregory, gives us some insight into the nature of his rule, and the motives and feelings which influenced him: it is too long to do more than extract portions of it.

BASIL TO GREGORY

Your letter brought you before me, just as one recognizes a friend in his children. It is just like you, to tell me it was but little to describe the place, without mentioning my habits and method of life, if I wished to make you desirous to join me; it was worthy of a soul which counts all things of earth as nothing, compared with that blessedness which the promises reserve for us. Yet really I am ashamed to tell you how I pass night and day in this lonely nook. Though I have left the city's haunts, as the source of innumerable ills, yet I have not yet learned to leave myself. I am like a man who, on account of sea-sickness, is angry with the size of his vessel as tossing overmuch, and leaves it for the pinnace or boat, and is sea-sick and miserable still, as carrying his delicacy of stomach along with him. So I have got no great good from this retirement. However, what follows is an account of what I proposed to do, with a view of tracking the footsteps of Him who is our guide unto salvation, and who has said: "If any one will come after Me, let him deny himself, and take up his cross, and follow Me."

We must strive after a quiet mind. As well might the eye ascertain an object put before it, while it is wandering restless up and down, and sideways, without fixing a steady gaze upon it, as a mind, distracted by a thousand worldly cares, be able clearly to apprehend the truth. He who is not yet yoked in the bonds of matrimony, is harassed by frenzied cravings, and rebellious impulses, and hopeless attachments; he who has found his mate is encompassed with his own tumult of cares: if he is childless, there is desire of children; has he children, anxiety about their education; attention to his wife, care of his house, oversight of his servants, misfortunes in trade, quarrels with his neighbours, lawsuits, the risks of the merchant, the toil of the farmer. Each day, as it comes, darkens the soul in its own way; and night after night takes up the day's anxieties, and cheats the mind with corresponding illusions. Now, one way of escaping all this is separation from the whole world; that is, not bodily separation, but the severance of the soul's sympathy with the body, and so to live without city, home, goods, society, possessions, means of life, business, engagements, human learning, that the heart may readily receive every impress of divine teaching. Preparation of heart is the unlearning the prejudices of evil converse. It is the smoothing the waxen tablet before attempting to write on it. Now, solitude is of the greatest use for this purpose, inasmuch as it stills our passions, and gives opportunity to our reason to cut them out of the soul.

This then is the meaning and drift of monasteries and monastic life, to serve God without distraction:—

Pious exercises nourish the soul with divine thoughts. What state can be more blessed than to imitate on earth the choruses of Angels?—to begin the day with prayer, and honour our Maker with hymns and songs?—as the day brightens, to betake ourselves, with prayer attending on it throughout, to our labours, and to sweeten our work with hymns, as if with salt? Soothing hymns compose the mind to a cheerful and calm state. Quiet, then, as I have said, is the first step in our sanctification; the tongue purified from the gossip of the world; the eyes unexcited by fair colour or comely shape; the ear not relaxing the tone of the mind by voluptuous songs, nor by that especial mischief, the talk of light men and jesters. Thus the mind, saved from dissipation from without, nor, through the senses, thrown upon the world, falls back upon itself, and thereby ascends to the contemplation of God.

The study of inspired Scripture is the chief way of finding our duty; for in it we find both instruction about conduct, and the lives of blessed men delivered in writing, as some breathing images of godly living, for the imitation of their good works. Hence, in whatever respect each one feels himself deficient, devoting himself to this imitation, he finds, as from some dispensary, the due medicine for his ailment. He who is enamoured of chastity, dwells upon the history of Joseph, and from him learns chaste actions finding him not only able to master the assaults of pleasure, but virtuous by habit. He is taught endurance from Job. Or, should he be inquiring how to be at once meek and great-hearted, hearty against sin, meek towards men, he will find David noble in warlike exploits, meek and unruffled as regards revenge on enemies. Such, too, was Moses, rising up with great heart upon sinners against God, but with meek soul bearing their evil-speaking against himself.

He would make the monk to be the true gentleman for he continues:—

This, too, is a very principal point to attend to,—knowledge how to converse; to interrogate without over-earnestness; to answer without desire of display; not to interrupt a profitable speaker, nor to desire ambitiously to put in a word of one's own; to be measured in speaking and hearing; not to be ashamed of receiving, or to be grudging in giving, information, nor to disown what one has learned from others, as depraved women practise with their children, but to refer it candidly to the true parent. The middle tone of voice is best, neither so low as to be inaudible, nor ill-bred from its high pitch. One should reflect first what one is going to say, and then give it utterance; be courteous when addressed, amiable in social intercourse; not aiming to be pleasant by smartness, but cultivating gentleness in kind admonitions. Harshness is ever to be put aside, even in censuring.—*Ep.* 2.

These last remarks are curious, considering the account which, as we have seen, Gregory has left us of Basil's own manner. In another epistle, of an apologetic character, he thus speaks of the devotional exercises of his monastery:—

Our people rise, while it is yet night, for the house of prayer; and after confessing to God, in distress and affliction and continued tears, they rise up and turn to psalm-singing. And now, being divided into two, they respond to each other, thereby deepening their study of the holy oracles, and securing withal attention of heart without wandering. Next, letting one lead the chant, the rest follow him; and thus, with variety of psalmody, they spend the night, with prayers interspersed; when day begins to dawn, all in common, as from one mouth and one heart, lift up to the Lord the psalm of confession, each making the words of repentance his own.—*Ep.* 207.

Such was Basil's life till he was called to the priesthood which led to his leaving his retirement for Cæsarea: by night, prayer; by day, manual labour, theological study, and mercy to the poor.

6

THE NEXT KINDLY INTERCOURSE between Basil and Gregory took place on occasion of the difference between Basil and his bishop, Eusebius; when, as has been already related, Gregory interfered successfully to reconcile them. And the next arose out of circumstances which followed the death of Gregory's brother, Cæsarius. On his death-bed he had left all his goods to the poor; a bequest which was thwarted, first, by servants and others about him, who carried off at once all the valuables on which they could lay hands; and, after Gregory had come into possession of the residue, by the fraud of certain pretended creditors, who appealed to the law on his refusing to satisfy them. Basil, on this occasion, seconded his application to the Prefect of Constantinople, who was from Cæsarea, and had known the friends intimately there, as well as at Athens.

We now come to the election of Basil to the Exarchate of Cappadocia, which was owing in no small degree to the exertions of Gregory and his father in his favour. This event, which was attended with considerable hazard of defeat, from the strength of the civil party, and an episcopal faction opposed to Basil, doubtless was at the moment a cause of increased affection between the friends, though it was soon the occasion of the difference and coolness which I spoke of in the beginning of this chapter. Gregory, as I have said, was of an amiable temper, fond of retirement and literary pursuits, and of cultivating Christianity in its domestic and friendly aspect, rather than amid the toils of ecclesiastical warfare. I have also said enough to show that I have no thought whatever of accusing so great a Saint of any approach to selfishness; and his subsequent conduct at Constantinople made it clear how well he could undergo and fight up against persecution in the quarrel of the Gospel. But such scenes of commotion were real sufferings to him, even independently of the personal risks which they involved; he was unequal to the task of ruling, and Basil in vain endeavoured to engage him as his assistant and comrade in the government of his exarchate. Let the following letter of Gregory explain his feelings:—

GREGORY TO BASIL

I own I was delighted to find you seated on the high throne, and to see the victory of the Spirit, in lifting up a light upon its candlestick, which even before did not shine dimly. Could I be otherwise, seeing the general interests of the Church so depressed, and so in need of a guiding hand like yours? However, I did not hasten to you at once, nor will I; you must not ask it of me. First, I did not, from delicacy towards your own character, that you might not seem to be collecting your partisans about you with indecency and heat, as objectors would say; next, for my own peace and reputation. Perhaps you will say, "When, then, will you come, and till when will you delay?" Till God bids, till the shadows of opposition and jealousy are passed. And I am confident it cannot be long before the blind and the lame give way, who are shutting out David from Jerusalem.—*Ep.* 45.

At length Gregory came to Cæsarea, where Basil showed him all marks of affection and respect: and when Gregory declined any public attentions, from a fear of the jealousy it might occasion, his friend let him do as he would, regardless, as Gregory observes, of the charge which might fall on himself, of neglecting Gregory, from those who were ignorant of the circumstances. However, Basil could not detain him long in the metropolitan city, as the following letter shows, written on occasion of a charge of heterodoxy, which a monk of Nazianzus advanced against Basil, and which Gregory had publicly and indignantly opposed, sending, however, to Basil to gain a clearer explanation from himself. Basil was much hurt to find he had anything to explain to Gregory. He answers in the following letter:—

BASIL TO GREGORY

I have received the letter of your religiousness, by the most reverend brother Hellenius; and what you have intimated, he has told me in plain terms. How I felt on hearing it, you cannot doubt at all. However, since I have determined that my affection for you shall outweigh my pain, whatever it is, I have accepted it as I ought to do, and I pray the Holy God, that my remaining days or hours may be as carefully conducted in their disposition towards you as they have been in past time, during which, my conscience tells me, I have been wanting to you in nothing, small or great.

After saying that his life was a practical refutation of the calumny, that a brief letter would not do what years had failed in doing, and hinting that the matter ought never to have been brought before him, and that they who listen to tales against others will have tales told of themselves, he continues:—

I know what has led to all this, and have urged every topic to hinder it; but now I am sick of the subject, and will say no more about it;—I mean, our little intercourse. For had we kept our old promise to each other, and had we had due regard to the claims which the churches have on us, we should have been the greater part of the year together; and then there would have been no opening for these calumniators. Pray have nothing to say to them; let me persuade you to come here and assist me in my labours, particularly in my contest with the individual who is now assailing me. Your very appearance would have the effect of stopping him; as soon as you show these disturbers of our country that you will, by God's blessing, place yourself at the head of our friends, you will break up their cabal, and you will "shut every unjust mouth that speaketh lawlessly against God." And thus facts will show who are your followers in good, and who it is that halts and betrays through cowardice the word of truth. If, however, the Church be betrayed, why then I shall care little to set men right about myself by means of words, who account of me as men would naturally account who have not yet learned to measure themselves. Perhaps, in a short time, by God's grace, I shall be able to refute their slanders by very deed, for it seems likely that I shall have soon to suffer somewhat for the truth's sake more than usual; the best I can expect is banishment. Or, if this hope fails, after all, Christ's judgment-seat is not far distant.—*Ep.* 71.

7

THE ALLUSION in the last sentences is to the attempts upon him of the Emperor Valens, which were then impending. We have seen in a former chapter how they were encountered and baffled by Basil's intrepidity; Valens appeared to be reconciled to him; but his jealousy of him led him to a measure which involved consequences to Basil, worse than any worldly loss, the loss of Gregory. To lessen Basil's power, Valens divided Cappadocia into two parts. This was about two years after Basil's elevation. In consequence, a dispute arose between him and Anthimus, Bishop of Tyana. Anthimus contended that an ecclesiastical division must necessarily follow the civil, and that, in consequence, he himself, as holding the chief see in the second Cappadocia, was now the rightful metropolitan of that province. The justice of the case was with Basil, but he was opposed by the party of bishops who were secretly Arianizers, and had already opposed themselves to his election. Accordingly, having might on his side, Anthimus began to alienate the monks from Basil, to appropriate those revenues of the Church of Cæsarea which lay in his province, and to expel or gain over the presbyters, giving, as an excuse, that respect and offerings ought not to be paid to heterodox persons.

Gregory at once offered his assistance to his friend, hinting to him, at the same time, that some of those about him had some share of blame in the dispute. It happened unfortunately for their friendship that they were respectively connected with distinct parties in the Church. Basil knew and valued, and gained over many of the Semi-Arians, who dissented from the Catholic doctrine more from over-subtlety, or want of clearness of mind, than from unbelief. Gregory was in habits of intimacy with the monks of Nazianzus, his father's see, and these were eager for the Nicene formula, almost as a badge of party. In the letter last cited, Basil reflects upon these monks; and, on this occasion, Gregory warned him in turn against Eustathius and his friends, whose orthodoxy was suspicious, and who, being ill-disposed towards Anthimus, were likely to increase the difference between the latter and Basil. It may be observed that it was this connexion between Basil and Eustathius to which Anthimus alluded, when he spoke against paying offerings to the heterodox.

Gregory's offer of assistance to Basil was frankly made, and seems to have been as frankly accepted. "I will come, if you wish me," he had said, "if so be, to advise with you, if the sea wants water, or you a counsellor; at all events, to gain benefit, and to act the philosopher, by bearing ill usage in your company."—*Ep.* 47. Accordingly, they set out together for a district of Mount Taurus, in the second Cappadocia, where there was an estate or Church dedicated to St. Orestes, the property of the see of Cæsarea. On their return with the produce of the farm, they were encountered by the retainers of Anthimus, who blocked up the pass, and attacked their company. This warfare between Christian bishops was obviously a great scandal in the Church, and Basil adopted a measure which he considered would put an end to it. He increased the number of bishoprics in that district, considering that residents might be able to secure the produce of the estate without disturbance, and moreover to quiet and gain over the minds of those who had encouraged Anthimus in his opposition. Sasima was a village in this neighborhood, and here he determined to place his friend Gregory, doubtless considering that he could not show him a greater mark of confidence than to commit to him the management of the quarrel, or could confer on him a post, to his own high spirit more desirable, than the place of risk and responsibility.

Gregory had been unwilling even to be made a priest; but he shrank with fear from the office of a bishop. He had upon him that overpowering sense of the awfulness of the ministerial commission which then commonly prevailed in more serious minds. "I feel myself to be unequal to this warfare," he had said on his ordination, "and therefore have hid my face, and slunk away. And I sought to sit down in solitude, being filled with bitterness, and to keep silence from a conviction that the days were evil, since God's beloved have kicked against the truth, and we have become revolting children. And besides this, there is the eternal warfare with one's passions, which my body of humiliation wages with me night and day, part hidden, part open;—and the tossing to and fro and whirling, through the senses and the delights of life; and the deep mire in which I stick fast; and the law of sin warring against the law of the spirit, and striving to efface the royal image in us, and whatever of a divine effluence has been vested in us. Before we have subdued with all our might the principle which drags us down, and have cleansed the mind duly, and have surpassed others much in approach to God, I consider it unsafe either to undertake cure of souls, or mediatorship between God and man, for some such thing is a priest."—*Or.* 2.

With these admirable feelings the weakness of the man mingled itself: at the urgent command of his father he had submitted to be consecrated; but the reluctance which he felt to undertake the office was now transferred to his occupying the see to which he had been appointed. There seems something indeed conceited in my arbitrating between Saints, and deciding how far each was right and wrong. But I do not really mean to do so: I am but reviewing their external conduct in its historical development. With this explanation I say, that an ascetic, like Gregory, ought not to have complained of the country where his see lay, as deficient in beauty and interest, even though he might be allowed to feel the responsibility of a situation which made him a neighbour of Anthimus. Yet such was his infirmity; and he repelled the accusations of his mind against himself, by charging Basil with unkindness in placing him at Sasima. On the other hand, it is possible that Basil, in his eagerness for the settlement of his exarchate, too little consulted the character and taste of Gregory; and, above all, the feelings of duty which bound him to Nazianzus. This is the account which Gregory gives of the matter, in a letter which displays much heat, and even resentment, against Basil:—

> Give me, [he says,] peace and quiet above all things. Why should I be fighting for sucklings and birds, which are not mine, as if in a matter of souls and canons? Well, play the man, be strong, turn everything to your own glory, as rivers suck up the mountain torrent, thinking little of friendship or intimacy, compared with high aims and piety, and disregarding what the world will think of you for all this, being the property of the Spirit alone; while, on my part, so much shall I gain from this your friendship, not to trust in friends, nor to put anything above God.—*Ep*. 48.

In the beginning of the same letter, he throws the blame upon Basil's episcopal throne, which suddenly made him higher than Gregory. Elsewhere he accuses him of ambition, and desire of aggrandizing himself. Basil, on the other hand, seems to have accused him of indolence, slowness, and want of spirit.

8

SUCH WAS THE MELANCHOLY CRISIS of an estrangement which had been for some time in preparation. Henceforth no letters, which are preserved, passed between the two friends; and but one act of intercourse is discoverable in their history. That exception indeed is one of much interest: Basil went to see Gregory at Nazianzus in A.D. 374, on the death of Gregory's father. But this was only like a sudden gleam, as if to remind us that charity still was burning within them; and scarcely mitigates the sorrowful catastrophe, from the point of view in which history presents it. Anthimus appointed a rival bishop to the see of Sasima; and Gregory, refusing to contest the see with him, returned to Nazianzus. Basil laboured by himself. Gregory retained his feeling of Basil's unkindness even after his death; though he revered and admired him not less, or even more, than before, and attributed his conduct to a sense of duty. In his commemorative oration, after praising his erection of new sees, he says:—

> To this measure I myself was brought in by the way. I do not seem bound to use a soft phrase. For admiring as I do all he did, more than I can say, this one thing I cannot praise,—for I will confess my feeling, which is in other ways not unknown to the world, —his extraordinary and unfriendly conduct towards me, of which time has not removed the pain. For to this I trace all the irregularity and confusion of my life, and my not being able, or not seeming, to command my feelings, though the latter of the two is a small matter; unless, indeed, I may be suffered to make this excuse for him, that, having views beyond this earth, and having departed hence even before life was over, he viewed everything as the Spirit's; and knowing how to reverence friendship, then only slighted it, when it was a duty to prefer God, and to make more account of the things hoped for than of things perishable.—*Orat.* 43.

These lamentable occurrences took place before two years of Basil's episcopate had run out, and eight or nine years before his death; he had before and after them many trials, many sorrows; but this loss of Gregory probably was the greatest of all.

CHAPTER IV

RISE AND FALL OF GREGORY

"Who will give me in the wilderness a lodging-place of wayfaring men, and I will leave my people and depart from them. Because they are all adulterers, an assembly of transgressors; and they have bent their tongue, as a bow, for lies, and not for truth."

1

"THIS, O BASIL, to thee, from me,"—thus Gregory winds up his sermon upon Basil,—"this offering to thee from a tongue once most dear to thee! thy fellow in honour and in age! If it approaches to be worthy of thee, the praise is thine; for, relying upon thee, I have set about this oration concerning thee. But if it be beneath and much beside my hope, what is to be expected from one worn down with years, sickness, and regret for thee? However, the best we can is acceptable to God. But O that thou, divine and sacred heart, mayest watch over me from above, and that thorn of my flesh, which God has given for my discipline, either end it by thy intercessions, or persuade me to bear it bravely! and mayest thou direct my whole life towards that which is most convenient! and when I depart hence, then mayest thou receive me into thy tabernacles!"—*Orat.* 43.

Gregory delivered this discourse on his return to Cæsarea from Constantinople, three years after St. Basil's death; a busy, turbulent, eventful three years, in which he had been quite a different man from what he was before, though it was all past and over now, and was about to be succeeded by the same solitude in which Basil's death found him.

Gregory disliked the routine intercourse of society; he disliked ecclesiastical business, he disliked publicity, he disliked strife, he felt his own manifold imperfections, he feared to disgrace his profession, and to lose his hope; he loved the independence of solitude, the tranquillity of private life; leisure for meditation, reflection, self-government, study, and literature. He admired, yet he playfully satirized, Basil's lofty thoughts and heroic efforts. Yet, upon Basil's death, Basil's spirit, as it were, came into him; and within four months of it, he had become a preacher of the Catholic faith in an heretical metropolis, had formed a congregation, had set apart a place for orthodox worship, and had been stoned by the populace. Was it Gregory, or was it Basil, that blew the trumpet in Constantinople, and waged a successful war in the very seat of the enemy, in despite of all his fluctuations of mind, misgivings, fastidiousness, disgust with self, and love of quiet? Such was the power of the great Basil, triumphing in his death, though failing throughout his life. Within four or five years of his departure to his reward, all the objects were either realized, or in the way to be realized, which he had so vainly attempted, and so sadly waited for. His eyes had failed in longing; they waited for the morning, and death closed them ere it came. He died on the 1st of January, 379; on the 19th of the same month the glorious Emperor Theodosius was invested with the imperial purple; by the 20th of April, Gregory had formed a Church in Constantinople; in February, in the following year, Theodosius declared for the Creed of Nicæa; in November he restored the Churches of Constantinople to the Catholics. In the next May he convoked, in that city, the second General Council, which issued in the pacification of the Eastern Church, in the overthrow of the great heresy which troubled it, and (in a measure, and in prospect) in its union with the West. "*Pretiosa in conspectu Domini mors sanctorum ejus.*"

It was under such circumstances, when our Saint had passed through many trials, and done a great work, when he, a recluse hitherto, had all at once been preacher, confessor, metropolitan, president of a General Council, and now was come back again to Asia as plain Gregory—to be what he had been before, to meditate and to do penance, and to read, and to write poems, and to be silent as in former years, except that he was now lonely,[1]—his friend dead, his father dead, mother dead, brother Cæsarius, sister Gorgonia dead, and himself dead to this world, though still to live in the flesh for some eight dreary years,—in such a time and in such a place, at Cæsarea, the scene of Basil's labours, he made the oration to which I have referred above, and invoked Basil's glorified spirit; and his invocation ends thus:—"And when I depart hence, mayest thou receive me into thy tabernacles, so that, living together with one another, and beholding together more clearly and more perfectly the Holy and Blessed Trinity, whose vision we now receive in poor glimpses, we may there come to the end of all our desires, and receive the reward of the warfare which we have waged, which we have endured! To thee, then, these words from me; but me who will there be to praise, leaving life after thee? even should I do aught praiseworthy, in Christ Jesus our Lord, to whom be glory for ever.—Amen."

2

THE CIRCUMSTANCES which brought Gregory to Constantinople were the following:—It was now about forty years since the Church of Constantinople had last had the blessing of orthodox teaching and worship. Paul, who had been elected bishop at the beginning of this period, had been visited with four successive banishments from the Arian party, and at length with martyrdom. He had been superseded in his see, first by Eusebius, the leader of the Arians, who denied our Lord's divinity; then by Macedonius, the head of those who denied the divinity of the Holy Spirit; and then by Eudoxius, the Arianizer of the Gothic tribes. On the death

[1] Vide Greg. Ep. 80, and Carm. p. 990.

of the last-mentioned, A.D. 370, the remnant of the Catholics elected for their bishop, Evagrius, who was immediately banished by the Emperor Valens; and, when they petitioned him to reverse his decision, eighty of their ecclesiastics, who were the bearers of their complaints, were subjected to an atrocious punishment for their Christian zeal, being burned at sea in the ship in which they had embarked. In the year 379, the orthodox Theodosius succeeded to the empire of the East; but this event did not at once alter the fortunes of the Church in his metropolis. The body of the people, nay, the populace itself, and, what is stranger, numbers of the female population, were eagerly attached to Arianism, and menaced violence to any one who was bold enough to preach the true doctrine. Such was the internal state of the Church; in addition to which must be added, the attitude of its external enemies:—the Novatians, who, orthodox themselves in doctrine, yet possessed a schismatical episcopacy, and a number of places of worship in the city;—the Eunomians, professors of the Arian heresy in its most undisguised blasphemy, who also had established a bishop there;—and the Semi-Arians and Apollinarists, whose heretical sentiments have been referred to in my foregoing pages. This was the condition of Constantinople when the orthodox members of its Church, under the sanction and with the coöperation of the neighbouring bishops, invited Gregory, whose gifts, religious and intellectual, were well known to them, to preside over it, instead of the heretical Demophilus, whom Valens, three years before, had placed there.

The history of Gregory's doings and fortunes at Constantinople may be told in a few words. A place of worship was prepared for him by the kindness of a relative. There he began to preach the true doctrine,—first, amid the contempt, then amid the rage and violence, of the Arian population. His congregation increased; he was stoned by the multitude, and brought before the civil authorities on the charge of creating a riot. At length, however, on Theodosius visiting the capital, he was recognized by him as bishop, and established in the temporalities of the see. However, upon the continued opposition of the people, and the vexatious combinations against him of his brother bishops, he resigned his see during the session of the second General Council, and retired to Asia Minor.

I do not intend to say more upon St. Gregory's public career; but, before leaving the subject, I am tempted to make two reflections.

First, he was fifty years old when he was called to Constantinople; a consolatory thought for those who see their span of life crumbling away under their feet, and they apparently doing nothing. Gregory was nothing till he was almost an old man; had he died at Basil's age, he would have done nothing. He seems to have been exactly the same age as Basil; but Basil had done his work and was taken away before Gregory had begun his.

The second reflection that suggests itself is this: in what a little time men move through the work which is, as it were, the end for which they are born, and which is to give a character to their names with posterity. They are known in history as the prime movers in this work, or as the instruments of that; as rulers, or politicians, or philosophers, or warriors; and when we examine dates, we often find that the exploits, or discoveries, or sway, which make them famous, lasted but a few years out of a long life, like plants that bloom once, and never again. Their ethical character, talents, acquirements, actions seem concentrated on a crisis, and give no sign of their existence as far as the world's annals are concerned, whether before or after. Gregory lived sixty years; his ecclesiastical life was barely three.

3

WHEN, TURNING FROM that ecclesiastical life, we view Gregory in his personal character, we have before us the picture of a man of warm affections, amiable disposition, and innocent life. As a son, full of piety, tenderness, and watchful solicitude; as a friend or companion, lively, cheerful, and open-hearted; overflowing with natural feelings, and easy in the expression of them; simple, good, humble, primitive. His aspirations were high, as became a saint, his life ascetic in the extreme, and his conscience still more sensitive of sin and infirmity. At the same time, he was subject to alternations of feeling; was deficient all along in strength of mind and self-control; and was harassed, even in his old age, by irritability, fear, and other passions, which one might think that even years, not to say self-discipline, would have brought into subjection. Such mere temptations and infirmities in no way interfere with his being a Saint, and, since they do not, it is consolatory to our weak hearts and feeble wills to find from the precedent of Gregory, that, being what we are, we nevertheless may be in God's favour. These then are some of the conspicuous points in Gregory's character; and the following extracts from his writings, in verse and prose, are intended in some measure to illustrate them.

At first sight, many persons may feel surprised at the rhetorical style of his sermons, or orations, as they are more fitly called: the following passage accounts for this characteristic of them. He considered he had gained at Athens, while yet in the world, a rare talent, the science of thought and speech; and next he considered that what had cost him so much, should not be renounced, but consecrated to religious uses.

This I offer to God, [he says,] this I dedicate, which alone I have left myself, in which only I am rich. For all other things I have surrendered to the commandment and the Spirit; and I have exchanged for the all-precious pearl whatever I had; and I have become, or rather long to become, a great merchant, buying things great and imperishable with what is small and will certainly decay. Discourse alone I retain, as being the servant of the Word, nor should I ever willingly neglect this possession; rather I honour and embrace and take more pleasure in it than in all other things in which the many take pleasure; and I make it my life's companion, and good counsellor, and associate, and guide heavenward, and ready comrade. I have said to Wisdom, "Thou art my sister." With this I bridle my impetuous anger, with this I appease wasting envy, with this I lull to rest sorrow, the chain of the heart; with this I sober the flood of pleasure, with this I put a measure, not on friendship, but on dislike. This makes me temperate in good fortune, and high-souled in poverty; this encourages me to run with the prosperous traveller, to stretch a hand to the falling, to be weak with the weak, and to be merry with the strong. With this, home and foreign land are all one to me, and change of places, which are foreign to me equally, and not mine own. This makes me see the difference between two worlds, withdraws me from one, joins me to the other.—*Orat.* 6.6.

When he was ordained priest, he betook himself in haste to Pontus, and only after a time returned to Nazianzus. He thus speaks of this proceeding:—

The chief cause was my surprise at the unexpected event; as they who are astounded by sudden noises, I did not retain my power of reflection, and therefore I offended against modesty, which I had cherished my whole time. Next, a certain love insinuated itself, of the moral beauty of quiet, and of retirement; for of this I had been enamoured from the beginning, more perhaps than any who have studied letters, and in the greatest and most severe of dangers, I had vowed to pursue it, nay, had even reached so far as to be on its threshold. Accordingly, I did not endure being tyrannized over, and being thrust into the midst of tumult, and dragged forcibly away from this mode of life, as if from some sacred asylum. For nothing seemed to me so great, as by closing up the senses, and being rid of flesh and world, and retiring upon one's self, and touching nothing human, except when absolutely necessary, and conversing with one's self and God, to live above things visible, and to bear within one the divine vision always clear, pure from the shifting impressions of earth,—a true mirror unsullied of God and the things of God, now and ever, adding light to light, the brighter to the dimmer, gathering even now in hope the blessedness of the world to come,—and to associate with Angels, while still on earth, leaving the earth and raised aloft by the spirit. Whoso of you is smitten with this love, knows what I say, and will be indulgent to my feeling at that time.—*Orat.* 2.

He professes that he could not bring himself to make a great risk, and to venture ambitiously, but preferred to be safe and sure.

Who is there, when he has not yet devoted himself and learned to receive God's hidden wisdom in mystery, being as yet a babe, yet fed on milk, yet unnumbered in Israel, yet unenlisted in God's army, yet unable to take up Christ's Cross as a man, not yet an honoured member of Him at all, who would, in spite of this, submit with joy and readiness to be placed at the head of the fulness of Christ? [1] No one, if I am to be the counsellor; for this is the greatest of alarms, this the extremest of dangers, to every one who understands how great a thing it is to succeed, and how ruinous to fail. Let another sail for traffic, so I said, and cross the expanse of ocean, and keep constant company with winds and waves, to gain much, if so be, and to risk much. This may suit a man apt in sailing, apt in trafficking; but what I prefer is to remain on land, to plough a small glebe and a dear one, to pay distant compliments to lucre and the sea, and thus to live, as I may be able, with a small and scanty loaf, and to linger along a life safe and surgeless, not to hazard a vast and mighty danger for mighty gains. To a lofty mind, indeed, it is a penalty not to attempt great things, not to exercise its powers upon many persons, but to abide in what is small, as if lighting a small house with a great light, or covering a child's body with a youth's armour; but to the small it is safety to carry a small burden, nor, by undertaking things beyond his powers, to incur both ridicule and a risk; just as to build a tower becomes him only who has wherewith to finish.—*Orat.* 2.

[1] Vide Eph. i. 23.

4

IT IS PLAIN THAT the gentle and humble-minded Gregory was unequal to the government of the Church and province of Constantinople, which were as unworthy, as they were impatient, of him. Charges of his incompetency formed part of the ground on which a successful opposition was made to him in the second General Council. What notions, however, his enemies had of fitness, is plain from the following extract. The truth is, Gregory was in no sense what is called, rightly or wrongly, a party man; and while he was deficient, perhaps, in the sagacity, keenness, vigour, and decision for which a public man too often incurs the reproach of that name, he also had that kindness of heart, dispassionateness, and placability, which more justly avail to rescue a person from it. It was imputed to him that he was not severe enough with his fallen persecutors. He thus replies:

Consider what is charged against me. "So much time is passed," they say, "of your governing the Church, at the critical moment, with the emperor's favour, which is of such importance. What symptom of the change is there? How many persecutors had we before! what misery did we not suffer! what insults, what threats, what exiles, what plunderings, what confiscations, what burnings of our clergy at sea, what temples profaned with blood of saints, and instead of temples made charnel-houses! What has followed? We have become stronger than our persecutors, and they have escaped!" So it is. For me it is enough of vengeance upon our injurers to have the power of retaliation. But these objectors think otherwise; for they are very precise and righteous in the matter of reprisals, and therefore they expect the advantage of the opportunity. "What prefect," they ask, "has been punished? or populace brought to its senses? or what incendiaries? what fear of ourselves have we secured to us for the time to come?"—*Orat.* 42.

Gregory had by far too little pomp and pretence to satisfy a luxurious and fastidious city. They wanted "a king like the nations;" a man who had a presence, who would figure and parade and rustle in silk, some Lord Mayor's preacher or West-end divine, who could hold forth and lay down the law, and be what is thought dignified and grand; whereas they had no one but poor, dear, good Gregory, a monk of Nazianzus, a personage who, in spite of his acknowledged learning and eloquence, was but a child, had no knowledge of the world, no manners, no conversation, and no address; who was flurried and put out in high society, and who would have been a bad hand at a platform speech, and helpless in the attempt to keep a modern vestry in order.

Perhaps, too, [he continues,] they may cast this slur upon me, as indeed they have, that I do not keep a good table, nor dress richly; and that there is a want of style when I go abroad, and a want of pomp when people address me. Certainly, I forgot that I had to rival consuls and prefects and illustrious commanders, who have more wealth than they know what to do with. If all this is heinous, it has slipped my mind; forgive me this wrong; choose a ruler instead of me, who will please the many; restore me to solitude, to rusticity, and to God, whom I shall please, though I be parsimonious.

And shortly before,—

This is my character: I do not concur in many points with the many; I cannot persuade myself to walk their pace; this may be rudeness and awkwardness, but still it is my character. What to others are pleasures, annoy me; and what I am pleased with, annoys others. Indeed, it would not surprise me, even were I put into confinement as a nuisance, and were I considered to be without common wits by the multitude, as is said to have happened to a Greek philosopher, whose good sense was accused of being derangement, because he made jest of all things, seeing that the serious objects of the many were really ridiculous; or if I were accounted full of new wine, as Christ's disciples, from their speaking with tongues, the power of the Spirit being mistaken in them for excitement of mind.—*Ibid.*

He has a similar passage, written, after his resignation, in verse, which must here be unworthily exhibited in prose.

This good, [he says,] alone will be free and secure from restraint or capture,—a mind raised up to Christ. No more shall I be entertained at table by mortal prince, as heretofore,—I Gregory, to pack a few comforts into me, placed in the midst of them, bashful and speechless, not breathing freely, feasting like a slave. No magistrate shall punish me with a seat, either near him, or below him, giving its due place to a grovelling spirit. No more shall I clasp blood-stained hands, or take hold of beard, to gain some small favour. Nor, hurrying with a crowd to some sacred feast of birthday, burial, or marriage, shall I seize on all that I can, some things for my jaws, and some for attendants with their greedy palms, like Briareus's; and then carrying myself off, a breathing grave, late in the evening, drag along homeward my ailing carcass, worn out, panting with satiety, yet hastening to another fat feast, before I have shaken off the former infliction.—*Carm.* ii. 17.

One who is used to bread and water is overset by even a family dinner; much less could Gregory bear a city feast or conservative banquet.

5

On his return to Asia, first he had stayed for a time at Nazianzus; thence he went to Arianzus, the place of his birth. Here he passed the whole of Lent without speaking, with a view of gaining command over his tongue, in which, as in other respects, he painfully felt or fancied his deficiency. He writes the following notes to a friend:—"You ask what my silence means? it means measurement of speaking, and not speaking. For he who can do it in whole, will more easily do it in part. Besides, it allays anger, when it is not brought out into words, but is extinguished in itself."—*Ep.* 96. Again: "I do not forbid your coming to me; though my tongue be still, my ears shall be gladly open to your conversation; since to hear what is fitting is not less precious than to speak it."—97. And again: "I am silent in conversation, as learning to speak what I ought to speak; moreover, I am exercising myself in mastery of the passions. If this satisfies the inquirer, it is well;

if not, at least silence brings this gain, that I have not to enter into explanations."—98.

Gregory was now fifty-two or three; there is something remarkable in a man so advanced in life taking such vigorous measures to overcome himself.

The following passages from his poems allude to the same, or similar infirmities:—

I lost, O Lord, the use of yesterday;
Anger came on, and stole my heart away.
O may this morning's light until the evening stay!

Again:

The serpent comes anew! I hold Thy feet.
Help, David! help, and strike thy harp-strings sweet!
Hence! choking spirit, hence! to thine own hell retreat.

Some temptation or other is alluded to in the following poems; though perhaps it is not fair to make a poet responsible, in his own person, for all he speaks as if from himself.

Here are his thoughts for the

MORNING

I rise, and raise my claspèd hands to Thee.
Henceforth the darkness hath no part in me,
Thy sacrifice this day;
Abiding firm, and with a freeman's might
Stemming the waves of passion in the fight.
Ah! should I from Thee stray,
My hoary head, Thy table where I bow,
Will be my shame, which are mine honour now.
Thus I set out;—Lord, lead me on my way!

And then, after "the burden of the day, and the heat," we find him looking back when he comes to the

EVENING

O Holiest Truth, how have I lied to Thee!
I vowed this day Thy festival should be;
Yet I am dim ere night.

Surely I made my prayer, and I did deem
That I could keep in me Thy morning beam
Immaculate and bright.
But my foot slipped, and, as I lay, he came,
My gloomy foe, and robbed me of heaven's flame.
Help Thou my darkness, Lord, till I am light.

In the verses on Morning an allusion may be observed to his priesthood. The following lines bear a more express reference to it, and perhaps to Penance also:—

In service o'er the mystic feast I stand,
I cleanse Thy victim-flock, and bring them near
In holiest wise, and by a bloodless rite.
O Fire of Love! O gushing Fount of Light!
(As best I know, who need Thy cleansing hand),
Dread office this, bemirèd souls to clear
Of their defilement, and again make bright.

These lines may have an allusion which introduces us to the following:—

As viewing sin, e'en in its faintest trace,
Murder in wrath, and in the wanton oath
The perjured tongue, and therefore shunning them,
So deem'd I safe a strict virginity.
And hence our ample choir of holiest souls
Are followers of the unfleshly seraphim,
And Him who 'mid them reigns in lonely light.
These, one and all, rush towards the thought of death,
And hope of second life, with single heart,
Loosed from the law and chain of marriage vow.
For I was but a captive at my birth,
Sin my first life, till its base discipline
Revolted me towards a nobler path.
Then Christ drew near me, and the Virgin-born
Spoke the new call to join His virgin-train.
So now towards highest heaven my innocent brow
I raise exultingly, sans let or bond,
Leaving no heir of this poor tabernacle
To ape me when my proper frame is broke;

But solitary with my only God,
And truest souls to bear me company.

6

IT SO HAPPENS that we have a vast deal of Gregory's poetry, which he doubtless never intended for publication, but which formed the recreation of his retirement. From one of these compositions the following playful extract, on the same subject, is selected:—

As when the hand some mimic form would paint,
It marks its purpose first in shadows faint,
And next its store of varied hues applies,
Till outlines fade, and the full limbs arise;
So in the earlier school of sacred lore
The virgin life no claim of honour bore,
While in Religion's youth the Law held sway
And traced in symbols dim that better way.
But, when the Christ came by a virgin-birth,—
His radiant passage from high heaven to earth,—
And, spurning father for His mortal state,
Did Eve and all her daughters consecrate;
Solved fleshly laws, and in the letter's place
Gave us the spirit and the word of grace;—
Then shone the glorious Celibate at length,
Robed in the dazzling lightnings of its strength,
Surpassing spells of earth and marriage vow,
As soul the body, heaven this world below,
The eternal peace of saints life's troubled span,
And the high throne of God the haunts of man.
So now there circles round the King of Light
A heaven on earth, a blameless court and bright,
Aiming as emblems of their God to shine,
Christ in their heart, and on their brow His sign,
Soft funeral lights in the world's twilight dim,
Seeing their God, and ever one with Him.

Ye countless multitude, content to bow
To the soft thraldom of the marriage vow!

I mark your haughty step, your froward gaze,
Gems deck your hair, and silk your limbs arrays;
Come, tell the gain which wedlock has conferred
On man; and then the single shall be heard.

The married many thus might plead, I ween;
Full glib their tongue, right confident their mien:—
"Hear, all who live! to whom the nuptial rite
Has brought the privilege of life and light,
We, who are wedded, but the law obey,
Stamped at creation on our blood and clay,
What time the Demiurge our line began,
Oped Adam's side, and out of man drew man.
Thenceforth let children of a mortal sod
Honour the law of earth, the primal law of God.

"List, you shall hear the gifts of price that lie
Gathered and bound within the marriage tie.
What taught the arts of life, the truths that sleep
In earth, or highest heaven, or vasty deep?
What filled the mart, and urged the vessel brave
To link in one far countries o'er the wave?
What raised the town?—what gave the type and germ
Of social union, and of sceptre firm?
Who the first husbandman, the glebe to plough,
And rear the garden, but the marriage vow?

"Nay, list again! who seek its kindly chain,
A second self, a double presence gain;
Hands, eyes, and ears, to act or suffer here,
Till e'en the weak inspire both love and fear—
A comrade's sigh, to soothe when cares annoy—
A comrade's smile, to elevate his joy.

"Nor say it weds us to a carnal life;
When want is urgent, fears and vows are rife.
Light heart is his, who has no yoke at home,
Scant prayer for blessings as the seasons come.
But wife, and offspring, goods which go or stay,
Teach us our need, and make us trust and pray.

Take love away, and life would be defaced,
A ghastly vision on a howling waste,
Stern, heartless, reft of the sweet spells, which swage
The throes of passion, and which gladden age.
No child's sweet pranks, once more to make us young;
No ties of place about our heart-strings flung;
No public haunts to cheer; no festive tide,
Where harmless mirth and smiling wit preside;
A life, which scorns the gifts which Heaven assign'd,
Nor knows the sympathy of human kind.

"Prophets and teachers, priests and victor kings,
Decked with each grace which heaven-taught nature brings,
These were no giant offspring of the earth,
But to the marriage-promise owe their birth:—
Moses and Samuel, David, David's son,
The blessed Thesbite, and more blessed John,
The sacred twelve in apostolic choir,
Strong-hearted Paul, instinct with seraph-fire,
And others, now or erst, who to high heaven aspire.
Bethink ye; should the single state be best,
Yet who the single, but my offspring blest?
My sons, be still, nor with your parents strive,
They coupled in their day, and so ye live."

Thus Marriage pleads. Now let her rival speak;
Dim is her downcast eye, and pale her cheek;
Untrimmed her gear; no sandals on her feet;
A sparest form for austere tenant meet.
She drops her veil her modest face around,
And her lips open, but we hear no sound.
I will address her:—"Hail! O child of heaven,
Glorious within! to whom a post is given
Hard by the throne, where Angels bow and fear,
E'en while thou hast a name and mission here,
O deign thy voice, unveil thy brow, and see
Thy ready guard and minister in me.
Oft hast thou come heaven-wafted to my breast,
Bright Spirit! so come again, and give me rest!"

. . . "Ah! who has hither drawn my backward feet,
Changing for worldly strife my lone retreat?
Where, in the silent chant of holy deeds,
I praise my God, and tend the sick soul's needs;
By toils of day, and vigils of the night,
By gushing tears, and blessed lustral rite.
I have no sway amid the crowd, no art
In speech, no place in council or in mart;
Nor human law, nor judges throned on high,
Smile on my face, and to my words reply.
Let others seek earth's honours; be it mine
One law to cherish, and to track one line;
Straight on towards heaven to press with single bent,
To know and love my God, and then to die content."
etc., etc.

It would take up too much time to continue the poem, of which I have attempted the above rude and free translation (or rather paraphrase, as indeed are all the foregoing); or to introduce any other specimens of the poetical talents of this accomplished Father of the Church.

I end with one or two stanzas, which give an account of the place and circumstances of his retirement. I am obliged again to warn the reader, that he must not fancy he has gained an idea of Gregory's poetry from my attempts at translation; and should it be objected that this is not treating Gregory well, I answer, that at least I am as true to the original as if I exhibited it in plain prose.

Some one whispered yesterday
Of the rich and fashionable,
"Gregory, in his own small way,
Easy was, and comfortable.

Had he not of wealth his fill,
Whom a garden gay did bless,
And a gently trickling rill,
And the sweets of idleness?"

I made answer: "Is it ease
  Fasts to keep, and tears to shed?
Vigil hours and wounded knees,
  Call you these a pleasant bed?

Thus a veritable monk
  Does to death his fleshly frame;
Be there who in sloth are sunk,
  They have forfeited the name."

And thus I take leave of St. Gregory, a man who is as great theologically as he is personally winning.

CHAPTER V

ANTONY IN CONFLICT

"He found him in a desert land, in a place of horror and of wilderness; He led him about, and taught him; and He kept him as the apple of His eye."

1

IT WOULD BE A GREAT MISTAKE for us to suppose that we need quit our temporal calling, and go into retirement, in order to serve God acceptably. Christianity is a religion for this world, for the busy and influential, for the rich and powerful, as well as for the poor. A writer of the age of Justin Martyr expresses this clearly and elegantly:—"Christians differ not," he says, "from other men, in country, or language, or customs. They do not live in any certain cities, or employ any particular dialect, or cultivate peculiar habits of life. They dwell in cities, Greek and barbarian, each where he finds himself placed; and while they submit to the fashion of their country in dress and food, and the general conduct of life, still they maintain a system of interior polity, which, beyond all controversy, is admirable and strange. The countries they inhabit are their own, but they dwell like aliens. They marry, like other men, and do not exclude their children from their affections; their table is open to all around them; they live in the flesh, but not according to the flesh; they walk on earth, but their conversation is in heaven."—*Ad Diogn.* 5.

Yet, undeniable as it is, that there is never an obligation upon Christians in general to leave, and often an obligation against leaving, their worldly engagements and possessions, still it is as undeniable that such an abandonment is often praiseworthy, and in particular cases a duty. Our Saviour expressly told one, who was rich and young, "to sell all, and give to the poor;" and surely He does not speak in order to immortalize exceptions or extreme cases, or fugitive forms of argument, refutation, or censure. Even looking at the subject in a merely human light, one may pronounce it to be a narrow and shallow system, that Protestant philosophy, which forbids all the higher and more noble impulses of the mind, and forces men to eat, drink, and be merry, whether they will or no. But the mind of true Christianity is expansive enough to admit high and low, rich and poor, one with another.

If the primitive Christians are to be trusted as witnesses of the genius of the Gospel system, certainly it is of that elastic and comprehensive character which removes the more powerful temptations to extravagance, by giving, as far as possible, a sort of indulgence to the feelings and motives which lead to it, correcting them the while, purifying them, and reining them in, ere they get excessive. Thus, whereas our reason naturally loves to expatiate at will to and fro through all subjects known and unknown, Catholicism does not oppress us with an irrational bigotry, prescribing to us the very minutest details of thought, so that a man can never have an opinion of his own; on the contrary, its creed is ever what it was, and never moves out of the ground which it originally occupied, and it is cautious and precise in its decisions, and distinguishes between things necessary and things pious to believe, between wilfulness and ignorance. At the same time, it asserts the supremacy of faith, the guilt of unbelief, and the divine mission of the Church; so that reason is brought round again and subdued to the obedience of Christ, at the very time when it seems to be launching forth without chart upon the ocean of speculation. And it pursues the same course in matters of conduct. It opposes the intolerance of what are called "*sensible* Protestants." It is shocked at the tyranny of those who will not let a man do anything out of the way without stamping him with the name of fanatic. It deals softly with the ardent and impetuous, saying, in effect—"My child, you may do as many great things as you will; but I have already made a list for you to select from. You are too docile to pursue ends merely because they are of your own choosing; you seek them because they are *great*. You wish to live above the common course of a Christian;—I can teach you to do this, yet without arrogance." Meanwhile the sensible Protestant divine keeps to his point, hammering away on his own ideas, urging every one to be as every one else, and moulding all minds upon his one small model; and when he has made his ground good to his own admiration, he finds that half his flock have after all turned Wesleyans or Independents, by way of searching for something divine and transcendental.

2

THESE REMARKS ARE INTENDED as introductory to some notice of the life of St. Antony, the first monk, who finished his work in Egypt just about the time that St. Basil was renewing that work in Asia Minor. The words "monk," "monastic," mean "solitary," and, if taken literally, certainly denote a mode of life which is so far contrary to nature as to require some special direction or inspiration for its adoption. Christ sent His Apostles by two and two; and surely He knew what was in man from the day that He said—"It is not good for him to be alone." So far, then, Antony's manner of life may be ill-fitted to be a rule for others; but his pattern in this respect was not adopted by his followers, who by their numbers were soon led to the formation of monastic societies, nay, who, after a while, entangled even Antony himself in the tie of becoming in a certain sense their religious head and teacher. Monachism consisting, not in solitariness, but in austerities, prayers, retirement, and obedience, had nothing in it, surely, but what was perfectly Christian, and, under circumstances, exemplary; especially when viewed in its connexion with the relative duties, which were soon afterwards appropriated to it, of being almoner of the poor, of educating the clergy, and of defending the faith. In short, Monachism became, in a little while, nothing else than a peculiar department of the Christian ministry—a ministry not of the sacraments, but especially of the word and doctrine; not indeed by any formal ordination to it, for it was as yet a lay profession, but by the common right, or rather duty, which attaches to all of us to avow, propagate, and defend the truth, especially when such zeal for it has received the countenance and encouragement of our spiritual rulers.

St. Antony's life, written by his friend, the great Athanasius, has come down to us. Some critics, indeed, doubt its genuineness, or consider it interpolated. Rivetus and others reject it; Du Pin decides, on the whole, that it is his, but with additions; the Benedictines and Tillemont ascribe it to him unhesitatingly. I conceive no question can be raised with justice about its *substantial* integrity; and on rising from the perusal of it, all candid readers will pronounce Antony a wonderful man. Enthusiastic he certainly must be accounted, according to English views of things; and had he lived a Protestant in this Protestant day, he would have been exposed to a serious temptation of becoming a fanatic. Longing for some higher rule of life than any which the ordinary forms of society admit, and finding our present lines too rigidly drawn to include any character of mind that is much out of the way, any rule that is not "gentlemanlike," "comfortable," and "established," and hearing nothing of the Catholic Church, he might possibly have broken what he could not bend. The question is not, whether such impatience is not open to the charge of wilfulness and self-conceit; but whether, on the contrary, such special resignation to worldly comforts as we see around us, is not often the characteristic of nothing else than selfishness and sloth;—whether there are not minds with ardent feelings, keen imaginations, and undisciplined tempers, who are under a strong irritation prompting them to run wild,—whether it is not our duty (so to speak) to play with such, carefully letting out line enough lest they snap it,—and whether the Protestant Establishment is as indulgent and as wise as might be desired in its treatment of such persons, inasmuch as it provides no occupation for them, does not understand how to turn them to account, lets them run to waste, tempts them to dissent, loses them, is weakened by the loss, and then denounces them.

But to return to Antony. Did I see him before me, I might be tempted, with my cut and dried opinions, and my matter-of-fact ways, and my selfishness and pusillanimity, to consider him somewhat of an enthusiast; but what I desire to point out to the reader, and especially to the Protestant, is the subdued and Christian form which was taken by his enthusiasm, if it must be so called. It was not vulgar, bustling, imbecile, unstable, undutiful; it was calm and composed, manly, intrepid, magnanimous, full of affectionate loyalty to the Church and to the Truth.

3

ANTONY WAS BORN A.D. 251, while Origen was still alive, while Cyprian was bishop of Carthage, Dionysius bishop of Alexandria, and Gregory Thaumaturgus of Neocæsarea; he lived till A.D. 356, to the age of 105, when Athanasius was battling with the Emperor Constantius, nine years after the birth of St. Chrysostom, and two years after that of St. Augustine. He was an Egyptian by birth, and the son of noble, opulent, and Christian parents. He was brought up as a Christian, and, from his boyhood, showed a strong disposition towards a solitary life. Shrinking from the society of his equals, and despising the external world in comparison of the world within him, he set himself against what is considered a liberal education—that is, the study of philosophy and of foreign languages. At the same time, he was very dutiful to his parents, simple and self-denying in his habits, and attentive to the sacred services and readings of the Church.

Before he arrived at man's estate he had lost both his parents, and was left with a sister, who was a child, and an ample inheritance. His mind at this time was earnestly set upon imitating the Apostles and their converts, who gave up their possessions and followed Christ. One day, about six months after his parents' death, as he went to church, as usual, the subject pressed seriously upon him. The Gospel of the day happened to contain the text—"If thou wilt be perfect, go sell all that thou hast." Antony applied it to himself, and acted upon it. He had three hundred acres,[1] of especial fertility, even for Egypt; these he at once made over to the use of the poor of his own neighbourhood. Next, he turned into money all his personal property, and reserving a portion for his sister's use, gave the rest to the poor. After a while he was struck by hearing in church the text—"Be not solicitous for to-morrow;" and considering he had not yet fully satisfied the Evangelical counsel, he gave away what he had reserved, placing his sister in the care of some women, who had devoted themselves to the single state.

He commenced his ascetic life, according to the custom then observed, by retiring to a place not far from his own home. Here he remained for a while to steady and fix his mind in his new habits, and to gain what advice he could towards the perfect formation of them, from such as had already engaged in the like object. This is a remarkable trait, as Athanasius records it, as showing how little he was influenced by self-will or a sectarian spirit in what he was doing, how ardently he pursued an ascetic life as in itself good, and how willing he was to become the servant of any who might give him directions in pursuing it. But this will be best shown by an extract:—

There was, in the next village, an aged man who had lived a solitary life from his youth. Antony, seeing him, "was zealous in a good thing," and first of all adopted a similar retirement in the neighbourhood of the village. And did he hear of any zealous person anywhere, he would go and seek him out, like a wise man; not returning home till he had seen him, and gained from him

[1] *Arura*—Three quarters of an English acre.—*Gibbon.*

some stock, as it were, for his journey towards holiness. He laboured with his hands, according to the words—"if anyone will not work, neither let him eat;" laying out part of his produce in bread, part on the poor. He prayed continually, having learned that it is a duty to pray in private without ceasing. So attentive, indeed, was he to sacred reading, that he let no part of the Scripture fall from him to the ground, but retained all, memory serving in place of book. In this way he gained the affections of all; he, in turn, subjecting himself sincerely to the zealous men whom he visited, and marking down, in his own thoughts, the special attainment of each in zeal and ascetic life—the refined manners of one, another's continuance in prayer, the meekness of a third, the kindness of a fourth, the long vigils of a fifth, the studiousness of a sixth. This one had a marvellous gift of endurance, that of fasting and sleeping on the ground; this was gentle, that long-suffering; and in one and all he noted the devotion towards Christ, and love one towards another. Thus furnished, he returned to his own ascetic retreat, henceforth combining in himself their separate exercises, and zealously minded to exemplify them all. This, indeed, was his only point of emulation with those of his own age, viz. that he might not come off second to them in good things; and this he so pursued as to annoy no one, rather to make all take delight in him. Accordingly, all the villagers of the place, and religious persons who were acquainted with him, seeing him such, called him God's beloved, and cherished him as a son or as a brother.—§ 4.

Of course this acount is the mere relation of a fact; but, over and above its historical character, it evidently is meant as the description of a type of character which both the writer and those for whom he wrote thought eminently Christian. Taking it then as being, in a certain line, the *beau ideal* of what Protestants would call the enthusiasm of the time, I would request of them to compare it with the sort of religion into which the unhappy enthusiast of the present day is precipitated by the high and dry system of the Establishment; and he will see how much was gained to Christianity, in purity, as well as unity, by that monastic system, the place of which in this country is filled by methodism and dissent.

After a while, our youth's enthusiasm began to take its usual course. His spirits fell, his courage flagged; a reaction followed, and the temptations of the world which he had left assaulted him with a violence which showed that as yet he had not mastered the full meaning of his profession. Had he been nothing more than an enthusiast, he would have gone back to the world. The property he had abandoned, the guardianship of his sister, his family connexions, the conveniences of wealth, worldly reputation, disgust of the sameness and coarseness of his food, bodily infirmity, the tediousness of his mode of living, and the absence of occupation, presented themselves before his imagination, and became instruments of temptation. Other and fiercer assaults succeeded. However, his faith rose above them all, or rather, as Athanasius says, "not himself, but the grace of God that was in him." His biographer proceeds:—

Such was Antony's first victory over the devil, or rather the Saviour's glorious achievement in him, "who hath condemned sin in the flesh, that the justification of the law may be fulfilled in us, who walk not according to the flesh, but according to the Spirit." Not, however, as if Antony, fancying the devil was subdued, was neglectful afterwards, and secure; knowing from the Scriptures that there are many devices of the enemy, he was persevering in his ascetic life. He was the more earnest in chastising his body, and bringing it into subjection, lest, triumphing in some things, in others he might be brought low. His vigils were often through the whole night. He ate but once in the day, after sunset; sometimes after two days, often after four: his food was bread and salt,—his drink, water only. He never had more than a mat to sleep on, but generally lay down on the ground. He put aside oil for anointing, saying that the youthful ought to be forward in their asceticism, and, instead of seeking what might relax the body, to accustom it to hardships, remembering the Apostle's words—"When I am weak, then am I powerful." He thought it unsuitable to measure either holy living, or retirement for the sake of it, by length of time; but by the earnest desire and deliberate resolve of being holy. Accordingly, he never himself used to take any account of the time gone by; but, day by day, as if ever fresh beginning his exercise, he made still greater efforts to advance, repeating to himself continually the saying of the Apostle, "forgetting the things that are behind, and stretching forth myself to those that are before."—§ 7.

4

SUCH WAS HIS LIFE for about fifteen years. At the end of this time, being now thirty-five, he betook himself to the desert, having first spent some days in prayers and holy exercises in the tombs. Here, however, I am compelled to introduce another subject, which has already entered into Athanasius's text, though it has not been necessary to notice it,—his alleged conflicts with the evil spirits; to it, then, let us proceed.

It is quite certain, then, that Antony believed himself to be subjected to sensible and visible conflicts with evil spirits. It would not be consistent with our present argument to rescue him from the imputation of enthusiasm: he must be here considered an enthusiast, else I cannot make use of him; the very drift of my account of him being to show how enthusiasm is sobered and refined by being submitted to the discipline of the Church, instead of being allowed to run wild externally to it. I say, if he were not an enthusiast, or at least in danger of being such, we should lose one chief instruction which his life conveys. To maintain, however, that he was an enthusiast, is far from settling the question to which the narrative of his spiritual conflicts gives rise; so I shall first make some extracts descriptive of them, and then comment upon them.

The following is the account of his visit to the tombs:—

Thus bracing himself after the pattern of Elias, he set off to the tombs, which were some distance from his village; and giving directions to an acquaintance to bring him bread after some days' interval, he entered into one of them, suffered himself to be shut in, and remained there by himself. This the enemy not enduring, yea, rather dreading, lest before long he should engross the desert also with his holy exercise, assaulted him one night with a host of spirits, and so lashed him, that he lay speechless on the ground from the torture, which, he declared, was far more severe than from strokes which man could inflict. But, by God's Providence, who does not overlook those who hope in Him, on the next day his acquaintance came with the bread; and, on opening the door, saw him lying on the ground as if dead. Whereupon he carried him to the village church, and laid him on the ground; and many of his relations and the villagers took their places by the body, as if he were already dead. However, about midnight his senses returned, and collecting himself, he observed that they were all asleep except his aforesaid acquaintance; whereupon he beckoned him to his side, and asked of him, without waking any of them, to carry him back again to the tombs.

The man took him back: and when he was shut in, as before, by himself, being unable to stand from his wounds, he lay down, and began to pray. Then he cried out loudly, "Here am I, Antony; I do not shun your blows. Though ye add to them, yet nothing shall separate me from the love of Christ." And then he began to sing, "If armies in camp should stand together against me, my heart shall not fear." The devil has no trouble in devising diverse shapes of evil. During the night, therefore, the evil ones made so great a tumult, that the whole place seemed to be shaken, and, as if they broke down the four walls of the building, they seemed to rush in in the form of wild beasts and reptiles. . . . But Antony, though scourged and pierced, felt indeed his bodily pain, but the rather kept vigil in his soul. So, as he lay groaning in body, yet a watcher in his mind, he spoke in taunt—"Had ye any power, one of you would be enough to assail me; you try, if possible, to frighten me with your number, because the Lord has spoiled you of your strength. Those pretended forms are the proofs of your impotence. Our seal and wall of defence is faith in our Lord." After many attempts, then, they gnashed their teeth at him, because they were rather making themselves a sport than him. But the Lord a second time remembered the conflict of Antony, and came to his help. Raising his eyes, he saw the roof as if opening, and a beam of light descending towards him; suddenly the devils vanished, his pain ceased, and the building was whole again. Upon this Antony said, "Where art Thou, Lord? why didst Thou not appear at the first, to ease my pain?" A voice answered, "Antony, I was here, but waited to see thy bearing in the contest; since, therefore, thou hast sustained and not been worsted, I will be to thee an aid for ever, and I will make thy name famous in every place."—§§ 9, 10.

After this preliminary vigil, Antony made for the desert, where he spent the next twenty years in solitude. Athanasius gives the following account of his life there:—

The following day he left the tombs, and his piety becoming still more eager, he went to the old man before mentioned, and prayed him to accompany him into the desert. When he declined by reason of his age and the novelty of the proposal, he set off for the mountain by himself . . . and finding beyond the river a strong place, deserted so long a while that venomous reptiles abounded there, he went thither, and took possession of it, they farther retreating, as if one pursued them. Blocking up the entrance, and laying in bread for six months (as the Thebans are wont, often keeping their bread a whole year), and having a well of water indoors, he remained, as if in a shrine, neither going abroad himself, nor seeing any of those who came to him. . . . He did not allow his acquaintance to enter; so, while they remained often days and nights without, they used to hear noises within; blows, pitiable cries, such as "Depart from our realm! what part hast thou in the desert? thou shalt perforce yield to our devices." At first they thought he was in dispute with some men who had entered by means of ladders; but when they had contrived to peep in through a chink, and saw no one, then they reckoned it was devils that they heard, and, in terror, called Antony. He cared for them more than for the spirits, and coming at once near the door, bade them go away, and not fear; "for," he said, "the devils make all this feint to alarm the timid. Ye, then, sign yourselves, and depart in confidence, and let them make game of themselves." —§§ 12, 13.

5

TO ENTER INTO THE STATE of opinion and feeling which such accounts imply, it is necessary to observe, that, as regards the Church's warfare with the devil, the primitive Christians, as Catholics since, considered themselves to be similarly circumstanced with the Apostles. They did not draw a line, as is the fashion with Protestants, between the condition of the Church in their day and in the first age, but believed that what she had been, such she was still in her trials and in her powers; that the open assaults of Satan, and their own means of repelling them, were such as they are described in the Gospels. Exorcism was a sacred function with them, and the energumen took his place with catechumens and penitents, as in the number of those who had the especial prayers, and were allowed some of the privileges, of the Christian body. Our Saviour speaks of the power of exorcising as depending on fasting and prayer, in certain special cases, and thus distinctly countenances the notion of a direct conflict between the Christian athlete and the powers of evil,—a conflict, carried on, on the side of the former, by definite weapons, for definite ends, and not that indirect warfare merely which an ordinary religious course of life implies. "This kind can go out by nothing but by prayer and fasting." Surely none of Christ's words are chance words; He spoke *with a purpose*, and the Holy Spirit guided the Evangelists in their selection of them *with a purpose;* and if so, this text is a rule and an admonition, and was acted upon as such by the primitive Christians, whether from their received principles of interpretation or the traditionary practice of the Church.

In like manner, whether from their mode of interpreting Scripture, or from the opinions and practices which came down to them, they conceived the devil to be allowed that power over certain brute animals which Scripture sometimes assigns to him. He is known on one memorable occasion to have taken the form of a serpent; at another time, a legion of devils possessed a herd of swine. These instances may, for what we know, be revealed *specimens* of a whole side of the Divine Dispensation, viz., the interference of spiritual agencies, good and bad, with the course of the world, under which, perhaps, the speaking of Balaam's ass falls; and the early Christians, whether so understanding Scripture, or from their traditionary system, acted as if they really were such specimens. They considered that brute nature was widely subjected to the power of spirits; as, on the other hand, there had been a time when even the Creator Spirit had condescended to manifest Himself in the bodily form of a dove. Their notions concerning local demoniacal influences as existing in oracles and idols, in which they were sanctioned by Scripture, confirmed this belief. Accordingly, they took passages like the following literally, and used them as a corroborative proof: "Behold, I have given you power to tread upon *serpents* and *scorpions*, and upon all the power of the enemy." "They shall take up *serpents*, and if they drink any deadly thing, it shall not hurt them." "Your adversary, the devil, as a roaring *lion*, goeth about, seeking whom he may devour." "I saw three unclean spirits, like *frogs* . . . they are the spirits of devils, working signs." Add to these, Daniel's vision of the four beasts; and the description of leviathan, in the book of Job, which was interpreted of the evil spirit.

Moreover, there is a ground of deep philosophy on which such notions may be based, and which appears to have been held by these primitive Christians; viz., that visible things are types and earnests of things invisible. The elements are, in some sense, symbols and tokens of spiritual agents, good and bad. Satan is called the prince of this air. Still more mysterious than inanimate nature is the family of brute animals, whose limbs and organs are governed by some motive principle unknown. Surely there is nothing abstractedly absurd in considering certain hideous developments of nature as tokens of the presence of the unseen author of evil, as soon as we once admit that he exists. Certainly the sight of a beast of prey, with his malevolent passions, savage cruelty, implacable rage, malice, cunning, sullenness, restlessness, brute hunger, irresistible strength, though there cannot be sin in any of these qualities themselves, awakens very awful and complicated musings in a religious mind. Thus a philosophical view of nature would be considered, in the times I speak of, to corroborate the method of Scripture interpretation which those same times adopted.

But, moreover, Scripture itself seemed, in the parallel case of demoniacs, to become its own interpreter. It was notorious that in the Apostolic age devils made human beings their organs; why, then, much more, should not brute beasts be such? The simple question was, whether the state of things in the third century was substantially the same as it was in the first; and this, I say, the early Christians *assumed* in the affirmative, and certainly, whether they were judges of this question or not, I suppose they were as good judges as Protestants are. The case of demoniacs should be carefully considered, since their sufferings often seem to have been neither more nor less than what would now be hastily attributed to natural diseases, and would be treated by medical rules. The demoniac whom the Apostles could not cure had certain symptoms which in another would have been called epileptic. Again, the woman who was bowed together for eighteen years, and was cured by Christ, is expressly said to have had "a spirit of infirmity," to have been "bound by Satan." If, then, what looks like disease may sometimes be the token of demoniacal presence and power, though ordinarily admitting of medical treatment, why is it an objection to the connexion of the material or animal world with spirits, that the laws of mineral agents, or the peculiarities of brute natures, can also be drawn out into system on paper, and can be anticipated and reckoned on by our knowledge of that system? The same objection lies, nay, avails, against the one and the other. The very same scoffing temper which rejects the teaching of the Church, primitive and modern, concerning Satan's power, as "Pagan," "Oriental," and the like, does actually assail the inspired statements respecting it also, explains away demoniacal possessions as unreal, and maintains that Christ and His Apostles spoke by way of accommodation, and in the language of their day, when they said that Satan bound us with diseases and plagues, and was "prince of the power of the air."

Dreams are another department of our present state of being, through which, as Scripture informs us, the Supernatural sometimes acts; and in the same general way; *i.e.* not always, and by ascertainable rules, but by the virtue of occasional, though real, connexion with them.

6

On the whole, then, I am led to conclude, that, supposing I found a narrative, such as Antony's, of *the Apostles' age,* it would be sufficiently agreeable to the narratives of Scripture to make me dismiss from my mind all *antecedent* difficulties in believing it. On the other hand, did the miracle of the swine occur in the life of St. Antony, I venture to maintain that men of this scientific day would not merely suspend their judgment, or pronounce it improbable (which they might have a right to do), but would at once, and peremptorily, pronounce it altogether incredible and false: so as to make it appear that

> There are more things in heaven and earth, Horatio,
> Than are dreamt of in your philosophy.

I have no wish to trifle, or argue with subtlety upon a very deep subject. This earth had become Satan's kingdom; our Lord came to end his usurpation; but Satan retreated only inch by inch. The Church of Christ is hallowed ground, but external to it is the kingdom of darkness. Many serious persons think that the evil spirits have, even now, extraordinary powers in heathen lands, to say nothing of the remains of their ancient dominion in countries now Christian. There are strange stories told in heathen populations of sorcerers and the like. Nay, how strange are the stories which only in half-heathen, or even Christian places, have come perhaps to our own knowledge! How unaccountable to him who has met with them are the sudden sounds, the footsteps, and the noises which he has heard in solitary places, or when in company with others!

These things being considered, were I a candid Protestant, I would judge of Antony's life thus:—I should say: "There may be enthusiasm here; there may be, at times, exaggerations and misconceptions of what, as they really happened, meant nothing. And still, it may be true also that that conflict, begun by our Lord when He was interrogated and assaulted by Satan, was continued in the experience of Antony, who lived not so very long after Him. How far the evil spirit acted, how far he was really present in material forms, how far on the other hand was dream, how far imagination, is little to the purpose. I see, anyhow, the root of a great truth here, and think that those are wiser who admit something than those who deny everything. I see Satan frightened at the invasions of the Church upon his kingdom; I see him dispossessed by fasting and prayer, as was predicted; I see him retreating step by step; and I see him doing his utmost in whatever way to resist. Nor is there anything uncongenial to the Gospel system, that so direct a war, with such definite weapons, should be waged upon him; a war which has not the ordinary duties of life and of society for its subject-matter and instruments. That text about fasting and prayer is a canon in sanction of it: our Saviour too Himself was forty days in the wilderness; and St. Peter at Joppa, and St. John at Patmos, show us that duties of this world may be providentially suspended under the Gospel, and a direct intercourse with the next world may be opened upon the Christian."

And if so much be allowed, certainly there is nothing in Antony's life to make us suspicious of him personally. His doctrine surely was pure and unimpeachable; and his temper is high and heavenly,—without cowardice, without gloom, without formality, and without self-complacency. Superstition is abject and crouching, it is full of thoughts of guilt; it distrusts God, and dreads the powers of evil. Antony at least has nothing of this, being full of holy confidence, divine peace, cheerfulness, and valorousness, be he (as some men may judge) ever so much an enthusiast. But on this subject I shall say something in the next chapter.

CHAPTER VI

ANTONY IN CALM

"The land that was desolate and impassable shall be glad, and the wilderness shall rejoice and shall flourish like the lily. And that which was dry land shall become a pool, and the thirsty land springs of water."

1

I HAVE SAID ENOUGH about St. Antony's history; let me now introduce the reader to his character, which I shall best do by setting before him some unconnected passages, as they occur in the narrative of his life.

It is remarkable that his attempts at curing diseases were not always successful; his prayers being *experimental*, not, as in the case of the Apostles, immediately suggested by the same Power which was about miraculously to manifest Itself. Of course there were then in the Church, as at all times, extraordinary and heavenly gifts; but still they were distinct from those peculiar powers which we ascribe to the Apostles, as immediate ministers of the Revelation.

He united in sympathy and prayer with those who were in suffering, [says Athanasius,] and *often*, and in many cases, the Lord heard him. When heard, he did not boast; *when unsuccessful*, he did not murmur; but, under all circumstances, he gave thanks himself to the Lord, and exhorted the sufferers to be patient, and to be assured that their cure was out of the power of himself, and indeed of any man, and lay with God only, *who wrought when He would, and towards whom He chose*. The patients in consequence accepted *even the words* of the old man as a medicine, learning themselves not to despise the means, but rather to be patient, while those who were healed were instructed not to give thanks to Antony but to God only.—§ 56.

This passage deserves notice also, as showing the unvarnished character of the narrative. Superstitious and fabulous histories are not candid enough to admit such failures as are implied in it. The following is to the same purpose. He was asked to allow a paralytic woman and her parents to visit him, with the hope of a cure, and he refused, on the ground that, if her life was to be preserved, her own prayers might be efficacious without him.

Go, [he humbly answered,] and, *unless she be dead already*, you will find her cured. This happy event is not my doing, that she should come to me, a miserable man, to secure it; but the cure is from the Saviour, who shows mercy *in every place*, on those who call upon Him. *To her prayers*, then, the Lord has been gracious, to me is but revealed, by his loving-kindness, that He means to cure her where she is.—§ 58.

Antony held that faith had power with God for any work: and he took delight in contrasting with this privilege of exercising faith that poor measure of knowledge which is all that sight and reason open on us at the utmost. He seems to have felt there was a divine spirit and power in Christianity such as irresistibly to commend it to religious and honest minds, coming home to the heart with the same conviction which any high moral precept carries with it, and leaving argumentation behind as comparatively useless, except by way of curiously investigating motives and reasons for the satisfaction of the philosophical analyst. And then, when faith was once in operation, it was the instrument of gaining the knowledge of truths which reason could but feebly presage, or could not even have imagined.

Some philosophers came to discourse with him; he says to them:

"Since you prefer to insist on demonstrative argument, and, being skilled in the science of it, would have us also refrain from worshipping God without a demonstrative argument, tell me first, how is the knowledge of things in general, and especially of religion, absolutely ascertained? Is it by a demonstration of argument, or through an operative power of faith? And which of the two will you put first?" They said, Faith, owning that it was absolute knowledge. Then Antony rejoined, "Well said, for faith results from a disposition of the soul; but dialectics are from the science of the disputant. They, then, who possess the operative power of faith can supersede, nay, are but cumbered with demonstration in argument; for what we apprehend by faith, you are merely endeavouring to arrive at by argument, and sometimes cannot even express what we apprehend. Faith, then, which operates, is better and surer than your subtle syllogisms."—§ 77.

Again:

Instead of demonstrating in the persuasive arguments of Gentile wisdom, as our Teacher says, we persuade by faith, which vividly anticipates a process of argument.—§ 80.

After curing some demoniacs with the sign of the cross, he adds:

Why wonder ye at this? It is not we who do it, but Christ, by means of those who believe on Him. Do ye too believe, and ye shall see that our religion lies not in some science of argument, but in faith, which operates through love towards Jesus Christ; which if ye attained, ye too would no longer seek for demonstrations drawn from argument, but would account faith in Christ all-sufficient.—*Ibid.*

Antony, as we have already seen, is far from boasting of his spiritual attainments:

It is not right to glory in casting out devils, nor in curing diseases, nor to make much of him only who casts out devils, and to undervalue him who does not. On the contrary, study the ascetic life of this man and that, and either imitate and emulate or improve it. For to do miracles is not ours, but the Saviour's; wherefore He said to His disciples, "Rejoice not that spirits are subject unto you," etc. To those who take confidence, not in holiness but in miracles, and say, "Lord, did we not cast out devils in

Thy name?" He makes answer, "I never knew you," for the Lord does not acknowledge the ways of the ungodly. On the whole, then, we must pray for the gift of discerning spirits, that, as it is written, we may not believe every spirit.—§ 38.

In like manner he dissuades his hearers from seeking the gift of prophecy; in which he remarkably differs from heathen ascetics, such as the Neo-platonists, who considered a knowledge of the secret principles of nature the great reward of their austerities.

What is the use of hearing beforehand from the evil ones what is to happen? Or, why be desirous of such knowledge, even though it be true? It does not make us better men; nor is it a token of religious excellence at all. None of us is judged for what he does not know, nor accounted happy for his learning and acquirements; but in each case the question is this, whether or not he has kept the faith, and honestly obeyed the commandments? Wherefore we must not account these as great matters, nor live ascetically for the sake of them—viz. in order to know the future; but to please God by a good conversation. But if we are anxious at all to foresee what is to be, it is necessary to be pure in mind. Certainly I believe that that soul which is clean on every side, and established in its highest nature, becomes keen-sighted, and is able to see things more and further than the devils, having the Lord to reveal them to it. Such was the soul of Eliseus, which witnessed Giezi's conduct, and discerned the heavenly hosts which were present with it.—§ 34.

2

THESE EXTRACTS HAVE incidentally furnished some evidence of the calmness, and I may say coolness of Antony's judgment—*i.e.* waiving the question of the truth of the principles and facts from which he starts. I am aware that an objector would urge that this is the very peculiarity of aberrations of the intellect, to reason correctly upon false premisses; and that Antony in no way differs from many men nowadays, whom we consider unable to take care of themselves. Yet surely, when we are examining the evidence for the divine mission of the Apostles, we do think it allowable to point out their good sense and composure of mind, though they assume premisses as Antony does. And, considering how extravagant and capricious the conduct of enthusiasts commonly is, how rude their manners, how inconstant their resolutions, how variable their principles, it is certainly a recommendation to our solitary to find him so grave, manly, considerate, and refined,—or, to speak familiarly, so gentlemanlike in the true sense of that word. We see something of this in the account which Athanasius gives us of his personal appearance after his twenty years' seclusion, which has nothing of the gaunt character, or the uncouth expression, of one who had thrown himself out of the society of his fellow-men. I shall be obliged to make a long extract, if I begin; and yet I cannot help hoping that the reader will be pleased to have it.

He had now spent nearly twenty years exercising himself thus by himself, neither going abroad nor being seen for any time by any one. But at this date, many longing to copy his ascetic life, and acquaintances coming and forcibly breaking down and driving in the door, Antony came forth as from some shrine, fully perfect in its mysteries, and instinct with God. This was his first appearance outside the enclosure, and those who had come to see him were struck with surprise at the little change his person had undergone, having neither a full habit, as being without exercise, nor the shrivelled character which betokens fasts and conflicts with the evil ones. He was the same as they had known him before his retreat. His mind also was serene, neither narrowed by sadness nor relaxed by indulgence, neither over-merry nor melancholy. He showed no confusion at the sight of the multitude, no elation at their respectful greetings. The Lord gave him grace in speech, so that he comforted many who were in sorrow, and reconciled those who were at variance, adding in every case, that they ought to set nothing of this world before love towards Christ. And while he conversed with the people, and exhorted them to remember the bliss to come, and God's loving-kindness to us men in not sparing His own Son, but giving Him up for us all, he persuaded many to choose the monastic life. And from that time monasteries have been raised among the mountains, and the desert is made a city by monks leaving their all and enrolling themselves in the heavenly citizenship.

His biographer then goes on to record one of his discourses. It was spoken in the Egyptian language, and ran as follows:

Holy Scripture is sufficient for teaching, yet it is good to exhort one another in the faith, and refresh one another with our discourses. You then, as children, bring hither to your father whatever you have learned; and I in turn, as being your elder, will now impart to you what I have experienced. Let this preeminently be the common purpose of every one of you, not to give in when once you have begun, not to faint in your toil, not to say, "We have been long enough at these exercises." Rather as though, day after day, we were beginning for the first time, let our zeal grow stronger; for even the whole of human life is very short compared with eternity, or rather nothing. And every thing in this world has its price, and you get no more than an equivalent; yet the promise of everlasting life is bought at a trifling purchase. "The days of our years are three score and ten years," as Scripture says, "and if, in the strong, they be four score;" yet, did we persist in our exercises for the whole four score, or for a hundred, this would not be the measure of our reign in glory. Instead of a hundred years, we shall reign for ages upon ages; not upon this poor earth upon which is our struggle, but our promised inheritance is in heaven. We lose a corruptible body to receive it back incorruptible.

Wherefore, my children, let us not worry, nor think we have been a long while toiling, or that we are doing any great thing; for our present sufferings are not to be compared to the glory that shall be revealed in us. Let us not look at the world, or reckon we have made great sacrifices, for even the whole earth is but a small spot compared to the expanse of heaven. Though we had possessed it all, and had given it all up, it is nothing to the kingdom of heaven. It is no more than a man's making little of one copper coin in order to gain a hundred gold ones; thus he who is lord of the whole earth, and bids it farewell, does but give up little and gains a hundredfold. But if the whole earth be so little, what is it to leave a few acres? or a house? or a store of gold? Surely we should not boast or be dejected upon such a sacrifice. If we do not let these things go for virtue's sake, at death at length we shall leave them, and often to whom we would not, as says Ecclesiastes. What gain is it to acquire what we cannot carry away with us? Far different are prudence, justice, temperance, fortitude, understanding, charity, love of the poor, faith towards Christ, gentleness, hospitality; obtain we these, and we shall find them there before us, making ready a dwelling for us in the country of the meek.

After reminding his brethren that they have the Lord to work with them, and that they must fulfil the Apostles' rule of dying daily,—by rising as though they should not last till evening, and going to rest as though they should never rise, "life being of an uncertain nature, doled out by Providence from day to day," he continues:

Therefore, having now set out upon the path of virtue, let us rather stretch forward to what is before. Be not alarmed when you hear speak of virtue, nor feel towards the name as if you were strangers to it; for it is not far from us, it is not external to us; the work is in us, and the thing is easy, if we have but the will. Greeks travel beyond the sea to learn letters,—we need not travel for the kingdom of heaven, or cross the sea for virtue. Christ anticipates us, "The kingdom of heaven (He says) is within you;" virtue needs but the will.

We have able and subtle enemies, the evil spirits; with these we must wrestle, as the Apostle says. There is need of much prayer and self-discipline to gain, through the Holy Spirit, the gift of discerning of spirits, to detect their nature, viz. which of them are the less abandoned, which the more, what is the aim of each, what each affects, and how each is overthrown and ejected. When the Lord came on earth, the enemy fell, and his power waxed weak; therefore, as being a tyrant, though powerless, he keeps not quiet even in his fall, but threats, for he can do no more. Let each of you consider this, and he may scorn the evil spirits. Behold, we are here met together and speak against them, and they know that, as we make progress, they will grow feebler. Had they then leave, they would suffer none of us Christians to live; had they power, they would not come on with a noise, or put forth phantoms, or change their shapes to further their plans; one of them would be enough, did he come, to do what he could and wished to do. Such as have power do not make a display in order to kill another, nor alarm by noises, but use their power to effect at once what they wish. But evil spirits, since they can do nothing, are but as actors in a play, changing their shapes and frightening children by their tumult and their make-belief; whereas the true Angel of the Lord, sent by Him against the Assyrians, needed not tumult, appearance, noise, or clatter, but, in that quiet exercise of his power, he slew at once a hundred four score and five thousand. But the devils have not power even over the swine: much less over man made in God's image.—§§ 14–29.

3

WHAT CAN BE MORE CALM, more fearless, more noble than his bearing in this passage? Call his life a romance, if you think fit; still, I say, at least, we have in the narrative the ideal of a monk, according to the teaching of the fourth century. You cannot say that Anthony was a savage self-tormentor, an ostentatious dervise;[1] that he had aught of pomposity or affectation, aught of cunning and hypocrisy. According to Athanasius's description—who was personally acquainted with him—

His countenance had a great and extraordinary beauty in it. This was a gift from the Saviour; for, if he was in company with a number of monks, and any stranger wished to have a sight of him, directly that he came to them, he would pass by the rest, and run to Antony, as being attracted by his appearance. Not that he was taller or larger than others; but there was a peculiar composure of manner and purity of soul in him. For, being unruffled in soul, all his outward expressions of feeling were free from perturbation also; so that the joy of his soul made his very face cheerful, and from the gestures of the body might be understood the composure of his soul, according to the text, "A glad heart maketh a cheerful countenance;

[1] Archaic for "dervish."—[Ed.]

but by grief of mind the spirit is cast down." Thus Jacob detected Laban's treachery, and said to his wives, "I see your father's countenance, that it is not towards me as yesterday." Thus Samuel, too, discovered David; for he had beaming eyes, and teeth white as milk. In like manner one might recognise Antony; for he was never agitated, his soul being in deep calm,—never changed countenance, from his inward joyfulness.—§ 67.

His own words assign one of the causes of this tranquillity. He says:

The vision granted us of the holy ones is not tumultuous; for "He shall not contend, nor cry out," nor shall any one hear their voice. So quietly and gently does it come, that the soul is straightway filled with joy, exultation, and confidence, knowing that the Lord is with them, who is our joy, and God the Father's power. And its thoughts are preserved from tumult and tempest; so that, being itself illuminated fully, it is able of itself to contemplate the beings that appear before it. A longing after divine and future things takes possession of it, till it desires altogether to be joined unto them, and to depart with them. Nay, and if there be some who, from the infirmity of man, dread the sight of these good ones, such apparitions remove their alarm at once by their love, as Gabriel did to Zacharias, and the Angel at the divine tomb to the women, and that other who said to the shepherds in the Gospel, "Fear not."—§ 35.

Such sentiments, beautiful as they are, might in another be ascribed to mere mysticism; but not so in the case of Antony, considering his constant profession and practice of self-denying and active virtue, and the plain practical sense of his exhortations. He took a vigorous part in the religious controversies of his day, reverencing the authorities of the Church, and strenuously opposing both the Meletian schismatics and the Arians. The following is an account of another of his interviews with heathen philosophers. They came with the hope of jeering at his ignorance of literature:

Antony said to them, "What do you say? which is prior, the mind or letters? And which gives rise to which, mind to letters, or letters to mind?" When they answered that mind was prior, and invented letters, Antony replied, "He, then, whose mind is in health, does not need letters." This answer struck all who were present, as well as the philosophers. They went away surprised that an uneducated man should show such understanding. For, indeed, he had nothing of the wildness of one who had lived and grown old on a mountain; but was polished in his manners, and a man of the world.—§ 73.

It has sometimes been objected, that hagiographists commonly fail in point of dignity, in the miracles which they introduce into their histories. I am not called here to consider the force of this objection; but Antony at least is clear of the defect; had his miracles and visions been ascribed to St. Peter or St. Paul, I conceive they would not have been questioned, evidence being supposed. For instance:

Once, when he was going to take food, having stood up to pray, about the ninth hour, he felt himself carried away in spirit, and, strange to say, he saw himself, as if out of himself, while he stood looking on, and borne into the air by certain beings. Next, he saw some hateful and terrible shapes, stationed in the air, and stopping the way to prevent his passing on. His conductors resisted, but they asked whether he was not impeachable. But on their beginning to reckon up from his birth, his conductors interrupted them, saying, "The Lord has wiped out all his earlier sins; but a reckoning may lawfully be made from the time he became a monk, and promised himself to God." His accusers hereupon began; but, when they could prove nothing, the way became clear and open; and immediately he found himself returned, as it were, to himself, and forming with himself one Antony as before. Then forgetting his meal, he remained the rest of that day, and the whole of the following night, groaning and praying; for he was astonished at finding against how many we have to wrestle, and by what an effort we must pass through the air heavenward. He remembered that this is what the Apostle said, "the prince of the power of this air,"—and his special exhortation in consequence, "Put on the panoply of God, that ye may be able to resist in the evil day." When we heard it, we called to mind the Apostle's words,

"Whether in the body, or out of the body, I know not; God knoweth."—§ 65.

Again:

He had had a discussion with some persons, who had come to him, concerning the passage of the soul, and the abode which was allotted to it. On the following night, some one calls him from above in these words, "Antony, rise, go forth, and behold." Accordingly he went forth, knowing whom he should obey, and, looking up, he saw a huge something, unsightly and horrid, standing and reaching up to the clouds, and beings were ascending as if with wings, and it was catching at them with its hands. Of these, it brought some to a stand; while others, flying past it, went upwards without further trouble. In such cases, that huge monster would gnash its teeth; rejoicing, on the other hand, over those whom it cast down. Immediately Antony heard a voice, saying, "Look, and understand." And his mind was opened, and he comprehended that he saw the passage of souls, and the enemy, envious of the faithful, seizing and stopping those whom he had an advantage over, but foiled in his attempts upon those who had not obeyed him. After this vision, taking it as a warning, he made still more strenuous efforts to advance forward daily.—§ 66.

Once more:

Once, when he was sitting and working, he fell into a trance, and groaned much at the sight he saw. After a while, he turned to those who were with him groaning, and prayed with much trembling, remaining a long time on his knees. When, at length, he rose, the old man began to weep. His friends, trembling and in great alarm themselves, begged to know what it was, and urged him till he was forced to tell. "O, my children," he said at length, with a deep sigh, "it were better to die before that vision is fulfilled." On their pressing him, he continued with tears, "Wrath is about to overtake the Church, which is to be given over to men like irrational brutes. For I saw the table of the Lord's house hemmed in by mules, who were striking about with their hoofs at everything within, as is the way with unmannered beasts. You see, now, why I groaned so much; for I heard a voice, saying, My altar shall be polluted." This the old man saw; two years after, the assaults of the Arians took place, when they plundered the churches, and gave the sacred vessels to heathens to carry, and compelled the heathens from the workshops to attend their religious meetings with them, and in their presence wanton insults offered to the Lord's table. –§ 82.

4

At length the hour came for him to die; and Antony and his monks made their respective preparations for it. The narrative runs thus:

The brethren urging him to remain with them, and there finish his course, he would not hear of it, as for other reasons, which were evident, even though he did not mention them, so especially because of the custom of the Egyptians in respect to the dead. For the bodies of good men, especially of the holy martyrs, they used to enfold in linen cloths; and, instead of burying, to place them upon biers, and keep them within their houses, thinking thus to honour the departed. Antony had applied even to bishops on this subject, begging them to admonish their people; and had urged it upon laymen, and had rebuked women, saying, that the practice was consistent neither with received rule, nor at all with religion. "The bodies of patriarchs and prophets are preserved to this day in sepulchres; and the Lord's body itself was laid in a tomb, and a stone at the entrance kept it hidden till He rose the third day." By such arguments he showed the irregularity of not burying the dead, however holy; "for what can be more precious or holy than the Lord's body?" And he persuaded many to bury for the future, giving thanks to the Lord for such good instruction.

This was a matter of discipline and of discretion, as to which the custom of the Church may vary at different times; but with that we are not concerned here; to proceed:

Antony, then, being aware of this, and fearing lest the same should be done to his own body, bidding farewell to the monks in the outer mountain, made hastily for the inner mountain, where he commonly dwelt, and after a few months, fell ill. Then calling to him two who lived with him, as ascetics, for fifteen years past, and ministered to him on account of his age, he said to them, "I, as it is written, go the way of my fathers; for I perceive I am called by the Lord. You, then, be sober, and forfeit not the reward of your long asceticism; but, as those who have made a beginning, be diligent to hold fast your earnestness. Ye know the assaults of the evil spirit, how fierce they are, yet how powerless. Fear them not; rather breathe the spirit of Christ, and believe in Him always. Live as if dying daily; take heed to yourselves, and remember the admonitions you have heard from me. Have no fellowship with the schismatics, nor at all with the heretical Arians. Be diligent the rather to join yourselves, first of all, to the Lord, next to the Saints, that after death they may receive you as friends and intimates into the eternal habitations. Such be your thoughts, such your spirit; and if you have any care for me, remember me as a father. Do not let them carry my body into Egypt, lest they store it in their houses. One of my reasons for coming to this mountain was to hinder this. You know I have ever reproved those who have done this, and charged them to cease from the custom. Bury, then, my body in the earth, in obedience to my word, so that no one may know the place, except yourselves. In the resurrection of the dead it will be restored to me incorruptible by the Saviour. Distribute my garments as follows:—let Athanasius, the bishop, have the one sheep-skin and the garment I sleep on, which he gave me new, and which has grown old with me. Let Serapion, the bishop, have the other sheep-skin. As to the hair-shirt, keep it for yourselves. And now, my children farewell; Antony is going, and is no longer with you."

After these words, they kissed him. Then he stretched himself out, and seemed to see friends come to him, and to be very joyful at the sight (to judge from the cheerfulness of his countenance as he lay), and so he breathed his last, and was gathered to his fathers. His attendants, as he had bidden them, wrapped his body up, and buried it: and no one knows yet where it lies, except these two. As to the two friends who were bequeathed a sheep-skin a-piece of the blessed Antony, and his tattered garment, each of them preserves it as a great possession. For when he looks at it, he thinks he sees Antony; and when he puts it on, he is, as it were, carrying about him his instruction with joy.—§§ 90, 92.

Such was in life and death the first founder of the monastic system; and his example, both as seen, and far more in the narrative of his biographer, was like a fire kindled in Christendom, which "many waters could not quench." Not that I would defend the details of any popular form of religion, considering that its popularity implies some condescension to the weaknesses of human nature; yet, if I must choose between the fashionable doctrines of one age and of another, certainly I shall prefer that which requires self-denial, and creates hardihood and contempt of the world, to some of the religions now in esteem, which rob faith of all its substance, its grace, its nobleness, and its strength, and excuse self-indulgence by the arguments of spiritual pride, self-confidence, and security;—which, in short, make it their boast that they are more *comfortable* than that ancient creed which, together with joy, leads men to continual smiting on the breast, and prayers for pardon, and looking forward to the judgment-day, as to an event really to happen to themselves individually.

The following is Athanasius's account of the effect produced by Antony in Egypt, even in his lifetime; and perhaps in his lifetime it was not only in its beginning, but in its prime. For all things human tend not to be, and the first fervour of zeal and love is the most wonderful. Yet even when its original glory had faded, the monastic home was ever, as now, the refuge of the penitent and the school of the saint. But let us hear Athanasius:

> Among the mountains there were monasteries, as if tabernacles filled with divine choirs, singing, studying, fasting, praying, exulting in the hope of things to come, and working for almsdeeds, having love and harmony one towards another. And truly it was given one there to see a peculiar country of piety and righteousness. Neither injurer nor injured was there, nor chiding of the tax-collector; but a multitude of ascetics, whose one fceling was towards holiness. So that a stranger, seeing the monasteries and their order, would be led to cry out, "How beauteous are thy homes, O Jacob, and thy tabernacles, O Israel; as shady groves, as a garden on a river, as tents which the Lord has pitched, and as cedars by the waters."—§ 44.

CHAPTER VII

AUGUSTINE AND THE VANDALS

"The just perisheth, and no man layeth it to heart; and men of mercy are taken away, for there is none to understand; for the just man is taken away from before the face of evil."

1

I BEGAN BY DIRECTING the reader's attention to the labours of two great bishops, who restored the faith of Christianity where it had long been obscured. Now, I will put before him, by way of contrast, a scene of the overthrow of religion,—the extinction of a candlestick,—effected, too, by champions of the same heretical creed which Basil and Gregory successfully resisted. It will be found in the history of the last days of the great Augustine, bishop of Hippo, in Africa. The truth triumphed in the East by the power of preaching; it was extirpated in the South by the edge of the sword.

Though it may not be given us to appropriate the prophecies of the Apocalypse to the real events to which they belong, yet it is impossible to read its inspired pages, and then to turn to the dissolution of the Roman empire, without seeing a remarkable agreement, on the whole, between the calamities of that period and the sacred prediction. There is a plain announcement in the inspired page, of "Woe, woe, woe, to the inhabitants of the earth;" an announcement of "hail and fire mingled with blood," the conflagration of "trees and green grass," the destruction of ships, the darkening of the sun, and the poisoning of the rivers over a third of their course. There is a clear prophecy of revolutions on the face of the earth and in the structure of society. And, on the other hand, let us observe how fully such general foretokenings are borne out, among other passages of history, in the Vandalic conquest of Africa.

The coast of Africa, between the great desert and the Mediterranean, was one of the most fruitful and opulent portions of the Roman world. The eastern extremity of it was more especially connected with the empire, containing in it Carthage, Hippo, and other towns, celebrated as being sees of the Christian Church, as well as places of civil importance. In the spring of the year 428, the Vandals, Arians by creed, and barbarians by birth and disposition, crossed the Straits of Gibraltar, and proceeded along this fertile district, bringing with them devastation and captivity on every side. They abandoned themselves to the most savage cruelties and excesses. They pillaged, ravaged, burned, massacred all that came in their way, sparing not even the fruit trees, which might have afforded some poor food to the remnant of the population, who had escaped from them into caves, the recesses of the mountains, or into vaults. Twice did this desolating pestilence sweep over the face of the country.

The fury of the Vandals was especially exercised towards the memorials of religion. Churches, cemeteries, monasteries, were objects of their fiercest hatred and most violent assaults. They broke into the places of worship, cut to pieces all internal decorations, and then set fire to them. They tortured bishops and clergy with the hope of obtaining treasure. The names of some of the victims of their ferocity are preserved. Mansuetus, bishop of Utica, was burnt alive; Papinianus, bishop of Vite, was laid upon red-hot plates of iron. This was near upon the time when the third General Council was assembling at Ephesus, which, from the insecure state of the roads, and the universal misery which reigned among them, the African bishops were prevented from attending. The Clergy, the religious brotherhoods, the holy virgins, were scattered all over the country. The daily sacrifice was stopped, the sacraments could not be obtained, the festivals of the Church passed unnoticed. At length, only three cities remained unvisited by the general desolation,—Carthage, Hippo, and Cirtha.

2

HIPPO WAS THE SEE of St. Austin, then seventy-four years of age (forty almost of which had been passed in ministerial labours), and warned, by the law of nature, of the approach of dissolution. It was as if the light of prosperity and peace were fading away from the African Church, as sank the bodily powers of its great earthly ornament and stay. At this time, when the terrors of the barbaric invasion spread on all sides, a bishop wrote to him to ask whether it was allowable for the ruler of a Church to leave the scene of his pastoral duties in order to save his life. Different opinions had heretofore been expressed on this question. In Augustine's own country Tertullian had maintained that flight was unlawful, but he was a Montanist when he so wrote. On the other hand, Cyprian had actually fled, and had defended his conduct when questioned by the clergy of Rome. His contemporaries, Dionysius of Alexandria, and Gregory of Neocæsarea, had fled also; as had Polycarp before them, and Athanasius after them.

Athanasius also had to defend his flight, and he defended it, in a work still extant, thus:—First, he observes, it has the sanction of numerous Scripture precedents. Thus, in the instance of confessors under the old covenant, Jacob fled from Esau, Moses from Pharao, David from Saul; Elias concealed himself from Achab three years, and the sons of the prophets were hid by Abdias in a cave from Jezebel. In like manner under the Gospel, the disciples hid themselves for fear of the Jews, and St. Paul was let down in a basket over the wall at Damascus. On the other hand, no instance can be adduced of overboldness and headstrong daring in the saints of Scripture. But our Lord Himself is the chief exemplar of fleeing from persecution. As a child in arms He had to flee into Egypt. When He returned, He still shunned Judea, and retired to Nazareth. After raising Lazarus, on the Jews seeking His life, "He walked no more openly among them," but retreated to the neighbourhood of the desert. When they took up stones to cast at Him, He hid Himself; when they attempted to cast Him down headlong, He made His way through them; when He heard of the Baptist's death, He retired across the lake into a desert place, apart. If it be said that He did so, because His time was not yet come, and that when it was come, He delivered up Himself, we must ask, in reply, how a man can know that his time is come, so as to have a right to act as Christ acted? And since we do not know, we must have patience; and, till God by His own act determines the time, we must "wander in sheep-skins and goat-skins," rather than take the matter into our own hands; as even Saul, the persecutor, was left by David in the hands of God, whether He would "strike him, or his day should come to die, or he should go down to battle and perish."

If God's servants, proceeds Athanasius, have at any time presented themselves before their persecutors, it was at God's command: thus Elias showed himself to Achab; so did the prophet from Juda, to Jeroboam; and St. Paul appealed to Cæsar. Flight, so far from implying cowardice, requires often greater courage than not to flee. It is a greater trial of heart. Death is an end of all trouble; he who flees is ever expecting death, and dies daily. Job's life was not to be touched by Satan, yet was not his fortitude shown in what he suffered? Exile is full of miseries. The after-conduct of the saints showed they had not fled for fear. Jacob, on his deathbed, contemned death, and blessed each of the twelve Patriarchs; Moses returned, and presented himself before Pharao; David was a valiant warrior; Elias rebuked Achab and Ochazias; Peter and Paul, who had once hid themselves, offered themselves to martyrdom at Rome. And so acceptable was the previous flight of these men to Almighty God, that we read of His showing them some special favour during it. Then it was that Jacob had the vision of Angels; Moses saw the burning bush; David wrote his prophetic Psalms; Elias raised the dead, and gathered the people on Mount Carmel. How would the Gospel ever have been preached throughout the world, if the Apostles had not fled? And, since their time, those, too, who have become martyrs, at first fled; or, if they advanced to meet their persecutors, it was by some secret suggestion of the Divine Spirit. But, above all, while these instances abundantly illustrate the rule of duty in persecution, and the temper of mind necessary in those who observe it, we have that duty itself declared in a plain precept by no other than our Lord: "When they shall persecute you in this city," He says, "flee into another;" and "let them that are in Judea flee unto the mountains."

Thus argues the great Athanasius, living in spirit with the saints departed, while full of labour and care here on earth. For the arguments on the other side, let us turn to a writer, not less vigorous in mind, but less subdued in temper. Thus writes Tertullian on the same subject, then a Montanist, a century and a half earlier:—Nothing happens, he says, without God's will. Persecution is sent by Him, to put His servants to the test; to divide between good and bad: it is a trial; what man has any right to interfere? He who gives the prize, alone can assign the combat. Persecution is more than permitted, it is actually appointed by Almighty God. It does the Church much good, as leading Christians to increased seriousness while it lasts. It comes and goes at God's ordering. Satan could not touch Job, except so far as God gave permission. He could not touch the Apostles, except as far as an opening was allowed in the words, "Satan hath desired to have you, but I have prayed for thee," Peter, "and thou, being once converted, confirm thy brethren." We pray, "Lead us not into temptation, but deliver us from evil;" why, if we may deliver ourselves? Satan is permitted access to us, either for punishment, as in Saul's case, or for our chastisement. Since the persecution comes from God, we may not lawfully avoid it, nor can we avoid it. We cannot, because He is all powerful; we must not, because He is all good. We should leave the matter entirely to God. As to the command of fleeing from city to city, this was temporary. It was intended to secure the preaching of the Gospel to the nations. While the Apostles preached to the Jews,—till they had preached to the Gentiles,—they were to flee; but one might as well argue, that we now are not to go "into the way of the Gentiles," but to confine ourselves to "the lost sheep of the house of Israel," as that we are now to "flee from city to city." Nor, indeed, was going from city to city a flight; it was a continued preaching; not an accident, but a rule: whether persecuted or not, they were to go about; and before they had gone through the cities of Israel, the Lord was to come. The command contemplated only those very cities. If St. Paul escaped out of Damascus by night, yet afterwards, against the prayers of the disciples and the prophecy of Agabus, he went up to Jerusalem. Thus the command to flee did not last even through the lifetime of the Apostles; and, indeed, why should God introduce persecution, if He bids us retire from it? This is imputing inconsistency to His acts. If we want texts to justify our not fleeing, He says, "Whoso shall confess Me before men, I will confess him before My Father." "Blessed are they that suffer persecution;" "He that shall persevere to the end, he shall be saved;" "Be not afraid of them that kill the body;" "Whosoever does not carry his cross and come after Me, cannot be My disciple." How are these texts fulfilled when a man flees? Christ, who is our pattern, did not more than pray, "If it be possible, let this chalice pass:" we, too, should both stay and pray as He did. And it is expressly told us, that "We also ought to lay down our lives for the brethren." Again, it is said, "Perfect charity casteth out fear;" he who flees, fears; he who fears, "is not perfected in charity." The Greek proverb is sometimes urged, "He who flees, will fight another day;" yes, and he may flee another day, also. Again, if bishops, priests, and deacons flee, why must the laity stay? or must they flee also? "The good shepherd," on the contrary, "layeth down his life for his sheep;" whereas, the bad shepherd "seeth the wolf coming, and leaveth the sheep, and fleeth." At no time, as Jeremiah, Ezekiel, and Zechariah tell us, is the flock in greater danger of being scattered than when it loses its shepherd. Tertullian ends thus:—"This doctrine, my brother, perhaps appears to you hard; nay, intolerable. But recollect that God has said, 'He that can take, let him take it;' that is, he who receives it not, let him depart. He who fears to suffer cannot belong to Him who has suffered. He who does not fear to suffer is perfect in love, that is, of God. Many are called, few are chosen. Not he who would walk the broad way is sought out by God, but he who walks the narrow." Thus the ingenious and vehement Tertullian.

3

WITH THESE REMARKS for and against flight in persecution, we shall be prepared to listen to Augustine on the subject;—I have said, it was brought under his notice by a brother bishop, with reference to the impending visitation of the barbarians. His answer happily is preserved to us, and extracts from it shall now be set before the reader.

TO HIS HOLY BROTHER AND FELLOW-BISHOP HONORATUS,
AUGUSTINE SENDS HEALTH IN THE LORD

I thought the copy of my letter to our brother Quodvultdeus, which I sent to you, would have been sufficient, dear brother, without the task you put on me of counselling you on the proper course to pursue under our existing dangers. It was certainly a short letter; yet I included every question which it was necessary to ask and answer, when I said that no persons were hindered from retiring to such fortified places as they were able and desirous to secure; while, on the other hand, we might not break the bonds of our ministry, by which the love of Christ has engaged us not to desert the Church, where we are bound to serve. The following is what I laid down in the letter I refer to:—"It remains, then," I say, "that, though God's people in the place where we are be ever so few, yet, if it does stay, we, whose ministration is necessary to its staying, must say to the Lord, Thou art our strong rock and place of defence."

But you tell me that this view is not sufficient for you, from an apprehension lest we should be running counter to our Lord's command and example, to flee from city to city. Yet is it conceivable that He meant that our flocks, whom He bought with His own blood, should be deprived of that necessary ministration without which they cannot live? Is He a precedent for this, who was carried in flight into Egypt by His parents when but a child, before He had formed Churches which we can talk of His leaving? Or, when St. Paul was let down in a basket through a window, lest the enemy should seize him, and so escaped his hands, was the Church of that place bereft of its necessary ministration, seeing there were other brethren stationed there to fulfil what was necessary? Evidently it was their wish that he, who was the direct object of the persecutor's search, should preserve himself for the sake of the Church. Let, then, the servants of Christ, the ministers of His word and sacraments, do in such cases as He enjoined or permitted. Let such of them, by all means, flee from city to city, as are special objects of persecution; so that they who are not thus attacked desert not the Church, but give meat to those their fellow-servants, who they know cannot live without it. But in a case when all classes—I mean bishops, clergy, and people—are in some common danger, let not those who need the aid of others be deserted by those whom they need. Either let one and all remove into some fortified place, or, if any are obliged to remain, let them not be abandoned by those who have to supply their ecclesiastical necessity, so that they may survive in common, or suffer in common what their Father decrees they should undergo.

Then he makes mention of the argument of a certain bishop, that "if our Lord has enjoined upon us flight, in persecutions which may ripen into martyrdom, much more is it necessary to flee from barren sufferings in a barbarian and hostile invasion," and he says, "this is true and reasonable, in the case of such as have no ecclesiastical office to tie them;" but he continues:

Why should men make no question about obeying the precept of fleeing from city to city, and yet have no dread of "the hireling who seeth the wolf coming, and fleeth, because he careth not for the sheep?" Why do they not try to reconcile (as they assuredly can) these two incontrovertible declarations of our Lord, one of which suffers and commands flight, the other arraigns and condemns it? And what other mode is there of reconciling them than that which I have above laid down? viz., that we, the ministers of Christ, who are under the pressure of persecution, are *then* at liberty to leave our posts, when no flock is left for us to serve; or again, when, though there be a flock, yet there are others to supply our necessary ministry, who have not the same reason for fleeing,—as in the case of St. Paul; or, again, of the holy Athanasius, bishop of Alexandria, who was especially sought after by the emperor Constantius, while the Catholic people, who remained together in Alexandria, were in no measure deserted by the other ministers. But when the people remain, and the ministers flee, and the ministration is suspended, what is that but the guilty flight of hirelings, who care not for the sheep? For then the wolf will come,—not man, but the devil, who is accustomed to persuade such believers to apostasy, who are bereft of the daily ministration of the Lord's Body; and by your, not knowledge, but ignorance of duty, the weak brother will perish, for whom Christ died.

Let us only consider, when matters come to an extremity of danger, and there is no longer any means of escape, how persons flock together to the Church, of both sexes, and all ages, begging for baptism, or reconciliation, or even for works of penance, and one and all of them for consolation, and the consecration and application of the sacraments. Now, if ministers are wanting, what ruin awaits those, who depart from this life unregenerate or unabsolved! Consider the grief of their believing relatives, who will not have them as partakers with themselves in the rest of eternal life; consider the anguish of the whole multitude, nay, the cursings of some of them, at the absence of ministration and ministers.

It may be said, however, that the ministers of God ought to avoid such imminent perils, in order to preserve themselves for the profit of the Church for more tranquil times. I grant it where others are present to supply the ecclesiastical ministry, as in the case of

Athanasius. How necessary it was to the Church, how beneficial, that such a man should remain in the flesh, the Catholic faith bears witness, which was maintained against the Arians by his voice and his love. But when there is a common danger, and when there is rather reason to apprehend lest a man should be thought to flee, not from purpose of prudence, but from dread of dying, and when the example of flight does more harm than the service of living does good, it is by no means to be done. To be brief, holy David withdrew himself from the hazard of war, lest perchance he should "quench the light of Israel," at the instance of his people, not on his own motion. Otherwise, he would have occasioned many imitators of an inactivity which they had in that case ascribed, not to regard for the welfare of others, but to cowardice.

Then he goes on to a further question, what is to be done in a case where all ministers are likely to perish, unless some of them take to flight? or when persecution is set on foot only with the view of reaching the ministers of the Church? This leads him to exclaim:

O, that there may be then a quarrel between God's ministers, *who* are to remain, and *who* to flee, lest the Church should be deserted, whether by all fleeing or all dying! Surely there will ever be such a quarrel, where each party burns in its own charity, yet indulges the charity of the other. In such a difficulty, the lot seems the fairest decision, in default of others. God judges better than man in perplexities of this sort; whether it be His will to reward the holier among them with the crown of martyrdom, and to spare the weak, or again, to strengthen the latter to endure evil, removing those from life whom the Church of God can spare the better. Should it, however, seem inexpedient to cast lots,—a measure for which I cannot bring precedent,—at least, let no one's flight be the cause of the Church's losing those ministrations which, in such dangers, are so necessary and so imperative. Let no one make himself an exception, on the plea of having some particular grace, which gives him a claim to life, and therefore to flight.

It is sometimes supposed that bishops and clergy, remaining at their posts in dangers of this kind, mislead their flocks into staying, by their example. But it is easy for us to remove this objection or imputation, by frankly telling them not to be misled by our remaining. "We are remaining for your sake," we must say, "lest you should fail to obtain such ministration, as we know to be necessary to your salvation in Christ. Make your escape, and you will then set us free." The occasion for saying this is when there seems some real advantage in retiring to a safer position. Should all or some make answer, "We are in His hands from whose anger no one can flee anywhere; whose mercy every one may find everywhere, though he stir not, whether some necessary tie detains him, or the uncertainty of safe escape deters him;" most undoubtedly such persons are not to be left destitute of Christian ministrations.

I have written these lines, dearest brother, in truth, as I think, and in sure charity, by way of reply, since you have consulted me; but not as dictating, if perchance, you may find some better view to guide you. However, better we cannot do in these perils than pray the Lord our God to have mercy upon us.—*Ep.* 228.

4

THE LUMINOUS JUDGMENT, the calm faith, and the single-minded devotion which this letter exhibits, were fully maintained in the conduct of the far-famed writer, in the events which followed. It was written on the first entrance of the Vandals into Africa, about two years before they laid siege to Hippo; and during this interval of dreadful suspense and excitement, as well as of actual suffering, amid the desolation of the Church around him, with the prospect of his own personal trials, we find this unwearied teacher carrying on his works of love by pen, and word of mouth,—eagerly, as knowing his time was short, but tranquilly, as if it were a season of prosperity. He commenced a fresh work against the opinions of Julian, a friend of his, who, beginning to run well, had unhappily taken up a bold profession of Pelagianism; he wrote a treatise on Predestination, at the suggestion of his friends, to meet the objections urged against former works of his on the same subject; sustained a controversy with the Arians; and began a history of heresies. What makes Augustine's diligence in the duties of his episcopate, at this season, the more remarkable, is, that he was actually engaged at the same time in political affairs, as a confidential friend and counsellor of Boniface, the governor of Africa (who had first invited and then opposed the entrance of the Vandals), and accordingly was in circumstances especially likely to unsettle and agitate the mind of an aged man.

At length events hastened on to a close. Fugitive multitudes betook themselves to Hippo. Boniface threw himself into it. The Vandals appeared before it, and laid siege to it. Meanwhile, Augustine fell ill. He had about him many of the African bishops, and among other friends, Possidius, whose account of his last hours is preserved to us. "We used continually to converse together," says Possidius, "about the misfortunes in which we were involved, and contemplated God's tremendous judgments which were before our eyes, saying, 'Thou art just, O Lord, and Thy judgment is right.' One day, at meal time, as we talked together, he said, 'Know ye that in this our present calamity, I pray God to vouchsafe to rescue this besieged city, or (if otherwise) to give His servants strength to bear His will, or, at least, to take me to Himself out of this world.' We followed his advice, and both ourselves, and our friends and the whole city offered up the same prayer with him. On the third month of the siege he was seized with a fever, and took to his bed, and was reduced to the extreme of sickness."

Thus, the latter part of his prayer was put in train for accomplishment, as the former part was subsequently granted by the retreat of the enemy from Hippo. But to continue the narrative of Possidius:—"He had been used to say, in his familiar conversation, that after receiving baptism, even approved Christians and priests ought not to depart from the body without a fitting and sufficient course of penance. Accordingly, in the last illness, of which he died, he set himself to write out the special penitential psalms of David, and to place them four by four against the wall, so that, as he lay in bed, in the days of his sickness, he could see them. And so he used to read and weep abundantly. And lest his attention should be distracted by any one, about ten days before his death, he begged us who were with him to hinder persons entering his room except at the times when his medical attendants came to see him, or his meals were brought to him. This was strictly attended to, and all his time given to prayer. Till this last illness, he had been able to preach the word of God in the church without intermission with energy and boldness, with healthy mind and judgment. He slept with his fathers in a good old age, sound in limb, unimpaired in sight and hearing, and, as it is written, while we stood by, beheld, and prayed with him. We took part in the sacrifice to God at his funeral, and so buried him."

Though the Vandals failed in their first attack upon Hippo, during Augustine's last illness, they renewed it shortly after his death, under more favourable circumstances. Boniface was defeated in the field, and retired to Italy; and the inhabitants of Hippo left their city. The Vandals entered and burned it, excepting the library of Augustine, which was providentially preserved.

The desolation which, at that era, swept over the face of Africa, was completed by the subsequent invasion of the Saracens. Its five hundred churches are no more. The voyager gazes on the sullen rocks which line its coast, and discovers no token of Christianity to cheer the gloom. Hippo [1] has ceased to be an episcopal city; but its great Teacher, though dead, yet speaks; his voice is gone out into all lands, and his words unto the ends of the world. He needs no dwelling-place, whose home is the Catholic Church; he fears no barbarian or heretical desolation, whose creed is destined to last unto the end.

[1] Since this was written, the French have reinstated the see.

CHAPTER VIII

CONVERSION OF AUGUSTINE

"Thou hast chastised me and I was instructed, as a steer unaccustomed to the yoke. Convert me, and I shall be converted, for Thou art the Lord my God. For after Thou didst convert me, I did penance, and after Thou didst show unto me, I struck my thigh. I am confounded and ashamed, because I have borne the reproach of my youth."

I

A CHANCE READER may ask, What was the history of that celebrated Father, whose last days were the subject of my last chapter? What had his life been, what his early years, what his labours? Surely he was no ordinary man, whose end, in all its circumstances, is so impressive. We may answer in a few words, that Augustine was the son of a pious mother, who had the pain of witnessing, for many years, his wanderings in doubt and unbelief, who prayed incessantly for his conversion, and at length was blessed with the sight of it. From early youth he had given himself up to a course of life quite inconsistent with the profession of a catechumen, into which he had been admitted in infancy. How far he had fallen into any great excesses is doubtful. He uses language of himself which may have the worst of meanings, but may, on the other hand, be but the expression of deep repentance and spiritual sensitiveness. In his twentieth year he embraced the Manichæan heresy, in which he continued nine years. Towards the end of that time, leaving Africa, his native country, first for Rome, then for Milan, he fell in with St. Ambrose; and his conversion and baptism followed in the course of his thirty-fourth year. This memorable event, his conversion, has been celebrated in the Western Church from early times, being the only event of the kind thus distinguished, excepting the conversion of St. Paul.

His life had been for many years one of great anxiety and discomfort, the life of one dissatisfied with himself, and despairing of finding the truth. Men of ordinary minds are not so circumstanced as to feel the misery of irreligion. That misery consists in the perverted and discordant action of the various faculties and functions of the soul, which have lost their legitimate governing power, and are unable to regain it, except at the hands of their Maker. Now the run of irreligious men do not suffer in any great degree from this disorder, and are not miserable; they have neither great talents nor strong passions; they have not within them the materials of rebellion in such measure as to threaten their peace. They follow their own wishes, they yield to the bent of the moment, they act on inclination, not on principle, but their motive powers are neither strong nor various enough to be troublesome. Their minds are in no sense under rule; but anarchy is not in their case a state of confusion, but of deadness; not unlike the internal condition as it is reported of eastern cities and provinces at present, in which, though the government is weak or null, the body politic goes on without any great embarrassment or collision of its members one with another, by the force of inveterate habit. It is very different when the moral and intellectual principles are vigorous, active, and developed. Then, if the governing power be feeble, all the subordinates are in the position of rebels in arms; and what the state of a mind is under such circumstances, the analogy of a civil community will suggest to us. Then we have before us the melancholy spectacle of high aspirations without an aim, a hunger of the soul unsatisfied, and a never-ending restlessness and inward warfare of its various faculties. Gifted minds, if not submitted to the rightful authority of religion, become the most unhappy and the most mischievous. They need both an object to feed upon, and the power of self-mastery; and the love of their Maker, and nothing but it, supplies both the one and the other. We have seen in our own day, in the case of a popular poet, an impressive instance of a great genius throwing off the fear of God, seeking for happiness in the creature, roaming unsatisfied from one object to another, breaking his soul upon itself, and bitterly confessing and imparting his wretchedness to all around him. I have no wish at all to compare him to St. Augustine; indeed, if we may say it without presumption, the very different termination of their trial seems to indicate some great difference in their respective modes of encountering it. The one dies of premature decay, to all appearance, a hardened infidel; and if he is still to have a name, will live in the mouths of men by writings at once blasphemous and immoral: the other is a Saint and Doctor of the Church. Each makes confessions, the one to the saints, the other to the powers of evil. And does not the difference of the two discover itself in some measure, even to our eyes, in the very history of their wanderings and pinings? At least, there is no appearance in St. Augustine's case of that dreadful haughtiness, sullenness, love of singularity, vanity, irritability, and misanthropy, which were too certainly the characteristics of our own countryman. Augustine was, as his early history shows, a man of affectionate and tender feelings, and open and amiable temper; and, above all, he sought for some excellence external to his own mind, instead of concentrating all his contemplations on himself.

2

But let us consider what his misery was;—it was that of a mind imprisoned, solitary, and wild with spiritual thirst; and forced to betake itself to the strongest excitements, by way of relieving itself of the rush and violence of feelings, of which the knowledge of the Divine Perfections was the true and sole sustenance. He ran into excess, not from love of it, but from this fierce fever of mind. "I sought what I might love,"[1] he says in his *Confessions*, "in love with loving, and safety I hated, and a way without snares. For within me was a famine of that inward food, Thyself, my God; yet throughout that famine I was not hungered, but was without any longing for incorruptible sustenance, not because filled therewith, but the more empty, the more I loathed it. For this cause my soul was sickly and full of sores; it miserably cast itself forth, desiring to be scraped by the touch of objects of sense."—iii. 1.

O foolish man that I then was, [he says elsewhere,] enduring impatiently the lot of man! So I fretted, sighed, wept, was distracted; had neither rest nor counsel. For I bore about a shattered and bleeding soul, impatient of being borne by me, yet where to repose it I found not; not in calm groves, nor in games and music, nor in fragrant spots, nor in curious banquetings, nor in indulgence of the bed and the couch, nor, finally, in books or poetry found it repose. All things looked ghastly, yea, the very light. In groaning and tears alone found I a little refreshment. But when my soul was withdrawn from them, a huge load of misery weighed me down. To Thee, O Lord, it ought to have been raised, for Thee to lighten; I knew it, but neither could nor would; the more, since when I thought of Thee, Thou wast not to me any solid or substantial thing. For Thou wert not Thyself, but a mere phantom, and my error was my God. If I offered to discharge my load thereon, that it might rest, it glided through the void, and came rushing down against me; and I had remained to myself a hapless spot, where I could neither be, nor be from thence. For whither should my heart flee from my heart? whither should I flee from myself? whither not follow myself? And yet I fled out of my country; for so should mine eyes look less for *him*, where they were not wont to see him. —iv. 12.

He is speaking in this last sentence of a friend he had lost, whose death-bed was very remarkable, and whose dear familiar name he apparently has not courage to mention. "He had

[1] Most of these translations are from the Oxford edition of 1838.

grown up from a child with me," he says, "and we had been both schoolfellows and playfellows." Augustine had misled him into the heresy which he had adopted himself, and when he grew to have more and more sympathy in Augustine's pursuits, the latter united himself to him in a closer intimacy. Scarcely had he thus given him his heart, when God took him.

Thou tookest him, [he says,] out of this life, when he had scarce completed one whole year of my friendship, sweet to me above all sweetness in that life of mine. A long while, sore sick of a fever, he lay senseless in the dews of death, and being given over, he was baptized unwitting; I, meanwhile little regarding, or presuming that his soul would retain rather what it had received of me than what was wrought on his unconscious body.

The Manichees, it should be observed, rejected baptism. He proceeds:

But it proved far otherwise; for he was refreshed and restored. Forthwith, as soon as I could speak with him (and I could as soon as he was able, for I never left him, and we hung but too much upon each other), I essayed to jest with him, as though he would jest with me at that baptism, which he had received, when utterly absent in mind and feeling, but had now understood that he had received. But he shrunk from me, as from an enemy; and with a wonderful and sudden freedom bade me, if I would continue his friend, forbear such language to him. I, all astonished and amazed, suppressed all my emotions till he should grow well, and his health were strong enough for me to deal with him as I would. But he was taken away from my madness, that with Thee he might be preserved for my comfort: a few days after, in my absence, he was attacked again by fever, and so departed.—iv. 8.

3

FROM DISTRESS OF MIND Augustine left his native place, Thagaste, and came to Carthage, where he became a teacher in rhetoric. Here he fell in with Faustus, an eminent Manichean bishop and disputant, in whom, however, he was disappointed; and the disappointment abated his attachment to his sect, and disposed him to look for truth elsewhere. Disgusted with the licence which prevailed among the students at Carthage, he determined to proceed to Rome, and disregarding and eluding the entreaties of his mother, Monica, who dreaded his removal from his own country, he went thither. At Rome he resumed his profession; but inconveniences as great, though of another kind, encountered him in that city; and upon the people of Milan sending for a rhetoric reader, he made application for the appointment, and obtained it. To Milan then he came, the city of St. Ambrose, in the year of our Lord 385.

Ambrose, though weak in voice, had the reputation of eloquence; and Augustine, who seems to have gone with introductions to him, and was won by his kindness of manner, attended his sermons with curiosity and interest. "I listened," he says, "not in the frame of mind which became me, but in order to see whether his eloquence answered what was reported of it: I hung on his words attentively, but of the matter I was but an unconcerned and contemptuous hearer."—v. 23. His impression of his style of preaching is worth noticing: "I was delighted with the sweetness of his discourse, more full of knowledge, yet in manner less pleasurable and soothing, than that of Faustus." Augustine was insensibly moved: he determined on leaving the Manichees, and returning to the state of a catechumen in the Catholic Church, into which he had been admitted by his parents. He began to eye and muse upon the great bishop of Milan more and more, and tried in vain to penetrate his secret heart, and to ascertain the thoughts and feelings which swayed him. He felt he did not understand him. If the respect and intimacy of the great could make a man happy, these advantages he perceived Ambrose to possess; yet he was not satisfied that he was a happy man. His celibacy seemed a drawback: what constituted his hidden life? or was he cold at heart? or was he of a famished and restless spirit? He felt his own malady, and longed to ask him some questions about it. But Ambrose could not easily be spoken with. Though accessible to all, yet that very circumstance made it difficult for an individual, especially one who was not of his flock, to get a private interview with him. When he was not taken up with the Christian people who surrounded him, he was either at his meals or engaged in private reading. Augustine used to enter, as all persons might, without being announced; but after staying awhile, afraid of interrupting him, he departed again. However, he heard his expositions of Scripture every Sunday, and gradually made progress.

He was now in his thirtieth year, and since he was a youth of eighteen had been searching after truth; yet he was still "in the same mire, greedy of things present," but finding nothing stable.

To-morrow, [he said to himself,] I shall find it; it will appear manifestly, and I shall grasp it: lo, Faustus the Manichee will come and clear every thing! O you great men, ye academics, is it true, then, that no certainty can be attained for the ordering of life? Nay, let us search diligently, and despair not. Lo, things in the ecclesiastical books are not absurd to us now, which sometimes seemed absurd, and may be otherwise taken and in a good sense. I will take my stand where, as a child, my parents placed me, until the clear truth be found out. But where shall it be sought, or when? Ambrose has no leisure; we have no leisure to read; where shall we find even the books? where, or when, procure them? Let set times be appointed, and certain hours be ordered for the health of our soul. Great hope has dawned; the Catholic faith teaches not what we thought; and do we doubt to knock, that the rest may be opened? The forenoons, indeed, our scholars take up; what do we during the rest of our time? why not this? But if so, when pay we court to our great friend, whose favours we need? when compose what we may sell to scholars? when refresh ourselves, unbending our minds from this intenseness of care?

Perish every thing: dismiss we these empty vanities; and betake ourselves to the one search for truth! Life is a poor thing, death is uncertain; if it surprises us, in what state shall we depart hence? and when shall we learn what here we have neglected? and shall we not rather suffer the punishment of this negligence? What if death itself cut off and end all care and feeling? Then must this be ascertained. But God forbid this! It is no vain and empty thing, that the excellent dignity of the Christian faith has overspread the whole world. Never would such and so great things be wrought for us by God, if with the body the soul also came to an end. Wherefore delay then to abandon worldly hopes, and give ourselves wholly to seek after God and the blessed life? But wait: even those things are pleasant; they have some and no small sweetness. We must not lightly abandon them, for it were a shame to return again to them. See, how great a matter it is now to obtain some station, and then what should we wish for more? We have store of powerful friends; if nothing else offers, and we be in much haste, at least a presidency may be given us; and a wife with some fortune, that she increase not our charges; and this shall be the bound of desire. Many great men, and most worthy of imitation, have given themselves to the study of wisdom in the state of marriage.—vi. 18, 19.

4

IN SPITE OF THIS RELUCTANCE to give up a secular life, yet in proportion as the light of Christian truth opened on Augustine's mind, so was he drawn on to that higher Christian state on which our Lord and His Apostle have bestowed special praise. So it was, and not unnaturally in those times, that high and earnest minds, when they had found the truth, were not content to embrace it by halves; they would take all or none, they would go all lengths, they would covet the better gifts, or else they would remain as they were. It seemed to them absurd to take so much trouble to find the truth, and to submit to such a revolution in their opinions and motives as its reception involved; and yet, after all, to content themselves with a second-best profession, unless there was some plain duty obliging them to live the secular life they had hitherto led. The cares of this world, and the deceitfulness of riches, the pomp of life, the pride of station, and the indulgence of sense, would be tolerated by the Christian, then only, when it would be a sin to renounce them. The pursuit of gain may be an act of submission to the will of parents; a married life is the performance of a solemn and voluntary vow; but it may often happen, and did happen in Augustine's day especially, that there are no religious reasons against a man's giving up the world, as our Lord and His Apostles renounced it. When his parents were heathen, or were Christians of his own high temper, when he had no fixed engagement or position in life, when the State itself was either infidel or but partially emerging out of its old pollutions, and when grace was given to desire and strive after, if not fully to reach, the sanctity of the Lamb's virginal company, duty would often lie, not in shunning, but in embracing an ascetic life. Besides, the Church in the fourth century had had no experience yet of temporal prosperity; she knew religion only amid the storms of persecution, or the uncertain lull between them, in the desert or the catacomb, in insult, contempt, and calumny. She had not yet seen how opulence, and luxury, and splendour, and pomp, and polite refinement, and fashion, were compatible with the Christian name; and her more serious children imagined, with a simplicity or narrowness of mind which will in this day provoke a smile that they ought to imitate Cyprian and Dionysius in their mode of living and their habits, as well as in their feelings, professions, and spiritual knowledge. They thought that religion consisted in deeds, not words. Riches, power, rank, and literary eminence, were then thought misfortunes, when viewed apart from the service they might render to the cause of truth; the atmosphere of the world was thought unhealthy:—Augustine then, in proportion as he approached the Church, ascended towards heaven.

Time went on; he was in his thirty-second year; he still was gaining light; he renounced his belief in fatalism; he addressed himself to St. Paul's Epistles. He began to give up the desire of distinction in his profession: this was a great step; however, still his spirit mounted higher than his heart as yet could follow.

I was displeased, [he says,] that I led a secular life; yea, now that my desires no longer inflamed me, as of old, with hopes of honour and profit, a very grievous burden it was to undergo so heavy a bondage. For in comparison of Thy sweetness, and "the beauty of Thy honour, which I loved," these things delighted me no longer. But I still was enthralled with the love of woman: nor did the Apostle forbid me to marry, although he advised me to something better, chiefly wishing that all men were as he himself. But I, being weak, chose the more indulgent place; and, because of this alone, was tossed up and down in all beside, faint and wasted with withering cares, because in other matters I was constrained, against my will, to conform myself to a married life, to which I was given up and enthralled. I had now found the goodly pearl, which, selling all that I had, I ought to have bought; and I hesitated.—viii. 2.

Finding Ambrose, though kind and accessible, yet reserved, he went to an aged man named Simplician, who seems to have baptized St. Ambrose, and eventually succeeded him in his see. He opened his mind to him, and happening in the course of his communications to mention Victorinus's translation of some Platonic works, Simplician asked him if he knew that person's history. It seems he was a professor of rhetoric at Rome, was well versed in literature and philosophy, had been tutor to many of the senators, and had received the high honour of a statue in the Forum. Up to his old age he had professed, and defended with his eloquence, the old pagan worship. He was led to read the Holy Scriptures, and was brought, in consequence, to a belief in their divinity. For a while he did not feel the necessity of changing his profession; he looked upon Christianity as a philosophy, he embraced it as such, but did not propose to join what he considered the Christian sect, or, as Christians would call it, the Catholic Church. He let Simplician into his secret; but whenever the latter pressed him to take the step, he was accustomed to ask, "whether walls made a Christian." However, such a state could not continue with a man of earnest mind: the leaven worked; at length he unexpectedly called upon Simplician to lead him to church. He was admitted a catechumen, and in due time baptized, "Rome wondering, the Church rejoicing." It was customary at Rome for the candidates for baptism to profess their faith from a raised place in the church, in a set form of words. An offer was made to Victorinus, which was not unusual in the case of bashful and timid persons, to make his profession in private. But he preferred to make it in the ordinary way. "I was public enough," he made answer, "in my profession of rhetoric, and ought not to be frightened when professing salvation." He continued the school which he had before he became a Christian, till the edict of Julian forced him to close it. This story went to Augustine's heart, but it did not melt it. There was still the struggle of two wills, the high aspiration and the habitual inertness.

I was weighed down with the encumbrance of this world, pleasantly, as one is used to be with sleep; and my meditations upon Thee were like the efforts of men who would awake, yet are steeped again under the depth of their slumber. And as no one would wish always to be asleep, and, in the sane judgment of all, waking is better, yet a man commonly delays to shake off sleep, when a heavy torpor is on his limbs, and though it is time to rise, he enjoys it the more heartily while he ceases to approve it: so, in spite of my conviction that Thy love was to be obeyed rather than my own lusts, yet I both yielded to the approval, and was taken prisoner by the enjoyment. When Thou saidst to me, "Rise, thou that sleepest, and arise from the dead, and Christ will enlighten thee," and showedst the plain reasonableness of Thy word, convinced by its truth, I could but give the slow and sleepy answer, "Presently;" "yes, presently;" "wait awhile;" though that presently was never present, and that awhile became long. It was in vain that I delighted in Thy law in the inner man, while another law in my members fought against the law of my mind, and led me captive to the law of sin, which was in my members.—viii. 12.

5

One day, when he and his friend Alypius were together at home, a countryman, named Pontitian, who held an office in the imperial court, called on him on some matter of business. As they sat talking, he observed a book upon the table, and on opening it found it was St. Paul's Epistles. A strict Christian himself, he was agreeably surprised to find an Apostle, where he expected to meet with some work bearing upon Augustine's profession. The discourse fell upon St. Antony, the celebrated Egyptian solitary, and while it added to Pontitian's surprise to find that they did not even know his name, they, on the other hand, were still more struck with wonder at the relation of his life, and the recent date of it. Thence the conversation passed to the subject of monasteries, the purity and sweetness of their discipline, and the treasures of grace which through them had been manifested in the desert. It turned out that Augustine and his friend did not even know of the monastery, of which Ambrose had been the patron, outside the walls of Milan. Pontitian went on to give an account of the conversion of two among his fellow-officers under the following circumstances. When he was at Treves, one afternoon, while the emperor was in the circus, he happened to stroll out, with three companions, into the gardens close upon the city wall. After a time they split into two parties, and while he and another went their own way, the other two came upon a cottage, which they were induced to enter. It was the abode of certain recluses, "poor in spirit," as Augustine says, "of whom is the kingdom of heaven;" and here they found the life of St. Antony, which Athanasius had written about twenty years before (A.D. 364–366). One of them began to peruse it; and, moved by the narrative, they both of them resolved on adopting the monastic life.

The effect produced by this relation on Augustine was not less than was caused by the history of Antony itself upon the imperial officers, and almost as immediately productive of a religious issue. He felt that they did but represent to him, in their obedience, what was wanting in his own, and suggest a remedy for his disordered and troubled state of mind. He says:

> The more ardently I loved these men, whose healthful state of soul was shown in surrendering themselves to Thee for healing, so much the more execrable and hateful did I seem to myself in comparison of them. For now many years had passed with me, as many perhaps as twelve, since my nineteenth, when, upon reading Cicero's "Hortensius," I was first incited to seek for wisdom; and still I was putting off renunciation of earthly happiness, and simple search after a treasure which, even in the search, not to speak of the discovery, was better than the actual possession of heathen wealth and power, and than the pleasures of sense poured around me at my will. But I, wretched, wretched youth, in that springtime of my life, had asked indeed of Thee the gift of chastity, but had said, "Give me chastity and continence, but not at once." I feared, alas, lest Thou shouldst hear me too soon, and cure a thirst at once, which I would fain have had satisfied, not extinguished. . . . But now . . . disturbed in countenance as well as mind, I turn upon Alypius, "What ails us?" say I, "what is this? what is this story? See; the unlearned rise and take heaven by violence, while we, with all our learning, all our want of heart, see where we wallow in flesh and blood! Shall I feel shame to follow their lead, and not rather to let alone what alone is left to me?" Something of this kind I said to him, and while he eyed me in silent wonder, I rushed from him in the ferment of my feelings.—viii. 17–19.

He betook himself to the garden of the house where he lodged, Alypius following him, and sat for awhile in bitter meditation on the impotence and slavery of the human will. The thought of giving up his old habits of life once for all pressed upon him with overpowering force, and, on the other hand, the beauty of religious obedience pierced and troubled him. He says:

> The very toys of toys, and vanities of vanities, my old mistresses, kept hold of me; they plucked my garment of flesh, and whispered softly, "Are you indeed giving us up? What! from this moment are

we to be strangers to you *for ever?* This and that, shall it be allowed you from this moment *never again?*" Yet, what a view began to open on the other side, whither I had set my face and was in a flutter to go; the chaste majesty of Continency, serene, cheerful, yet without excess, winning me in a holy way to come without doubting, and ready to embrace me with religious hands full stored with honourable patterns! So many boys and young maidens, a multitude of youth and every age, grave widows and aged virgins, and Continence herself in all, not barren, but a fruitful mother of children, of joys by Thee, O Lord, her Husband. She seemed to mock me into emulation, saying, "Canst not thou what these have done, youths and maidens? Can they in their own strength or in the strength of their Lord God? The Lord their God gave me unto them. Why rely on thyself and fall? Cast thyself upon His arm. Be not afraid. He will not let you slip. Cast thyself in confidence, He will receive thee and heal thee." Meanwhile Alypius kept close to my side, silently waiting for the end of my unwonted agitation.

He then proceeds to give an account of the termination of this struggle:

At length burst forth a mighty storm, bringing a mighty flood of tears; and to indulge it to the full, even unto cries, in solitude, I rose up from Alypius, . . . who perceived from my choked voice how it was with me. He remained where we had been sitting, in deep astonishment. I threw myself down under a fig-tree, I know not how, and allowing my tears full vent, offered up to Thee the acceptable sacrifice of my streaming eyes. And I cried out to this effect:—"And Thou, O Lord, how long, how long, Lord, wilt Thou be angry? For ever? Remember not our old sins!" for I felt that they were my tyrants. I cried out, piteously, "How long? how long? to-morrow and to-morrow? why not *now?* why not in this very hour put an end to this my vileness?" While I thus spoke, with tears, in the bitter contrition of my heart, suddenly I heard a voice, as if from a house near me, of a boy or girl chanting forth again and again, "TAKE UP AND READ, TAKE UP AND READ!" Changing countenance at these words, I began intently to think whether boys used them in any game, but could not recollect that I had ever heard them. I left weeping and rose up, considering it a divine intimation to open the Scriptures and read what first presented itself. I had heard that Antony had come in during the reading of the Gospel, and had taken to himself the admonition, "Go, sell all that thou hast," etc., and had turned to Thee at once, in consequence of that oracle. I had left St. Paul's volume where Alypius was sitting, when I rose thence. I returned thither, seized it, opened, and read in silence the following passage, which first met my eyes, "*Not in rioting and drunkenness, not in chambering and impurities, not in contention and envy, but put ye on the Lord Jesus Christ, and make not provision for the flesh in its concupiscences.*" I had neither desire nor need to read farther. As I finished the sentence, as though the light of peace had been poured into my heart, all the shadows of doubt dispersed. Thus hast Thou converted me to Thee, so as no longer to seek either for wife or other hope of this world, standing fast in that rule of faith in which Thou so many years before hadst revealed me to my mother.—viii. 26–30.

The last words of this extract relate to a dream which his mother had had some years before, concerning his conversion. On his first turning Manichee, abhorring his opinions, she would not for a while even eat with him, when she had this dream, in which she had an intimation that where she stood, there Augustine should one day be with her. At another time she derived great comfort from the casual words of a bishop, who, when importuned by her to converse with her son, said at length with some impatience, "Go thy ways, and God bless thee, for it is not possible that the son of these tears should perish!" It would be out of place, and is perhaps unnecessary, to enter here into the affecting and well-known history of her tender anxieties and persevering prayers for Augustine. Suffice it to say, she saw the accomplishment of them; she lived till Augustine became a Catholic; and she died in her way back to Africa with him. Her last words were, "Lay this body anywhere; let not the care of it in any way distress you; this only I ask, that wherever you be, you remember me at the Altar of the Lord."

May she, [says her son, in dutiful remembrance of her words,] rest in peace with her husband, before and after whom she never had any; whom she obeyed, with patience bringing forth fruit unto Thee, that she might win him also unto Thee. And inspire, O Lord my God, inspire Thy servants, my brethren,—Thy sons, my masters,—whom, in heart, voice, and writing I serve, that so many as read these confessions, may at Thy altar remember Monica, Thy handmaid, with Patricius, her sometime husband, from whom Thou broughtest me into this life; how, I know not. May they with pious affection remember those who were my parents in this transitory light,—my brethren under Thee, our Father, in our Catholic Mother, —my fellow-citizens in the eternal Jerusalem, after which Thy pilgrim people sigh from their going forth unto their return: that so, her last request of me may in the prayers of many receive a fulfilment, through my confessions, more abundant than through my prayers.—ix. 37.

6

But to return to St. Augustine himself. His conversion took place in the summer of 386 (as seems most probable), and about three weeks after it, taking advantage of the vintage holidays, he gave up his school, assigning as a reason a pulmonary attack which had given him already much uneasiness. He retired to a friend's villa in the country for the rest of the year, with a view of preparing himself for baptism at the Easter following. His religious notions were still very imperfect and vague. He had no settled notion concerning the nature of the soul, and was ignorant of the mission of the Holy Ghost. And still more, as might be expected, he needed correction and reformation in his conduct. During this time he broke himself of a habit of profane swearing, and, in various ways, disciplined himself for the sacred rite for which he was a candidate. It need scarcely be said that he was constant in devotional and penitential exercises.

In due time the sacrament of baptism was administered to him by St. Ambrose, who had been the principal instrument of his conversion; and he resolved on ridding himself of his worldly possessions, except what might be necessary for his bare subsistence, and retiring to Africa, with the purpose of following the rule of life which it had cost him so severe a struggle to adopt. Thagaste, his native place, was his first abode, and he stationed himself in the suburbs, so as to be at once in retirement and in the way for usefulness, if any opening should offer in the city. His conversion had been followed by that of some of his friends, who, together with certain of his fellow-citizens, whom he succeeded in persuading, joined him, and who naturally looked up to him as the head of their religious community. Their property was cast into a common stock, whence distribution was made according to the need of each. Fasting and prayer, almsgiving and Scripture-reading, were their stated occupations; and Augustine took upon himself the task of instructing them and variously aiding them. The consequence naturally was, that while he busied himself in assisting others in devotional habits, his own leisure was taken from him. His fame spread, and serious engagements were pressed upon him of a nature little congenial with the life to which he had hoped to dedicate himself. Indeed, his talents were of too active and influential a character to allow of his secluding himself from the world, however he might wish it.

Thus he passed the first three years of his return to Africa, at the end of which time, A.D. 389, he was admitted into holy orders. The circumstances under which this change of state took place are curious, and, as in the instance of other Fathers, characteristic of the early times. His reputation having become considerable, he was afraid to approach any place where a bishop was wanted, lest he should be forcibly consecrated to the see. He seems to have set his heart on remaining for a time a layman, from a feeling of the responsibility of the ministerial commission. He considered he had not yet mastered the nature and the duties of it. But it so happened, that at the time in question, an imperial agent or commissioner, living at Hippo, a Christian and a serious man, signified his desire to have some conversation with him, as to a design he had of quitting secular pursuits and devoting himself to a religious life. This brought Augustine to Hippo, whither he went with the less anxiety, because that city had at that time a bishop in the person of Valerius. However, it so happened that a presbyter was wanted there, though a bishop was not; and Augustine, little suspicious of what was to happen, joined the congregation in which the election was to take place. When Valerius addressed the people and demanded whom they desired for their pastor, they at once named the stranger, whose reputation had already spread among them. Augustine burst into tears, and some of the people, mistaking the cause of his agitation, observed to him that though the presbyterate was lower than his desert, yet, notwithstanding, it stood next to the episcopate. His ordination followed, as to which Valerius himself, being a Greek, and unable to speak Latin fluently, was chiefly influenced by a wish to secure an able preacher in his own place. It may be remarked, as a singular custom in the African Church hitherto, that presbyters either never preached, or never in the presence of a bishop. Valerius was the first to break through the rule in favour of Augustine.

On his coming to Hippo, Valerius gave him a garden belonging to the Church to build a monastery upon; and shortly afterwards we find him thanking Aurelius, bishop of Carthage, for bestowing an estate either on the brotherhood of Hippo or of Thagaste. Soon after we hear of monasteries at Carthage, and other places, besides two additional ones at Hippo. Others branched off from his own community, which he took care to make also a school or seminary of the Church. It became an object with the African Churches to obtain clergy from him. Possidius, his pupil and friend, mentions as many as ten bishops out of his own acquaintance, who had been supplied from the school of Augustine.

7

Little more need be said to conclude this sketch of an eventful history. Many years had not passed before Valerius, feeling the infirmities of age, appointed Augustine as his coadjutor in the see of Hippo, and in this way secured his succeeding him on his death; an object which he had much at heart, but which he feared might be frustrated by Augustine's being called to the government of some other church. This elevation necessarily produced some change in the accidents of his life, but his personal habits remained the same. He left his monastery, as being too secluded for an office which especially obliges its holder to the duties of hospitality; and he formed a religious and clerical community in the episcopal house. This community consisted chiefly of presbyters, deacons, and sub-deacons, who gave up all personal property, and were supported upon a common fund. He himself strictly conformed to the rule he imposed on others. Far from appropriating to any private purpose any portion of his ecclesiastical income, he placed the whole charge of it in the hands of his clergy, who took by turns the yearly management of it, he being auditor of their accounts. He never indulged himself in house or land, considering the property of the see as little his own as those private possessions, which he had formerly given up. He employed it, in one way or other, directly or indirectly, as if it were the property of the poor, the ignorant, and the sinful. He had "counted the cost," and he acted like a man whose slowness to begin a course was a pledge of zeal when he had once begun it.

II

THE LAST YEARS OF ST. CHRYSOSTOM

CHAPTER I

INTRODUCTORY

1

I CONFESS TO A DELIGHT in reading the lives, and dwelling on the characters and actions, of the Saints of the first ages, such as I receive from none besides them; and for this reason, because we know so much more about them than about most of the Saints who come after them. People are variously constituted; what influences one does not influence another. There are persons of warm imaginations, who can easily picture to themselves what they never saw. They can at will see Angels and Saints hovering over them when they are in church; they see their lineaments, their features, their motions, their gestures, their smile or their grief. They can go home and draw what they have seen, from the vivid memory of what, while it lasted, was so transporting. I am not one of such; I am touched by my five senses, by what my eyes behold and my ears hear. I am touched by what I read about, not by what I myself create. As faith need not lead to practice, so in me mere imagination does not lead to devotion. I gain more from the life of our Lord in the Gospels than from a treatise *de Deo*. I gain more from three verses of St. John than from the three points of a meditation. I like a Spanish crucifix of painted wood more than one from Italy, which is made of gold. I am more touched by the Seven Dolours than by the Immaculate Conception; I am more devout to St. Gabriel than to one of Isaiah's seraphim. I love St. Paul more than one of those first Carmelites, his contemporaries, whose names and acts no one ever heard of; I feel affectionately towards the Alexandrian Dionysius, I do homage to St. George. I do not say that my way is better than another's; but it is my way, and an allowable way. And it is the reason why I am so specially attached to the Saints of the third and fourth century, because we know so much about them. This is why I feel a devout affection for St. Chrysostom. He and the rest of them have written autobiography on a large scale; they have given us their own histories, their thoughts, words, and actions, in a number of goodly folios, productions which are in themselves some of their meritorious works.

I do not know where else to find the daily life, the secret heart, of such favoured servants of God, unveiled to their devout disciples in such completeness and fidelity. Modern times afford some instances of the kind: St. Theresa is one of them; St. Francis de Sales is another: still, on the whole, what should we have known of the generality of the great Saints of the later centuries, had we been left to themselves for the information? We should of course have had the treasure of their recorded visions, prophecies, and meditations; but these are portions of their divine, not their human life, and rather belong to what God did for them, than to what they did for themselves. There is one circumstance, indeed, which tells in their favour; we have their portraits. This, I grant, is in favour of the moderns; certainly we have no idea at all of the personal appearance, the expression of countenance, or the bearing of St. Athanasius or St. Hilary. It is assuredly a great point, if the case be so, that we have likenesses of the modern Saints. But I am not sure that we have; often there was no attempt at all made to take their likenesses in their lifetime; sometimes they would not let themselves be taken when there was. St. Philip Neri once caught an artist in the very commission of that great offence, and stopped him; and the unfinished picture hangs up to this day at the *Pellegrini,* a memorial of a painter's devotion and a saint's modesty. Sometimes, again, there may be a good likeness; but, perhaps, however interesting in itself, it was taken before the Saint's conversion, and can only satisfy a human curiosity: sometimes it was taken, indeed, but has been lost, and the copies, if there are any, are not to be trusted. Sometimes the artist's veneration has idealized the countenance, or the popular demand has vulgarized it. How has a devout poetry embellished some of the ordinary portraits of the great St. Carlo! how does the original likeness of St. Ignatius differ from the military countenance and figure which ordinary pencils have bestowed upon him! You cannot thus wander from the original, in the new edition you put to press of St. Ambrose or the blessed Theodoret.

I repeat, what I want to trace and study is the real, hidden but human, life, or the *interior,* as it is called, of such glorious creations of God; and this I gain with difficulty from mere biographies. Those biographies are most valuable both as being true and as being edifying; they are true to the letter, as far as they record facts and acts; I know it: but actions are not enough for sanctity; we must have saintly motives; and as to these motives, the actions themselves seldom carry the motives along with them. In consequence, they are often supplied simply by the biographer out of his own head; and with good reason supplied, from the certainty which he feels that, since it is the act of a Saint which he is describing, therefore it must be a saintly act. Properly and naturally supplied, I grant: but I can do that as well as he; and ought to do it for myself, and shall be sure to do it, if I make the Saint my meditation. The biographer in that case is no longer a mere witness and reporter; he has become a commentator. He gives me no insight into the Saint's *interior;* he does but tell me to infer that the Saint acted in some transcendent way from the reason of the case, or to hold it on faith because he has been canonized. For instance: When I read in such a life, "The Saint, when asked a question, was silent from humility," or "from compassion for the ignorance of the speaker," or "in order to give him a gentle rebuke,"—I find a motive assigned, whichever of the three is selected, which is the biographer's own, and perhaps has two chances to one against its being the right one. We read of an occasion on which St. Athanasius said nothing, but smiled, when a question was put to him: it was another Saint who asked the question, and who has recorded the smile; but he does not more than doubtfully explain it. Many a biographer would, simply out of piety, have pronounced the reason of that smile. I should not blame him for doing so; but it was more than he could do as a biographer; if he did it, he would do it, not as an historian, but as a spiritual writer.

On the other hand, when a Saint is himself the speaker, he interprets his own action; and that is what I find done in such fulness in the case of those early luminaries of the Church to whom I am referring. I want to hear a Saint converse; I am not content to look at him as a statue; his words are the index of his hidden life, as far as that life can be known to man, for "out of the abundance of the heart the mouth speaketh." This is why I exult in the folios of the Fathers. I am not obliged to read the whole of them, I read what I can and am content. Though I may not have advanced into their *interior* more than a certain way, still, what I have read is good so far as it goes. It does not derogate from the reality of that knowledge and love of a Saint which I have actually got from what I have read already of his writings, that there is much more of those writings to be read and much more of him to be loved. Cannot we know and love the King of Saints? Yet we ever can know more and more about Him, and gain further motives for loving Him.

2

NOW THE ANCIENT SAINTS have left behind them just that kind of literature which more than any other represents the abundance of the heart, which more than any other approaches to conversation; I mean correspondence. Why is it that we feel an interest in Cicero which we cannot feel in Demosthenes or Plato? Plato is the very type of soaring philosophy, and Demosthenes of forcible eloquence; Cicero is something more than orator and a sage; he is not a mere ideality, he is a man and a brother; he is one of ourselves. We do not merely believe it, or infer it, but we have the enduring and living evidence of it—how? In his letters. He can be studied, criticized if you will; but still dwelt upon and sympathized with also. Now the case of the Ancient Saints is parallel to that of Cicero. We have their letters in a marvellous profusion. We have above 400 letters of St. Basil's; above 200 of St. Augustine's. St. Chrysostom has left us about 240; St. Gregory Nazianzen the same number; Pope St. Gregory as many as 840. St. Nilus close on 1400 short ones; St. Isidore, 1440. The blessed Theodoret, 146; St. Leo, 140; St. Cyprian, 80 or 90; St. Paulinus, 50; St. Jerome, above 100; St. Ambrose, 90. St. Bernard, the last of the fathers, supplies 444; and St. Anselm, the first of the schoolmen, nearly the same number. I am passing beyond the early Saints; so I might go on to certain modern, as St. Francis Xavier; but they all belong to one school of literature, which is now well-nigh extinct.

These letters are of very various characters, compared one with another: a large portion of them were intended simply for the parties to whom they are addressed; a large portion consist of brief answers to questions asked of the writer, or a few words of good counsel or spiritual exhortation, disclosing his character either by the topic selected, or his mode of dealing with it. Many are doctrinal; great numbers, again, are strictly ecclesiastical and *ex cathedrâ.* Many are historical and biographical; some might be called state-papers; some narrate public transactions, and how the writer felt towards them, or why he took part in them. Pope Gregory's epistles give us the same sort of insight into the holy solicitude for the universal Christian people which possessed him, that minute vigilance, yet comprehensive superintendence of the chief pastor, which in a very different field of labour is seen in the Duke of Wellington's despatches on campaign, which tell us so much more about him than any panegyrical sketch. Those of St. Isidore and St. Nilus consist of little more than one or two terse, pithy, pregnant sentences, which may be called sermonets, and are often as vivid as if we heard them. St. Chrysostom's are for the most part crowded into the three memorable years in which the sufferings of exile gradually ripened into a virtual martyrdom. Others, as some of those of St. Jerome and St. Ambrose, are meditations on mystical subjects. Those of St. Dionysius of Alexandria, which are but fragments, recount the various trials of the time, and are marked with a vigorous individuality which invests the narrative with an interest far higher than historical.

This manifestation of themselves the Ancient Saints carry with them into other kinds of composition, where it was less to be expected. Instead of writing formal doctrinal treatises, they write controversy; and their controversy, again, is correspondence. They mix up their own persons, natural and supernatural, with the didactic or polemical works which engaged them. Their authoritative declarations are written, not on stone tablets, but on what Scripture calls "the fleshly tables of the heart." The line of their discussion traverses a region rich and interesting, and opens on those who follow them in it a succession of instructive views as to the aims, the difficulties, the disappointments, under which they journeyed on heavenward, their care of the brethren, their anxieties about contemporary teachers of error. Dogma and proof are in them at the same time hagiography. They do not write a *summa theologiæ,* or draw out a *catena,* or pursue a single thesis through the stages of a scholastic disputation. They wrote for the occasion, and seldom on a carefully-digested plan.

The same remark holds of their comments upon Scripture. A speaker and an audience are prominent throughout them; and we gain an insight into their own character and the circumstances of their times, while we are indoctrinated in the sacred text. When Pope Gregory comments upon Ezechiel, he writes about the Lombards, his own people, and himself. What a vivid idea we have of St. Chrysostom! partly from his style, partly from his matter; yet we gain it from his formal expositions of Scripture. His expositions are discourses; his discourses, whether he will or no, are manifestations. St. Gregory Nazianzen has written discourses too, by means of which he has gained for himself the special title of "Theologus"; yet these same orations give us also a large range of information about his own life, his kindred and friends, his feelings and his fortunes; and, as if this were not enough, he has bequeathed to us, besides his letters, his poems, a huge collection of miscellaneous verse, full of himself and his times. They are his confessions.

Here I am reminded of the celebrated work of St. Augustine's which bears that name, and which has no parallel in sacred literature. Of the same character are portions of the correspondence of St. Basil, and, again, of St. Jerome. It is remarkable, on the other hand, that certain ancient writers, who, able and learned as they are, have no title to be called Saints, such as Tertullian and Eusebius, afford as few instances as possible in their works, as far as I know, of that tenderness and simplicity of character which leads their saintly contemporaries to an unstudied self-manifestation.

3

It is perhaps presumptuous in me to have spoken of the Fathers thus universally, and I may have made mistakes in detail; but I have confidence in my general principle, and its general exemplification in their case. Words are the exponents of thoughts, and a silent Saint is the object of faith rather than of affection. If he speaks, then we have the original before us; if he is silent, we must put up with a copy, done with more or less skill according to the painter. But in saying this, I do not mark off the Saints into two distinct classes, those who speak and those who are silent; I am only contrasting two kinds of exhibition which are variously fulfilled in them, taken one by one. Nor is a silent Saint one who does not write, but one who does not speak; and some of them may manifest themselves by their short sayings and their single words more graphically than if they had written a volume.

When St. Philip Neri excused his abstemiousness on the ground of his fear lest he should get as fat as his friend Francesco Scarletti, or hid his religious tears with the jest, "Mayn't a poor orphan weep, who has neither father nor mother?" or made Consolini read out loud a storybook to him, when certain great lords of Poland came to see a Saint, he let us into his character better than by many treatises. Nor are any words at all necessary in some cases; for I suppose the Martyrs, who are the most ancient Saints of all, speak by their deaths; whereas some of the Fathers, as St. Isidore of Seville, and various medieval Saints, have written many large books, and tell us, alas! about themselves nothing. And further still, in the present state of education among us, I do not see how it is possible we should enjoy that personal knowledge of the Saints which seems to me so desirable. The bulk of the faithful have nothing at all to do with Saints' lives or writings, for this simple reason, because they cannot read, or do not like reading. They are devout to a Saint, as they are devout to their Guardian Angel, because he is a work of God, full of grace and glory, and able to protect them. I recollect an Irishman of the humblest class complaining of the sermon of a Religious because it had nothing in it about the Saints: the fact was not so at all, and in the pulpit from which the sermon was preached there had been much about Saints Sunday after Sunday. But it turned out that the complainant was devout to St. Joseph; and his real grievance was, that St. Joseph was not mentioned in the sermon. Nor did he want more than the mention of his glorious patron's name; his very name inspired devotion, he needed no life of him. I wish we, with all our learning, were sure of having this poor man's devotion; but that wish is nothing to the purpose in my present argument, in which I am not contrasting educated and uneducated piety, but the popular biographies of Saints and their actual writings.

Nor must it be supposed that I think lightly of the debt of gratitude which we owe to their biographers. It is not their fault if their Saint has been silent; all that we know about him, be it much, be it little, we owe to them. As I was saying just now, some of those saints who have written most have told us least. There is St. Thomas; he was called in his youth the Bos Siculus for his silence; it is one of the few personal traits which we have of him, and for that very reason, though it does but record the privation of which I am complaining, it is worth a good deal. It is a great consolation to know that he was the Bos Siculus; it makes us feel a sympathy with him, and leads us to trust that perhaps he will feel some sympathy for us, who for one reason or other are silent at times when we should like to be speaking. But it is the sole consolation for that forlorn silence of his, since, although at length he broke it to some purpose, as regards theology, and became a marvel (according to the proverb in such cases), still he is as silent as before in regard to himself. The Angel of the schools! how overflowing he must have been, I say to myself, in all bright supernatural visions, and beautiful and sublime thoughts! how serene in his contemplation of them! how winning in his communication! but he has not helped me ever so little in apprehending what I firmly believe about him. He wrote his *Summa* and his *Hymns* under obedience, I suppose; and no obedience was given him to speak of himself. So we are thrown upon his biographers, and but for them, we should speak of him as we speak of the author of the *Imitation* or of the *Veni Creator,* only as of a great unknown benefactor. All honour, then, and gratitude to the writers of Saints' lives. They have done what they could. It would not have improved matters if they had been silent as well as the Saint; still, they cannot make up for their Saint's silence; they do not deprive me of my grievance, that at present I do not really know those to whom I am devout, whom I hope to see in heaven.

4

A SAINT'S WRITINGS are to me his real "Life"; and what *is called* his "Life" is not the outline of an individual, but either of the *auto-saint* or of a myth. Perhaps I shall be asked what I mean by "Life." I mean a narrative which impresses the reader with the idea of moral unity, identity, growth, continuity, personality. When a Saint converses with me, I am conscious of the presence of one active principle of thought, one individual character, flowing on and into the various matters which he discusses, and the different transactions in which he mixes. It is what no memorials can reach, however skilfully elaborated, however free from effort or study, however conscientiously faithful, however guaranteed by the veracity of the writers. Why cannot art rival the lily or the rose? Because the colours of the flower are developed and blended by the force of an inward life; while on the other hand, the lights and shades of the painter are diligently laid on from without. A magnifying glass will show the difference. Nor will it improve matters, though not one only, but a dozen good artists successively take part in the picture; even if the outline is unbroken, the colouring is muddy. Commonly, what is called "the Life," is little more than a collection of anecdotes brought together from a number of independent quarters; anecdotes striking, indeed, and edifying, but valuable in themselves rather than valuable as parts of a biography; valuable whoever was the subject of them, not valuable as illustrating a particular Saint. It would be difficult to mistake for each other a paragraph of St. Ambrose, or of St. Jerome, or of St. Augustine; it would be very easy to mistake a chapter in the life of one holy missionary or nun for a chapter in the life of another.

An almsgiving here, an instance of meekness there, a severity of penance, a round of religious duties,—all these things humble me, instruct me, improve me; I cannot desire any thing better of their kind; but they do not necessarily coalesce into the image of a person. From such works I do but learn to pay devotion to an abstract and typical perfection under a certain particular name; I do not know more of the real Saint who bore it than before. Saints, as other men, differ from each other in this, that the multitude of qualities which they have in common are differently combined in each of them. This forms one great part of their personality. One Saint is remarkable for fortitude; not that he has not other heroic virtues by *concomitance,* as it may be called, but by virtue of that one gift in particular he has won his crown. Another is remarkable for patient hope, another for renunciation of the world. Such a particular virtue may be said to give form to all the rest which are grouped round it, and are moulded and modified by means of it. Thus it is that often what is right in one would be wrong in another; and, in fact, the very same action is allowed or chosen by one, and shunned by another, as being consistent or inconsistent with their respective characters,—pretty much as in the combination of colours, each separate tint takes a shade from the rest, and is good or bad from its company. The whole gives a meaning to the parts; but it is difficult to rise from the parts to the whole. When I read St. Augustine or St. Basil, I hold converse with a beautiful grace-illumined soul, looking out into this world of sense, and leavening it with itself; when I read a professed life of him, I am wandering in a labyrinth of which I cannot find the centre and heart, and am but conducted out of doors again when I do my best to penetrate within.

This seems to me, to tell the truth, a sort of pantheistic treatment of the Saints. I ask something more than to stumble upon the *disjecta membra* of what ought to be a living whole. I take but a secondary interest in books which chop up a Saint into chapters of faith, hope, charity, and the cardinal virtues. They are too scientific to be devotional. They have their great utility, but it is not the utility which they profess. They do not manifest a Saint, they mince him into spiritual lessons. They are rightly called spiritual reading, that is just what they are, and they cannot possibly be any thing better; but they are not any thing else. They contain a series of points of meditation on particular virtues, made easier because those points are put under the patronage and the invocation of a Saint. With a view to learning real devotion to him, I prefer (speaking for myself) to have any one action or event of his life drawn out minutely, with his own comments upon it, than a score of virtues, or of acts of one virtue, strung together in as many sentences. Now, in the ancient writings I have spoken of, certain transactions are thoroughly worked out. We know all that happened to a Saint on such or such an occasion, all that was done by him. We have a view of his character, his tastes, his natural infirmities, his struggles and victories over them, which in no other way can be attained. And therefore it is that, without quarrelling with the devotion of others, I give the preference to my own.

This is why it is so difficult to be patient with such Church histories as Mosheim's, putting out of the question his Protestant prejudices. When you have read through a century of him, you have as little distinct idea of what he has been about, as when you began. You have been hurried about from subject to subject, from external history to internal, from ceremonies to divines, from heresies to persecutions, till you find that you have gained nothing but to be fatigued. If history is to mirror the actual course of time, it must also be a course itself; it must not be the mere emptying out of a portfolio of unconnected persons and events, which are not synchronous, nor coordinate, nor correlative, but merely arranged, if arrangement it can be called, according to the convenience of the author. And I have a parallel difficulty in the case of hagiographers, when they draw out their materials, not according to years, but according to virtues. Such reading is not history, it is moral science; nay, hardly that: for chronological considerations will be neglected; youth, manhood, and age, will be intermingled. I shall not be able to trace out, for my own edification, the solemn conflict which is waging in the soul between what is divine and what is human, or the eras of the successive victories won by the powers and principles which are divine. I shall not be able to determine whether there was heroism in the young, whether there was not infirmity and temptation in the old. I shall not be able to explain actions which need explanation, for the age of the actors is the true key for entering into them. I shall be wearied and disappointed, and I shall go back with pleasure to the Fathers.

Here another great subject opens upon us, when I ought to be bringing these remarks to an end; I mean the endemic perennial fidget which possesses us about giving scandal; facts are omitted in great histories, or glosses are put upon memorable acts, because they are thought not edifying, whereas of all scandals such omissions, such glosses, are the greatest. But I am getting far more argumentative than I thought to be when I began; so I lay my pen down, and retire into myself.

CHAPTER II

THE SEPARATION

1

JOHN OF ANTIOCH, from his sanctity and his eloquence called Chrysostom, was approaching sixty years of age, when he had to deliver himself up to the imperial officers, and to leave Constantinople for a distant exile. He had been the great preacher of the day now for nearly twenty years; first at Antioch, then in the metropolis of the East; and his gift of speech, as in the instance of the two great classical orators before him, was to be his ruin. He had made an Empress his enemy, more powerful than Antipater,—as passionate, if not so vindictive, as Fulvia. Nor was this all; a zealous Christian preacher offends not individuals merely, but classes of men, and much more so when he is pastor and ruler too, and has to punish as well as to denounce. Eudoxia, the Empress, might be taken off suddenly,—as indeed she was taken off a few weeks after the Saint arrived at the place of exile, which she personally, in spite of his entreaties, had marked out for him;—but her death did but serve to increase the violence of the persecution directed against him. She had done her part in it, perhaps she might have even changed her mind in his favour; probably the agitation of a bad conscience was, in her critical condition, the cause of her death. She was taken out of the way; but her partisans, who had made use of her, went on vigorously with the evil work which she had begun. When Cucusus would not kill him, they sent him on his travels anew, across a far wilder country than he had already traversed, to a remote town on the eastern coast of the Euxine; and he sank under this fresh trial.

The Euxine! that strange mysterious sea, which typifies the abyss of outer darkness, as the blue Mediterranean basks under the smile of heaven in the centre of civilization and religion. The awful, yet splendid drama of man's history has mainly been carried on upon the Mediterranean shores; while the Black Sea has ever been on the very outskirts of the habitable world, and the scene of wild unnatural portents; with legends of Prometheus on the savage Caucasus, of Medea gathering witch-herbs in the moist meadows of the Phasis, and of Iphigenia sacrificing the shipwrecked stranger in Taurica; and then again, with the more historical, yet not more grateful visions of barbarous tribes, Goths, Huns, Scythians, Tartars, flitting over the steppes and wastes which encircle its inhospitable waters. To be driven from the bright cities and sunny clime of Italy or Greece to such a region, was worse than death; and the luxurious Roman actually preferred death to exile. The suicide of Gallus, under this dread doom, is well known; Ovid, too cowardly to be desperate, drained out the dregs of a vicious life on the cold marshes between the Danube and the sea. I need scarcely allude to the heroic Popes who patiently lived on in the Crimea, till a martyrdom, in which they had no part but the suffering, released them.

But banishment was an immense evil in itself. Cicero, even though he had liberty of person, the choice of a home, and the prospect of a return, roamed disconsolate through the cities of Greece, because he was debarred access to the senate-house and forum. Chrysostom had his own *rostra,* his own *curia;* it was the Holy Temple, where his eloquence gained for him victories not less real, and more momentous, than the detection and overthrow of Catiline. Great as was his gift of oratory, it was not by the fertility of his imagination, or the splendour of his diction that he gained the surname of "Mouth of Gold." We shall be very wrong if we suppose that fine expressions, or rounded periods, or figures of speech, were the credentials by which he claimed to be the first doctor of the East. His oratorical power was but the instrument, by which he readily, gracefully, adequately expressed,—expressed without effort and with felicity,—the keen feelings, the living ideas, the earnest practical lessons which he had to communicate to his hearers. He spoke, because his heart, his head, were brimful of things to speak about. His elocution corresponded to that strength and flexibility of limb, that quickness of eye, hand, and foot, by which a man excels in manly games or in mechanical skill. It would be a great mistake, in speaking of it, to ask whether it was Attic or Asiatic, terse or flowing, when its distinctive praise was that it was natural. His unrivalled charm, as that of every really eloquent man, lies in his singleness of purpose, his fixed grasp of his aim, his noble earnestness.

A bright, cheerful, gentle soul; a sensitive heart, a temperament open to emotion and impulse; and all this elevated, refined, transformed by the touch of heaven,—such was St. John Chrysostom; winning followers, riveting affections, by his sweetness, frankness, and neglect of self. In his labours, in his preaching, he thought of others only. "I am always in admiration of that thrice-blessed man," says an able critic,[1] "because he ever in all his writings puts before him as his object, to be useful to his hearers; and as to all other matters, he either simply put them aside, or took the least possible notice of them. Nay, as to his seeming ignorant of some of the thoughts of Scripture, or careless of entering into its depths, and similar defects, all this he utterly disregarded in comparison of the profit of his hearers."

There was as little affectation of sanctity in his dress or living as there was effort in his eloquence. In his youth he had been one of the most austere of men; at the age of twenty-one, renouncing bright prospects of the world, he had devoted himself to prayer and study of the Scriptures. He had retired to the mountains near Antioch, his native place, and had lived among the monks. This had been his home for six years, and he had chosen it in order to subdue the daintiness of his natural appetite. "Lately," he wrote to a friend at the time,—

[1] Photius, p. 387.

"lately, when I had made up my mind to leave the city and betake myself to the tabernacle of the monks, I was for ever inquiring and busying myself how I was to get a supply of provisions; whether it would be possible to procure fresh bread for my eating, whether I should be ordered to use the same oil for my lamp and for my food, to undergo the hardship of peas and beans, or of severe toil, such as digging, carrying wood or water, and the like; in a word, I made much account of bodily comfort." [1] Such was the nervous anxiety and fidget of mind with which he had begun: but this rough discipline soon effected its object, and at length, even by preference, he took upon him mortifications which at first were a trouble to him. For the last two years of his monastic exercise, he lived by himself in a cave; he slept, when he did sleep, without lying down; he exposed himself to the extremities of cold. At length he found he was passing the bounds of discretion, nature would bear no more; he fell ill, and returned to the city.

A course of ascetic practice such as this would leave its spiritual effects upon him for life. It sank deep into him, though the surface might not show it. His duty at Constantinople was to mix with the world; and he lived as others, except as regards such restraints as his sacred office and station demanded of him. He wore shoes, and an under garment; but his stomach was ever delicate, and at meals he was obliged to have his own dish, such as it was, to himself. However, he mixed freely with all ranks of men; and he made friends, affectionate friends, of young and old, men and women, rich and poor, by condescending to all of every degree. How he was loved at Antioch, is shown by the expedient used to transfer him thence to Constantinople. Asterius, count of the East, had orders to send for him, and ask his company to a church without the city. Having got him into his carriage, he drove off with him to the first station on the high-road to Constantinople, where imperial officers were in readiness to convey him thither. Thus he was brought upon the scene of those trials

[1] Ad Demetrium, i. 6.

which have given him a name in history, and a place in the catalogue of the Saints. At the imperial city he was as much followed, if not as popular, as at Antioch. "The people flocked to him," says Sozomen, "as often as he preached; some of them to hear what would profit them, others to make trial of him. He carried them away, one and all, and persuaded them to think as he did about the Divine Nature. They hung upon his words, and could not have enough of them; so that, when they thrust and jammed themselves together in an alarming way, every one making an effort to get nearer to him, and to hear him more perfectly, he took his seat in the midst of them, and taught from the pulpit of the Reader." [1] He was, indeed, a man to make both friends and enemies; to inspire affection, and to kindle resentment; but his friends loved him with a love "stronger" than "death," and more burning than "hell;" and it was well to be so hated, if he was so beloved.

2

HERE HE DIFFERS, as far as I can judge, from his brother saints and doctors of the Greek Church, St. Basil and St. Gregory Nazianzen. They were scholars, shy perhaps and reserved; and though they had not given up the secular state, they were essentially monks. There is no evidence, that I remember, to show that they attached men to their persons. They, as well as John, had a multitude of enemies; and were regarded, the one with dislike, the other perhaps with contempt; but they had not, on the other hand, warm, eager, sympathetic, indignant, agonized friends. There is another characteristic in Chrysostom, which perhaps gained for him this great blessing. He had, as it would seem, a vigour, elasticity, and, what may be called, sunniness of mind, all his own. He was ever sanguine, seldom sad. Basil had a life-long malady, involving continual gnawing pain and a weight of

[1] Hist. viii. 5.

physical dejection. He bore his burden well and gracefully, like the great Saint he was, as Job bore his; but it was a burden like Job's. He was a calm, mild, grave, autumnal day; St. John Chrysostom was a day in springtime, bright and rainy, and glittering through its rain. Gregory was the full summer, with a long spell of pleasant stillness, its monotony relieved by thunder and lightning. And St. Athanasius figures to us the stern persecuting winter, with its wild winds, its dreary wastes, its sleep of the great mother, and the bright stars shining overhead. He and Chrysostom have no points in common; but Gregory was a dethroned Archbishop of Constantinople, like Chrysostom, and, again, dethroned by his brethren the Bishops. Like Basil, too, Chrysostom was bowed with infirmities of body; he was often ill; he was thin and wizened; cold was a misery to him; heat affected his head; he scarcely dared touch wine; he was obliged to use the bath; obliged to take exercise, or rather to be continually on the move. Whether from a nervous or febrile complexion, he was warm in temper; or at least, at certain times, his emotion struggled hard with his reason. But he had that noble spirit which complains as little as possible; which makes the best of things; which soon recovers its equanimity, and hopes on in circumstances when others sink down in despair.

Every one has his own gifts. I often muse upon, I have quoted, I here would copy what is told us of St. Antony; how the young ascetic went first to this holy man, and then to that, according as each was qualified to teach him; "marking down in his own thoughts the special attainment of each; his refinement, or his continuance in prayer, or his meekness, or his kindness, or his power of long-watching, or his studiousness." And thus there was in Basil tenderness, gravity, self-possession, resignation, penance; in Gregory, innocence, amiableness, an inward peace, a self-resource, an independence of external things; and all these graces in both Saints grafted upon Christian perfection, and raised to an heroic standard. The Giver of all good suits His gifts to the circumstances of the recipient. John, in like manner, was endowed with those which John required.

But now all these fragrant and beautiful flowers of grace are to be hurried where, to all seeming, they will "waste their sweetness on the desert air," and then wither away, as far as this earth is concerned. The eloquent voice is to be mute: Chrysostom has preached his last sermon; for the last time crowds of devoted followers—holy bishops, zealous priests, youths whom he is training to virtue, noble ladies who have become deaconesses of the Church,—for the last time the court, the populace, his faithful poor,—have lingered on the sound of his touching accents. They shall never hear him again. The silver cord is to be broken; the golden fillet is to shrink; he is vanishing from the eyes of men. It was just at the summer solstice, in the year 404, that the order came to him from the Emperor to go. He had resisted a like order already; but now the state of things was so near upon a bloody quarrel, that it seemed expedient to obey. He went into his church for the last time; to take leave, as he said, of the Angel who had the charge of it. Then he bade farewell to some ecclesiastics, his intimate friends: "I am going to take some rest," he said, so calling his exile; "but do you remain here." And then, lastly, he took leave in the baptistery of some heart-broken pious women, to whom he spoke with greater sadness and effusion of heart. "O my daughters," he said, "come and hear what I have to say; my matters have an end, as I see well. I have finished my course; it may be, you will not see my face again. But one thing I ask of you, continue your services to the church; and, if there be one put into my place against his will, and without his seeking, and with the consent of all, him obey as if he were John; for a church cannot be without a Bishop: so shall ye find mercy. And remember me in your prayers."[1] Then, ordering the beast he rode to the western gate of the ecclesiastical buildings, to mislead

[1] Pallad. p. 35, etc.

his people, who were keeping guard over his person, he issued by the eastern, and, with a protest, surrendered himself to the imperial guard. He was at once put into a boat, and carried over into Asia. Oh, how down was his heart, and what sorrowful thoughts chased one another across it; and how his life seemed to him a dream, and his long labours to have done nothing at all, and to be lost, as he landed on the opposite coast, and was conducted up the country to Nicæa, there to stay awhile, till his place of banishment was finally determined!

3

His sadness, however, was of no long duration; "weeping may take place in the evening, but there is gladness in the morning." The change of air and scene, the quiet, and above all, his own cheerful spirit, came to his aid; and he began to hope again. Men of gentle and generous tempers cannot understand how any one can be a good hater; and certainly our Saint did not realise the inveterate malice and the savage determination of his enemies. He might forgive them; they could not forgive him. This, however, was not as yet a matter of experience with him; accordingly he began to speculate on the possibility of the Emperor's relenting, and changing his place of exile to some neighbouring city. He was soon undeceived in his anticipation. He was to prepare for a long journey. Scythia was mentioned as his destination; then Sebaste in Pontus; at length, Cucusus. It was his custom in all his afflictions, as we shall see in his letters, to use the words "Glory to God" upon every event; and he now soon reconciled himself to his disappointment. He had to remain at Nicæa about a fortnight, and during that delay wrote various letters to Constantinople, some of which have been preserved.

One of his most devoted of friends, and most zealous of correspondents, was St. Olympias. This celebrated lady was the daughter of Count Seleucus, and the grand-child of

Ablavius, the powerful minister in the reign of Constantine. She had been left an orphan and a pagan; and she did not change her single state for marriage before she had relieved her worse desolateness by entering into the family of Saints and Angels. In St. Chrysostom's words, she "deserted to Christian truth from the ranks of an ungodly family." Her husband, who was Prefect of Constantinople, died not many months after the marriage; on which, in spite of her great friends, she became a deaconess of the Church. At this time she was between thirty and forty years of age. The exiled Bishop wrote to her from Nicæa as follows:

TO OLYMPIAS

My consolation increases with my trial. I am sanguine about the future. Every thing is going on prosperously, and I am sailing with a fair wind. There are, indeed, hidden rocks; there are tempests, the night is moonless, the darkness thick, and crags and cliffs are before me; yet, though I am navigating a sea like this, still I am not at all in worse case than many a man who is tossing about in harbour. Reflect on this, my religious lady, and rise above these alarms and troubles; and please to tell me about your own health: for myself, I am in health and in spirits. I find myself stronger than I was; I breathe a pure air; the soldiers of the prefecture, who are to accompany me, are so attentive as to leave me no need even of domestics, for they take on themselves domestic duties. They actually volunteered this charge of me for love of me; and wherever I go I have a body-guard, each of them thinking himself happy in such a ministry. I have one drawback; my anxiety for your health. Inform me on this point.—*Ep.* 11.

He writes to her again a few days later:

TO OLYMPIAS

Have no fear about this either, I mean my journey; as I have already written you word, I am improved in health and strength. The climate has agreed with me; and my conductors have shown every wish, and done all in their power—more, indeed, than I desired myself—to make me comfortable. I have written this when on the point of starting from Nicæa, the 3rd of July. Give me some account from time to time of your own health; and also tell me that the cloud of despondency has passed away from you. If I were assured of this from yourself, I should write more frequently to you, under a feeling that my letters might be of service; but, so it is, many persons have crossed to this place who might have brought me a letter from you, and it has been a great sorrow that I have received nothing.—*Ep.* 10.

Perhaps he exaggerated his own hopefulness, in order to increase hers. He describes his state of feeling more exactly, and reveals more fully what occupied his thoughts, in a letter of about the same date to Constantius, a priest of Antioch, and intimate friend, who had taken a forward part together with the Saint in extending Christianity to Phœnicia. This, as so many of his other letters, shows us how little his personal troubles had damped his evangelical zeal or his pastoral solicitude.

TO CONSTANTIUS

I am to set off on July 4 from Nicæa. I send you this letter to urge you, as I never cease to urge, though the storm increase in fury and the waves mount higher, not to fail to do your part in the matter which you originally undertook,—I mean the destruction of the Greek worship, the erection of churches, and the care of souls; and not to let the difficulties of things throw you upon your back. For myself, if I do not take my share of the work, but am remiss, I shall not be able to excuse myself by my present trouble; for Paul in prison and in the stocks fulfilled the office which fell to him, and Jonas inside the monster, and the Three Children in the midst of the furnace. You, then, my lord, remembering this, do not give over your duties towards Phœnicia, Arabia, and the churches of the East, knowing that your reward will only be the greater if, amid so great hindrances, you contribute towards the work.

And do not be backward in writing to me from time to time, nay, very frequently; for I now know that I am sent, not to Sebaste, but to Cucusus, whither it will be easier for you to get letters to me. Write me word how many churches are built every year, and what holy men have passed into Phœnicia, and what progress they have made. As to Salamis in Cyprus, which is beset by the Marcionite heretics, I should have treated with the proper persons, and set every thing right, but for my banishment. Urge those especially who have familiar speech with God, to use much prayer with much perseverance, for the stilling of the tempest which is at present wrecking the whole world.—*Ep.* 221.

4

THUS HE SET OFF INTO EXILE. He could not fully realize what was coming upon him; nor was the prospect of things so threatening as to suggest grave apprehension. Cucusus, his destination, was not so bad as Sebaste, much better than Scythia. It was on the high military way into Mesopotamia; it was a place at which two lines of road met from Asia Minor and Armenia, not to say a third from Issus on the Mediterranean. After the junction, the above roads passed on, as it would seem, to Melitene on the Euphrates, which afterwards, if not then, was a principal emporium in the commercial intercourse between Europe and Asia. Moreover, it was the seat of a bishopric; and, what was of more consequence, was in the neighbourhood, and within easy reach, of his friends at Antioch. That city lay about 120 miles due south of Cucusus: those who visited him thence would pass by the high road through the Amanus or Black Mountain to Pagræ, and then, crossing or skirting round the Bay of Issus, to the mouth of the Pyramus, would ascend the valley of that river till they came to Cucusus. Nor was the journey thither from Nicæa at first sight formidable, except that the season was against him. It lay all the way along the great high-road of the Empire, passing from Nicæa to Dadastana or to Dorylæum; thence to Ancyra, the capital of Galatia; then, turning to the southeast, down to Cæsarea, the capital of Cappadocia; then to Comana, the chief city in Cataonia; and thence, over the Taurus, to

Cucusus, which was the first town out of Asia Minor, opening upon the valley of the Euphrates.

And, as he would have to pass along a noble road, so would he pass through rich towns in a fertile country. Ancyra was finely situated in the middle of an extensive plain, which, even under the Turkish yoke, is described by Tournefort as beautiful, well watered, and in parts well cultivated. Cæsarea, in the century before St. Chrysostom, had counted 400,000 inhabitants. Comana was placed in the richest of valleys, to which the Turks have given the name of Bostan, or the Garden. Nor was the journey less adapted for spiritual than for mental refreshment. It lay through Cæsarea, the see and tomb of St. Basil; and through Nyssa, the like home in life and death of St. Gregory his brother. Nazianzus lay to the right. The country of Cappadocia and Pontus was classical to an oriental Christian, for the great Saints who had adorned it. Meanwhile he was gaining strength in Nicæa, a magnificent city magnificently placed; and, moreover, as full of religious inspirations as any city in the East. There it was that the Great Council had been held eighty years before, in which Arianism had been condemned, and the faith of the Apostles solemnly proclaimed, for the edification of all faithful souls in the many years of turbulence and temptation which were to follow.

CHAPTER III

THE JOURNEY

I

I left St. John Chrysostom turning his face eastward, and leaving the shores of the Propontis for his distant exile. He had been banished on the pretence of his resumption of the episcopal functions before the legitimate reversal of a synodical decree, which had condemned and deposed him; and such an offence, by a recent imperial law, was punished by banishment to a distance of at least a hundred miles. In consequence, he might have been simply told to vanish from Constantinople, and make his way to the prescribed limit as best he could; but a definite place having been assigned to him, Cucusus, on the eastern slope of the Taurus, it was necessary, and even considerate, to send guides and protectors with him. Two soldiers seem to have been named by the Prefect for this purpose; and, as we have seen, he speaks well of them. They might have been better, perhaps; but they certainly might have been worse. He might have suffered ill-treatment at their hands, as he did from his guards on his second journey; and without their aid and countenance it is probable he never would have reached his destination. They had their share, of course, in many of the hardships to which he was exposed, yet they seem to have borne their share with temper, if not with spirit; and the Saint appears to have liked them at the end of his expedition as well as at the beginning. This was no slight merit in them or in him; for many a time it happens, as all must know who have experience of travelling, that the persons we fall in with in what may be called an official capacity, or the acquaintance we make, are much more amiable and satisfactory at first, and can more easily be got on with, than when our relations have continued with them through a certain space of time. Such persons often do not excite pleasant memories in the retrospect. It is worth recording, then, that, writing back, some time after his arrival at Cucusus, to a friend at Constantinople, the Saint speaks of one of them as "my honoured lord Theodorus, of the prefecture, who took me to Cucusus;" and he implies that he had talked confidently with him.

He must have left the beautiful Nicæa with regret, except as rejoicing to suffer in the cause of religion. Rich in marble edifices and works which were carried even into the Ascanian lake, it lay on an eminence in the midst of a well-wooded, flower-embellished country, with the clear bright waters at its foot, and successive tiers of mountains behind, which terminated in the snow-capped Olympus. He took a last look of the last fair place which he was to see on earth; and, as he passed out by the south-eastern gate to begin a pilgrimage which was to end in the gate of heaven, the scene at once changed. He entered a valley, which, as travellers tell us, rose and fell again through a succession of wild crags and distant peaks, till at length he reached a cultivated track, and then a forest region. Let him enjoy it while it lasts, for signs of volcanic action are multiplying on every side of him; and even though he travels in the evening or at night, the bare lava and limestone rock, like some vast oven, retain the intolerable heat of the July day. Nor is the traveller's prospect much better when he has reached the high table-land of the Asian peninsula, nearly 2,000 feet above the level of the sea, which stretches for hundreds of miles in every direction. Fertile as this vast plateau may be, and verdant and well watered, at an earlier season, it presents from June to the end of October an arid and scorched surface; and on it lies the road of St. Chrysostom for months, till he comes to the spurs of the Taurus, on the farther side of Cæsarea. Perhaps on the third or fourth night after starting he rested at Dorylæum.

2

WELL HAD IT BEEN FOR HIM if the Emperor, or any of his great officers, had allowed him the use of the *cursus publicus,* or government conveyance. It would have carried him on with fair speed, and without expense of his own. This privilege, indeed, could hardly have been expected by one who was in the place of a criminal; yet the same sanguine spirit which led him to hope for a sojourn at Cyzicus or Nicomedia, easily might, when a distant exile was decreed, have contemplated such an alleviation. He had had trial of that "public course," at an earlier date, on one of the few real journeys which he had ever made in his life,—and, ah, under what opposite circumstances!—on that memorable occasion, I mean, when an imperial summons impetuously hurried him away from his dear Antioch. The splendid circumstances of that journey seem to have impressed themselves on his imagination; and in one of his works, speaking of the merit of Abraham's pilgrimage from Mesopotamia to Palestine, he contrasts with it the facility with which travelling was performed along the military lines of road in his own day. "The distance," he says, "between place and place is what it was; but the condition of the roads is very different. For now the line passes through stations placed at intervals, and through cities and farms, and is crowded with wayfarers, who avail for the security of travel not less than farms, towns, and stations. Moreover, by order of the city magistrates, a provincial police is raised,—picked men, as well skilled in the javelin and sling as bowmen are adepts in the arrow, and the heavy-armed in the lance,—with commanders over them, and that for the express purpose of protecting the roads. Further still, as an additional security, buildings are placed a mile from each other, as guard-houses; this watch and ward being the most complete defence against the attacks of plunderers. In the time of Abraham there were none of these."[1] And so he proceeds, rejoicing, as it were, in

[1] Ad Stag. ii. 6.

his picture of a state of convenience and security, which the Roman empire alone could boast, but which in the event was to be so strikingly reversed in every particular in the melancholy journey which was to close his labours.

Left, then, to himself to find his own conveyance, he chose the *basterna,* which answered pretty nearly to the Sicilian *lettiga,* being a sort of car or palanquin carried between two mules, one before and one behind. Such, at least, was his style of carriage at a later part of his journey; and he would advance by means of it at the rate of from three to four miles an hour. The distance between Dorylæum and Ancyra he may be supposed to have accomplished within eight days; at least, such is the time which a caravan employs upon it. If Tournefort's account is to be taken, the route has few attractions, even at a better season. He speaks of a beautiful plain, of villages, streams, gentle undulations of surface, but with a notable absence of wood. It was the ancient Phrygia, and celebrated as a corn country. Mount Dindymus, famous for the fanatical worship of Cybele, rose on his left, an outpost, apparently, of the north Olympic range. At length the temples and public buildings of Ancyra, nobly situated on an elevated terrace, greeted his weary eyes in the distant horizon.

So far his course seems to have been prosperous; nothing, at least, is recorded to the contrary. He would travel at his own hours, and at his own pace; with rumours, indeed, of the evils which were coming upon him, but probably with no foretaste of them. The villages, however, of Phrygia had within a few years been devastated by the insurgent Goth Tribigildus, and this might affect the convenience of his lodging and his halts; and at all times the inns would be a great difficulty to any respectable traveller, not to say a saintly Bishop. They were of the lowest description, and contained the worst of company; and it was usual for those who had good connections to avail themselves of the country houses of their friends, as, indeed, St. Chrysostom did in the sequel.

3

When he got to Ancyra his troubles began; we have but a confused account of them. Leontius, Bishop of that city, was one of the very foremost of his enemies, and in some way or other nearly brought about his death. The Isaurians, too, had just descended from their mountain-holds, and spread themselves over the country. The interior of Asia Minor was a scene of disorder: the country people were flying, the cities fortifying themselves, the road-stations deserted, the guards gone. On leaving Ancyra, our traveller had to make for Cæsarea as quickly as he could, in order to avoid the danger of falling into the enemy's hands. He travelled night and day; from fatigue and anxiety he fell ill; a tertian fever seized on him; wholesome food and water could not be obtained; with much difficulty and in the greatest distress he accomplished the 200 miles between the two cities, and found himself in the metropolis of Cappadocia.

It is very observable that, in spite of the indescribable confusion of the populations through which he passed, Christian zeal and charity did not allow their personal sufferings to interfere with the homage and interest due from them to the presence of so illustrious a confessor. They poured out upon his line of road to greet him and condole with him. At this time, as I shall show presently in his own words, he was in extreme weakness and distress of body; but, as the poor people neglected their own temporal troubles, so did he his. It was a triumph of the supernatural on both sides. His sufferings, too, so far from making him selfish, left him at liberty to write. The following letter to Olympias, written as he was approaching Cæsarea, is striking for the sympathy which it breathes both for her and for the generous people he writes about:

TO OLYMPIAS

When I see whole populations of men and women, in the highway, at the road-stations, and in the cities, pouring out to see me, and weeping at the sight, I am able to comprehend your grief at home. For if these people, who now see me for the first time, are thus broken with sorrow (so that they could not be comforted, but when I besought them, and exhorted, and admonished them, their hot tears did but stream the more), most certainly on you the storm is beating more violently still. But the greater also will be your reward, if you persevere under it with thanksgiving and with becoming fortitude, as you do. You know this well, my religious lady; therefore beware of surrendering yourself to the tyranny of sorrow. You can command yourself; the tempest is not beyond your skill. And send me a letter to tell me this; that, though I live in a strange land, I may enjoy much cheerfulness from the assurance that you bear your trials with the understanding and wisdom which becomes you. I write this when not far from Cæsarea.—*Ep*. 9.

In a second letter, written apparently about the same time, he again complains of her silence, which seemed to him a token of excessive grief; and he adds, in like manner: "I see that not even my removal from Constantinople can release me from distress; for those who meet me on my journey, some from the east, some from Armenia, some from other parts, are drowned in tears at the sight of me, and follow me with piercing laments as I travel onwards."—*Ep*. 8. Not a word about his own sufferings.

He seems to have had a special fear of frightening Olympias, and takes care to write when he has good news to communicate, either about himself or about things around him. Accordingly, he selects the most favourable moment of his sojourn at Cæsarea to send her an account of his state and circumstances. This, too, I will submit to the reader, before addressing myself to those of a more painful character belonging to the very same days. It runs as follows:

TO OLYMPIAS

Now that I have got rid of the ailment which I suffered on my journey, the remains of which I carried with me into Cæsarea, and am already restored to perfect health, I write to you from that place. I have had the advantage here of much careful treatment at the hands of the first and most celebrated physicians, who nevertheless did even more for me by their sympathy and soothing kindness than by their skill. One of them went so far as to promise to accompany me on my journey; so, indeed, did also many other persons of consideration. Now I am often writing to you of my own matters; and you, as I have already complained, are very remiss in that respect yourself. I can prove to you that it is your own neglect, and not the want of letter-carriers; for my honoured lord, the brother of Bishop Maximus of blessed memory, arrived here two days since, and, on my asking him if he brought me letters, he made answer that there was no one who had any to send by him, nay, that when he expressly applied to Tigrius, the presbyter, the latter brought him none. I wish you would inflict this upon him, and upon that true and warm friend of mine, and on all the rest who are about Bishop Cyriacus. As to my changing my place of abode, do not trouble him or any one else about it. I accept their kindness: perhaps they wished, and could not effect it. Glory be to God for all things. I will never cease saying this, whatever befalls me. But suppose they could not effect it, still could they not at least write? Thank in my name my ladies, the sisters of my most honoured lord Bishop Pergamius, for the great trouble they have taken about me. For yourself, write me word frequently how you are, and about my friends; but as for me, have no anxiety about me, for I am in health and in good spirits, and in the enjoyment of much repose up to this day.—*Ep.* 12.

It is the case with most people who leave home, even in this day, when the arrangements of the letter-post are so complete, that the friends whom they have left seem never to write to them, and they get impatient at the supposed neglect. St. John Chrysostom, who lived in his friends, and knew what persecution they were enduring, was especially open to this misconception during his journey; and he shows his sense of it much more openly in the following letter to Theodora, to whom he does not think it necessary to show the tender consideration which Olympias required. He writes to her, when at the worst, on his first arrival at Cæsarea, and takes no pains to hide a distress which he did hide from others, and which perhaps he found a relief in expressing:

TO THEODORA

I am done for; I am simply spent; I have died a thousand deaths. On this point the bearers of this will be the best informants, though they were with me only for a very short time. In truth, I was not in a state to converse with them ever so little, being prostrated by continual fever. In this condition I was forced to travel on night and day, stifled by the heat, worn out with sleeplessness, at death's door for want both of necessaries and of persons to attend to me. I have suffered and suffer worse even than men who labour at the mines, or who are confined to prison. Hardly and at length I arrived at Cæsarea; and I find the place like a calm, like a port after a storm. Not that it set me up all at once, after the severe handling which preceded it; but still, now that I am at Cæsarea, I have recovered a little, since I drink clean water, bread that can be chewed, and is not offensive to the senses. Moreover, I no longer wash myself in broken crockery, but have contrived some sort of bath; also I have got a bed, to which I can confine myself.—*Ep.* 120.

He goes on to bring out the feelings which are obscurely intimated in his letter to Olympias. For the moment he certainly thought his friends unkind, because, rich and powerful as they were, they could do nothing towards securing him the cheap indulgence, which even convicts obtained, of some place of banishment more tolerable and nearer home, some place where there would be nothing to try so severely his bodily strength, or to inflict the terrors which he experienced from the Isaurians. However, he adds, "Even for this, glory be to God: I will not cease glorifying Him for all things; blessed be His Name for ever." And then he goes on to complain of Theodora herself for not writing. "I am astonished at you," he says; "this is the fourth, if not the fifth, letter I have sent you; and you have sent me but one. It pains me much to think that you have so soon forgotten me."

Poor Theodora had doubtless been in continual prayers

and tears, and could give her own account of her silence, as the others could also. Tigrius, for instance, whose silence he wonders at in his letter to Olympias, had, in spite of his informant, been scourged and racked, and lay probably between life and death. His martyrdom is commemorated in the Martyrology on January 12. However, we are not concerned here with any confessors but St. John Chrysostom; so I go on to explain who the Isaurians were, and how it was that the fear of them made him travel night and day for two hundred miles at midsummer, when a fever lay upon him, and death seemed to threaten. In fact, the country through which his route lay was the theatre of war, for the outbreak of the barbarians could be called nothing less; in the very month, almost in the very days, when he was passing through Cæsarea, a battle had taken place, perhaps in the neighbourhood, between the Romans and the insurgent forces; and I shall require a page or two to set before the reader how things came to this pass.

4

IN TRUTH, THE ISAURIANS were not insurgents, unless that name can be given to a people who had never fairly been conquered. The passes of Mount Taurus had ever sheltered a wild independent people, whom the student of history naturally connects with those Cilician pirates who so audaciously insulted the Roman republic, and were at last punished and suppressed by Pompey. Even after the lapse of four centuries, however, the Isaurians had not given up their old craft; and we find them in the reign of Constantius seizing and plundering the vessels which passed along their coast. However, the direction of their rapacity was on the whole turned landwards after Pompey's time; and the whole continent, from the Egean almost to Egypt, was kept in a state of unsettlement and insecurity down to the time of Justinian by the fitful devastations of these freebooters. After a time of nominal subjection to the Roman power, in the middle of the third century they placed themselves under the rule of Trebellian, one of the Thirty Tyrants, as they are called; proclaimed independence, coined money, and when Trebellian was killed in battle, worshipped him as a god. For a time they formed, together with Galatia, part of the empire of Zenobia. After her fall they returned, under various bold and skilful leaders, to their raids and depredations; till the imperial government, despairing of carrying the war into their mountainous recesses with effect, contented themselves with surrounding them with a *cordon* of forts, while they kept a large force in the interior, and a stronghold on the coast to secure communication with the sea. In the reign of Probus they had extended themselves along Pamphylia and Lycia. Under Constantius, besides their piracy, which I have already noticed, they had overrun the plains of the interior towards Pontus. Under Valens, they cut to pieces a Roman force commanded by the Vicar of Asia, and were only stemmed in their onward course by the local militia. Within a dozen years after, they appear to have poured down again, if St. Basil speaks of them when he describes the country as being full of plunderers, and the roads unsafe from Cappadocia to Constantinople. If we may take the Canons in evidence, which are contained in one of the epistles of the same Father, they forced their captives to renounce the faith and to take part in idolatrous rites. At another time their raid extended as far as the Euxine on the north, and as far south as Damascus.

One of their most formidable outbreaks was precisely at the time when Chrysostom was sent into the countries bordering on them; and it would greatly increase the guilt of his persecutors, if they knowingly exposed him to this additional misery. But the movements of barbarian mountaineers are ordinarily sudden, and the imperial court was probably as much taken by surprise by the Isaurians as by the contemporary irruption of the Huns. On this occasion they spread themselves along the coast from Caria to Phœnicia, so as even to threaten Jerusalem; and, what is more to our purpose to observe, they poured over the interior of the country till they found themselves in the neighborhood of the river Kur and the Caspian. In spite of partial successes, two Roman generals failed before them; and this terrible scourge continued till the year after the Saint's death. His years of exile were spent in the very scene, almost in the heart, of these horrors.

I have said it was doubtless the neighbourhood of these free-booters which forced St. John Chrysostom to hurry over the ground between Ancyra and Cæsarea when he was so little able to bear it. He looked forward to Cæsarea as a harbour after the storm, as he says in his letter to Theodora; and at first he found it so; but troubles arose of another kind. The Bishop of Cæsarea, though pretending to be his friend, really wished to get rid of him. Chrysostom became a centre of attraction to all the religious feeling of the place, and the prelate did not relish this; he did not like the Saint's lingering in his own city; he determined to send him on his journey without delay, at all costs; and, when he could not do so peaceably, he did not scruple, as we shall see, at violent measures. He forgot somehow the text about receiving Angels unawares, and the promise attached to those who welcome a prophet in the name of a prophet, and the just in the name of the just. I shall draw out the account of what took place chiefly in the Saint's own words, as contained in letters from him to Olympias after he had arrived at Cucusus, his destination. It will be recollected that in his last letter to her from Cæsarea he spoke of his health and good spirits and repose, his only trouble being that he had no news how she and his other friends were getting on at Constantinople. Now that he was safe at Cucusus, we shall find him writing about his condition at that same date in far different terms.

TO OLYMPIAS

Hardly at length do I breathe again, now that I have reached Cucusus, from which place I write to you; hardly at length am I in the use of my eyes after the phantoms and the various clouds of ill which beset me during my journey. Now then, since the pain is passed, I will give you an account of it; for while I was under it I was loth to do so, lest I should distress you too much. For near thirty days, or even more, I was wrestling with a most severe fever; and, during my long and severe journey, was beset besides with a most severe ailment of the stomach; and this when I was without physicians, baths, necessaries, or relief of any kind, and in continual alarm about the Isaurians, besides having the ordinary anxieties of travel. However, all these troubles are at an end. On arriving at Cucusus I got rid of all my ailments, and all that appertained to them, and am now in the most perfect health.—*Ep.* 13.

After this introduction, and more of the same character, he resumes the subject in a second letter:

When I got rid of our Galatian friend [the Bishop of Ancyra] (who, indeed, almost threatened me with death), and was on the point of entering Cappadocia, I met many persons on the road who said, "My lord Pharetrius [Bishop of Cæsarea] is expecting to see you, and is going here and there in his fear of missing you; and is taking great pains to see and embrace you, and show you all love. He has even set in motion the monasteries and nunneries." I, however, did not anticipate any thing of the kind; rather I formed just the contrary surmises in my own breast: however, I did not say a word to that effect to those who brought me the news.

At length, when I arrived at Cæsarea in a state of prostration, a mere cinder, in the fiercest flame of my fever, in the deepest depression, in extremities, I found a lodging in the outskirts of the city; and I did my best to get medical advice for the quenching of this furnace, for I entered the place almost a corpse. And then, to be sure, the whole clergy, the people, monks, nuns, physicians, at once came about me; I had an abundance of attention, all of them doing all in their power in the way of ministration and service. Even with all this care, I was altogether delirious in the burning heat, and lay in imminent danger. At length, by degrees, the malady gave way and retired. All this while Pharetrius was not to be found; he was but looking out for my departure, I cannot tell why.—*Ep.* 14.

5

CHRYSOSTOM HAD BEEN EAGER to proceed, wishing to get his journey over, and to be at last at rest at Cucusus; and scarcely was he better when he thought of moving. Then came the news that the Isaurians were approaching, and made him hesitate.

While I was in this state, suddenly the tidings came that the Isaurians are overrunning the neighbourhood of Cæsarea in great force; that they have burned a large village, inflicting every evil on the people. On receipt of the news, the city commander, with such soldiers as he had with him, went out to meet them; for they were even apprehensive of an attack on the city. Indeed, all persons were in a state of great alarm, in great excitement, their native soil being in jeopardy; so that even aged men took part in guarding the walls. Things were in this state when on a sudden, at the break of dawn, down comes a battalion of monks (I can use no better word to express their fury), beset the house where I was, and threaten to set fire to it, to burn it down, to do me all possible mischiefs, unless I took myself off; and neither did the danger from the Isaurians, nor my own serious state of body, no, nor anything else, avail to disarm their violence.

Here I interpose a word of explanation. Nothing which has been hitherto said of the monastic bodies would lead one to expect such a sudden movement as this. The monks, as we have seen, generally treated the Saint with great consideration and reverence, as he passed in their neighbourhood. But at this time, it must be confessed, they were a very rude and excitable set of men, at least in certain places; they were not under the strict discipline which afterwards prevailed; and they were sometimes, as here, at the command of their Bishop, sometimes actuated by strong local or national feelings. Moreover there was a vast number of fanatical monks at that day, whom the Church did not recognise, and who were exposed to the influence of any wild calumnies or absurd tales which might be circulated to the prejudice of Chrysostom. However, be the explanation of this incident what it may, this monastic troop played a chief part in worrying the Saint out of Cæsarea. He continues:

Nor did any thing avail to disarm their violence; but they urged their point with such an explosion of wrath as even to frighten my companions, the soldiers of the prefecture. For they threatened to beat even them; and they boasted that many were the Prefect's soldiers before now whom they had badly beaten. When my soldiers heard this, they came to me, and begged and prayed that, though they should in consequence fall into the hands of the Isaurians, I would rid them of these wild beasts. The mayor of the city also heard what was going on, and he hastened to my house with the wish to assist me; but the monks would not listen to his entreaties, and he too was unsuccessful. Upon this, feeling the dilemma in which matters were, not daring to advise me either to go out of the city to certain death, or to remain within it, exposed as I was to the fury of the monks, he sent to Pharetrius, entreating him to give me a few days' grace, both by reason of my illness, and of the danger which lay in my way. However, he was not able to obtain even this, for on the next day the monks came with still greater violence; and no one of the presbyters ventured to stand by me or succour me; but with shame and a blush on their faces (for they said they acted on the orders of Pharetrius), they shuffled away and kept out of sight, and refused to answer when I appealed to them. Why many words? Though such dangers threatened me, and death was almost in sight, and my fever was preying on me, I threw myself into my *lectica*, noontide as it was, and set off amid the wailings and laments of the whole people.

However, he had one more chance: at this moment Seleucia, the wife of one of the principal persons of Cæsarea, sent to offer him the use of her suburban villa, at a distance of five miles from the city; a kindness which he joyfully accepted. This good lady, moreover, gave orders to her steward to gather together the labourers on her farms round about, if the monks showed any disposition to repeat their violence, and fairly to give them battle. Nay, she had a fortified building on her ground, where she wished to place him; where neither the monks nor the Bishop could reach him. However, the Bishop was too much both for her and St. Chrysostom. He terrified her by threats into submission to his will; and a priest, one of his creatures, was sent to the Saint. The sequel shall be told in his own words:

At midnight Evethius, the presbyter, came into my room when I was asleep; he woke me, and cried out loudly, "Up, I pray you, the barbarians are coming; they are close at hand." Fancy what my perplexity was at these words. I said to him, "What is to be done? It is impossible to make for the city; for I should fare worse there than at the hands of the Isaurians." He began to urge me to set off on my journey. There was no moon; it was midnight; it was dark, pitch dark: this, again, was a great perplexity. I had no one to aid me; they all had deserted me. However, compelled by the danger, and expecting instant death, I rose from my bed, overwhelmed with misery as I was, and ordered torches. Evethius insisted they should be put out again: he said, "The barbarians will be attracted by the light, and will fall upon us;" so put out the torches were. The way was broken, steep, and stony. The mule, which was carrying my litter, fell; down came the litter, and I in it; and I had near been killed. I jumped out of it, and began to crawl along. Evethius dismounted, and got hold of me; and thus I was assisted or rather dragged forward; for I could not possibly walk on such difficult ground, amid formidable mountains, and in the middle of the night.

The Saint's military friends do not play a specially brilliant part in this affair; and their conduct tempts one to think that his praise of them is rather owing to his cheerful forgiving spirit, sanguine before trouble, and buoyant after it, than to any merit of theirs. We may suppose they did not go to Seleucia's villa with him; if they did, it is strange he does not mention them in the last scene. After this we know nothing more of his adventures before he reached Cucusus, though he had still much heavy travelling over the mountains; he proceeds thus:

Who can describe the other troubles which befell me on my journey—the alarms, the risks? I think of them every day, and always carry them about with me; and am transported with joy, and my heart leaps to think of the great treasure I have laid up. Do you rejoice also over it, and give glory to God, who has honoured me with these sufferings. But keep it all to yourself, and tell no one, though the soldiers are able to fill the city with their tales; especially as they were in extreme peril themselves.

However, let no one know these matters from you; and stop the mouths of those who talk about them. And if you are pained at this memorial of my hardships, know for certain I am now clean rid of them all; and I am stronger in health than I was in Constantinople. Why are you anxious about the cold? My dwelling is most comfortably built, and my lord Dioscorus busies himself in every way that I may not have the very slightest feeling of the cold. If I may conjecture from the trial I have had of it, the climate seems to me quite oriental, just like that of Antioch; such is the temperature, such the character of the air. Nor need you fear the Isaurians from this time; they have returned to their country: the Prefect has left nothing undone to effect this. I am much safer here than I was at Cæsarea. Henceforth I fear no one but the Bishops; a few of them excepted. How is it that you say, you have received no letters from me? I have sent you three; one by the soldiers of the prefecture, one by Antony, one by your domestic Anatolius: they were long ones.

It is curious to see, that while he was complaining of the silence of his friends at home, they were complaining of his.[1] But now we may fairly stop, having brought the great confessor, whose trials we are tracing, to his place of exile.

[1] *Vid.* also Ep. 137.

CHAPTER IV

THE EXILE

1

AT LENGTH OUR GREAT CONFESSOR has arrived at his appointed place of exile. He reached it faint and exhausted in body and soul; but, as was usual with him, he soon rallied, and began to colour every thing about him with his own sweet, cheerful, thankful temper. In two days he had recovered his equanimity. He was pleased with all that was in any way pleasant; he made the best of what was bad; he blotted out the trials of the past; he fed his imagination with good hopes for the future. He generously and gallantly threw himself upon his lot, and tenderly embraced the cross; and though, as we shall see, the miseries of Cucusus grew on him, in spite of himself, as time went on, still he was determined he would like the place; and he did like it as long as ever he could, and, after the manner of the exiled sovereign in the drama, "found sermons in stones, and good in every thing."

He wrote to Olympias, in letters from which I quoted in the foregoing Chapter, that the place promised well; that the climate was like Antioch; that he was too well housed to fear the winter, and too sure of the winter to fear the Isaurians; that he had had a hearty welcome on the spot; that Adelphius, the Bishop, was kind; that Sopater, the Prefect of Armenia, left nothing undone for his protection; that friends from Antioch had come over to receive him on his arrival; and, lastly, that he did not doubt that he should eventually be restored to Constantinople. If the trials of his journey still remained on his memory, it was in order to give a zest to his enjoyment of the repose which had now succeeded to them, and to indispose him to move again. Accordingly, he begged his friends not to attempt to gain from government his transference to any other place, unless, indeed, it was in the immediate neighbourhood of the imperial city. He was happy when he was let alone; but it was a tremendous penance to travel. Something of all this has already been given in his own words, and more shall now follow:

TO OLYMPIAS

. . . All these evils have vanished. On arriving at Cucusus, I got rid of all remains of my malady, and I am in most perfect health; and I am released from my fear of the Isaurians, for there is a strong force of soldiers here who are ready and eager for an engagement; and there is an abundance of all that is necessary, which flows in upon me on every side, all parties welcoming me with the greatest good will, in spite of the extreme desolateness of the place. My lord Dioscorus happened to be there; and he had even sent a domestic to me to Cæsarea for the very purpose of inviting, nay begging, me to accept his house and no other; and many others did the same. I availed myself by preference of his offer, as I felt I ought to do, and took up my abode with him; and he has been every thing to me, so that I have been continually protesting against the lavish expense which he has been at on my account. He has even left his house to me, and gone to live at some other place, in order to show me every attention possible; and he got the house into a condition to weather the winter, busying himself with this object in every way. In a word, he has left nothing undone which could be of service to me. Many others, too, agents and stewards, have received letters from their masters, ordering them to call upon me, as they have done continually, and in every way to study my comfort.

And now I have told you all about me, the distressing past and the favourable present, lest any friend should be precipitate in getting me removed elsewhere. If these persons, who wish to be kind to me, put into my own hands the choice where to dwell, instead of taking on themselves to assign the place, in that case I accept the favour. But if they remove me hence, in order to send me elsewhere, and there is to be another journey and another exile, this would be far more painful to me than my present condition--first, because of the chance of my relegation to a more distant or worse country; next, because travelling is to me worse than ten thousand banishments. For the inconveniences of my late journey brought me to the very gates of death; and now here I am in Cucusus, recruiting myself by an uninterrupted rest and quiet, and by that quiet nursing my long distress and my shattered bones and wearied flesh.

My lady the Deaconess Sabiniana arrived here the same day that I did, knocked up, indeed, and wearied out, as being of that advanced age when travel is a toil, but in her earnestness a girl, and making no account of suffering, and ready, as she said, to go as far as Scythia; for the report went that I was to be deported thither. And now her mind is made up, she says, never to go away again, but to remain wherever I am. The ecclesiastics of the place received her with much attention and kindness. Moreover, my honoured lord, the most religious priest Constantius, would have been here long ago; for he wrote to me asking my leave to come, because, he said, he would not venture on the step without my judgment, much as he desired it, and certain as it was he could not remain at home; for he is in hiding, such troubles, he says, are upon him. On this account I beg you not to exert yourself for the change of my abode, for here I am enjoying great relief,—so much so that, in the course of two days, all the troubles of my journey have been wiped out of my mind.—*Ep.* 43.

In a few days he wrote again to the same correspondent, in answer to a letter brought to him by Patricius:

Why do you bewail me? Why beat your breast, and abandon yourself to the tyranny of despondency? Why are you grieved because you have failed in effecting my removal from Cucusus? Yet, as far as your own part is concerned, you have effected it, since you have left nothing undone in attempting it. Nor have you any reason to grieve for your ill success; perhaps it has seemed good to God to make my race-course longer that my crown may be brighter. You ought to leap and dance and crown yourself for this, viz. that I should be accounted worthy of so great a matter, which far exceeds my merit. Does my present loneliness distress you? On the contrary, what can be more pleasant than my sojourn here? I have quiet, calm, much leisure, excellent health. To be sure, there is no market in the city, nor any thing on sale; but this does not affect me; for all things, as if from some fountains, flow in upon me. Here is my lord, the Bishop of the place, and my lord Dioscorus, making it their sole business to make me comfortable. That excellent person Patricius will tell you in what good spirits and lightness of mind, and amid what kind attentions, I am passing my time.—*Ep.* 14.

2

THE SAME IS HIS REPORT to his friends at Cæsarea, and the same are his expressions of gratitude and affection towards them. The following is addressed to the President of Cappadocia:

TO CARTERIUS

Cucusus is a place desolate in the extreme; however, it does not annoy me so much by its desolateness as it relieves me by its quiet and its leisure. Accordingly, I have found a sort of harbour in this desolateness; and have sat me down to recover breath after the miseries of the journey, and have availed myself of the quiet to dispose of what remained both of my illness and of the other troubles which I have undergone. I say this to your illustriousness, knowing well the joy you feel in this rest of mine. I can never forget what you did for me in Cæsarea, in quelling those furious and senseless tumults, and striving to the utmost, as far as your power extended, to place me in security. I give this out publicly wherever I go, feeling the liveliest gratitude to you, my most worshipful lord, for so great solicitude towards me.—*Ep.* 236.

To Hymnetius, who attended him in his illness at Cæsarea, he says: "I shall never give over my praises of you, in all companies, as a worthy man and the best of physicians, and a true friend. Whenever I have to speak here of my illness, of course you come into my story; and I am necessarily full of the benefits which I experienced from your great skill and kindness, which it is the greatest gratification to myself to enlarge upon."

He adds, "Well as I am, I would give a good sum to attract you here, were it only to get the sight of you."—*Ep.* 81.

To Firminus, another Cæsarean, he says: "Even to have been in your company once has served to make me love you dearly; and you are yourself the cause of it, for from the first moment you showed an extreme and enthusiastic affection towards me; and instead of leaving me to time to gain experience of you, you took me captive at sight, and bound me closely to you. This is why I write to you, and tell you what you are eager to hear. What is that? Why, that I am in health, that I finished my journey without accident, that I am revelling in perfect quiet and leisure, that I have met with great kindness from all parties, that I am enjoying unspeakable consolation."— *Ep.* 80.

And in like manner to Leontius: "From your city I was driven, from my love for you I have have not been driven; for it rested with others whether I should remain there or be cast out, but this thing depends upon me. Nor shall any one avail to deprive me of this privilege; but whithersoever I am carried, everywhere I carry with me the honey of my love for you, and revel in the recollection of you."—*Ep.* 83.

"I have reached Cucusus in health," he says to Faustinus, "and have found a place free from tumult, full of leisure and quiet, and without a soul to annoy me or to send me off. Nor is it wonderful that I should have these advantages here, when even the route hither from you, which is so desolate, so dangerous, of such ill repute, was traversed by me without alarms, without adventures, with the enjoyment of greater security than is found in the best-regulated cities."—*Ep.* 84.

While he had this keen sensibility towards the kindnesses done him on his journey, he had no remembrance of the injuries. As to his enemies generally, there is hardly a word against them in the multitude of his private letters which have been preserved. He had spoken of his military attendants with cheerful hopefulness at Nicæa; he speaks of them with satisfaction at Cucusus, though they had shown neither spirit nor generosity at Cæsarea. He was too humble to exact much; he was too resigned not to be content with little. But what is stranger is his bearing towards Evethius, who figures as the tool of his Bishop in frightening the Saint away, on what seems a false alarm, from Seleucia's hospitable villa, and in sending him out in the dark at midnight, with a fever upon him, to stumble among the mountains and to get an overturn in his litter. This priest, indeed, is considered by great authorities to have been, not a Cæsarean, but a friend of the Saint's, who accompanied him from Nicæa. There was such a friend with him at Cucusus, certainly; but he seems to me to have joined him at a later date; on the other hand, it is certain that Chrysostom knew two persons of the name, and that one of them lived at Cæsarea. Evethius, then, I consider, was one of those priests who had been civil to him up to the time that the Bishop forbade such civility, and who then took part with the Bishop. Chrysostom remembered his beginning rather than his end, as the following letter will show. It will be observed, too, that here, as in a letter I just now quoted, he has forgotten his "alarms and risks," as well as the priest's rough behaviour. Perhaps on reflection he thought he had been too hard upon him in his letter to Olympias, though in that letter he does no more than barely state what happened.

TO EVETHIUS

Though I am absent from you in body, yet in charity I am bound to your soul; so large a claim of friendship have you deposited with me, in the great attention and kindness which you showed towards me in your own city. Therefore, wherever I go, I never fail to make my acknowledgments to you. And I beg you to write to me frequently, and to give me good tidings about your health. As regards myself, I finished my whole journey without trouble or danger, and am now living at Cucusus, revelling in the quiet and leisure of the place, and enjoying great attention and kindness at the hands of its inhabitants.—*Ep.* 173.

What is a still stronger evidence of his placable spirit is the tone in which he speaks of the vile Pharetrius himself, in a letter to a friend, who seems to have held some high post at Constantinople, and who had taken a prominent part in defending the Saint from his enemies. Prudence also, it will be observed, dictated this course.

TO PÆANIUS

The matter of Pharetrius is certainly most painful; however, considering his presbyters have had no dealings with my enemies, as you say, nor have any wish to make common cause with them, but, on the contrary, profess still to be on my side, make no movement against them on this account, though what Pharetrius did to me is unpardonable. However, all his clergy felt pain, and gave open expression to their feeling, and were on my side of the question altogether. Lest, then, we cause a reaction among them, and make them violent, I advise you, after you have heard the whole matter from my soldiers, to keep it to yourself, and to deal with them very gently. I know your discreet ways; and so say for me that I have heard how much the bishop was distressed at what occurred, and how ready he was to undergo any suffering in order to put right all the flagrant acts which had been committed.

I am in good health, and have shaken off the remains of my illness; and, when I reflect what anxiety you have shown on this point, it is of itself a medicine to me to have gained so affectionate a friend in you. God reward you for the earnestness, love, zeal, and vigilance which you manifest in my cause, both in this world and in the next: may He defend and guard and protect you, and vouchsafe to you those His secret blessings. And may He grant me to see your dear face soon, and to enjoy your sweet spirit, and thus to hold the best of festivals. For you know well that it is a real festival to me, and a high day, to be allowed your most sweet and profitable converse once again.—*Ep.* 204.

3

THUS THE SAINT was ever forgetting his enemies in his friends. And, while it was his gift ever to be making new ones, he did not lose his old. His former people at Antioch vied in their services to him with his partisans at Constantinople and his newly-made acquaintance at Cæsarea. They came to see him, and returned home full of his praises. The enthusiasm which he inspired spread into Syria and Cilicia. Large sums of money were offered him for his support, both at Antioch and by rich persons in the neighbourhood of Cucusus. One or two letters of this date will serve as a specimen of many.

TO DIOGENES

Cucusus is indeed a desolate spot, and moreover unsafe to dwell in, from the continual danger to which it is exposed of brigands. You, however, though away, have turned it for me into a paradise. For, when I hear of your abundant zeal and charity in my behalf, so genuine and warm (it does not at all escape me, far removed as I am from you), I possess a great treasure and untold wealth in such affection, and feel myself to be dwelling in the safest of cities, by reason of the great gladness which bears me up, and the high consolation which I enjoy.—*Ep.* 144.

Diogenes was one of the friends who sent him supplies: he writes in answer:

"You know very well yourself that I have ever been one of your most warmly-attached admirers; therefore I beg you will not be hurt at my having returned your presents. I have pressed out of them and have quaffed the honour which they did me; and if I return the things themselves, it has been from no slight or distrust of you, but because I was in no need of them. I have done the same in the case of many others; for many others too, with a generosity like yours, ardent friends of mine, have made me the same offers; and the same apology has set me right with them which I now ask you to receive. If I am in want, I will ask these things of you with much freedom, as if they were my own property, nay with more, as the event will show. Receive them back, then, and keep them carefully; so that, if there is a call for them some time hence, I may reckon on them.—*Ep.* 50.

As a fellow to the above, I add one of his letters

TO CARTERIA

What are you saying? that your unintermitting ailments have hindered you from visiting me? but you *have* come, you *are* present with me. From your very intention I have gained all this, nor have you any need to excuse yourself in this matter. That warm and true charity of yours, so vigorous, so constant, suffices to make me very happy. What I have ever declared in my letters, I now declare again, that, wherever I may be, though I be transported to a still more desolate place than this, you and your matters I never shall forget. Such pledges of your warm and true charity have you stored up for me, pledges which length of time can never obliterate nor waste; but, whether I am near you or far away, ever do I cherish that same charity, being assured of the loyalty and sincerity of your affection for me, which has been my comfort hitherto.—*Ep.* 227.

No one could live in his friends more intimately than St. John Chrysostom; he had not a monk's spirit of detachment in such severity as to be indifferent to the presence, the handwriting, the doings, the welfare, soul and body, of those who were children of the same grace with him, and heirs of the same promise. He writes as if he considered that the more religious a man is, the more sensitive he will be of a separation from his friends in religion; and, by the very topics which he uses in handling the subject of bereavement, in one of his letters to Olympias, he betrays his own acute suffering under the trial. The passage is too long to quote, but I may attempt an abstract of it.

"It is not a light effort," he says (*Ep.* 2), "but it demands an energetic soul and a great mind to bear separation from one whom we love in the charity of Christ. Every one knows this who knows what it is to love sincerely, who knows the power of supernatural love. Take the blessed Paul: here was a man who had stripped himself of the flesh, and who went about the world almost with a disembodied soul, who had exterminated from his heart every wild impulse, and who imitated the passionless sereneness of the immaterial intelligences, and who stood on high with the Cherubim, and shared with them in their mystical music, and bore prisons, chains, transportations, scourges, stoning, shipwreck, and every form of suffering; yet he, when separated from one soul loved by him in Christian charity, was so confounded and distracted as all at once to rush out of that city, in which he did not find the beloved one whom he expected. 'When I was come to Troas,' he says, 'for the gospel of Christ, and a door was opened to me in the Lord, I had no rest in my spirit, because I found not Titus my brother; but bidding them farewell, I went into Macedonia.'

"Is it Paul who says this?" he continues; "Paul who, even when fastened in the stocks, when confined in a dungeon, when torn with the bloody scourge, did nevertheless convert and baptize and offer sacrifice, and was chary even of one soul which was seeking salvation? and now, when he has arrived at Troas, and sees the field cleansed of weeds, and ready for the sowing, and the floor full, and ready to his hand, suddenly he flings away the profit, though he came thither expressly for it. 'So it was,' he answers me, 'just so; I was possessed by a predominating tyranny of sorrow, for Titus was away; and this so wrought upon me as to compel me to this course.' Those who have the grace of charity are not content to be united in soul only, they seek for the personal presence of him they love.

"Turn once more to this scholar of charity, and you will find that so it is. 'We, brethren,' he says, 'being bereaved of you for the time of an hour, in sight, not in heart, have hastened the more abundantly to see your face with great desire. For we would have come unto you, I, Paul, indeed, once and again, but Satan hath hindered us. For which cause, forbearing no longer, we thought it good to remain at Athens alone, and we sent Timothy.' What force is there is each expression! That flame of charity living in his soul is manifested with singular luminousness. He does not say so much as 'separated from you,' nor 'torn,' nor 'divided,' nor 'abandoned,' but only 'bereaved;' moreover, not 'for a certain period,' but merely 'for the time of an hour;' and separated, 'not in heart, but in presence only;' again, 'have hastened the more abundantly to see your face.' What! it seems charity so captivated you that you desiderated their sight, you longed to gaze upon their earthly, fleshly countenance? 'Indeed I did,' he answers: 'I am not ashamed to say so; for in that seeing all the channels of the senses meet together. I desire to see your presence; for there is the tongue which utters sounds and announces the secret feelings; there is the hearing which receives words, and there the eyes which image the movements of the soul.' But this is not all: not content with writing to them letters, he actually sends to them Timothy, who was with him, and who was more than any letters. And, 'We thought it good to remain alone;' that is, when he is divided from one brother, he says, he is left alone, though he had so many others with him."

4

THE TONE OF THIS PASSAGE certainly makes it clear that, when the Saint so eagerly calls on his friends for letters, it is for his own sake, in order to supply, as best he may, the severe deprivation—the *pœna damni,* as it is called—which his absence from them became to him.

This feeling of isolation is expressed in the following letter:

TO BRISO

Near seventy days I passed on my journey, haunted on many sides with fear of the Isaurians, and fighting with intolerable fever; at length I reached Cucusus, the most desolate place in the whole world. I say this, not wishing you to be troublesome to any one in your attempts to effect my removal, for I have suffered my worst in suffering the hardship of the journey; but I ask you this favour, to write to me frequently, without allowing my distance from you to act in depriving me at least of this solace. For you know how great a comfort it is to me, however afflicted or badly circumstanced I may be, to hear how you are, who love me so well; to hear that you are in good spirits, and in health, and at your ease. As you would have me, then, on this score light of heart, write to me word of this frequently, for it will be no common restorative. You know well what joy I feel in your prosperity.—*Ep.* 234.

However, there was obviously another reason for his wishing to hear news about them of a different kind, at a time when so many friends of his were, as being his friends, under the stroke of a severe persecution.

To enumerate the sufferings of these friends would be to write the history of the years to which his banishment belongs. Two Bishops who had sided with him, on pretence of their being concerned in the fire which consumed the cathedral and senate-house, upon his crossing to Bithynia, were first imprisoned, and then sent into banishment. One of his lectors, a delicate youth, was, on the same charge, put on the rack, torn with hooks, scourged, and then scorched with torches till he died. Tigrius, of whom mention was made in a former chapter, was scourged and racked, and then banished. Somewhat later, the persecution embraced all those who would not communicate with the Bishops who were successively intruded into the see of Constantinople. An imperial rescript determined that any Bishop who would not communicate with the usurper should lose his property, and be cast into exile. "Those who were rich," says Fleury, "and cared for their estates, communicated with Atticus out of policy; and those who were poor and weak in the faith suffered themselves to be seduced by bribes. But there were others who nobly disregarded their riches, their country, and all temporal advantages, and fled to escape the persecution. Several of them repaired to Rome, and others retired to the mountains, or into monasteries. The edict against the laity ordained that whosoever was invested with any dignity should be dispossessed of it; that officers and military men should be broken, and the rest of the people and tradesmen condemned to pay a large fine and banished. Notwithstanding these menaces, the people who were faithful to St. Chrysostom, rather than communicate with Atticus, used to pray in the open air, exposed to many inconveniences." [1]

In this way, Cyriacus, Bishop of Emesa, was sent off to

[1] Book xxii. 9, Oxford translation.

Persia, Palladius to Syene, Demetrius to the Oasis; the soldiers who conducted them treating them with great indignity and cruelty. Serapion, Bishop of Heraclea, who had made himself especially obnoxious to the schismatical party, was scourged, tortured, and banished. Hilarius, an old ascetic, was scourged, and banished to the farthest part of Pontus. The priests were sent away as far as to Arabia, Mesopotamia, the Thebaid, and Africa. Stephen, a monk, was scourged, imprisoned, and then banished to Pelusium. The holy women who took part with the Saint, whether in Constantinople or elsewhere, had, at an earlier date, a share in the sufferings of his cause. Olympias especially, in spite of her high birth and connections, was summoned before the prefect of the imperial city, and was heavily fined. She withdrew to Cyzicus. Pentadia, another deaconess, widow of a man who had filled the consulate, was fined and imprisoned. Nicarete had to leave the city.

It is not surprising that outrages so extreme should have filled Chrysostom, not only with horror, but with the most cruel anxiety what was next to happen; and should have made him eager to learn from his correspondents the course of events without any delay. We have various letters of his, written to Bishops and others under persecution; in others he makes application in their behalf in powerful quarters, and on their liberation from prison he sends about the news of it. His exhortations to them are characteristic of the writer. He calls them "champions who are nobly fighting for the peace of the world."—*Ep.* 148. And he realizes what it is to be a champion. He understands well that their prison was not merely a building, or a chamber, or a courtyard with a strong door to it, an honourable confinement, or the *surveillance* of an officer: "You are the inmates of a prison," he writes; "you are encompassed with chains, shut up with foul and filthy men. Who, then, can be more blessed than you? What have bright and spacious mansions to compare in value with that murky, filthy, fetid, and tormenting prison, undergone for God's sake?"—*Ep.* 118. And he entreats them not to lose heart, but "day by day to prosecute their labours for the churches of the world, that there may be such a settlement of matters as is suitable, and no abandonment of their cause because of their being so few and so baited on every side."—*Ep.* 174.

5

He set the example himself of what he preached; he never thought of dispensing himself from the ordinary oversight of his church, so far as it was possible, even though he had been removed, as he says, to the extremity of the Roman world. He had thoughts to bestow even on the remissness of individual ecclesiastics at Constantinople. Several of his letters are devoted to the case of two of his priests, who, whether from fear of the court or other reason, had during his absence seldom preached or been present at the public devotions. "It has given me no common pain," he writes to one of them, "that both you and the priest Theophilus should have relaxed in your duties. I have been informed that one of you has only preached five homilies up to October, and the other none at all. This news has tried me more than my desolate state here. Please to tell me, then, if I am mistaken; if not, make a reformation. How are you excusable if, at a time when others are in persecution, sent into exile, and variously harassed, you neither by your presence nor your teaching exert yourselves for your distressed people?"—*Ep.* 203. He sends equally strong remonstrances to Theophilus. "Now," he says, "is the very time for glory and much gain. The merchant does not get together his cargo by sitting down in harbour, but by venturing across open seas."—*Ep.* 119. And he writes to a friend to complain of his not having been told the state of things. "I am informed," he says, "that the one from indolence, the other from cowardice, has not attended the sacred assembly. To Theophilus I have written severely; Sallust I refer to you, for I know, and am pleased to know, how much you are attached to him. And I am pained that you have not even informed me, much less set him right, as you should have done. Now I beg you to do both yourself and me the great kindness of giving him a startling notice, and not to suffer him to sleep or to be idle. For if he does not show becoming courage in our present tempestuous weather, what good will he be to us when calm and peace succeed?"—*Ep.* 210.

While he thus kept his eyes on his clergy at home, he was exemplifying the same zeal for the conversion of the heathen which we have seen in him at Nicæa. At that time he had been busying himself in the extension of religion in Phœnicia; and though Cucusus was, as he says, at the extremity of the empire, it was on that very account only the more central place for missionary enterprises in the wide range of countries which bordered upon it. As to Phœnicia, he obtained funds for the missionaries, he sent relics for their new churches, he encouraged them to perseverance in persecution, and he provided them with fresh labourers. One of his letters to a friend is a recommendation to him of a holy priest, who had succeeded in converting the pagans of Mount Amanus,—the Black Mountain, between himself and Antioch,—and had built churches and monasteries among them. He interested himself also in the conversion of the Goths, who at that time were on the left bank of the Don, and still adhered to their nomad habits. He endeavoured to secure them a successor to their Bishop, who was lately dead; and he wrote to some Goths in a monastery at Constantinople on the subject. He enters upon it in that letter to Olympias in which he details the sufferings of his journey. Those sufferings, however keen, had no power to divert his mind for however short a time from the apostolical duties of his Patriarchate. In the same letter he also speaks of the prospect which was then opening of the conversion of the Persians, and makes mention of St. Maruthas, who was at the time doing so much for the extension of the faith among them. Maruthas, from misinformation, had allied himself with the enemies of St. Chrysostom; and the latter was very desirous both to gain him and to forward his work. He had written two letters to Maruthas, without getting an answer; and as the zealous missionary was at this time at Constantinople, he wrote to Olympias to make acquaintance with him. "Do not fail," he says, "to show all the attention in your power to the Bishop Maruthas, in order to draw him out of that pit. I have the greatest need of him for the affairs of Persia; and learn from him, if you can, what success he has had there."—*Ep.* 14. He did not forget, in these more expansive thoughts, the welfare of the poor people who were his immediate neighbours. We have seen him refusing sums of money when offered to him by friends; one of the channels into which he contrived to divert their liberality was the supply of the wants of the poor round about him, especially during a famine which happened while he was at Cucusus. He also redeemed from slavery many who had been taken captive by the Isaurian robbers, and sent them to their homes.

6

AMID THESE VARIOUS EXERCISES of faith and piety he had not been neglectful of the duties of the cause for which he suffered banishment. It was incumbent upon him to rouse Christendom in his own behalf, and he had been prompt and earnest in doing so. We have letters written by him to the Bishops of Thessalonica, Corinth, Synnada, Laodicea, Mopsuestia, Jerusalem, Carthage, Milan, Brescia, and Aquileia. Above all, he addressed himself to the Holy See, and his friends zealously prosecuted the appeal which he initiated. Many of them had fled to Rome; and though Pope Innocent did not at once decide on the main points at issue between the Saint and his enemies, yet he had no scruple in acknowledging him and communicating with him as Bishop of Constantinople, and by consequence in rejecting the pretensions of the schismatical party which had taken possession of his see. Innocent could do no more at the moment; but it was easy to prophesy what his ultimate determination would be. Every thing then seemed turning out in the Saint's favour; his reputation, his celebrity, his influence, had been greatly increased by the measures which his enemies had taken to ruin him. He was doing greater things at Cucusus than he had done at Constantinople. Debarred from the exercise of his special gift, his eloquent voice, he moved more forcibly the hearts of men by his very absence from the scene of the world; and he had the opportunity of showing how little he depended on the breath of popular favour, how much on himself and on his God, for that vigour and energy which had been the characteristics of his public life.

Habitually sanguine, he shared the belief of his friends that the triumph of his cause was at hand. As he had no resentments in respect to his persecutors, so he had no misgivings about his coming victory over them; and if his hopefulness forfeits for him the praise of prophecy, it evinces the more excellent grace of patience and trust. He was as easy about the future at Cucusus as he had been at Nicæa. He writes to Olympias thus:

> I do not despair of happier times, considering that He is at the helm of the universe who overcomes the storm, not by human skill, but by His *fiat*. If He does not do so at once, this is because it is His rule to take this course; and, when evils have increased and reached their fullness, and a change is despaired of by the many, then to work His marvellous and strange work, manifesting that power which is His prerogative, while exercising withal the endurance of the afflicted. Never be cast down, then; for one thing alone is fearful, that is, sin.—*Ep.* 1.

Again:

> Cherish a full conviction that you will see me again, and will be released from your present distress, and will receive the great gain, now as hitherto, which follows from it.—*Ep.* 2.

And still more strikingly in the following interesting and touching passage, which belongs to a later year of his exile, when he was no longer at Cucusus:

I speak not for the sake of consoling you, but I know that so it absolutely shall be. For, unless it were so to be, long ago, as it seems to me, should I have departed hence, so far as the trials go which have come upon me. For, not to speak of all that I suffered in Constantinople, you may easily understand how many things have happened to me since I left the city, in my long and painful journey hitherto, most of which were enough to cause my death; how many things after I arrived here, how many things after my dislodgment from Cucusus, how many things during my stay at Arabissus. Yet I got through them all, and am now in health and in all safety, to the astonishment of all the Armenians, that a frame so feeble, so spider-like, should be able to bear such unbearable cold, should be able to breathe in it, when even those who are accustomed to sharp winters are seriously affected by it. Nevertheless I have remained unharmed even to this day, and have escaped the hands of brigands in their many inroads; and have been preserved amid want of the necessaries of life, and without even a bath to recruit me, although when I was in Constantinople I had constant need of one; yet here I have found my state of body such that I have not even had a desire for this refreshment, and have been all the healthier. And no insalubrity of air, nor desolateness of place, nor absence of stores, nor scarcity of drugs, nor unskilfulness of physicians, nor difficulty of baths, nor absolute confinement, or rather imprisonment, in one room, nor want of exercise, which was always necessary to me, nor my atmosphere of smoke, nor alarms of robbers, nor the state of siege, nor any other hardship, has availed to destroy me; but I am in better health here than I was with you, though I then took such care of myself. Think over all this, and shake off the despondency with which my trial has oppressed you, and give over your needless and painful self-inflictions.—*Ep.* 4.

And then he goes on to bid her read a treatise which he sends her, and which has for its title the noble maxim, "Be true to yourself, and no one can harm you."

And here I pause in my sketch of the last years of this many-gifted Saint, this most natural and human of the creations of supernatural grace.

CHAPTER V

THE DEATH

1

WHENCE IS THIS DEVOTION to St. John Chrysostom, which leads me to dwell upon the thought of him, and makes me kindle at his name, when so many other great Saints, as the year brings round their festivals, command indeed my veneration, but exert no personal claim upon my heart? Many holy men have died in exile, many holy men have been successful preachers; and what more can we write upon St. Chrysostom's monument than this, that he was eloquent and that he suffered persecution? He is not an Athanasius, expounding a sacred dogma with a luminousness which is almost an inspiration; nor is he Athanasius, again, in his romantic life-long adventures, in his sublime solitariness, in his ascendency over all classes of men, in his series of triumphs over material force and civil tyranny. Nor, except by the contrast, does he remind us of that Ambrose who kept his ground obstinately in an imperial city, and fortified himself against the heresy of a court by the living rampart of a devoted population. Nor is he Gregory or Basil, rich in the literature and philosophy of Greece, and embellishing the Church with the spoils of heathenism. Again, he is not an Augustine, devoting long years to one masterpiece of thought, and laying, in successive controversies, the foundations of theology. Nor is he a Jerome, so dead to the world that he can imitate the point and wit of its writers without danger to himself or scandal to his brethren. He has not trampled upon heresy, nor smitten emperors, nor beautified the house or the service of God, nor knit together the portions of Christendom, nor founded a religious order, nor built up the framework of doctrine, nor expounded the science of the Saints; yet I love him, as I love David or St. Paul.

How am I to account for it? It has not happened to me, as it might happen to many a man, that I have devoted time and toil to the study of his writings or of his history, and cry up that upon which I have made an outlay, or love what has become familiar to me. Cases may occur when our admiration for an author is only admiration of our own comments on him, and when our love of an old acquaintance is only our love of old times. For me, I have not written the life of Chrysostom, nor translated his works, nor studied Scripture in his exposition, nor forged weapons of controversy out of his sayings or his doings. Nor is his eloquence of a kind to carry any one away who has ever so little knowledge of the oratory of Greece and Rome. It is not force of words, nor cogency of argument, nor harmony of composition, nor depth or richness of thought, which constitutes his power,—whence, then, has he this influence, so mysterious, yet so strong?

I consider St. Chrysostom's charm to lie in his intimate sympathy and compassionateness for the whole world, not only in its strength, but in its weakness; in the lively regard with which he views every thing that comes before him, taken in the concrete, whether as made after its own kind or as gifted with a nature higher than its own. Not that any religious man,—above all, not that any Saint,—could possibly contrive to abstract the love of the work from the love of its Maker, or could feel a tenderness for earth which did not spring from devotion to heaven; or as if he would not love every thing just in that degree in which the Creator loves it, and according to the measure of gifts which the Creator has bestowed upon it, and pre-eminently for the Creator's sake. But this is the characteristic of all Saints; and I am speaking, not of what St. Chrysostom had in common with others, but what he had special to himself; and this specialty, I conceive, is the interest which he takes in all things, not so far as God has made them alike, but as He has made them different from each other. I speak of the discriminating affectionateness with which he accepts every one for what is personal in him and unlike others. I speak of his versatile recognition of men, one by one, for the sake of that portion of good, be it more or less, of a lower order or a higher, which has severally been lodged in them; his eager contemplation of the many things they do, effect, or produce, of all their great works, as nations or as states; nay, even as they are corrupted or disguised by evil, so far as that evil may in imagination be disjoined from their proper nature, or may be regarded as a mere material disorder apart from its formal character of guilt. I speak of the kindly spirit and the genial temper with which he looks round at all things which this wonderful world contains; of the graphic fidelity with which he notes them down upon the tablets of his mind, and of the promptitude and propriety with which he calls them up as arguments or illustrations in the course of his teaching as the occasion requires. Possessed though he be by the fire of divine charity, he has not lost one fibre, he does not miss one vibration, of the complicated whole of human sentiment and affection; like the miraculous bush in the desert, which, for all the flame that wrapt it round, was not thereby consumed.

Such, in a transcendent perfection, was the gaze, as we may reverently suppose, with which the loving Father of all surveyed in eternity that universe even in its minutest details which He had decreed to create; such the loving pity with which He spoke the word when the due moment came, and began to mould the finite, as He created it, in His infinite hands; such the watchful solicitude with which He now keeps His catalogue of the innumerable birds of heaven, and counts day by day the very hairs of our head and the alternations of our breathing. Such, much more, is the awful contemplation with which He encompasses incessantly every one of those souls on whom He heaps His mercies here, in order to make them the intimate associates of His own eternity hereafter. And we too, in our measure, are bound to imitate Him in our exact and vivid apprehension of Himself and of His works. As to Himself, we love Him, not simply in His nature, but in His triple personality, lest we become mere pantheists. And so, again, we choose our patron Saints, not for what they have in common with each other (else there could be no room for choice at all), but for what is peculiar to them severally. That which is my warrant, therefore, for particular devotions at all, becomes itself my reason for devotion to St. John Chrysostom. In him I recognize a special pattern of that very gift of discrimination. He may indeed be said in some sense to have a devotion of his own for every one who comes across him,—for persons, ranks, classes, callings, societies, considered as divine works and the subjects of his good offices or good will, and therefore I have a devotion for him.

It is this observant benevolence which gives to his exposition of Scripture its chief characteristic. He is known in ecclesiastical literature as the expounder, above all others, of its literal sense. Now in mystical comments the direct object which the writer sets before him is the Divine Author Himself of the written Word. Such a writer sees in Scripture, not so much the works of God, as His nature and attributes; the Teacher more than the definite teaching, or its human instruments, with their drifts and motives, their courses of thought, their circumstances and personal peculiarities. He loses the creature in the glory which surrounds the Creator. The problem before him is not what the inspired writer directly meant, and why, but, out of the myriad of meanings present to the Infinite Being who inspired him, which it is that is most illustrative of that Great Being's all-holy attributes and solemn dispositions. Thus, in the Psalter, he will drop David and Israel and the Temple together, and will recognise nothing there but the shadows of those greater truths which remain for ever. Accordingly, the mystical comment will be of an objective character; whereas a writer who delights to ponder human nature and human affairs, to analyse the workings of the mind, and to contemplate what is subjective to it, is naturally drawn to investigate the sense of the sacred writer himself, who was the organ of the revelation, that is, he will investigate the literal sense. Now, in the instance of St. Chrysostom, it so happens that literal exposition is the historical characteristic of the school in which he was brought up; so that if he commented on Scripture at all, he any how would have adopted that method; still, there have been many literal expositors, but only one Chrysostom. It is St. Chrysostom who is the charm of the method, not the method that is the charm of St. Chrysostom.

That charm lies, as I have said, in his habit and his power of throwing himself into the minds of others, of imagining with exactness and with sympathy circumstances or scenes which were not before him, and of bringing out what he has apprehended in words as direct and vivid as the apprehension. His page is like the table of a *camera lucida,* which represents to us the living action and interaction of all that goes on around us. That loving scrutiny, with which he follows the Apostles as they reveal themselves to us in their writings, he practises in various ways towards all men, living and dead, high and low, those whom he admires and those whom he weeps over. He writes as one who was ever looking out with sharp but kind eyes upon the world of men and their history; and hence he has always something to produce about them, new or old, to the purpose of his argument, whether from books or from the experience of life. Head and heart were full to overflowing with a stream of mingled "wine and milk," of rich vigorous thought and affectionate feeling. This is why his manner of writing is so rare and special; and why, when once a student enters into it, he will ever recognize him, wherever he meets with extracts from him.

2

BUT I MUST GO ON with the history of his banishment, which I have left in order to enlarge upon the character of his mind and of his teaching. The evils which he first denounced at Antioch came to a crisis at Constantinople, and he himself was the principal victim of them. His cause was that of the strict party in the Church, and the fire of envy and malice, of which he had spoken, burst forth against him as its representative. For a time, in a city which boasted that it never had been pagan, the goodly fabric of Christianity was little better than a heap of ruins. The transportation of its saintly Bishop was the signal for a schism which it took years to heal; and, worse still, it was a triumph of the secular party, which has never been reversed down to this day. In the present state of the Greek Church we read the moral of the conflict in which St. Chrysostom was engaged. Accordingly, there was much of significance in the coincidence that, on the very day on which he was carried over to Asia, fire literally did break out in the cathedral, where he had so lately preached, and in his very pulpit. "There suddenly appeared," to use the words of Fleury, "a great flame in the church, from the pulpit from which he used to preach. The fire ascended to the roof, and then burst forth on the outside, so that it was burnt to the ground. The flames, driven by a violent wind, spanned the square like a bridge, seized upon the palace where the senate assembled, and burnt it down in three hours. The Catholics looked upon it as a miracle; some accused the schismatical party of it; they, and after them the pagans, imputed it to the Catholics." However originating, it typified the spiritual devastation of the Church of Constantinople.

The court party would perhaps give the catastrophe a different application; they might see in it the fortunes of St. Chrysostom himself. Thus blazed and burnt out, they might say, the glories of that eloquent preacher, who had been so hastily brought to the imperial city. It was a great pity that he had ever left Antioch; for what had he done since he came but create confusion in the Church? No one denied his oratorical powers; but he had neither discretion nor patience; and, after two or three years, here was the end of it. As some brilliant meteor, he had glared and disappeared. He thought, forsooth, to get back from banishment; but that never would be. His enemies were far too strong and too determined to allow him the chance of it. They were resolved utterly to blot out his name and his memory; he would be written in the sand; posterity would not know him, except as one who had caused great scandals, and had undergone the penalty of them.

Such anticipations, plausible as they were, have been falsified by the event; the cause of truth and sanctity cannot utterly be defeated, however poor be the measure of justice which is accorded to it even on the long-run. The Saint, however, was over-sanguine, as we have seen, in his anticipations of a contrary kind. Certainly at length he was brought back in triumph to his see; but he was brought back in his coffin. That first momentary presentiment, when he took leave of his deaconesses at Constantinople, was the true one. His earthly career was coming to an end. Here, then, we are come round to the point from which I have digressed, and I resume the narrative where I left off.

3

The reader may recollect that St. Chrysostom got to Cucusus in the autumn. His enemies seemed to have hoped that the winter would complete for them what they had begun; he, on the contrary, looked forward to it with cheerfulness. Both parties were disappointed; it did not kill him, but it inflicted on him great suffering; it told most for his enemies, for they would infer that he could not possibly bear the recurrence of many such trials.

In the early spring of the following year (405) he wrote to Olympias thus:

I write to you after a recovery from the very gates of death; on this account it was a great joy to me that your servants have not reached me till now, when I am getting into port; for, had they come while I was still tossing out at sea, and shipping the heavy waves of my illness, it would not have been easy for me to deceive you with good tidings, when there could only be bad. The winter was more severe than usual, and brought on, what was worse than itself, my stomach complaint; and for two whole months I was no better than the dead, or even worse. So far I lived as to be alive to the miseries that encompassed me; day, dawn, and noon, all were night to me; I was confined to my bed all day. With a thousand contrivances, I could not avoid the mischief which the cold did me; though I had a fire, and submitted to the oppressive smoke, and imprisoned myself in one room, and had coverings without number, and never ventured to pass the threshold, nevertheless I used to suffer in the most grievous way from continual vomitings, headache, disgust at food, and obstinate sleeplessness, through the long interminable nights. But I will not distress you longer with this account of my troubles; I am now rid of them all.—*Ep.* 6.

Later in the spring he reports that the marauding bands had again made their appearance:

TO THEODOTUS

It was no slight relief in the desolateness of this place to be able to write frequently to you; but even this resource has been cut off by the circumstance of these Isaurian troubles. For, as soon as spring came, the brigands shot forth with it, and spread themselves out over all the roads, to the stoppage of all traffic. Free women were carried off and men slain. I know how anxious you are to know about my health. After serious suffering in the past winter, I am now somewhat getting round, though I am still distressed by the changes in the weather. Winter is in force even now; however, I look forward to be rid of the remains of my illness when summer is fairly come. Indeed, nothing so tries me as cold, nothing does me so much good as summer and the comfort of being warm.—*Ep.* 140.

In thus speaking hopefully of the approaching summer, he did but show his cheerful temper; for, when it actually came, he was forced to confess to some friends, "The summer distresses me not less than the cold."—*Ep.* 146. Earth and sea temper the sky for us, and keep the atmosphere in a due medium of heat and cold. But Chrysostom was in a desert country, which gave him no protection against weather of any kind, neither against the sun nor against the frost.

Yet his spirit did not sink under his disappointing experience of the climate, as the following letter shows:

TO CASTOR

I know well it will be a great pleasure to you to learn how I fare. I am rid of my weakness of stomach; I am well; and, in spite of beleaguering, raids, loneliness, and a host of misfortunes, I am in no depression or trouble of mind, and am in the enjoyment of security, leisure, quiet, and keep your matters daily in my thoughts, and talk of them with all who visit me.—*Ep.* 130.

However, as autumn drew on, and his first year was completed, the face of things altered. Whether the barbarians were stronger, or the garrison at Cucusus had been weakened or removed; whether it was some scheme of the Saint's enemies to bring about a death which as yet they had not effected, so it was, that at the beginning of winter he was persuaded, or he found, that he was not safe at Cucusus; the gates of the city were thrown open to him, and he was advised or obliged to leave it for the mountain region in the neighbourhood. Old as he was, enfeebled by recent illness, ignorant of the country and sensitive to the climate, and, as it would appear, without attendants, he had to face the wild winter as he best could, and to wander from village to village, according as the alarm of the Isaurians chased him to and fro. In this way he advanced at length to the distance of sixty miles from Cucusus, to a city called Arabissus. He knew the Bishop of this place, and it was professedly defended by a fortress, which at least served for its own defence. Into this fortress he threw himself; it was a prison rather than a place of refuge, but at least it was secure; and when he fell ill again of the cold there, he got some sort of medical aid, though medicines were not to be procured. At this time he writes as follows:

TO NICOLAS

Lately I have been flitting from place to place in the very depth of winter, now in towns, now in ravines and woods, driven to and fro by the inroads of the Isaurians. When this disturbance had at length abated a little, I left these desolate places, and betook myself to Arabissus; not to the town, for that is quite as unsafe as they are, but to the fortress, which, however, in spite of its being safer, was a worse dwelling than any prison. And, besides the imminent prospect of death day by day from the Isaurians, who were making their attacks in every direction, and destroying human beings and houses by fire and sword, I am in dread of famine too, from our want of resources, and the number who have taken refuge here. And I have had to endure a tedious illness, brought on by the winter and my incessant wanderings, and I still carry the remains of it, though I have recovered from its violence.—*Ep.* 69.

And to Polybius:

I lament your separation from me as a heavier trial than this desolateness, my illness, and the winter. The winter, indeed, has added to it; for it has deprived me of that intercourse by letter, which was my sole relief of your most painful absence; roads being blocked up by vast drifts of snow, and the passage interrupted, whether from the outward world hither, or from hence to you. And now the same obstruction is caused by fear of the Isaurians; nay, much greater, increasing the desolateness, putting into confusion, flight, and exile the whole population. No one any longer endures to remain at home; all leave their dwellings and scamper off. The cities are but walls and roofs; and the ravines and woods are cities. We, who dwell in Armenia, are obliged to run from place to place day after day, living the life of nomads and strollers, from fear to settle any where; such confusion reigns. When the plunderers come up, they slaughter, burn, enslave; when they are even rumoured, they put to flight the inhabitants of the cities, nay, I may say, murder them also; for the young children, who have been suddenly forced to fly, as if smoked out of their houses, in the dead of night, often in hard frost, have needed no Isaurian sword, but have been frozen to death in the snow.—*Ep.* 127.

To another friend he says, "In whatever direction you go, you will see torrents of blood, heaps of corpses, houses demolished, cities sacked."—*Ep.* 68. He seems to have been besieged at Arabissus, from the following passage:

TO THEODOTUS

The troubles of the siege increase daily, and here we are seated in this fort as in a trap. Just at midnight, when no one expected it, a band of three hundred Isaurians spread through the city, and were all but getting possession of me. However, the hand of God took them off again before I knew any thing about it, so that I escaped the alarm as well as the danger; and, when day was come, then at last I heard what had chanced.—*Ep.* 133.

At length the storm blew over, and he was in comparative security, and he remained in the place for nearly the whole of his second year of exile (A.D. 406). He was able to employ himself in teaching the poor people, and he contrived, as I have said before, by means of the money sent him by friends, to relieve their wants when a famine set in. Before the year was over, he returned to Cucusus.

A third winter came, and brought its usual hardships along with it. We find the Saint again weak and suffering at the beginning of A.D. 407; but by this time he was in some measure acclimated to the place, and he was able to express content at the state of his health:

TO ELPIDIUS

I have learned at last to bear the Armenian winter, with some suffering, indeed, such as may be expected in the instance of so feeble a frame, but still with real success. This is, by means of rigidly confining myself indoors when the cold is unbearable. As to the other seasons, I find them most pleasant and enjoyable, so as to enable me comfortably to recover from the illness brought on by the winter.—*Ep.* 142.

And to Olympias:

Do not be anxious on my account. It is true that the winter was what the season is in Armenia; one need say no more; but it has not done me any great harm, since I take great precautions against it. I keep up a constant fire, and have every part of my small room closed. I put on a great deal of clothing, and I never stir out. A few days ago, nothing would stay on my stomach, from the severity of the weather. I took, among other remedies, the medicine which Syncletium gave me, and, after using it, I got well by the end of three days. I had a second attack; I used it again, and got completely well. Do not, then, make yourself anxious about my wintering here, for I feel much easier and better than I did last year.—*Ep.* 4.

It was at this date that he wrote to the same correspondent the striking letter, part of which I quoted in my foregoing Chapter; in which he confidently foretells his return from banishment, on the ground of his having been so wonderfully preserved hitherto, and enabled to triumph over the accumulated trials which bodily weakness, the seasons, and his wanderings and privations brought upon him. So hopefully for him, so unsatisfactorily for his enemies, opened the third year of his exile at the place which was to have been his death.

4

But the fairer were his prospects, the more certain was their disappointment. He was in their hands; they had sentenced him to die, and only hesitated how his death was to be brought about. They had no wish to do the deed themselves, if it could be done without them; but do it they must, if circumstances would not do it for them. Cucusus promised to spare them the odium of his murder; and doubtless they would listen with complacency to the complaints about his discomforts and his ailments which from time to time he transmitted to Constantinople. It was easy to fancy them the tokens of a broken spirit, and the harbingers of the consummation they desired, when they were but his protests against injustice and cruelty, and the spontaneous relief of a soul too great to care about being misinterpreted. When time went on, and the end did not come, when even his wanderings in the mountains and his flight to Arabissus did not subdue him, they were prompted to more violent and summary dealings with him.

He must be carried off to some still more inhospitable region; he must undergo the slow torture of a still more exhausting journey. Cold and heat, wind and rain, night-air, bad lodging, unwholesome water, long foot-marches, rough-paced mules,—these were to be the instruments of his martyrdom. He was to die by inches; want of sleep, want of rest, want of food and medicine, and the collapse certain to follow, were to extinguish the brave spirit which hitherto had risen superior to all sorrows. A rescript was gained from the Emperor Arcadius, banishing him to Pityus upon the north-east coast of the Euxine.

In that sentence the curtain falls upon the history of the Saint. His correspondence ceases; the letter, so full of sunshine, to which I have several times referred, was apparently his last. He leaves us with the language of hope upon his lips. It is well that he should thus close the great drama, in which he was the chief actor. Bright, pleasant thoughts, nought but what is radiant, nought but what is enlivening and consolatory, attaches to the historical memory of St. Chrysostom. But the devout heart seeks to lift the veil; it desires even amid the changes of mortality *notas audire et reddere voces:* it would fain be near to comfort him in his agony, and to hear his last cry.

It may not be; when his letters would be most precious, they are, as I have said, denied to us. In the case of a Saint, we are left to faith. It has been otherwise with others. There was a Protestant missionary, in the first years of this century, who, after attempting the conversion of a Mahometan country, was committed to the rough charge of a Tartar courier, not for exile, but for return to his own England. Hurried on by forced journeys, and having at the time a deadly malady upon him, he gradually sank under the cruel punishment, and breathed out his wearied spirit at the very spot which, 1400 years before, had witnessed the death of John Chrysostom. Let us trust that that zealous preacher came under the shadow of the Catholic doctor, that he touched the bones of Eliseus, and that, all errors forgiven, he lives to God through the intercession of the Confessor, to whom in place and manner of death he was united. The friends of Henry Martyn are in possession of his journal up to within ten days of his death; for us, we must wait till we are admitted to the company of St. Chrysostom above, if such be our blessedness, before we know the last sufferings, the last thoughts, the prayers and consolations, the patience, sweetness, gentleness, and charity in his death, of that great mind.

5

LET US GLEAN WHAT WE CAN from history and tradition of that last unknown journey.

First, we know that Pityus is on the very verge of the Roman empire, to the north of Colchis, close to Sarmatia, and under the Caucasus. It had been a large and rich city in an earlier century, and was situated in a region so peculiarly a border country, that in Dioscurias, which lay south of it, as many as seventy languages or dialects were spoken. From that city it was distant about fifty miles, and Dioscurias was distant as much as 280 miles from Trapezus.[1] This portion, however, of his journey was held in reserve for the Saint's destruction: he never got so far as Trapezus; and it concerns us more to

[1] Smith's Dictionary.

consider how he travelled towards it. There were three routes from Cucusus thither; the most direct lay through Melitene and Satala; but this he certainly did not pursue, or he could not have died in the neighbourhood of Neocæsarea. To direct this course to Neocæsarea, he must have passed through Sebaste, and Sebaste he might reach by either of two routes,—by Cæsarea or by Melitene. Both of these were high military roads, and beyond Sebaste he might be helped on still further by another high road at least as far as Sebastopolis, which is either 365 or 330 miles from Cucusus, according to the route which was chosen for him. Thus we may say, that it took, more or less, 400 miles to kill him. The narrative which I shall presently transcribe says that his journey lasted three months, which is hardly conceivable, unless he was detained from time to time by illness or other causes on the way.

So much for his route; next, as to the place of his death, we have historical information that he died at Comana in Pontus; and thence it was that his sacred body was conveyed some years afterwards to Constantinople.

Then, as to the day: Socrates tells us that it was the 14th of September, the day since set apart, in consequence of the events of later history, as the feast of the Exaltation of the Holy Cross.

So far we can speak without hesitation; but when we set ourselves to trace the occurrences of his closing months, and the particulars of his journey, we find ourselves without any materials for the undertaking. We have neither public documents nor the private letters of himself or of his friends to assist us in the task. The narrative which commonly, and by great authorities, is received as authentic, is written by one of his contemporaries and friends; but he was no eye-witness of what he relates, nor does he tell us how he got his information. However, I present it to the reader as it stands:

6

"THE RESCRIPT," said Palladius, "ordered that he should be transported to Pityus, a most wild place of the Tyanians, lying on the coast of the Euxine. And the Prætorian soldiers, who conveyed him, urged him forward on his journey with such haste, saying that it was according to their orders, that it appeared as if their promotion depended on his dying in the course of it. One, indeed, of them, having less solicitude for this earthly warfare, secretly showed him some sort of kindness; but the other carried his brutality so far as even to take as an affront the very attentions which were shown to himself by strangers, with the hope of softening him towards his prisoner, having this solicitude, and no other, that John should miserably die. So, when rain was profuse, the man went on, not caring for it, so that floods of water poured down the bishop's back and breast; and again, the fierce heat of the sun he considered a treat, as knowing that the bald head of blessed Eliseus would suffer from it. Moreover at city or village, where the refreshment of a bath was to be found, the wretch would not consent to stop for a moment.

"And all these sufferings the Saint endured for three months, travelling that most difficult way with the brightness of a star, baked red by the sun as fruit upon the top branches of a tree. And when they came to Comana, they passed through it as if its street were no more than a bridge, and halted outside the walls at the shrine, which is five or six miles in advance.

"In that very night the martyr of the place stood before him, Basiliscus by name, who had been Bishop of Comana, and died by martyrdom in Nicomedia, in the reign of Maximinus, together with Lucian of Bithynia, who had been a priest of Antioch. And he said, 'Be of good heart, brother John, for to-morrow we shall be together.' It is said that the martyr had already made the same announcement to the priest of the place: 'Prepare the place for brother John, for he is coming.' And John, believing the divine oracle, upon the morrow besought his guards to remain there until the fifth hour. They refused, and set forward; but when they had proceeded about thirty stadia, he was so ill that they returned back to the martyr's shrine whence they had started.

"When he got there, he asked for white vestments, suitable to the tenor of his past life; and taking off his clothes of travel, he clad himself in them from head to foot, being still fasting, and then gave away his old ones to those about him. Then, having communicated in the symbols of the Lord, he made the closing prayer *'On present needs.'* He said his customary words, 'Glory be to God for all things;' and having concluded it with his last Amen, he stretched forth those feet of his which had been so beautiful in their running, whether to convey salvation to the penitent or reproof to the hardened in sin. . . . And being gathered to his fathers, and shaking off this mortal dust, he passed to Christ."

The translation of his relics to Constantinople took place a little more than thirty years afterwards. "A great multitude of the faithful," says Theodoret, "crowded the sea in vessels, and lighted up a part of the Bosphorus, near the mouth of the Propontis, with torches. These sacred treasures were brought to the city by the present emperor (Theodosius the Younger). He laid his face upon the coffin, and entreated that his parents might be forgiven for having so unadvisedly persecuted the Bishop." [1]

So died, and so was buried, St. John Chrysostom, one of that select company whom men begin to understand and honour when they are removed from them. It is the general law of the world, which the new law of the Gospel has not reversed:

Virtutem incolumem odimus,
Sublatam ex oculis quærimus, invidi.

[1] Bohn's transl.

III

THE BENEDICTINE SCHOOLS

CHAPTER I

THE MISSION OF ST. BENEDICT[1]

1

AS THE PHYSICAL UNIVERSE is sustained and carried on in dependence on certain centres of power and laws of operation, so the course of the social and political world, and of that great religious organization called the Catholic Church, is found to proceed for the most part from the presence or action of definite persons, places, events, and institutions, as the visible cause of the whole. There has been but one Judæa, one Greece, one Rome; one Homer, one Cicero; one Cæsar, one Constantine, one Charlemagne. And so, as regards Revelation, there has been one St. John the Divine, one Doctor of the Nations. Dogma runs along the line of Athanasius, Augustine, Thomas. The conversion of the heathen is ascribed, after the Apostles, to champions of the truth so few, that we may almost count them, such as Martin, Patrick, Augustine, Boniface. Then there is St. Antony, the father of monachism; St. Jerome, the interpreter of Scripture; St. Chrysostom, the great preacher.

Education follows the same law: it has its history in Christianity, and its doctors or masters in that history. It has had three periods:—the ancient, the medieval, and the modern; and there are three Religious Orders in those periods respectively, which succeed, one the other, on its public stage, and represent the teaching given by the Catholic Church during the time of their ascendancy. The first period is that long series of centuries, during which society was breaking or had broken up, and then slowly attempted its own re-construction;

[1] From the *Atlantis* of January, 1858.—[Ed.]

the second may be called the period of re-construction; and the third dates from the Reformation, when that peculiar movement of mind commenced, the issue of which is still to come. Now, St. Benedict has had the training of the ancient intellect, St. Dominic of the medieval; and St. Ignatius of the modern. And in saying this, I am in no degree disrespectful to the Augustinians, Carmelites, Franciscans, and other great religious families, which might be named, or to the holy Patriarchs who founded them; for I am not reviewing the whole history of Christianity, but selecting a particular aspect of it.

Perhaps as much as this will be granted to me without great hesitation. Next, I proceed to contrast these three great masters of Christian teaching with each other. To St. Benedict, then, who may fairly be taken to represent the various families of monks before his time and those which sprang from him (for they are all pretty much of one school), to this great Saint let me assign, for his discriminating badge, the element of Poetry; to St. Dominic, the Scientific element; and to St. Ignatius, the Practical.

These characteristics, which belong respectively to the schools of the three great Teachers, grow out of the circumstances under which they respectively entered upon their work. Benedict, entrusted with his mission almost as a boy, infused into it the romance and simplicity of boyhood. Dominic, a man of forty-five, a graduate in theology, a priest and a canon, brought with him into religion that maturity and completeness of learning which he had acquired in the schools. Ignatius, a man of the world before his conversion, transmitted as a legacy to his disciples that knowledge of mankind which cannot be learned in cloisters. And thus the three several Orders were (so to say), the births of Poetry, of Science, and Practical Sense.

And here another coincidence suggests itself. I have been giving these three attributes to the three Patriarchs whom I have specified, severally, from a *bonâ-fide* regard to their history, and without at all having any theory of philosophy in my eye. But after having so described them, it certainly did strike me that I had unintentionally been illustrating a somewhat popular notion of the day, the like of which is attributed to authors with whom I have as little sympathy as with any persons who can be named. According to these speculators, the life, whether of a race or of an individual of the great human family, is divided into three stages, each of which has its own ruling principle and characteristic. The youth makes his start in life, with "*hope* at the prow, and *fancy* at the helm;" he has nothing else but these to impel or direct him; he has not lived long enough to exercise his reason, or to gather in a store of facts; and, because he cannot do otherwise, he dwells in a world which he has created. He begins with illusions. Next, when at length he looks about for some surer footing than imagination gives him, he may have recourse to reason, or he may have recourse to facts; now facts are external to him, but his reason is his own: of the two, then, it is easier for him to exercise his reason than to ascertain facts. Accordingly, his first mental revolution, when he discards the life of aspiration and affection which has disappointed him, and the dreams of which he has been the sport and victim, is to embrace a life of logic: this, then, is his second stage,—the metaphysical. He acts now on a plan, thinks by system, is cautious about his middle terms, and trusts nothing but what takes a scientific form. His third stage is when he has made full trial of life; when he has found his theories break down under the weight of facts, and experience falsify his most promising calculations. Then the old man recognizes at length, that what he can taste, touch, and handle, is trustworthy, and nothing beyond it. Thus he runs through his three periods of Imagination, Reason, and Sense; and then he comes to an end, and is not;—a most impotent and melancholy conclusion.

Undoubtedly a Catholic has no sympathy in so heartless a view of life, and yet it seems to square with what I have been saying of the three great Patriarchs of Christian teaching. And certainly there is a truth in it, which gives it its plausibility. However, I am not concerned here to do more than to put my finger on the point at which I should diverge from it, both in what I have been saying and what I must say concerning them. It is true, then, that history, as viewed in these three Saints, is, somewhat after the manner of the theory I have mentioned, a progress from poetry through science to practical sense or prudence; but then this important *proviso* has to be borne in mind at the same time, that what the Catholic Church once has had, she never has lost. She has never wept over, or been angry with, time gone and over. Instead of passing from one stage of life to another, she has carried her youth and middle age along with her, on to her latest time. She has not changed possessions, but accumulated them, and has brought out of her treasure-house, according to the occasion, things new and old. She did not lose Benedict by finding Dominic; and she has still both Benedict and Dominic at home, though she has become the mother of Ignatius. Imagination, Science, Prudence, all are good, and she has them all. Things incompatible in nature, coëxist in her; her prose is poetical on the one hand, and philosophical on the other.

Coming now to the historical proof of the contrast I have been instituting, I am sanguine in thinking that one branch of it is already allowed by the consent of the world, and is undeniable. By common consent, the palm of religious Prudence, in the Aristotelic sense of that comprehensive word, belongs to the School of Religion of which St. Ignatius is the Founder. That great Society is the classical seat and fountain (that is, in religious thought and the conduct of life, for of ecclesiastical politics I speak not), the school and pattern of discretion, practical sense, and wise government. Sublimer conceptions or more profound speculations may have been created or elaborated elsewhere; but, whether we consider the illustrious Body in its own constitution, or in its rules for instruction and direction, we see that it is its very genius to prefer this most excellent prudence to every other gift, and to think little both of poetry and of science, unless they happen to be useful. It is true that, in the long catalogue of its members, there are to be found the names of the most consummate theologians, and of scholars the most elegant and accomplished; but we are speaking here, not of individuals, but of the body itself. It is plain that the body is not over-jealous about its theological traditions, or it certainly would not suffer Suarez to controvert with Molina, Viva with Vasquez, Passaglia with Petavius, and Faure with Suarez, de Lugo, and Valentia. In this intellectual freedom its members justly glory; inasmuch as they have set their affections, not on the opinions of the Schools, but on the souls of men. And it is the same charitable motive which makes them give up the poetry of life, the poetry of ceremonies,—of the cowl, the cloister, and the choir,—content with the most prosaic architecture, if it be but convenient, and the most prosaic neighbourhood, if it be but populous. I need not then dwell longer on this wonderful Religion, but may confine the remarks which are to follow to the two Religions which historically preceded it—the Benedictine and the Dominican.[1]

One preliminary more, suggested by a purely fanciful analogy:—As there are three great Patriarchs on the high road and public thoroughfare of Christian Education, so there were three chief Patriarchs in the first age of the chosen people. Putting aside Noe and Melchisedec, and Joseph and his brethren, we recognize three venerable fathers,—Abraham, Isaac, and Jacob, and what are their characteristics? Abraham, the father of many nations; Isaac, the intellectual, living in solitary simplicity, and in loving contemplation; and Jacob, the persecuted and helpless, visited by marvellous providences, driven from place to place, set down and taken up again, ill-treated by those who were his debtors, suspected because of his sagacity, and betrayed by his eager faith, yet carried on

[1] Owing to the temporary suspension of the *Atlantis*, the article on the Dominican Order was not written.

and triumphing amid all troubles by means of his most faithful and powerful guardian-archangel.

2

ST. BENEDICT, THEN, like the great Hebrew Patriarch, was the "Father of many nations." He has been styled "the Patriarch of the West," a title which there are many reasons for ascribing to him. Not only was he the first to establish a perpetual Order of Regulars in Western Christendom; not only, as coming first, has he had an ampler course of centuries for the multiplication of his children; but his Rule, as that of St. Basil in the East, is the normal rule of the first age of the Church, and was in time generally received even in communities which in no sense owed their origin to him. Moreover, out of his Order rose, in process of time, various new monastic families, which have established themselves as independent institutions, and are able in their turn to boast of the number of their houses, and the sanctity and historical celebrity of their members. He is the representative of Latin monachism for the long extent of six centuries, while monachism was one; and even when at length varieties arose, and distinct titles were given to them, the change grew out of him;—not the act of strangers who were his rivals, but of his own children, who did but make a new beginning in all devotion and loyalty to him. He died in the early half of the sixth century; at the beginning of the tenth rose from among his French monasteries the famous Congregation of Cluni, illustrated by St. Majolus, St. Odilo, Peter the Venerable, and other considerable personages, among whom is Hildebrand, afterwards Pope Gregory the Seventh. Then came, in long succession, the Orders or Congregations of Camaldoli under St. Romuald, of Vallombrosa, of Citeaux, to which St. Bernard has given his name, of Monte Vergine, of Fontvrault; those of England, Spain, and Flanders; the Silverstrines, the Celestines, the Olivetans, the Humiliati, besides a multitude of institutes for women, as the Gilbertines and the Oblates of St. Frances, and then at length, to mention no others, the Congregation of St. Maur in modern times, so well known for its biblical, patristical, and historical works, and for its learned members, Montfaucon, Mabillon, and their companions. The panegyrists of this illustrious Order are accustomed to claim for it in all its branches as many as 37,000 houses, and, besides, 30 Popes, 200 Cardinals, 4 Emperors, 46 Kings, 51 Queens, 1,406 Princes, 1,600 Archbishops, 600 Bishops, 2,400 Nobles, and 15,000 Abbots and learned men.[1]

Nor are the religious bodies which sprang from St. Benedict the full measure of what he has accomplished,—as has been already observed. His Rule gradually made its way into those various monasteries which were of an earlier or of an independent foundation. It first coalesced with, and then supplanted, the Irish Rule of St. Columban in France, and the still older institutes which had been brought from the East by St. Athanasius, St. Eusebius, and St. Martin. At the beginning of the ninth century it was formally adopted throughout the dominions of Charlemagne. Pure, or with some admixture, it was brought by St. Augustine to England; and that admixture, if it existed, was gradually eliminated by St. Wilfrid, St. Dunstan, and Lanfranc, till at length it was received, with the name and obedience of St. Benedict, in all the Cathedral monasteries [2] (to mention no others), excepting Carlisle. Nor did it cost such regular bodies any very great effort to make the change, even when historically most separate from St. Benedict; for the Saint had taken up for the most part what he found, and his Rule was but the expression of the genius of monachism in those first times of the Church, with a more exact adaptation to their needs than could elsewhere be found.

So uniform indeed had been the monastic idea before his

[1] Helyot, Hist. Mon. Ziegelbauer, Litt. Hist. Soame's Mosheim, vol. ii., p. 26. Brockie, Præf. ad Regul. Buckingham's Bible in the Middle Ages, p. 81, etc., etc.

[2] Butler, June 22.

time, and so little stress had been laid by individual communities on their respective peculiarities, that religious men passed at pleasure from one body to another.[1] St. Benedict provides in his Rule for the case of strangers coming to one of his houses, and wishing to remain there. If such a one came from any monastery with which the monks had existing relations, then he was not to be received without letters from his Abbot; but, in the instance of "a foreign monk from distant parts," who wished to dwell with them as a guest, and was content with their ways, and conformed himself to them, and was not troublesome, "should he in the event wish to stay for good," says St. Benedict, "let him not be refused; for there has been room to make trial of him, during the time that hospitality has been shown to him: nay, let him even be invited to stay, that others may gain a lesson from his example; for in every place we are servants of one Lord and soldiers of one King." [2]

3

THE UNITY OF IDEA, which, as these words imply, is to be found in all monks in every part of Christendom, may be described as a unity of object, of state, and of occupation. Monachism was one and the same everywhere, because it was a reaction from that secular life, which has everywhere the same structure and the same characteristics. And, since that secular life contained in it many objects, many states, and many occupations, here was a special reason, as a matter of principle, why the reaction from it should bear the badge of unity, and should be in outward appearance one and the same everywhere. Moreover, since that same secular life was, when monachism arose, more than ordinarily marked by variety, perturbation and confusion, it seemed on that very account to justify emphatically a rising and revolt against itself, and a

[1] Thomassin, Disc. Eccl., t. i., p. 705. Calmet, Reg. Ben., t. ii., p. 25. Mabillon, Acta Sæc. iv., p. 1, præf., p. xxx. Annal., t. i., præf., § 19.

[2] Reg., c. 61.

recurrence to some state which, unlike itself, was constant and unalterable. It was indeed an old, decayed, and moribund world, into which Christianity had been cast. The social fabric was overgrown with the corruptions of a thousand years, and was held together, not so much by any common principle, as by the strength of possession and the tenacity of custom. It was too large for public spirit, and too artificial for patriotism, and its many religions did but foster in the popular mind division and scepticism. Want of mutual confidence would lead to despondency, inactivity, and selfishness. Society was in the slow fever of consumption, which made it restless in proportion as it was feeble. It was powerful, however, to seduce and deprave; nor was there any *locus standi* from which to combat its evils; and the only way of getting on with it was to abandon principle and duty, to take things as they came, and to do as the world did. Worse than all, this encompassing, entangling system of things, was, at the time we speak of, the seat and instrument of a paganism, and then of heresies, not simply contrary, but bitterly hostile, to the Christian profession. Serious men not only had a call, but every inducement which love of life and freedom could supply, to escape from its presence and its sway.

Their one idea then, their one purpose, was to be quit of it; too long had it enthralled them. It was not a question of this or that vocation, of the better deed, of the higher state, but of life and death. In later times a variety of holy objects might present themselves for devotion to choose from, such as the care of the poor, or of the sick, or of the young, the redemption of captives, or the conversion of the barbarians; but early monachism was flight from the world, and nothing else. The troubled, jaded, weary heart, the stricken, laden conscience, sought a life free from corruption in its daily work, free from distraction in its daily worship; and it sought employments as contrary as possible to the world's employments,—employments, the end of which would be in themselves, in which each day, each hour, would have its own completeness;—no elaborate undertakings, no difficult aims, no anxious ventures, no uncertainties to make the heart beat, or the temples throb, no painful combination of efforts, no extended plan of operations, no multiplicity of details, no deep calculations, no sustained machinations, no suspense, no vicissitudes, no moments of crisis or catastrophe;—nor again any subtle investigations, nor perplexities of proof, nor conflicts of rival intellects, to agitate, harass, depress, stimulate, weary, or intoxicate the soul.

Hitherto I have been using negatives to describe what the primitive monk was seeking; in truth monachism was, as regards the secular life and all that it implies, emphatically a negation, or, to use another word, a *mortification;* a mortification of sense, and a mortification of reason. Here a word of explanation is necessary. The monks were too good Catholics to deny that reason was a divine gift, and had too much common sense to think to do without it. What they denied themselves was the various and manifold exercises of the reason; and on this account, because such exercises were excitements. When the reason is cultivated, it at once begins to combine, to centralize, to look forward, to look back, to view things as a whole, whether for speculation or for action; it practises synthesis and analysis, it discovers, it invents. To these exercises of the intellect is opposed simplicity, which is the state of mind which does not combine, does not deal with premisses and conclusions, does not recognize means and their end, but lets each work, each place, each occurrence stand by itself,—which acts towards each as it comes before it, without a thought of anything else. This simplicity is the temper of children, and it is the temper of monks. This was their mortification of the intellect; every man who lives, must live by reason, as every one must live by sense; but, as it is possible to be content with the bare necessities of animal life, so is it possible to confine ourselves to the bare ordinary use of reason, without caring to improve it or make the most of it. These monks held both sense and reason to be the gifts of heaven, but they used each of them as little as they could help, reserving their full time and their whole selves for devotion;—for, if reason is better than sense, so devotion they thought to be better than either; and, as even a heathen might deny himself the innocent indulgences of sense in order to give his time to the cultivation of the reason, so did the monks give up reason, as well as sense, that they might consecrate themselves to divine meditation.

Now, then, we are able to understand how it was that the monks had a unity, and in what it consisted. It was a unity, I have said, of object, of state, and of occupation. Their object was rest and peace; their state was retirement; their occupation was some work that was simple, as opposed to intellectual, viz., prayer, fasting, meditation, study, transcription, manual labour, and other unexciting, soothing employments. Such was their institution all over the world; they had eschewed the busy mart, the craft of gain, the money-changer's bench, and the merchant's cargo. They had turned their backs upon the wrangling forum, the political assembly, and the pantechnicon of trades. They had had their last dealings with architect and habit-maker, with butcher and cook; all they wanted, all they desired, was the sweet soothing presence of earth, sky, and sea, the hospitable cave, the bright running stream, the easy gifts which mother earth, *justissima tellus*, yields on very little persuasion. "The monastic institute," says the biographer of St. Maurus, "demands *Summa Quies*, the most perfect quietness;"[1] and where was quietness to be found, if not in reverting to the original condition of man, as far as the changed circumstances of our race admitted; in having no wants, of which the supply was not close at hand; in the *nil admirari;* in having neither hope nor fear of anything below; in daily prayer, daily bread, and daily work, one day being just like another, except that it was one step nearer than the day just gone to that great Day, which would swallow up all days, the day of everlasting rest?

[1] Mabillon, Act. Benedict., t. iv., p. 1, p. xxxvii.

4

However, I have come into collision with a great authority, M. Guizot, and I must stop the course of my argument to make my ground good against him. M. Guizot, then, makes a distinction between monachism in its birth-place, in Egypt and Syria, and that Western institute, of which I have made St. Benedict the representative. He allows that the Orientals mortified the intellect, but he considers that Latin monachism was the seat of considerable mental activity. "The desire for retirement," he says, "for contemplation, for a marked rupture with civilized society, was the source and fundamental trait of the Eastern monks: in the West, *on the contrary,* and especially in Southern Gaul, where, at the commencement of the fifth century, the principal monasteries were founded, it was in order to live in common, *with a view to conversation* as well as to religious edification, that the first monks met. The monasteries of Lerins, of St. Victor, and many others, were especially great schools of theology, the focus of intellectual movement. It was by no means with solitude or with mortification, but with discussion and activity, that they there concerned themselves."[1] Great deference is due to an author so learned, so philosophical, so honestly desirous to set out Christianity to the best advantage; yet, I am at a loss to understand what has led him to make such a distinction between the East and West, and to assign to the Western monks an activity of intellect, and to the Eastern a love of retirement.

It is quite true that instances are sometimes to be found of monasteries in the West distinguished by much intellectual activity, but more, and more striking, instances are to be found of a like phenomenon in the East. If, then, such particular instances are to be taken as fair specimens of the state of Western monachism, they are equally fair specimens of the state of Eastern also; and the Eastern monks will be proved more

[1] History of Civilization, vol. ii., p. 65, Bohn; and so Ampère.

intellectual than the Western, by virtue of that greater interest in doctrine and in controversy which given individuals or communities among them have exhibited. A very cursory reference to ecclesiastical history will be sufficient to show us that the fact is as I have stated it. The theological sensitiveness of the monks of Marseilles, Lerins, or Adrumetum, it seems, is to be a proof of the intellectualism generally of the West: then, why is not the greater sensitiveness of the Scythian monks at Constantinople, and of their opponents, the Accœmetæ, an evidence in favour of the East? These two bodies of Religious actually came all the way from Constantinople to Rome to denounce one another, besieging, as it were, the Holy See, and the former of them actually attempting to raise the Roman populace against the Pope, in behalf of its own theological tenet. Does not this show activity of mind? I venture to say that, for one intellectual monk in the West, a dozen might be produced in the East. The very reproach, thrown out by secular historians against Greeks in general, of over-subtlety of intellect, applies in particular, if to any men, to certain classes or certain communities of Eastern monks. These were sometimes orthodox, quite as often heretical, but inexhaustible in their argumentative resources, whether the one or the other. If Pelagius be a monk in the West, on the other hand, Nestorius and Eutyches, both heresiarchs, are both monks in the East; and Eutyches, at the time of his heresy, was an old monk into the bargain, who had been thirty years abbot of a convent, and whom age, if not sanctity, might have saved from this abnormal use of his reason. His partizans were principally monks of Egypt; and they, coming up in force to the pseudo-synod of Ephesus, in aid of a theological thesis, kicked to death the patriarch of Constantinople, and put to flight the Legate of the Pope, all in consequence of their intellectual susceptibilities. A century earlier, Arius, on starting, carried away into his heresy as many as seven hundred nuns; [1] what have the Western convents to show, in the way of contro-

[1] Epiph. Hær., 69.

versial activity, comparable with a fact like this? I do not insist on the zealous and influential orthodoxy of the monks of Egypt, Syria, and Asia Minor in the fourth century, because it was probably nothing else but an honourable adhesion to the faith of the Church, without any serious exercise of mind; but turn to the great writers of Eastern Christendom, and consider how many of them figure at first sight as monks;—Chrysostom, Basil, Gregory Nazianzen, Epiphanius, Ephrem, Amphilochius, Isidore of Pelusium, Theodore, Theodoret, perhaps Athanasius. Among the Latin writers no great names occur to me but those of Jerome and Pope Gregory; I may add Paulinus, Sulpicius, Vincent, and Cassian, but Jerome is the only learned writer among them. I have a difficulty, then, even in comprehending, not to speak of admitting, M. Guizot's assertion, a writer who does not commonly speak without a meaning or a reason.

But, after all, however the balance of intellectualism may lie between certain convents or individuals in the East and the West, such particular instances of mental activity are nothing to the purpose, when taken to measure the state of the great body of the monks; certainly not in the West, with which in this paper I am exclusively concerned. In taking an estimate of the Benedictines, we need not trouble ourselves about the state of monachism in Egypt, Syria, Asia Minor, and Constantinople, as it existed after the fourth century, when the true monastic tradition was passing from the East to the West. In the fourth century, the Eastern Monks simply follow the defined and promulgated doctrine of the Church, and in following it are guilty of no exercise of reason; their intellectualism proper, which is foreign to the genius of their institute, begins with the fifth. Taking, then, the great tradition of St. Antony, St. Pachomius, and St. Basil in the East, and then tracing it into the West by the hands of St. Athanasius, St. Martin, and their contemporaries, we shall find no historical facts but what admit of a fair explanation, consistent with the views which we have laid down above about monastic simplicity, bearing in mind always, what holds in all matters of fact, that there never was a rule without its exceptions.

5

EVERY RULE HAS ITS EXCEPTIONS; but, further than this, when exceptions occur, they are commonly likely to be great ones. This is no paradox; illustrations of it are to be found everywhere. For instance, we may conceive a climate very fatal to children, and yet those who survive growing up to be strong men; and for a plain reason, because those alone could have passed the ordeal who had robust constitutions. Thus the Romans, so jealous of their freedom, when they resolved on the appointment of a supreme ruler for an occasion, did not do the thing by halves, but made him a Dictator. In like manner, a mere trifling occurrence, or an ordinary inward impulse, would be powerless to snap the bond which keeps the monk fast to his cell, his oratory, and his garden. Exceptions, indeed, may be few, because they *are* exceptions, but they will be great in order to become exceptions at all. It must be a serious emergence, a particular inspiration, a sovereign command, which brings the monk into political life; and he will be sure to make a great figure in it, else why should he have been torn from his cloister at all? This will account for the career of St. Gregory the Seventh or of St. Dunstan, of St. Bernard or of Abbot Suger, as far as it was political: the work they had to do was such as none could have done but a monk with his superhuman single-mindedness and his pertinacity of purpose. Again, in the case of St. Boniface, the Apostle of Germany, and in that of others of the missionaries of his age, it seems to have been a particular inspiration which carried them abroad; and it is observable after all how soon most of them settled down into the mixed character of agriculturists and pastors in their new country, and resumed the tranquil life to which they had originally devoted themselves. As to the early Greek Fathers, some of those whom we have instanced above are only *primâ facie* exceptions, as Chrysostom, who, though he lived with the monks most austerely for as many as six years, can hardly be said to have taken on himself the responsibilities of their condition, or to have simply abandoned the world. Others of them, as Basil, were scholars, philosophers, men of the world, before they were monks, and could not put off their cultivation of mind or their learning with their secular dress; and these would be the very men, in an age when such talents were scarce, who would be taken out of their retirement by superior authority, and who therefore cannot fairly be quoted as ordinary specimens of the monastic life.

Exceptio probat regulam: let us see what two Doctors of the Church, one Greek, one Latin, both rulers, both monks, say concerning the state, which they at one time enjoyed, and afterwards lost. "You tell me," says St. Basil, writing to a friend from his solitude, "that it was little for me to describe the place of my retirement, unless I mentioned also my habits and my mode of life; yet really I am ashamed to tell you how I pass night and day in this lonely nook. I am like one who is angry with the size of his vessel, as tossing overmuch, and leaves it for the boat, and is seasick and miserable still. However, what I propose to do is as follows, with the hope of tracing His steps who has said, 'If any one will come after Me, let him deny himself.' We must strive after a quiet mind. As well might the eye ascertain an object which is before it, while it roves up and down without looking steadily at it, as a mind, distracted with a thousand worldly cares, be able clearly to apprehend the truth. One who is not yoked in matrimony is harassed by rebellious impulses and hopeless attachments; he who is married is involved in his own tumult of cares: is he without children? he covets them; has he children? he has anxieties about their education. Then there is solicitude about his wife, care of his house, oversight of his servants, misfortunes in trade, differences with his neighbours, lawsuits, the merchant's risks, the farmer's toil. Each day, as it comes, darkens the soul in its own way; and night after night takes up the day's anxieties, and cheats us with corresponding dreams. Now, the only way of escaping all this is separation from the whole world, so as to live without city, home, goods, society, possessions, means of life, business, engagements, secular learning, that the heart may be prepared as wax for the impress of divine teaching. Solitude is of the greatest use for this purpose, as it stills our passions, and enables reason to extirpate them. Let then a place be found such as mine, separate from intercourse with men, that the tenor of our exercises be not interrupted from without. Pious exercises nourish the soul with divine thoughts. Soothing hymns compose the mind to a cheerful and calm state. Quiet, then, as I have said, is the first step in our sanctification; the tongue purified from the gossip of the world, the eyes unexcited by fair colour or comely shape, the ear secured from the relaxation of voluptuous songs, and that especial mischief, light jesting. Thus, the mind, rescued from dissipation from without, and sensible allurements, falls back upon itself, and thence ascends to the contemplation of God." [1] It is quite clear that at least St. Basil took the same view of the monastic state as I have done.

So much for the East in the fourth century; now for the West in the seventh. "One day," says St. Gregory, after he had been constrained, against his own wish, to leave his cloister for the government of the Universal Church, "one day, when I was oppressed with the excessive trouble of secular affairs, I sought a retired place, friendly to grief, where whatever displeased me in my occupations might show itself, and all that was wont to inflict pain might be seen at one view." While he was in this retreat, his "most dear son, Peter," with whom, ever since the latter was a youth, he had been intimate, surprised him, and he opened his grief to him. "My sad mind," he said, "labouring under the soreness of its engagements, remembers how it went with me formerly in this monastery, how all perishable things were beneath it, how it rose above all that

[1] Ep. 2. *Vid.* Supr. p. 63.

was transitory, and, though still in the flesh, went out in contemplation beyond that prison, so that it even loved death, which is commonly thought a punishment, as the gate of life and the reward of labour. But now, in consequence of the pastoral charge, it undergoes the busy work of secular men, and for that fair beauty of its quiet, is dishonoured with the dust of the earth. And often dissipating itself in outward things, to serve the many, even when it seeks what is inward, it comes home indeed, but is no longer what it used to be." [1] Here is the very same view of the monastic state at Rome which St. Basil had in Pontus, viz., retirement and repose. There have been great Religious Orders since, whose atmosphere has been conflict, and who have thriven in smiting or in being smitten. It has been their high calling; it has been their peculiar meritorious service; but, as for the Benedictine, the very air he breathes is peace.

6

I HAVE NOW SAID ENOUGH both to explain and to vindicate the biographer of St. Maurus, when he says that the object, and life, and reward of the ancient monachism was *summa quies*,—the absence of all excitement, sensible and intellectual, and the vision of Eternity. And therefore have I called the monastic state the most poetical of religious disciplines. It was a return to that primitive age of the world, of which poets have so often sung, the simple life of Arcadia or the reign of Saturn, when fraud and violence were unknown. It was a bringing back of those real, not fabulous, scenes of innocence and miracle, when Adam delved, or Abel kept sheep, or Noe planted the vine, and Angels visited them. It was a fulfilment in the letter, of the glowing imagery of prophets, about the evangelical period. Nature for art, the wide earth and the majestic heavens for the crowded city, the subdued and docile

[1] Dial., i. 1. *Vid.*, Essays, vol. ii., p. 284. [*Esays Critical and Historical,* 2 vols., 1871.—Ed.]

beasts of the field for the wild passions and rivalries of social life, tranquillity for ambition and care, divine meditation for the exploits of the intellect, the Creator for the creature, such was the normal condition of the monk. He had tried the world, and found its hollowness; or he had eluded its fellowship, before it had solicited him;—and so St. Antony fled to the desert, and St. Hilarion sought the sea shore, and St. Basil ascended the mountain ravine, and St. Benedict took refuge in his cave, and St. Giles buried himself in the forest, and St. Martin chose the broad river, in order that the world might be shut out of view, and the soul might be at rest. And such a rest of intellect and of passion as this is full of the elements of the poetical.

I have no intention of committing myself here to a definition of poetry; I may be thought wrong in the use of the term; but, if I explain what I mean by it, no harm is done, whatever be my inaccuracy, and each reader may substitute for it some word he likes better. Poetry, then, I conceive, whatever be its metaphysical essence, or however various may be its kinds, whether it more properly belongs to action or to suffering, nay, whether it is more at home with society or with nature, whether its spirit is seen to best advantage in Homer or in Virgil, at any rate, is always the antagonist to *science*. As science makes progress in any subject-matter, poetry recedes from it. The two cannot stand together; they belong respectively to two modes of viewing things, which are contradictory of each other. Reason investigates, analyzes, numbers, weighs, measures, ascertains, locates, the objects of its contemplation, and thus gains a scientific knowledge of them. Science results in system, which is complex unity; poetry delights in the indefinite and various as contrasted with unity, and in the simple as contrasted with system. The aim of science is to get a hold of things, to grasp them, to handle them, to comprehend them; that is (to use the familiar term), to *master* them, or to be superior to them. Its success lies in being able to draw a line round them, and to tell where each of them is to be found within that circumference, and how each lies relatively to all the rest. Its mission is to destroy ignorance, doubt, surmise, suspense, illusions, fears, deceits, according to the *Felix qui potuit rerum cognoscere causas* of the Poet, whose whole passage, by the way, may be taken as drawing out the contrast between the poetical and the scientific.[1] But as to the poetical, very different is the frame of mind which is necessary for its perception. It demands, as its primary condition, that we should not put ourselves above the objects in which it resides, but at their feet; that we should feel them to be above and beyond us, that we should look up to them, and that, instead of fancying that we can comprehend them, we should take for granted that we are surrounded and comprehended by them ourselves. It implies that we understand them to be vast, immeasurable, impenetrable, inscrutable, mysterious; so that at best we are only forming conjectures about them, not conclusions, for the phenomena which they present admit of many explanations, and we cannot know the true one. Poetry does not address the reason, but the imagination and affections; it leads to admiration, enthusiasm, devotion, love. The vague, the uncertain, the irregular, the sudden, are among its attributes or sources. Hence it is that a child's mind is so full of poetry, because he knows so little; and an old man of the world so devoid of poetry, because his experience of facts is so wide. Hence it is that nature is commonly more poetical than art, in spite of Lord Byron, because it is less comprehensible and less patient of definitions; history more poetical than philosophy; the savage than the citizen; the knight-errant

[1] Me verò primùm dulces ante omnia Musæ . . .
Accipiant, *cœlique vias et sidera monstrent,* etc., etc.
Sin, has ne possim naturæ accedere partes,
Frigidus obstiterit circùm præcordia sanguis,
Rura mihi et rigui placeant in vallibus amnes, etc.

And so again:

Felix, qui potuit rerum cognoscere *causas,* etc.
Fortunatus et ille, Deos qui novit agrestes, etc.

than the brigadier-general; the winding bridle-path than the straight railroad; the sailing vessel than the steamer; the ruin than the spruce suburban box; the Turkish robe or Spanish doublet than the French dress coat. I have now said far more than enough to make it clear what I mean by that element in the old monastic life, to which I have given the name of the Poetical.

Now, in many ways the family of St. Benedict answers to this description, as we shall see if we look into its history. Its spirit indeed is ever one, but not its outward circumstances. It is not an Order proceeding from one mind at a particular date, and appearing all at once in its full perfection, and in its extreme development, and in form one and the same everywhere and from first to last, as is the case with other great religious institutions; but it is an organization, diverse, complex, and irregular, and variously ramified, rich rather than symmetrical, with many origins and centres and new beginnings and the action of local influences, like some great natural growth; with tokens, on the face of it, of its being a divine work, not the mere creation of human genius. Instead of progressing on plan and system and from the will of a superior, it has shot forth and run out as if spontaneously, and has shaped itself according to events, from an irrepressible fulness of life within, and from the energetic self-action of its parts, like those symbolical creatures in the prophet's vision, which "went every one of them straight forward, whither the impulse of the spirit was to go." It has been poured out over the earth, rather than been sent, with a silent mysterious operation, while men slept, and through the romantic adventures of individuals, which are well nigh without record; and thus it has come down to us, not risen up among us, and is found rather than established. Its separate and scattered monasteries occupy the land, each in its place, with a majesty parallel, but superior, to that of old aristocratic houses. Their known antiquity, their unknown origin, their long eventful history, their connection with Saints and Doctors when on earth, the legends which hang about them, their rival ancestral honours, their extended sway perhaps over other religious houses, their hold upon the associations of the neighbourhood, their traditional friendships and compacts with other great landlords, the benefits they have conferred, the sanctity which they breathe,—these and the like attributes make them objects, at once of awe and of affection.

7

SUCH IS THE GREAT ABBEY of Bobbio, in the Apennines, where St. Columban came to die, having issued with his twelve monks from his convent in Benchor, county Down, and having spent his life in preaching godliness and planting monasteries in half-heathen France and Burgundy. Such St. Gall's, on the lake of Constance, so called from another Irishman, one of St. Columban's companions, who remained in Switzerland, when his master went on into Italy. Such the Abbey of Fulda, where lies St. Boniface, who, burning with zeal for the conversion of the Germans, attempted them a first time and failed, and then a second time and succeeded, and at length crowned the missionary labours of forty-five years with martyrdom. Such Monte Cassino, the metropolis of the Benedictine name, where the Saint broke the idol, and cut down the grove, of Apollo. Ancient houses such as these subdue the mind by the mingled grandeur and sweetness of their presence. They stand in history with an accumulated interest upon them, which belongs to no other monuments of the past. Whatever there is of venerable authority in other foundations, in Bishops' sees, in Cathedrals, in Colleges, respectively, is found in combination in them. Each gate and cloister has had its own story, and time has engraven upon their walls the chronicle of its revolutions. And, even when at length rudely destroyed, or crumbled into dust, they live in history and antiquarian works, in the pictures and relics which remain of them, and in the traditions of their place.

In the early part of last century the Maurist Fathers, with a view of collecting materials for the celebrated works which they had then on hand, sent two of their number on a tour through France and the adjacent provinces. Among other districts the travellers passed through the forest of Ardennes, which has been made classical by the prose of Cæsar, and the poetry of Shakespeare. There they found the great Benedictine Convent of St. Hubert; [1] and, if I dwell awhile upon the illustration which it affords of what I have been saying, it is not as if twenty other religious houses which they visited would not serve my purpose quite as well, but because it has come first to my hand in turning over the pages of their volume. At that time the venerable abbey in question had upon it the weight of a thousand years, and was eminent above others in the country in wealth, in privileges, in name, and, not the least recommendation, in the sanctity of its members. The lands on which it was situated were its freehold, and their range included sixteen villages. The old chronicle informs us that, about the middle of the seventh century, St. Sigibert, the Merovingian, pitched upon Ardennes and its neighbourhood for the establishment of as many as twelve monasteries, with the hope of thereby obtaining from heaven an heir to his crown. Dying prematurely, he but partially fulfilled his pious intention, which was taken up by Pepin, sixty years afterwards, at the instance of his chaplain, St. Beregise; so far, at least, as to make a commencement of the abbey of which we are speaking. Beregise had been a monk of the Benedictine Abbey of St. Tron, and he chose for the site of the new foundation a spot in the midst of the forest, marked by the ruins of a temple dedicated to the pagan Diana, the goddess of the chase. The holy man exorcised the place with the sign of the Cross; and, becoming abbot of the new house, filled it either

[1] Voyage Littéraire. *Vid.* also Calmet, Lorraine, t. i., p. 1043. Moreri, art. S. Hubert. Gallia Christ., t. iii. p. 966. Mabillon. Annal. Bened., t. ii., pp. 16, 441, 606. Bucherii, Gest. Tungr. etc., t. i., p. 153. Helyot, Ordres Mon., t. vi., p. 296.

with monks, or, as seems less likely, with secular canons. From that time to the summer day, when the two Maurists visited it, the sacred establishment, with various fortunes, had been in possession of the land.

On entering its precincts, they found it at once full and empty: empty of the monks, who were in the fields gathering in the harvest; full of pilgrims, who were wont to come day after day, in never-failing succession, to visit the tomb of St. Hubert. What a series of events has to be recorded to make this simple account intelligible! and how poetical is the picture which it sets before us, as well as those events themselves, which it presupposes, when they come to be detailed! Were it not that I should be swelling a passing illustration into a history, I might go on to tell how strict the observance of the monks had been for the last hundred years before the travellers arrived there, since Abbot Nicholas de Fanson had effected a reform on the pattern of the French Congregation of St. Vanne. I might relate how, when a simple monk in the Abbey of St. Hubert, Nicholas had wished to change it for a stricter community, and how he got leave to go off to the Congregation just mentioned, and how then his old Abbot died suddenly, and how he himself to his surprise was elected in his place. And I might tell how, when his mitre was on his head, he set about reforming the house which he had been on the point of quitting, and how he introduced for that purpose two monks of St. Vanne; and how the Bishop of Liege, in whose diocese he was, set himself against his holy design, and how some of the old monks attempted to poison him; and how, though he carried it into effect, still he was not allowed to aggregate his Abbey to the Congregation whose reform he had adopted; but how his good example encouraged the neighbouring abbeys to commence a reform in themselves, which issued in an ecclesiastical union of the Flemish Houses.

All this, however, would not have been more than one passage, of course, in the adventures which had befallen the abbey and its abbots in the course of its history. It had had many seasons of decay before the time of Nicholas de Fanson, and many restorations, and from different quarters. None of them was so famous or important as the reform effected in the year 817, about a century after its original foundation, when the secular canons, who anyhow had got in, were put out, and the monks put in their place, at the instance of the then Bishop of Liege, who had a better spirit than his successor in the time of Nicholas. The new inmates were joined by some persons of noble birth from the Cathedral, and by their suggestion and influence the bold measure was taken of attempting to gain from Liege the body of the great St. Hubert, the Apostle of Ardennes. Great, we may be sure, was the resistance of the city where he lay; but Abbot Alreus, the friend and fellow-workman of St. Benedict of Anian, the first Reformer of the Benedictine Order before the date of Cluni, went to the Bishop, and he went to the Archbishop of Cologne; and then both prelates went to the Emperor Louis le Debonnaire, the son of Charlemagne, whose favourite hunting ground the forest was; and he referred the matter to the great Council of Aix-la-Chapelle, whence a decision came in favour of the monks of Ardennes. So with great solemnity the sacred body was conveyed by water to its new destination; and there in the Treasury, in memorial of the happy event, the Maurist visitors saw the very chalice of gold, and the beautiful copy of the Gospels, ornamented with precious stones, given to the Abbey by Louis at the time. Doubtless it was the handiwork of the monks of some other Benedictine House, as must have been the famous Psalter, of which the visitors speak also, written in letters of gold, the gift of Louis's son, the Emperor Lothaire; and there he sits in the first page, with his crown on his head, his sceptre in one hand, his sheathed sword in the other, and something very like a fleur-de-lys buckling on his ermine robe at the shoulder:—which precious gift, that is, the Psalter with all its pictures, two centuries after came most unaccountably into the possession of the Lady Helvidia of Aspurg, who gave it to her young son Bruno, afterwards Pope Leo the Ninth, to learn the Psalms by; but, as the young Saint made no progress in his task, she came to the conclusion that she had no right to the book, and so she ended by making a pilgrimage to St. Hubert with Bruno, and, not only gave back the Psalter, but made the offering of a Sacramentary besides.

But to return to the relics of the Saint; the sacred body was taken by water up the Maes. The coffin was of marble, and perhaps could have been taken no other way; but another reason, besides its weight, lay in the indignation of the citizens of Liege, who might have interfered with a land journey, and in fact did make several attempts, in the following years, to regain the body. In consequence, the good monks of Ardennes hid it within the walls of their monastery, confiding the secret of its whereabouts to only two of their community at a time; and they showed in the sacristy to the devout, instead, the Saint's ivory cross and his stole, the sole of his shoe and his comb, and Diana, Marchioness of Autrech, gave a golden box to hold the stole. This, however, was in after times; for they were very loth at first to let strangers within their cloisters at all; and in 838, when a long spell of rain was destroying the crops, and the people of the neighbourhood came in procession to the shrine to ask the intercession of the Saint, the cautious Abbot Sewold, availing himself of the Rule, would only admit priests, and them by threes and fours, with naked feet, and a few laymen with each of them. The supplicants were good men, however, and had no notion of playing any trick: they came in piety and devotion, and the rain ceased, and the country was the gainer by St. Hubert of Ardennes. And thenceforth others, besides the monks, became interested in his stay in the forest.

And now I have said something in explanation why the courtyard was full of pilgrims when the travellers came. St. Hubert had been an object of devotion for a particular benefit, perhaps ever since he came there, certainly as early as the eleventh century, for we then have historical notice of it. His preference of the forest to the city, which he had shown in his life-time before his conversion, was illustrated by the particular grace or miraculous service, for which, more than for any other, he used his glorious intercession on high. He is famous for curing those who had suffered from the bite of wild animals, especially dogs of the chase, and a hospital was attached to the Abbey for their reception. The sacristan of the Church officiated in the cure; and with rites which never indeed failed, but which to some cautious persons seemed to savour of superstition. Certainly they were startling at first sight; accordingly a formal charge on that score was at one time brought against them before the Bishop of Liege, and a process followed. The Bishop, the University of Louvain, and its Faculty of Medicine, conducted the inquiry, which was given in favour of the Abbey, on the ground that what looked like a charm might be of the nature of a medical regimen.

However, though the sacristan was the medium of the cure, the general care of the patients was left to externs. The hospital was served by secular priests, since the monks heard no confessions save those of their own people. This rule they observed, in order to reserve themselves for the proper duties of a Benedictine,–the choir, study, manual labour, and transcription of books; and, while the Maurists were ocular witnesses of their agricultural toils, they saw the diligence of their penmanship in its results, for the MSS. of their Library were the choicest in the country. Among them, they tell us, were copies of St. Jerome's Bible, the Acts of the Councils, Bede's History, Gregory and Isidore, Origen and Augustine.

The Maurists report as favourably of the monastic buildings themselves as of the hospital and library. Those buildings were a chronicle of past times, and of the changes which had taken place in them. First there were the poor huts of St. Beregise upon the half-cleared and still marshy ground of the forest; then came the building of a sufficient house, when St. Hubert was brought there; and centuries after that, St. Thierry, the intimate friend of the great Pope Hildebrand, had renewed it magnificently, at the time that he was Abbot. He was sadly treated in his lifetime by his monks, as Nicholas after him; but, after his death, they found out that he was a Saint, which they might have discovered before it; and they placed him in the crypt, and there he and another holy Abbot after him lay in peace, till the Calvinists broke into it in the sixteenth century, and burned both of them to ashes. There were marks too of the same fanatics on the pillars of the nave of the Church; which had been built by Abbot John de Wahart in the twelfth century, and then again from its foundations by Abbots Nicholas de Malaise and Romaclus, the friend of Blosius, four centuries later; and it was ornamented by Abbot Cyprian, who was called the friend of the poor; and doubtless the travellers admired the marble of the choir and sanctuary, and the silver candelabra of the altar given by the reigning Lord Abbot; and perhaps they heard him sing solemn Mass on the Assumption, as was usual with him on that feast, with his four secular chaplains, one to carry his Cross, another his mitre, a third his gremial, and a fourth his candle, and accompanied by the pealing organ and the many musical bells, which had been the gift of Abbot Balla about a hundred years earlier. Can we imagine a more graceful union of human with divine, of the sweet with the austere, of business and of calm, of splendour and of simplicity, than is displayed in a great religious house after this pattern, when unrelaxed in its observance, and pursuing the ends for which it was endowed?

8

THE MONKS HAVE BEEN accused of choosing beautiful spots for their dwellings; as if this were a luxury in ascetics, and not rather the necessary alleviation of their asceticism. Even when their critics are kindest, they consider such sites as chosen by a sort of sentimental, ornamental indolence. "Beaulieu river," says Mr. Warner in his topography of Hampshire, and, because he writes far less ill-naturedly than the run of authors, I quote him, "Beaulieu river is stocked with plenty of fish, and boasts in particular of good oysters and fine plaice, and is fringed quite to the edge of the water with the most beautiful hanging woods. In the area enclosed are distinct traces of various fishponds, formed for the use of the convent. Some of them continue perfect to the present day, and abound with fish. A curious instance occurs also of monkish luxury, even in the article of water; to secure a fine spring those monastics have spared neither trouble nor expense. About half a mile to the south-east of the Abbey is a deep wood; and at a spot almost inaccessible is a cave formed of smooth stones. It has a very contracted entrance, but spreads gradually into a little apartment, of seven feet wide, ten deep, and about five high. This covers a copious and transparent spring of water, which, issuing from the mouth of the cave, is lost in a deep dell, and is there received, as I have been informed, by a chain of small stone pipes, which formerly, when perfect, conveyed it quite to the Abbey. It must be confessed the monks in general displayed an elegant taste in the choice of their situations. Beaulieu Abbey is a striking proof of this. Perhaps few spots in the kingdom could have been pitched upon better calculated for monastic seclusion than this. The deep woods, with which it is almost environed, throw an air of gloom and solemnity over the scene, well suited to excite religious emotions; while the stream that glides by its side afforded to the recluse a striking emblem of human life: and at the same time that it soothed his mind by a gentle murmuring, led it to serious thought by its continual and irrevocable lesson." [1]

The monks were not so soft as all this, after all; and if Mr. Warner had seen them, we may be sure he would have been astonished at the stern, as well as sweet simplicity which characterized them. They were not dreamy sentimentalists, to fall in love with melancholy winds and purling rills, and waterfalls and nodding groves; but their poetry was the poetry of hard work and hard fare, unselfish hearts and charitable hands.

[1] Vol. i., p. 237, etc.

They could plough and reap, they could hedge and ditch, they could drain; they could lop, they could carpenter; they could thatch, they could make hurdles for their huts; they could make a road, they could divert or secure the streamlet's bed, they could bridge a torrent. Mr. Warner mentions one of their luxuries,—clear, wholesome water; it was an allowable one, especially as they obtained it by their own patient labour. If their grounds are picturesque, if their views are rich, they made them so, and had, we presume, a right to enjoy the work of their own hands. They found a swamp, a moor, a thicket, a rock, and they made an Eden in the wilderness. They destroyed snakes; they extirpated wild cats, wolves, boars, bears; they put to flight or they converted rovers, outlaws, robbers. The gloom of the forest departed, and the sun, for the first time since the Deluge, shone upon the moist ground. St. Benedict is the true man of Ross.

> Who hung with woods yon mountain's sultry brow?
> From the dry rock who made the waters flow?
> Whose causeway parts the vale with shady rows?
> Whose seats the weary traveller repose?
> He feeds yon almshouse, neat, but void of state,
> When Age and Want sit smiling at the gate;
> Him portioned maids, apprenticed orphans blessed,
> The young who labour, and the old who rest.

And candid writers, though not Catholics, allow it. Even English, and much more foreign historians and antiquarians, have arrived at a unanimous verdict here. "We owe the agricultural restoration of great part of Europe to the monks," says Mr. Hallam. "The monks were much the best husbandmen, and the only gardeners," says Forsyth. "None," says Wharton, "ever improved their lands and possessions more than the monks, by building, cultivating, and other methods." The cultivation of Church lands, as Sharon Turner infers from Doomsday Book, was superior to that held by other proprietors, for there was less wood upon them, less common pasture, and more abundant meadow. "Wherever they came," says Mr. Soames on Mosheim, "they converted the wilderness into a cultivated country; they pursued the breeding of cattle and agriculture, laboured with their own hands, drained morasses, and cleared away forests. By them Germany was rendered a fruitful country." M. Guizot speaks as strongly: "The Benedictine monks were the agriculturists of Europe; they cleared it on a large scale, associating agriculture with preaching." [1]

St. Benedict's direct object indeed in setting his monks to manual labour was neither social usefulness nor poetry, but penance; still his work was both the one and the other. The above-cited authors enlarge upon its use, and I in what I am writing may be allowed to dwell upon its poetry; we may contemplate both its utility to man and its service to God in the aspect of its poetry. How romantic then, as well as useful, how lively as well as serious, is their history, with its episodes of personal adventure and prowess, its pictures of squatter, hunter, farmer, civil engineer, and evangelist united in the same individual, with its supernatural colouring of heroic virtue and miracle! When St. Columban first came into Burgundy with his twelve young monks, he placed himself in a vast wilderness, and made them set about cultivating the soil. At first they all suffered from hunger, and were compelled to live on the barks of trees and wild herbs. On one occasion they were for five days in this condition. St. Gall, one of them, betook himself to a Swiss forest, fearful from the multitude of wild beasts; and then, choosing the neighbourhood of a mountain stream, he made a cross of twigs, and hung some relics on it, and laid the foundation of his celebrated abbey. St. Ronan came from Ireland to Cornwall, and chose a wood, full of wild beasts, for his hermitage, near the Lizard. The monks of St. Dubritius, the founder of the Welsh Schools, also

[1] Hallam, Middle Ages, vol. iii., p. 436. Forsyth, Antiqu., vol. i., pp. 37, 44, 179. Turner, Anglo-Sax., vol. ii., p. 167. Murdoch's Mosheim, vol. ii., p. 21, etc. Guizot, Hist. Civil., vol. ii., p. 75, Bohn.

sought the woods, and there they worked hard at manufactures, agriculture, and road making. St. Sequanus placed himself where "the trees almost touched the clouds." He and his companions, when they first explored it, asked themselves how they could penetrate into it, when they saw a winding footpath, so narrow and full of briars that it was with difficulty that one foot followed another. With much labour and with torn clothes they succeeded in gaining its depths, and stooping their heads into the darkness at their feet, they perceived a cavern, shrouded by the thick interlacing branches of the trees, and blocked up with stones and underwood. "This," says the monastic account, "was the cavern of robbers, and the resort of evil spirits." Sequanus fell on his knees, prayed, made the sign of the Cross over the abyss, and built his cell there. Such was the first foundation of the celebrated abbey called after him in Burgundy.[1]

Sturm, the Bavarian convert of St. Boniface, was seized with a desire, as his master before him in his English monastery, of founding a religious house in the wilds of Pagan Germany; and setting out with two companions, he wandered for two days through the Buchonian forest, and saw nothing but earth, sky, and large trees. On the third day he stopped and chose a spot, which on trial did not answer. Then, mounting an ass, he set out by himself, cutting down branches of a night to secure himself from the wild beasts, till at length he came to the place (described by St. Boniface as *locum silvaticum in eremo, vastissimæ solitudinis*), in which afterwards arose the abbey and schools of Fulda. Wunibald was suspicious of the good wine of the Rhine where he was, and, determining to leave it, he bought the land where Heidensheim afterwards stood, then a wilderness of trees and underwood, covering a deep valley and the sides of lofty mountains. There he proceeded, axe in hand, to clear the ground for his

[1] Neander, Memorials, pp. 436, 451, 473, Bohn. Rader, Bavaria Sacra. Calles, Ann. Germ., t. i., pp. 200, 276, 317, 318. Guizot, Civil., vol. ii., p. 134. Whitaker's Cornwall, vol. ii., p. 196. Fosbroke, Antiq., p. 16.

religious house, while the savage natives looked on sullenly, jealous for their hunting-grounds and sacred trees. Willibald, his brother, had pursued a similar work on system; he had penetrated his forest in every direction and scattered monasteries over it. The Irish Alto pitched himself in a wood, half way between Munich and Vienna. Pirminius chose an island, notorious for its snakes, and there he planted his hermitage and chapel, which at length became the rich and noble abbey and school of Augia Major or Richenau.[1]

The more celebrated School of Bec had a similar beginning at a later date, when Herluin, an old soldier, devoted his house and farm to an ecclesiastical purpose, and governed, as abbot, the monastery which he had founded. "You might see him," says the writer of his life, "when office was over in church, going out to his fields, at the head of his monks, with his bag of seed about his neck, and his rake or hoe in his hand. There he remained with them hard at work till the day was closing. Some were employed in clearing the land of brambles and weeds; others spread manure; others were weeding or sowing; no one ate his bread in idleness. Then when the hour came for saying office in church, they all assembled together punctually. Their ordinary food was rye bread and vegetables with salt and water; and the water muddy, for the well was two miles off." [2] Lanfranc, then a secular, was so edified by the simple Abbot, fresh from the field, setting about his baking with dirty hands, that he forthwith became one of the party; [3] and, being unfitted for labour, opened in the house a school of logic, thereby to make money for the community. Such was the cradle of the scholastic theology; the last years of the patristic, which were nearly contemporaneous, exhibit a similar scene,—St. Bernard founding his abbey of Clairvaux in a place called the Valley of Wormwood, in the heart of a savage

1 Meyrick's Willibald, p. 68. Bavaria Sacra, p. 119. Petri, Suevia Eccles., p. 96. Calles Ann. Germ., t. i., p. 191.

2 Butler's Lives, Aug. 20.

3 Apud. Mabillon Act. Bened.

forest, the haunt of robbers, and his thirteen companions clearing a homestead, raising a few huts, and living on barley or cockle bread with boiled beech leaves for vegetables.[1]

How beautiful is Simeon of Durham's account of Easterwine, the first abbot after Bennet of St. Peter's at Wearmouth! He was a man of noble birth, who gave himself to religion, and died young. "Though he had been in the service of King Egfrid," says Simeon, "when he had once left secular affairs, and lain aside his arms, and taken on him the spiritual warfare instead, he was nothing but the humble monk, just like any of his brethren, winnowing with them with great joy, milking the ewes and cows, and in the bakehouse, the garden, the kitchen, and all house duties, cheerful and obedient. And, when he received the name of Abbot, still he was in spirit just what he was before to every one, gentle, affable, and kind; or, if any fault had been committed, correcting it indeed by the Rule, but still so winning the offender by his unaffected earnest manner, that he had no wish ever to repeat the offence, or to dim the brightness of that most clear countenance with the cloud of his transgression. And often going here and there on business of the monastery, when he found his brothers at work, he would at once take part in it, guiding the plough, or shaping the iron, or taking the winnowing fan, or the like. He was young and strong, with a sweet voice, a cheerful temper, a liberal heart, and a handsome countenance. He partook of the same food as his brethren, and under the same roof. He slept in the common dormitory, as before he was abbot, and he continued to do so for the first two days of his illness, when death had now seized him, as he knew full well. But for the last five days he betook himself to a more retired dwelling; and then, coming out into the open air and sitting down, and calling for all his brethren, after the manner of his tender nature, he gave his weeping monks the kiss of peace, and died at night while they were singing lauds."[2]

[1] Thomass., Disc. Eccl., t. iii., p. 513.

[2] P. 93. The passage seems taken from Bede.

9

THIS GENTLENESS AND TENDERNESS of heart seems to have been as characteristic of the monks as their simplicity; and if there are some Saints among them, who on the public stage of history do not show it, it was because they were called out of their convents for some special purpose, and, as I have said above, exceptions to a rule are commonly great exceptions. Bede goes out of his way to observe of King Ethelbert, on St. Austin's converting him, that "he had learned from the teachers and authors of his salvation that men were to be drawn heavenwards and not forced." Aldhelm, when a council had been held about the perverse opinions of the British Christians, seconding the principle which the Fathers of it laid down, that "schismatics were to be convinced, not compelled," wrote a book upon their error and converted many of them. Wolstan, when the civil power failed in its attempts to stop the slave trade of the Bristol people, succeeded by his persevering preaching. In the confessional he was so gentle, that penitents came to him from all parts of England.[1] This has been the spirit of the monks from the first; the student of ecclesiastical history may recollect a certain passage in St. Martin's history, when his desire to shield the Spanish heretics from capital punishment brought him into great difficulties [2] with the usurper Maximus.

Works of penance indeed and works of mercy have gone hand in hand in the history of the monks; from the Solitaries in Egypt down to the Trappists of this day, it is one of the points in which the unity of the monastic idea shows itself. They have ever toiled for others, while they toiled for themselves; nor for posterity only, but for their poor neighbours, and for travellers who came to them. St. Augustine tells us that the monks of Egypt and of the East made so much by manual labour as to be able to freight vessels with provisions

[1] Bede, Hist. Eccles., i. 26. William of Malmesb. Ponfic. Angl.

[2] *Vid.* Supr. p. 198.

for impoverished districts. Theodoret speaks of a certain five thousand of them, who by their labour supported, besides themselves, innumerable poor and strangers. Sozomen speaks of the Monk Zeno, who, though a hundred years old, and the bishop of a rich Church, worked for the poor as well as for himself. Corbinian in a subsequent century surrounded his German Church with fruit trees and vines, and sustained the poor with the produce. The monks of St. Gall, already mentioned, gardened, planted, fished, and thus secured the means of relieving the poor and entertaining strangers. "Monasteries," says Neander, "were seats for the promotion of various trades, arts, and sciences. The gains accruing from their combined labour were employed for the relief of the distressed. In great famines, thousands were rescued from starvation." [1] In a scarcity at the beginning of the twelfth century, a monastery in the neighbourhood of Cologne distributed in one day fifteen hundred alms, consisting of bread, meat, and vegetables. About the same time St. Bernard founded his monastery of Citeaux, which, though situated in the waste district described above, was able at length to sustain two thousand poor for months, besides extraordinary alms bestowed on others. The monks offered their simple hospitality, uninviting as it might be, to high as well as low; and to those who scorned their fare, they at least could offer a refuge in misfortune or danger, or after casualties.

Duke William, ancestor of the Conqueror, was hunting in the woods about Jumieges, when he fell in with a rude hermitage.[2] Two monks had made their way through the forest, and with immense labour had rooted up some trees, levelled the ground, raised some crops, and put together their hut. William heard their story, not perhaps in the best humour, and flung aside in contempt the barley bread and water which they offered him. Presently he was brought back wounded and insensible: he had got the worst in an encounter

[1] Eccl. Hist., vol. vii., p. 331, Bohn.

[2] Duchesne, Script. North., p. 236.

with a boar. On coming to himself, he accepted the hospitality which he had refused at first, and built for them a monastery. Doubtless he had looked on them as trespassers or squatters on his domain, though with a religious character and object. The Norman princes were as good friends to the wild beasts as the monks were enemies: a charter still exists of the Conqueror, granted to the abbey of Caen,[1] in which he stipulates that its inmates should not turn the woods into tillage, and reserves the game for himself.

Contrast with this savage retreat and its rude hospitality the different, though equally Benedictine picture of the sacred grove of Subiaco, and the spiritual entertainment which it ministers to all comers, as given in the late pilgrimage of Bishop Ullathorne: "The trees," he says, "which form the venerable grove, are very old, but their old age is vigorous and healthy. Their great grey roots expose themselves to view with all manner of curling lines and wrinkles on them, and the rough stems bend and twine about with the vigour and ease of gigantic pythons. . . . Of how many holy solitaries have these trees witnessed the meditations! And then they have seen beneath their quiet boughs the irruption of mailed men, tormented by the thirst of plunder and the passion of blood, which even a sanctuary held so sacred could not stay. And then they have witnessed, for twelve centuries and more, the greatest of the Popes, the Gregories, the Leos, the Innocents, and the Piuses, coming one after another to refresh themselves from their labours in a solitude which is steeped with the inspirations and redolent with the holiness of St. Benedict."

What congenial subjects for his verse would the sweetest of all poets have found in scenes and histories such as the foregoing, he who in his *Georgics* has shown such love of a country life and country occupations, and of the themes and trains of thought which rise out of the country! Would that Christianity had a Virgil to describe the old monks at their

[1] Turner, Middle Ages, vol. v., p. 89.

rural labours, as it has had a Sacchi or a Domenichino to paint them! How would he have been able to set forth the adventures and the hardships of the missionary husbandmen, who sang of the Scythian winter, and the murrain of the cattle, the stag of Sylvia, and the forest home of Evander! How could he have pourtrayed St. Paulinus or St. Serenus in his garden, who could draw so beautiful a picture of the old Corycian, raising amid the thicket his scanty pot-herbs upon the nook of land, which was "not good for tillage, nor for pasture, nor for vines!" How could he have brought out the poetry of those simple labourers, who has told us of that old man's flowers and fruits, and of the satisfaction, as a king's, which he felt in those innocent riches! He who had so huge a dislike of cities, and great houses, and high society, and sumptuous banquets, and the canvass for office, and the hard law, and the noisy lawyer, and the statesman's harangue,—he who thought the country proprietor as even too blessed, did he but know his blessedness, and who loved the valley, winding stream, and wood, and the hidden life which they offer, and the deep lessons which they whisper,—how could he have illustrated that wonderful union of prayer, penance, toil, and literary work, the true *otium cum dignitate,* a fruitful leisure and a meek-hearted dignity, which is exemplified in the Benedictine! That ethereal fire which enabled the Prince of Latin poets to take up the Sibyl's strain, and to adumbrate the glories of a supernatural future,—that serene philosophy, which has strewn his poems with sentiments which come home to the heart,—that intimate sympathy with the sorrows of human kind and with the action and passion of human nature,—how well would they have served to illustrate the patriarchal history and office of the monks in the broad German countries, or the deeds, the words, and the visions of a St. Odilo or a St. Aelred!

What a poet deliberately chooses for the subject of his poems must be in its own nature poetical. A poet indeed is but a man after all, and in his proper person may prefer solid beef and pudding to all the creations of his own "fine frenzy," which, in his character of poet, are his meat and drink. But no poet will ever commit his poetical reputation to the treatment of subjects which do not admit of poetry. When, then, Virgil chooses the country and rejects the town, he shows us that a certain aspect of the town is uncongenial with poetry, and that a certain aspect of the country is congenial. Repose, intellectual and moral, is that quality of country life which he selects for his praises; and effort, and bustle, and excitement is that quality of a town life which he abhors. Herein then, according to Virgil, lies the poetry of St. Benedict, in the *secura quies et nescia fallere vita,* in the absence of anxiety and fretfulness, of schemes and scheming, of hopes and fears, of doubts and disappointments. Such a life,—living for the day without solicitude for the morrow, without plans or objects, even holy ones, here below; working, not (so to say) by the piece, but as hired by the hour; sowing the ground with the certainty, according to the promise, of reaping; reading or writing this present week without the consequent necessity of reading or writing during the next; dwelling among one's own people without distant ties; taking each new day as a whole in itself, an addition, not a complement, to the past; and doing works which cannot be cut short, for they are complete in every portion of them,—such a life may be called emphatically Virgilian. They, on the contrary, whose duty lies in what may be called *undertakings,* in science and system, in sustained efforts of the intellect or elaborate processes of action,—apologists, controversialists, disputants in the schools, professors in the chair, teachers in the pulpit, rulers in the Church,—have a noble and meritorious mission, but not so poetical a one. When the bodily frame receives an injury, or is seized with some sudden malady, nature may be expected to set right the evil, if left to itself, but she requires time; science comes in to shorten the process, and is violent that it may be certain. This may be taken to illustrate St. Benedict's mode of counteracting the miseries of life. He found the world, physical and social, in ruins, and his mission was to restore it in the way, not of science, but of nature, not as if setting about to do it, not professing to do it by any set time or by any rare specific or by any series of strokes, but so quietly, patiently, gradually, that often, till the work was done, it was not known to be doing. It was a restoration, rather than a visitation, correction, or conversion. The new world which he helped to create was a growth rather than a structure. Silent men were observed about the country, or discovered in the forest, digging, clearing, and building; and other silent men, not seen, were sitting in the cold cloister, tiring their eyes, and keeping their attention on the stretch, while they painfully deciphered and copied and re-copied the manuscripts which they had saved. There was no one that "contended, or cried out," or drew attention to what was going on; but by degrees the woody swamp became a hermitage, a religious house, a farm, an abbey, a village, a seminary, a school of learning, and a city. Roads and bridges connected it with other abbeys and cities, which had similarly grown up; and what the haughty Alaric or fierce Attila had broken to pieces, these patient meditative men had brought together and made to live again.

And then, when they had in the course of many years gained their peaceful victories, perhaps some new invader came, and with fire and sword undid their slow and persevering toil in an hour. The Hun succeeded to the Goth, the Lombard to the Hun, the Tartar to the Lombard; the Saxon was reclaimed only that the Dane might take his place. Down in the dust lay the labour and civilization of centuries,—Churches, Colleges, Cloisters, Libraries,—and nothing was left to them but to begin all over again; but this they did without grudging, so promptly, cheerfully, and tranquilly, as if it were by some law of nature that the restoration came, and they were like the flowers and shrubs and fruit trees which they reared, and which, when ill-treated, do not take vengeance, or remember evil, but give forth fresh branches, leaves, or blossoms, perhaps in greater profusion, and with richer quality, for the very reason that the old were rudely broken off. If one holy place was desecrated, the monks pitched upon another, and by this time there were rich or powerful men who remembered and loved the past enough to wish to have it restored in the future. Thus was it in the case of the monastery of Ramsey after the ravages of the Danes. A wealthy Earl, whose heart was touched, consulted his Bishop how he could best promote the divine glory: the Bishop answered that they only were free, serene, and unsolicitous, who renounced the world, and that their renunciation brought a blessing on their country. "By their merit," he said, "the anger of the Supreme Judge is abated; a healthier atmosphere is granted; corn springs up more abundantly; famine and pestilence withdraw; the state is better governed; prisons are opened; the fetters unbound; the shipwrecked relieved." He proceeded to advise him, as the best of courses, to give ground for a monastery, and to build and endow it. Earl Alwin observed in reply, that he had inherited some waste land in the midst of marshes, with a forest in the neighbourhood, some open spots of good turf, and others of meadow; and he took the Bishop to see it. It was in fact an island in the fens, and as lonely as religious men could desire. The gift was accepted, workmen were collected, the pious peasants round about gave their labour. Twelve monks were found from another cloister; cells and a chapel were soon raised. Materials were collected for a handsome church; stones and cement were given; a firm foundation was secured; scaffolding and machinery were lent; and in course of time a sacred edifice and two towers rose over the desolate waste, and renewed the past;—a learned divine from France was invited to preside over the monastic schools.[1]

[1] *Vid.* Turner, Anglo-Saxons, vol. iii., p. 468.

10

HERE THEN I AM LED, lastly, to speak of the literary labours of the Benedictines, but I have not room to do more than direct attention to the peculiar character of their work, and must leave the subject of their schools for some future opportunity. Here, as in other respects above noticed, the unity of monachism shows itself. What the Benedictines, even in their latest literary developments, have been, in St. Maur in the seventeenth century, and at Solesme now, such were the monks in their first years. One of the chief occupations of the disciples of St. Pachomius in Egypt was the transcription of books. It was the sole labour of the monks of St. Martin in Gaul. The Syrian solitaries, according to St. Chrysostom, employed themselves in making copies of the Holy Scriptures. It was the occupation of the monks of St. Equitius and of Cassiodorus, and of the nunnery of St. Cæsarius. We read of one holy man preparing the skins for writing, of another selling his manuscripts in order to gain alms for the poor, and of an abbess writing St. Peter's Epistles in letters of gold. St. David had shown the same reverence to St. John's Gospel. Abbot Plato filled his own and other monasteries with his beautifully written volumes.[1] During the short rule of Abbot Desiderius at Monte Cassino, his monks wrote out St. Austin's fifty Homilies, his Letters, his Comment upon the Sermon on the Mount, upon St. Paul and upon Genesis; parts of St. Jerome and St. Ambrose, part of St. Bede, St. Leo's Sermons, the Orations of St. Gregory Nazianzen; the Acts of the Apostles, the Epistles and the Apocalypse; various histories, including that of St. Gregory of Tours, and of Josephus on the Jewish War, Justinian's Institutes, and many ascetic and other works; of the Classics, Cicero *de Naturâ Deorum,* Terence, Ovid's *Fasti,* Horace, and Virgil, Maurus Lapi, a Camaldolese,

[1] Pallad, c. 39. Cassian, Inst., iv., 12. Calmet, Reg., t. ii., p. 150. Thomassin, Disc. Eccl., t. iii., p. 505. Ziegelbaur, Hist. Litt. Bened., t. ii., p. 510.

in the fifteenth century, copied a thousand volumes in less than fifty years. Jerome, a monk in an Austrian monastery, wrote so great a number of books that, it is said, a wagon with six horses would scarcely suffice to draw them. Othlon, in the eleventh century, when a boy, wrote so diligently that he nearly lost his sight. That was in France; he then went to Ratisbon, where he wrote nineteen missals, three books of the Gospel, two books of Epistle and Gospel, and many others. Many he gave to his friends, but the list is too long to finish. The Abbot Odo of Tournay "used to exult," according to his successor, "in the number of writers which the Lord had given him. Had you gone into his cloister, you might have seen a dozen young men sitting in perfect silence, writing at tables constructed for the purpose. All Jerome's Commentaries on the Prophets, all the works of St. Gregory, all that he could find of Austin, Ambrose, Isidore, Bede, and the Lord Anselm, Abbot of Bec, and afterwards Archbishop of Canterbury, he caused to be diligently transcribed." [1]

These tranquil labourers found a further field in the illumination and binding of the transcribed volumes, as they had previously been occupied in the practice necessary for the then important art of calligraphy. It was not running hand that the monks had to learn; for it was no ephemeral expression of their own thoughts which their writing was to convey, but the formal transcript, for the benefit of posterity, of the words of inspired teachers and Doctors of the Church. They were performing what has been since the printer's work; and it is said that from the English monks is derived the small letter of the modern Roman type. In France the abbeys of Fontenelle, Rheims, and Corbie were especially famed for beauty of penmanship in the age of Charlemagne,[2] when literature was in its most depressed state. Books intended for

[1] Annal. Camald., t. vii., p. 300: *vid.* other instances in Maitland's Dark Ages, and Buckingham's Bible in the Middle Ages, who, however, is deficient in references.

[2] Guizot's Hist. Civil., vol. ii., p. 236, Bohn.

presents, such as that which the mother of Leo the Ninth presented to St. Hubert, and, much more, if intended for sacred uses, were enriched with gold and silver plates and precious stones. Here was a commencement of the cultivation of the fine arts in those turbulent times,–a quiet, unexciting occupation, which went on inside the monasteries, whatever rivalries or heresies agitated Christendom outside of them, and which, though involving, of course, an improvement in the workmanship as time went on, yet in the case of every successive specimen, whatever exact degree of skill or taste each exhibited, had its end in itself, as though there had been no other specimen before or after.

Brower, in his work on the Antiquities of Fulda, gives us a lively picture of the various tranquil occupations which were going on at one time within the monastic walls. "As industrious bees," he says, "their work never flagging, did these monks follow out their calling. Some of them were engaged in describing, here and there upon the parchment, the special letters and characters which were to be filled in; others were wrapping or binding the manuscripts in handsome covers; others were marking out in red the remarkable sentences or the heads of the chapters. Some were writing fairly what had been thrown together at random, or had been left out in the dictation, and were putting every part in fair order. And not a few of them excelled in painting in all manner of colours, and in drawing figures." He goes on to refer to an old manuscript there, which speaks of the monks as decorating their church, and of their carpenters' work, sculpture, engraving, and brass work.

I have mentioned St. Dunstan in an earlier page, as called to political duties, which were out of keeping with the traditionary spirit of his Order; here, however, he shows himself in the simple character of a Benedictine. He had a taste of the arts generally, especially music. He painted and embroidered; his skill in smith's work is recorded in the well-known legend of his combat with the evil one. And, as the monks of Hilarion joined gardening with psalmody, and Bernard and his Cistercians joined field work with meditation, so did St. Dunstan use music and painting as directly expressive or suggestive of devotion. "He excelled in writing, painting, moulding in wax, carving in wood and bone, and in work in gold, silver, iron, and brass," says the writer of his life in Surius. "And he used his skill in musical instruments to charm away from himself and others their secular annoyances, and to rouse them to the thought of heavenly harmony, both by the sweet words with which he accompanied his airs, and by the concord of those airs themselves." [1] And then he goes on to mention how on one occasion, when he had hung his harp against the wall, and the wind brought out from its strings a wild melody, he recognized in it one of the antiphons in the Commune Martyrum, *Gaudete in Cœlis,* etc., and used it for his own humiliation.

As might be expected, the monasteries of the South of Europe would not be behind the North in accomplishments of this kind. Those of St. Gall, Monte Cassino, and Solignac, are especially spoken of as skilled in the fine arts. Monte Cassino excelled in illumination and in mosaic, the Camaldolese in painting, and the Olivetans in wood-inlaying.[2]

II

WHILE MANUAL LABOUR, applied to these artistic purposes, ministered to devotion, on the other hand, when applied to the transcription and multiplication of books, it was a method of instruction, and that peculiarly Benedictine, as being of a literary, not a scientific nature. Systematic theology had but a limited place in ecclesiastical study prior to the eleventh and twelfth centuries; Scripture and the Fathers were the received means of education, and these constituted the very text on which the pens of the monks were employed.

[1] *Vid.* also Whitaker's Cornwall, vol. i., p. 167, and the whole chapter.

[2] Meehan's Marchese, p. xxiv.

And thus they would be becoming familiar with that kind of knowledge which was proper to their vocation, at the same time that they were engaged in what was unequivocally a manual labour; and, in providing for the religious necessities of posterity, they were directly serving their own edification. And this again had been the practice of the monks from the first, and is included in the *unity* of their profession. St. Chrysostom tells us that their ordinary occupation in his time was "to sing and pray, to read Scripture, and to transcribe the sacred text." [1] As the works of the early Fathers gradually became the literary property of the Church, these, too, became the subject-matter of the reading and the writing of the monks. "For him who is going on to perfection," says St. Benedict in his Rule, "there are the lessons of the Holy Fathers, which lead to its very summit. For what page, what passage of the Old or New Testament, coming as it does with divine authority, is not the very exactest rule of life? What book of the Holy Catholic Fathers does not resound with this one theme, how we may take the shortest course to our Creator?" But I need not here insist on this characteristic of monastic study, which, especially as regards the study of Scripture, has been treated so fully and so well by Mr. Maitland in his *Essays on the Dark Ages.*

The sacred literature of the monks went a step further. They would be naturally led by their continual perusal of the Scriptures and the Fathers to attempt to compare and adjust these two chief sources of theological truth with each other. Hence resulted the peculiar character of the religious works of what may be especially called the Benedictine period, the five centuries between St. Gregory and St. Anselm. The age of the Fathers was well nigh over; the age of the Schoolmen was yet to come; the ecclesiastical writers of the intervening centuries employed themselves for the most part in arranging and digesting the patristical literature which had come down to them; they either strung together choice pas-

[1] Hist. Litter. de St. Maur, 1770, p. 21.

sages of the Fathers in *catenæ,* as a running illustration of the inspired text, or they formed them into a comment upon it. The *Summæ Sententiarum* of the same centuries were works of a similar character, while they also opened the way to the intellectual exercises of the scholastic period; for they were lessons or instructions arranged according to a scheme or system of doctrine, though they were still extracted from the works of the Fathers, and though the matter of those works suggested the divisions or details of the system. Moreover, such labours, as much as transcription itself, were Benedictine in their spirit, as well as in their subject-matter; for where there was nothing of original research, nothing of brilliant or imposing result, there would be nothing to dissipate, elate, or absorb the mind, or to violate the simplicity and tranquillity proper to the monastic state.

The same remark applies to a further literary employment in which the Benedictines allowed themselves, and which is the last I shall here mention, and that is the compilation of chronicles and annals, whether ecclesiastical, secular, or monastic. So prominent a place does this take in their literature, that the author of the *Asceticon,* in the fourth volume of Dom Francois's *Bibliothèque des Ecrivains Bénédictins,* does not hesitate to point to the historical writings of his Order as constituting one of its chief claims, after its Biblical works, on the gratitude of posterity. "This," he says, "is the praise especially due to the monks, that they have illustrated Holy Scripture, rescued history, sacred and profane, from the barbarism of the times, and have handed down to posterity so many lives both of Saints and of Bishops." [1] Here again is a fresh illustration of the Benedictine character; for first, those histories are of the most simple structure and most artless composition, and next, from the circumstance of their being commonly narratives of contemporary events, or compilations from a few definite sources of information which were at hand, they

[1] P. 379. Printing, another tranquil work, was introduced into Italy by the Benedictines of Subiaco. *Vid.* Dr. Ullathorne's Pilgrimage.

involved nothing of that laborious research and excitement of mind which is demanded of the writer who has to record a complex course of history, extending over many centuries and countries, and who aims at the discovery of truth, in the midst of deficient, redundant, or conflicting testimony. "The men who wrote history," says Mr. Dowling, speaking of the times in question, "did not write by rule; they only put down what they had seen, what they had heard, what they knew. Very many of them did what they did as a matter of moral duty. The result was something *sui generis;* it was not even what *we* call history at all. It was, if I may so speak, something more, an actual admeasurement rather than a picture; or, if a picture, it was painted in a style which had all the minute accuracy and homely reality of the most domestic of the Flemish masters, not the lofty hyperbole of the Roman school, nor the obtrusive splendour, not less unnatural, of the Venetian. In a word, history, as a subject of criticism, is an art, a noble and beautiful *art;* the historical writings of the middle ages is *nature.*" [1]

Mention is made in this passage of the peculiarity in monastic historiography, that it proceeded from the motive of religious duty. This must always have been the case in consequence of the monastic profession; however, we have here, in addition to the presumption, actual evidence, and not on one occasion only, of the importance which the Benedictine Order attached to these notices and memorials of past times. In the year 1082, for instance, the Abbot Marquand of New Corbie, in Saxony, seems to have sent an order to all churches and monasteries subject to his rule to send to him severally the chronicles of their own places. Abbot Wichbold repeated the order sixty years later, and Abbot Thierry in 1337 addressed to the provosts and rectors subject to him a like injunction.[2] Again, in 1481 the Abbot of Erfurdt addressed a letter to the Fathers of the Reform of Bursfeld, with the view

[1] Introd. Eccles. Hist., p. 56.

[2] Ziegelbaur, t. ii., p. 401.

of persuading them to take part in a similar work. "If you were to agree among yourselves," he says, "and make a statute to the effect that every Prelate is under an obligation to compose annals and histories of his monastery, what could be better, what more useful, what more interesting, whether for knowing or for reading?" [1]

It is easier to conjecture what those literary works would be, in which a Benedictine would find himself at liberty to engage, than to pretend to point out those from which his vocation would debar him; yet Mabillon, equally with de Rancé, implied that all subjects do not come alike to him. Here we are recalled to the well-known controversy between these two celebrated men. The Abbot of La Trappe, the Cistercian de Rancé, writing to his own people, put forth some statements on the subject of the studies proper to a monk, which seemed to reflect upon the learned Maurists. Mabillon, one of them, replied, in a learned vindication of himself and his brethren. The Abbot had maintained that study of whatever kind should be kept in strict subordination to manual labour, and should not extend to any books except the Scriptures and the ascetic treatises of the Fathers. Mabillon, on the other hand, without denying the necessity of manual labour, to which the Maurists themselves devoted an hour a day, seemed to allow to the Benedictine the free cultivation of the intellect, and an unlimited range of studies. When they explained themselves, each combatant would appear to have asserted more than he could successfully maintain; yet after all there was a considerable difference of view between them, which could not be removed. The critical question was whether certain historical instances, which Mabillon urged in his favour, were to be considered exceptions or not to the rule of St. Benedict. I have certainly maintained in an earlier page of this Essay that such instances as Alcuin, Paschasius, or

[1] *Ibid.*, t. i., p. 424. For lists of monastic histories, *vid.* Mr. Dowling, Introd. E. H., p. 260; the Asceticon as above, § 26. Ziegelbaur, t. ii., p. 398. Balmez., Prot. and Cath., p. 195.

Lanfranc are no fair specimens of the Benedictine profession, and must not be taken to represent the monks generally. Lest, however, in saying this, I may be thought to be evading the testimony of history, as adduced by a writer, authoritative at once by his learning and as spokesman of the great Congregation of St. Maur, I think it well to extract in my behalf some of his own admissions, which seem to me fully to bear out what I have been laying down above about the spirit and mission of his Order.

For instance, he frankly concedes, or rather maintains, that the scholastic method of teaching theology and philosophy is foreign to the profession of a Benedictine, as such. "Why," he asks, "need we cultivate these sciences in the way of disputation? Why not as positive sciences, explaining questions and resolving doubts as they occur? Why is it not more than enough for religious pupils to be instructed in the more necessary principles of the science, and thereby to make progress in the study of the Scriptures and the Fathers? What need of this perpetual syllogizing in form, and sharp answers to innumerable objections, as is the custom in the schools?" Elsewhere he contrasts the mode of teaching a subject, as adopted by the early Fathers, with that which the Schoolmen introduced. "The reasonings of the Fathers," he says, "are so full, so elegantly set forth, as to be everywhere redolent of the sweetness and vigour of Christian eloquence, whereas scholastic theology is absolutely dry and sterile." Elsewhere he says that "in the study of Holy Scripture consists the entire science of monks." Again, he says of Moral Theology, "As monks are rarely destined to the cure of souls, it does not seem necessary that they should give much time to the science of Morals." And though of course he does not forbid them the study of history, which we have seen to be so congenial to their calling, yet he observes of this study, when pursued to its full extent, "It seems to cause much dissipation of mind, which is prejudicial to that inward compunction of heart, which is so especially fitting to the holy life of a monk." Again, observing that the examination of ancient MSS. was the special occupation of the Maurists in his time, he says, "They who give themselves to this study have the more merit with God, in that they have so little praise with men. Moreover, it obliges them to devote the more time to solitude, which ought to be their chief delight. I confess it is a most irksome and unpleasant labour; however, it gives much less trouble than transcription, which was the most useful work of our early monks." Elsewhere, speaking of the celebrated Maurist editions of the Fathers, he observes, "Labour, such as this, which is undergone in silence and in quietness, is especially compatible with true tranquillity of mind and the mastery of the passions, provided we labour as a duty, and not for glory.[1]

I trust the reader will be so good as to keep in mind that I am all along speaking of the Benedictine life *historically*, and as I might speak of any other historical *fact;* not venturing at all on what would be the extreme presumption of any quasi-doctrinal or magisterial exposition of it, which belongs to those only who have actually imbibed its tradition. This being clearly understood, I think I may interpret Mabillon to mean that (be the range of studies lawful to a monk what it may) still, whatever literary work requires such continuous portions of time as not to admit of being suspended at a moment's notice, whatever is so interesting that other duties seem dull and heavy after it, whatever so exhausts the power of attention as to incapacitate for attention to other subjects, whatever makes the mind gravitate towards the creature, is inconsistent with monastic simplicity. Accordingly, I should expect to find that controversy was uncongenial to the Benedictine, because it excited the mind, and metaphysical investigations, because they fatigued it; and, when I met such instances as St. Paschasius or St. Anselm, I should deal with them as they came and as I could. Moreover, I should not look to a Benedictine for any elaborate and systematic work

[1] Stud. Monast., ed. 1732; t. i., pp. 52, 135; t. ii., p. 2; t. i., pp. 145, 147, 191, 64.

on the history of doctrine, or of heresy, or for any course of patristical theology, or any extended ecclesiastical history, or any philosophical disquisitions upon history, as implying a grasp of innumerable details, and the labour of using a mass of phenomena to the elucidation of a theory, or of bringing a range of multifarious reading to bear upon one point; and that, because such efforts of mind require either an energetic memory devoted to matters of time and place, or, instead of the tranquil and plodding study of one book after another, the presence of a large library, and the distraction of a vast number of books handled all at once, not for perusal, but for reference. Perhaps I am open to the charge of refining, in attempting to illustrate the principle which I seem to myself to detect in the Benedictine tradition; but the principle itself which I have before me is clear enough, and is expressed in the advice which is given to us by a sacred writer: "The words of the wise are as goads, and nails deeply fastened in; *more than these, my son, require not:* of making many books there is no end, and much study is an affliction of the flesh."

To test the truth of this view of the Benedictine mission, I cannot do better than appeal as a palmary instance to the Congregation of St. Maur, an intellectual school of Benedictines assuredly. Now what, in matter of fact, is the character of its works? It has no Malebranche, no Thomassin, no Morinus; it has no Bellarmine, no Suarez, no Petavius; it has no Tillemont or Fleury,—all of whom were more or less its contemporaries; but it has a Montfaucon, it has a Mabillon, it has a Sainte Marthe, a Coustant, a Sabbatier, a Martene,—men of immense learning and literary experience; it has collators and publishers of MSS. and of inscriptions, editors of the text and of the versions of Holy Scripture, editors and biographers of the Fathers, antiquarians, annalists, paleographists,—with scholarship indeed, and criticism, and theological knowledge, admirable as often as elicited by the particular subject on which they are directly employed, but conspicuously subordinate to it.

If we turn to other contemporary Congregations of St. Benedict we are met by the same phenomenon. Their labours have been of the same modest, patient, tranquil kind. The first name which occurs to me is that of Augustine Calmet, of the Congregation of St. Vanne. His works are biblical and antiquarian;—a literal Comment on Scripture with Dissertations, a dictionary of the Bible, a Comment on the Benedictine Rule, a history of Lorraine. I cast my eyes round the Library, in which I happen at the moment to be writing; what Benedictine authors meet them? There is Ceillier, also of the Congregation of St. Vanne; Bertholet, of the same Congregation; Cardinal Aguirre of Salamanca; Cressy of Douai; Pez of Mölk on the Danube; Lumper of St. George in the Hercynian Forest; Brockie of the Scotch College at Ratisbon; Reiner of the English Congregation. Their Works are of the same complexion,—historical, antiquarian, biographical, patristical,—calling to mind the line of study traditionally pursued by a modern ecclesiastical congregation, the Italian Oratory. I do not speak of Ziegelbauer, Francois, and other Benedictines, who might be added, because they have confined themselves to Benedictine Antiquities, and every Order will write about itself.

And so of the Benedictine Literature from first to last. Ziegelbauer, who has just been mentioned, has written four folio volumes on the subject. Now one of them is devoted to a catalogue and an account of Benedictine authors;—of these, those on Scripture and Positive Theology occupy 110 pages; those on history, 300; those on scholastic theology, 12; those on polemics, 12; those on moral theology, 6. This surprising contrast may be an exaggeration of the fact, because there is much of repetition and digression in his survey, and his biographical notices vary in length; but, after all allowances for such accidental unfairness in the list, the result must surely be considered as strikingly confirmatory of the account which I have been giving.

12

But I must cut short an investigation which, though imperfect for the illustration of its subject, is already long for the patience of the reader. All human works are exposed to vicissitude and decay; and that the great Order of which I have been writing should in the lapse of thirteen centuries have furnished no instances of that general law is the less to be expected, in proportion to the extent of its territory, the independence of its separate houses, and the local varieties of its constitution. To say that peace may engender selfishness, and humility become a cloak for indolence, and a country life may be an epicurean luxury, is only to enunciate the over-true maxim, that every virtue has a vice for its first cousin. *Usum non tollit abusus;* and the circumstance that Benedictine life admits of being corrupted into a mode of living which is not Benedictine, but is very contradictory, cannot surely be made an argument against its meritorious innocence, its resolute cheerfulness, and its strenuous tranquillity. We are told to be like little children; and where shall we find a more striking instance than is here afforded us of that union of simplicity and reverence, that clear perception of the unseen, yet recognition of the mysterious, which is the characteristic of the first years of human existence? To the monk heaven was next door; he formed no plans, he had no cares; the ravens of his father Benedict were ever at his side. He "went forth" in his youth "to his work and to his labour" until the evening of life; if he lived a day longer, he did a day's work more; whether he lived many days or few, he laboured on to the end of them. He had no wish to see further in advance of his journey than where he was to make his next stage. He ploughed and sowed, he prayed, he meditated, he studied, he wrote, he taught, and then he died and went to heaven. He made his way into the labyrinthine forest, and he cleared just so much of space as his dwelling required, suffering the high solemn trees and the deep pathless thicket to close him in. And when he began to build, his architecture was suggested by the scene,—not the scientific and masterly conception of a great whole with many parts, as the Gothic style in a later age, but plain and inartificial, the adaptation of received fashions to his own purpose, and an addition of chapel to chapel and a wayward growth of cloister, according to the occasion, with half-concealed shrines and unexpected recesses, with paintings on the wall as by a second thought, with an absence of display and a wild, irregular beauty, like that of the woods by which he was at first surrounded. And when he would employ his mind, he turned to Scripture, the book of books, and there he found a special response to the peculiarities of his vocation; for there supernatural truths stand forth as the trees and flowers of Eden, in a divine disorder, as some awful intricate garden or paradise, which he enjoyed the more because he could not catalogue its wonders. Next he read the Holy Fathers, and there again he recognized a like ungrudging profusion and careless wealth of precept and of consolation. And when he began to compose, still he did so after that mode which nature and revelation had taught him, avoiding curious knowledge, content with incidental ignorance, passing from subject to subject with little regard to system, or care to penetrate beyond his own homestead of thought,—and writing, not with the sharp logic of disputants, or the subtle analysis of philosophers, but with the one aim of reflecting in his pages, as in a faithful mirror, the words and works of the Almighty, as they confronted him, whether in Scripture and the Fathers, or in that "mighty maze" of deeds and events, which men call the world's history, but which to him was a Providential Dispensation.

Here the beautiful character in life and death of St. Bede naturally occurs to the mind, who is, in his person and his writings, as truly the pattern of a Benedictine as is St. Thomas of a Dominican; and with an extract from the letter of Cuthbert to Cuthwin concerning his last hours, which, familiarly as it is known, is always pleasant to read, I break off my subject for the present.

"He was exceedingly oppressed," says Cuthbert of St. Bede, "with shortness of breathing, though without pain, before Easter Day, for about a fortnight; but he rallied, and was full of joy and gladness, and gave thanks to Almighty God day and night and every hour, up to Ascension Day; and he gave us, his scholars, daily lectures, and passed the rest of the day in singing the Psalms, and the night too in joy and thanksgiving, except the scanty time which he gave to sleep. And as soon as he woke, he was busy in his customary way, and he never ceased with uplifted hands giving thanks to God. I solemnly protest, never have I seen or heard of any one who was so diligent in thanksgiving.

"He sang that sentence of the blessed Apostle Paul, 'It is a dreadful thing to fall into the hands of the Living God,' and many other passages of Scripture, in which he warned us to shake off the slumber of the soul, by anticipating our last hour. And he sang some verses of his own in English also, to the effect that no one could be too well prepared for his end, viz., in calling to mind, before he departs hence, what good or evil he has done, and how his judgment will lie. And he sang too the antiphons, of which one is, 'O King of Glory, Lord of Angels, who this day hast ascended in triumph above all the heavens, leave us not orphans, but send the promise of the Father upon us, the Spirit of Truth, alleluia.' And when he came to the words, 'leave us not orphans,' he burst into tears, and wept much. He said, too, 'God scourgeth every son whom He receiveth,' and, with St. Ambrose, 'I have not so lived as to be ashamed to have been among you, nor do I fear to die, for we have a good Lord.'

"In those days, besides our lectures and the Psalmody, he was engaged in two works; he was translating into English the Gospel of St. John, as far as the words, 'But what are these among so many,' and some extracts from the *Notæ* [1] of Isidore. On the Tuesday before Ascension Day he began to suffer still more in his breathing, and his feet were slightly swollen. However, he went through the day, dictating cheerfully, and he kept saying from time to time, 'Take down what I say quickly, for I know not how long I am to last, or whether my Maker will not take me soon.' He seemed to us to be quite aware of the time of his going, and he passed that night in giving of thanks, without sleeping. As soon as morning broke, that is on the Wednesday, he urged us to make haste with the writing which we had begun. We did so till nine o'clock, when we walked in procession with the Relics of the Saints, according to the usage of that day. But one of our party said to him, 'Dearest Master, one chapter is still wanting; can you bear our asking you about it?' He answered, 'I can bear it; take your pen and be ready, and write quickly.' At three o'clock he said to me, 'Run fast, and call our priests, that I may divide among them some little gifts which I have in my box.' When I had done this in much agitation, he spoke to each, urging and entreating them all to make a point of saying Masses and prayers for him. Thus he passed the day in joy until the evening, when the above-named youth said to him, 'Dear Master, there is yet one sentence not written;' he answered, 'Write quickly.' Presently the youth said, 'Now it is written;' he replied, 'Good, thou hast said the truth; *consummatum est;* take my head into thy hands, for it is very pleasant to me to sit facing my old praying place, and thus to call upon my Father.' And so, on the floor of his cell, he sang, 'Glory be to Father, Son, and Holy Ghost,' and, just as he had said 'Holy Ghost,' he breathed his last, and went to the realms above."

[1] The Bollandists have not been able to determine which of St Isidore's works is here intended. "Notæ" means "Musical Notes," according to Du Cange. According to Lebœuf in Ampère, Hist. Litter., t. iii., p. 253, the word means "penmanship."

It is remarkable that this flower of the Benedictine school died on the same day as St. Philip Neri,–May 26; Bede on Ascension Day, and Philip on the early morning after the feast of Corpus Christi. It was fitting that two saints should go to heaven together, whose mode of going thither was the same; both of them singing, praying, working, and guiding others, in joy and exultation, till their very last hour.

CHAPTER II

THE BENEDICTINE SCHOOLS[1]

1

WE READ IN HISTORY of great commanders, who, when an overwhelming force was directed against them on the plain, and success was for the time impossible, submitted to necessity, and, with plans afterwards to be developed, retired up the mountain passes in their rear, where nature had provided a safe halting-place for brave men who could not advance, and would not turn in flight. There, behind the lofty crag, the treacherous morass, and the thick wood, they nursed their confidence of victory, and waited patiently for an issue, which was not less certain because it was delayed. On came the haughty foe, with cries of defiance; and when at length he thought he had them at his mercy, he found that first he must do battle with the adamantine rocks, which sternly rose up in defence of fugitives who had invoked their aid. Then he stood for a while irresolute, till the difficulties of his position ended his deliberation, and forced upon him a retreat in his turn, while the lately besieged hosts were once more in motion, and pressed upon the baffled foe, who had neither plan of campaign nor base of operations to fall back upon.

Such is the history of Christian civilization. It gave way before the barbarians of the north and the fanatics of the south; it fled into the wilderness with its own books and those of the old social system which it was succeeding. It obeyed the direction given it in the beginning,—when persecuted in one place, to flee away to another; and then at length the hour of

[1] From the *Atlantis* of January, 1859.—[Ed.]

retribution came, and it advanced into the territories from which it had retired. St. Benedict is the historical emblem of its retreat, and St. Dominic of its return.

I do not say that its retreat in the first centuries was made with the intent of its return in the medieval. There was no oracular voice which proclaimed what would be the course and fortune of the war; no secret tradition which whispered to the initiated the tactic that ought to be pursued. It is a sufficient explanation of the double movement, that they who feel their weakness are used to give way, and they who feel their strength are used to push forward. The corruptions of Roman society caused Christians to despair of ever mending it, and to look out for that better world which was destined to supersede it. The evil which they experienced, the good for which they sighed, the promise in which they confided, wrought in them the persuasion that the end of all things was at hand; and this persuasion made them patient under inconveniences which they felt to be only temporary. "Behold, my brethren," says Pope Gregory about the year 600, "we already see with our eyes what we are used to hear in prophecy. Day by day is the world assaulted by fresh and thickening blows. Out of that innumerable Roman *plebs* what a mere remnant are ye at this day! yet incessant scourges are still in action; sudden adversities thwart you; new and unforeseen slaughters wear you away. For, as in youth, the body is in vigour, the chest is strong, the neck muscular, and the arms plump, but in old age the stature is bent, the neck is withered and stooping, the chest pants, the energies are feeble, and breath is wanting for the words; so the world too once was vigorous, robust for the increase of its kind, green in its health, and opulent in its resources, but now on the contrary it is laden with the weight of years, and is fast sinking into the grave by its ever-multiplying maladies. Beware, then, of giving your heart to that which, as even your senses tell you, cannot last for ever."[1] Commonly the presentiment wore a

[1] Hom. i. l.

more definitely supernatural expression than is found in this extract. Not sense merely, but the prophecies were directly invoked, which spoke of that great enemy of the Church, who was to be the herald of the Second Advent; and the rudiments of a new order of things were descried in the manifest tokens of an expiring world.

In all times, indeed, the multitude, whether from religious feeling or from superstition, is prone to portend some impending catastrophe from the occurrence of any startling phenomenon of nature. An eclipse, a comet, a volcanic eruption, is to them the omen of coming evil. But in the early centuries of the Church the expectation extended to the learned and the saintly. It was the posture of mind of confessors and doctors. As St. Gregory looked out for Antichrist in the sixth century, so had the Martyrs of Lyons in the second, St. Cyprian in the third, St. Hilary and St. Chrysostom in the fourth, and St. Jerome in the fifth. It was the sober judgment of the wisest and the most charitable, that the world was too bad to mend, and that destruction was close upon it.

What would be the practical result of such a belief? That which I have partly described in my remarks on the mission of St. Benedict; evidently, to leave the world to itself. Evils which threaten to continue we try to remedy; but what was the use of spending one's strength in reforming a state of things which would go to pieces, if let alone, and, if ever so much meddled with, would go to pieces too, nay, the sooner, perhaps, for the meddling? Hence it was the prevalent disposition, as I have said, of Christians of the first centuries, and no irrational disposition, either to leave the world or to put up with it, not to set about influencing it. "Let us go hence," said the Angels in the doomed sanctuary of the chosen people. "Come ye out of her, my people," was the present bidding of inspiration. Those who would be perfect obeyed it, and became monks. Monachism therefore was a sort of recognized emigration from the old world. St. Antony had found out a new coast, the true *eldorado* or gold country; and on the news of it thousands took their departure year after year for the diggings in the desert. The monks of Egypt alone soon became an innumerable host. As times got worse, Basil in the East, and Benedict in the West, put themselves at the head of fresh colonies, bound for the land of perpetual peace. There they sat them down, over against Babylon, and waited for the coming judgment and the end of all things. Those who remained in the world, waited too. To undergo patiently what was,—to make the best of it, to use it, as far as it could be used, for religious purposes,—was their wisdom and their resolve. If they took another course, they would be wasting strength and hope upon a shadow, and losing the present for a future which would never come. They had no large designs or profound policy. It was their aim that things should just last their time. They patched them up as best they might, they made shift, and lived from hand to mouth; and they followed events, rather than created them. Nor, when they undertook great labours and began works pregnant with consequences, did they perceive whither they were going.

How different in this respect is the spirit of the first Gregory, already cited, from that of Hildebrand, the seventh! Gregory the First did not understand his own act, when he converted the Anglo-Saxons; nor Ambrose, when he put Theodosius to penance. The great Christian Fathers laid anew the foundations of the world, while they thought that its walls were tottering to the fall, and that they already saw the fires of judgment through the chinks. They refuted Arianism, which they named the forerunner of the last woe, with reasonings which were to live for ages; and they denounced the preachers of a carnal millennium, without anticipating that wonderful temporal reign of the saints which was to be manifested in medieval times. They propounded broad principles, but did not carry them out into their inevitable consequences. How slow were they to define doctrine, when disputes arose about its meaning or its bearing! How patient they seem to us of imperial encroachments on ecclesiastical rights, when we view them by the side of the great Popes who came after them! How tamely do they conduct themselves when the civil magistrate interferes with their jurisdiction, or takes the initiative in points of discipline or order, in questions of property, and matrimonial causes! How contented or resigned are they to avail themselves of such education as the state provided for their use; sending their children to the pagan schools, before they have teachers of their own, and, even when at length they have them, adopting the *curriculum* of studies which those pagan schools had devised!

In fact, in the minds of those high saints, "the wish was father to the thought." Religious men will always desire, will always be prone to believe, the approach of that happier order of things, which sooner or later is to be. This hope was the form in which the deep devotion of those primitive times showed itself; and if it did not continue in its full expression beyond them, this was because experience had thrown a new light upon the course of Divine Providence in the world. With the multitude, indeed, as I have said, who know little of history, and in whom religious fear is a chief element, the anticipation of the Last Day revived, and revives, from time to time. At the end of the tenth century, when a thousand years had passed over the Church, the sense of impending destruction was so vivid as even to affect the transfer and disposal of property, and the repair of sacred buildings. However, when we seek in theologians for the apprehension, we shall find that it is a characteristic of the old Empire far more than of the barbarian kingdoms which succeeded to it. The barbarian world was young, as the Roman world was effete. Youth is the season of hope; and, according as things looked more cheerful, so did they look more lasting, and to-day's sunshine became the sufficient promise of a long summer. A fervent preacher here or there, St. Norbert or St. Vincent Ferrer, may have had forebodings of the end of all things; or an astrologer or a schismatizing teacher may have traded on the belief; but the men of gravity and learning after the time of Gregory the

First, for the most part, set their faces against speculations about the future.

Bede, after speaking of the six ages of the world, says, that "as no one of the former ages has consisted exactly of a thousand years, it follows that the sixth too, under which we live, is of uncertain length, known to Him alone who has bidden His servants watch. For," he continues, "whereas all saints naturally love the hour of His advent, and desire it to be near, still, we run into danger if we presume to conclude or to proclaim, either that the hour is near or that it is far off." [1] Raban and Adson, who witnessed or heard of the splendours of Charlemagne, go so far as to indulge the vision of a great king of the Franks, who, in time to come, is to reign religiously, ere the fulfilment of the bad times of the end.[2] Theodulf indeed predicts that they were coming; but, even when the popular excitement was at its height, in the last years of the tenth century, Richard and Abbo of Fleury, and the Adson above mentioned, set themselves against it. Hardly was the dreaded crisis over, when men took heart, and began to restore and decorate the Churches; hardly had the new century run its course, when Pope Paschal the Second held a Council at Florence against Raynerius, the archbishop of that city, who had preached of the coming end.[3] Such was the change of sentiment which followed after the Pontificate of St. Gregory, the last and saddest of a line of Fathers, who thought the world was on the verge of dissolution.

The names which I have been introducing show that, among these converts to a more hopeful view of things, were Benedictine monks, members of those very associations which had given up the world as lost, and had quitted it accordingly. And the position which they occupy in their own body is sufficient

[1] De Rat. Temp. 66, 67. Elsewhere, he speaks of *futura* tempora sub Antichristo, in Sam. iv., 2, p. 300.

[2] Raban, de Antichr. opp. t. vi., p. 178. Adson, ap. Alcuin, t. ii., p. 529.

[3] So Malvenda, t. i., p. 118, calling the prelate "Fluentinus"; *vid.* Ughelli, t. iii., p. 77.

evidence that what they held, their brethren held also; and that the actual changes which had taken place in the framework of society had been followed by a change of sentiment in these religious bodies. When we look into history, to see where these preachers of new hopes were, as well as who, we find the fact plain beyond all denial; for it is the monk Alcuin who was Charlemagne's instructor, and head of the school of the palace; the monk Theodulf who was a political *employé* of the same Emperor, and bishop of Orleans; and the monk Raban who was archbishop of Mayence. How could the cloister-loving monk have come to such places of station, unless he had experienced some singular change in his sentiments? And these instances, it must be allowed, are only samples of a phenomenon which is not uncommon in these centuries. Here then we have something to explain. Why should Benedictines leave those sweet country-homes which St. Benedict bequeathed to them for the haunts of men, the seats of learning, archiepiscopal sees, and king's courts? St. Jerome had said, when Monachism was young: "If the priest's office be your choice, if a bishop's work or dignity be your attraction, live a town life, and save your soul in saving others. But, if you wish to be a monk, that is a solitary, in fact as well as in name, what have you to do with towns?" "A monk's office," he says elsewhere, "is not a teacher's but mourner's, who bewails either himself or the world." [1] This, doubtless, was the primary aim and badge of the religious institute; and if, among uncongenial offices, there were one more uncongenial to it than another, it was that of a ruler or a master of the faithful. The monk did not lecture, teach, controvert, lay down the law, or give the word of command; and for this simple reason, because he did not speak at all, because he was bound to silence. He who had given up the use of his tongue, could neither be preacher nor disputant. It follows, we repeat, that a singular change must have taken place by the ninth century in the ecclesiastical position of a monk, when we find instances

[1] Ad Paulin. Ep. 58; adv. Vigil. fin.

of his acting so differently from St. Jerome's teaching and example in the fifth.

I touched, in the Essay to which I have already referred, upon this seeming anomaly in the history of the Benedictines, while I was describing them in outline; if I did not then dwell upon it and investigate its limits, this was because I thought it advisable first to trace out the general idea of the monastic state, with as little interruption as was possible, without risking the confusion which would arise in my delineation from a premature introduction of the historical modifications to which that idea has actually been subjected. Now, however, the time has come for taking up what in that former sketch I passed over; and I propose accordingly here, after a brief reference to the circumstances under which these modifications appeared, and to the extent to which they spread, to direct attention to the principal instance of them, viz., the literary employments of the monks, and to show how singularly, after all, these employments, as carried out, were in keeping with the main idea of the monastic rule, even though they seem at first sight scarcely contained in its letter. I stated, on that former occasion, that the substance of the monastic life was *summa quies;* that its object was rest, its state retirement, and its occupations such as were unexciting and had their end in themselves. That the literature in question was consistent with these conditions will be clearly seen, when I come to describe it; first, however, let me consider the circumstances which called for it, and the hold which it had upon the general body.

2

IT IS RARE, INDEED, TO FIND the profession and the history of any institution running exactly in one and the same groove. The political revolutions which issued in the rule of Charlemagne, changing, as they did, the currents of the world, and the pilotage of St. Peter's bark, became a severe trial of the consistency of an Order, like the Benedictine, of which the maxims and the aims are grave, definite, and fixed. Demands of action and work would be made on it by the exigencies of the times at variance with its genius, and it would find itself in the dilemma of failing in efficiency on the one hand, or in faithfulness to its engagements on the other. It would be incurring either the impatience of Society, which it disappointed, or the remonstrances of its own subjects, whom it might be considered to betray.

And indeed a greater shock can hardly be fancied than that which would overtake the peaceful inhabitant of the cloister, on his finding that, after all, he so intimately depended still upon this moribund world, which he had renounced for ever, that the changes which were taking place in its condition were affecting his own. Such men, whether senators like Paulinus, or courtiers like Arsenius, or legionaries like Martin, had one and all, in their respective places and times, left the responsibilities of earth for the anticipations of heaven.[1] They had sought, in the lonely wood or the silent mountain top, the fair uncorrupted form of nature, which spoke only of the Creator. They had retired into deserts, where they could have no enemies but such as fast and prayer could subdue. They had gone where the face of man was not, except as seen in pale, ascetic apparitions like themselves. They had secured some refuge, whence they might look round at the sick world in the distance, and see it die. But, when that last hour came, it did but frustrate all their hopes, for, instead of an old world at a distance, they found they had a young world close to them. The old order of things died, sure enough; but then a new order took its place, and they themselves, by no will or expectation of their own, were in no small measure its very life. The lonely Benedictine rose from his knees and found himself a city. This was the case, not merely here or there, but everywhere; Europe was new mapped, and the monks were the principle of mapping. They had grown into large com-

[1] "Omnibus idem propositus scopus erat, idemque finis, nempe secessus à sæculi tumultu et corruptelis." Mabillon, Annal. t. i., p. 215.

munities, into abbeys, into corporations with civil privileges, into landholders with tenants, serfs, and baronial neighbours; they had become centres of population, the schools of the most cherished truths, the shrines of the most sacred confidences. They found themselves priests, rulers, legislators, feudal lords, royal counsellors, missionary preachers, controversialists; and they comprehended that unless they fled anew from the face of man, as St. Antony in the beginning, they must bid farewell to the hope of leading St. Antony's life.

In this choice of difficulties, when there was a duty to stay and a duty to take flight, the monastic bodies were not unwilling to come to a compromise with the age, and, reserving their fidelity to St. Benedict, to undertake those functions to which both the world and the Church called them. Such, that is, for the most part, was the resolve of those who found themselves in this perplexity; but it could not be supposed that there were no Antonies on earth still, and that these would be satisfied to adopt it. On the contrary, there were holy men who were but impelled into a re-action of the most rigid asceticism by this semblance of a reconciliation between their brethren and the world. Such was St. Romuald in the tenth century, the founder of the Camaldolese, who, through a long life of incredible austerities, was ever forming new monastic stations, and leaving them when formed, from love of solitude. Such St. Bruno, the founder of the Carthusians, whose conversion, as described in the well-known legend, points to the union in his day of intellectual gifts and dissoluteness of life. "Come, dear friend," he is represented as saying to some companions, concerning the awful death which he had witnessed, "what is to become of us? If a man of this doctor's rank and repute, of such literary, such scientific attainments, of such seeming-virtuous life, of so wide a reputation, is thus indubitably damned, what is to become of poor creatures of no estimation, such as we are?" [1] Such, again, was St. Stephen of Grandimont, who, when two Cardinals came to see and

[1] Marten. Ampl. Coll. t. vi., p. 153.

wonder at him in his French desert, excused himself by saying, "How could we serve churches and undertake cures who are dead to the world, and have every member of our body cut off from this life, with neither feet to walk, nor tongues to speak withal?" [1] These, and others such, sought out for themselves a seclusion and silence, most congenial to the original idea of monachism, but incompatible with those active duties, —missions, the pastoral office, teaching in the schools, and disputations with heresy,—which at the time there were none but monks to fulfil.

Would that nothing worse than the demand of such sacred duties brought the monasteries into the world, and drove these reformers into the desert! The law of God was often broken by the monks, as well as the rule of St. Benedict. Grave moral disorders arose within their walls; and that partly indeed from the seductions of ease, wealth, and the homage of mankind, but in a great measure also from the political troubles of the times, which exposed them to the tyranny of the military chief or the violence of the marauder. Relaxation will easily take place in a religious community, when, from whatever circumstance, it cannot observe its rule; and what orderly observance could there be when the country round about was the seat of war and rapine? Nay, a simpler process of monastic degeneracy followed from the high hand of military power. Kings seized the temporalities of the abbeys for their favourites, and made licentious soldiers bishops and abbots; and these, by their terrors and their bribes, fostered a lax irreligious party in the heart of these communities up and down the country. This part of the history, however, does not concern us in these pages, which are devoted to the consideration of the real work of the Benedictine, not to the injuries or interruptions which it has sustained, or to corruptions which are not its own.

On the other hand, not kings alone interfered with St. Benedict. A not less forcible overruling of his tradition took

[1] *Ibid.*, p. 1063.

place from another quarter, where there was authority for the act, and where nothing would be done except on religious principles and with religious purposes. It was a more serious interference, for the very reason that it was a legal one, proceeding from the Church herself. According to the maxim, *sacramenta propter homines,* she has never hesitated to consider, in this sense of the maxim, that "the end justifies the means"; and since Regulars of whatever sort are her own creation, she can of course alter, or adapt, or change, or bring to nought, according as her needs require, the institutions which she has created. Necessity has no law, and charity has no reserves; and she has acted accordingly. She brought the Benedictine from his cloister into the political world; but, as far as she did so, let it be observed, it was her act and not his. If then, on account of the necessities of the day, she has overruled his resolve, and made him do what neither his tradition nor his wishes suggested, such instances cannot fairly be taken, either as specimens of Benedictine work, or as modifications of the Benedictine idea.

And such cases abound. St. Benedict himself had with difficulty contemplated the idea of a priest in the ranks of his children; laying it down in his Rule, "If a priest asks to be received in any monastery, his request must not quickly be granted; but if he persists, the whole discipline of the rule is binding on him without any relaxation."—*C.* 60. But Pope Gregory, who had himself been torn violently from the cloister to fill the Pontifical throne, spared his religious brethren as little as he had been spared himself. He made a number of them bishops. From his own convent on the Cælian he sent Augustine and his companions to be apostolic missionaries to the Anglo-Saxons, and he designed to put the entire episcopate and priesthood of the newly-converted race, and thereby their secular concerns, into the hands of the monks.[1] As to the Archbishops of Canterbury, they actually were monks

[1] Thomassin. Disc. Eccl., t. i., p. 674.

down to the twelfth century.[1] This is but a specimen of what was largely carried out by the Holy See on the continent in the centuries which followed Gregory; but, I repeat, the Pope's action is external to the Benedictines, who are as little compromised by his consecrating hand as by the iron glove of the feudal tyrant.

To whatever extent, however, these innovations went, whether they were simple profanations, or were made and ratified by the wise policy of those who had a right to make them, and whatever show they make in history from the circumstance of their necessary connection with public events, with principal cities, and with prominent men, we cannot speak of them as constituting any great exception to the monastic discipline, or as exerting any considerable influence on the monastic spirit, till we have surveyed the religious institutions of Christendom as a whole, and measured them by the side of the general view thus obtained. I had occasion in my former Essay to speak of the condition of the early monks, their various families, the rise of the Benedictines, and the process of assimilation and absorption, by which at length St. Benedict gathered under his own rule the disciples of St. Martin, St. Cæsarius, and St. Columban. And even when the whole monastic body was Benedictine, it was not on that account moulded upon one type, or dependent upon one centre. As it had not spread out from one origin, so neither was it homogeneous in its construction nor simple and concordant in its action. It propagated itself variously, and had much of local character in its secondary dispositions. We cannot be certain what it was in one place by knowing what it was in another. One house attained more nearly to what may be called its normal idea than another, and therefore we have no right to argue that such quasi-secularizations as I have

[1] "Uno excepto, qui ob hanc præsumptionem et alia depositus per Romanum Pontificem fuit." Eadmer ap. Nat. Alex. t. vi., p. 599. St. Thomas in consequence made himself a monk, when he came to the see.

noticed extended much further than those particular cases which history has handed down to us.

And then, on the other hand, we must bear in mind how vast was the whole multitude of persons who professed the monastic life, and, compared with it, how small was the number of those who were called away to active political duties or who gave themselves to literature or science. They might all be subtracted from the sum total of religious, and, as far as number goes, they would not have been missed. I have already referred to the exuberance of Egyptian monachism. Antony left to Pachomius the rule of 50,000. Posthumus of Memphis presided over 5,000; Ammon over 3,000. In the one city of Oxyrinchus there were 10,000. Hilarion in Syria had from 2,000 to 3,000. Martin of Gaul was followed to the grave by 2,000 of his disciples. At that date the sees of the whole of Christendom, according to Bingham, did not go much beyond 1,700.[1] If every bishop then had been a monk, the general character of monastic life would not have been much affected. In a later age, the monastery of Bangor contained 2,000; that of Banchor, county Down, according to St. Bernard, "many thousand monks," one of whom founded as many as 100 monasteries in various places.[2] Again, the Episcopal Sees of France are given in the *Gallia Christiana* as 160, including the provinces of Utrecht, Cologne, and Treves; and precisely that number of monastic houses is said to have been founded in that country by St. Maur alone, in the very first years of the Benedictines. Trithemius, at the end of the fifteenth century, numbers the Benedictine convents as 15,000; [3] and, though we are not to suppose that each of them had the 2,000 subjects which we find at Bangor, the lowest average will swell the sum total of monks to a vast multitude. In the beginning of the previous century, a census of the Benedictines

[1] Thomassin. Disc. Eccles. t. i., p. 702. Gibbon, ch. 37. Bingh. Antiqu. b. 9.

[2] Camden, Hist. vol. iii., p. 618.

[3] Milman, Latin Christ. vol. i., p. 398.

was taken by John the Twenty-second, to which Helyot refers, according to which the Order, from its commencement up to that time, had had 22,000 archbishops and bishops, and of saints alone, 40,000. Vague calculations or statements are sufficient to represent general truths; it is difficult to determine what is the per-centage of heroic virtue in a population of regulars; if we say at random, as many saints as one in the hundred, even at this rate the number of Benedictines would reach 4,000,000, and the Episcopal portion would be only the one hundred and eightieth part of the whole Order.

More data, then, than we need, will be left to us in history, to determine the monastic vocation, even though we strike out from the list of its disciples every monk who took any secular office, as of prelate, lecturer, or disputant; nay, though we formed all those who undertook such duties into evidence of an opposite mode of life. But in fact, these very men, who in one way or another were engaged in work, which St. Benedict has not recognized by name, are themselves specimens of fidelity to their founder, and impress the Benedictine type of sanctity upon their literary or political undertakings. The proverb, *naturam expellas furcâ,* etc., holds true of religion. Whatever has life has in it a conservative principle, and a power of assimilation. Where the religious spirit was strong, it would overcome obstacles in its exercise, and revive after overthrows, and would make for itself preternatural channels for its operations, when its legitimate course was denied to it. Neither the functions of an Apostle, nor of a schoolmaster, are much akin to those of a monk; nevertheless, in a given individual, they may be reconciled, or the one merged in the other. The Benedictine missionary soon relapsed into the laborious husbandman; the champion of the faith flung his adversary, and went back to his plough or his pen; the bishop, like Peter Damian, effected, or like Boniface, contemplated, a return in his old age to the cloister which he had left. As to the schools of learning, it will be my business now to show how undisputatious was the master, and how unexciting the studies.

3

THE RISE AND EXTENSION of these Schools seems to me as great an event in the history of the Order as the introduction of the sacerdotal office into the number of its functions. If Pope Gregory took a memorable step in turning the monks of his convent into missionary bishops, charged with the conversion of England, much more remarkable was the act of Pope Vitalian, in sending the old Greek monk Theodore to the same island, to fill the vacant see of Canterbury. I call it more remarkable, because it introduced an actual tradition into the Benedictine houses, and consecrated a system by authority. It is true that from an early date in the history of monachism, extensive learning had been combined with the profession of a monk. St. Jerome was only too fond of the Cicero and Horace, whom he put aside; and, if out of the whole catalogue of ecclesiastics I had to select a literary Father, the monk Jerome, *par excellence,* would be he. In the next century Claudian Mamercus, of Vienne, employed the leisure which his monastic profession gave him to gain an extensive knowledge of Greek and Latin literature. He collected a library of Greek, Roman, and Christian books, "*quam totam, monachus,*" says Sidonius of him, "*virente in ævo, secretâ bibit institutione.*" [1] And in the century after, Cassiodorus, the contemporary of St. Benedict, is well known for combining sacred and classical studies in his monastery. The tradition, however, of the cloister was up to that time against profane literature, and Theodore reversed it.

Theodore made his appearance at the end of the century which the missionary Augustine opened, and just about the time when the whole extent of England had been converted to the Christian faith. He brought with him Greek as well as Latin Classics, and set up schools for both the learned languages in various parts of the country. Henceforth the curriculum of the Seven Sciences is found in the Benedictine

[1] Mabillon. Annal. Bened. t. i., p. 32.

Schools. From Theodore[1] proceeded Egbert and the school of York; from Egbert came Bede and the school of Jarrow; from Bede, Alcuin and the schools of Charlemagne at Paris, Tours, and Lyons. From these came Raban and the school of Fulda; from Raban, Walafrid and the school of Richenau, Lupus and the school of Ferrières. From Lupus, Heiric, Remi, and the school of Rheims; from Remi, Odo of Cluni; from the dependencies of Cluni, the celebrated Gerbert, afterwards Pope Sylvester the Second, and Abbo of Fleury, whom I have already introduced to the reader's notice, though not by name, in the former part of this sketch, as repaying a portion of the debt which the Franks owed to the Anglo-Saxons, by opening the schools of Ramsey Abbey, after the inroad of the Danes.

In addressing myself, then, at length, to the question, how such studies can be considered in keeping with the original idea of the monastic state, I think it right to repeat an explanation which I made at an earlier stage of the discussion, to the effect that I am proposing nothing more than a survey of the venerable order of St. Benedict from without; and I claim leave to do as much as this by the same right by which the humblest among us may freely and without offence gaze on sun, moon, and stars, and form his own private opinion, true or false, of their materials and their motions. And with this proviso, I remind the reader, if I have not sufficiently done so already, that the one object, immediate as well as ultimate, of Benedictine life, as history presents it to us, was to live in purity and to die in peace. The monk proposed to himself no great or systematic work, beyond that of saving his soul. What he did more than this was the accident of the hour, spontaneous acts of piety, the sparks of mercy or beneficence, struck off in the heat, as it were, of his solemn religious toil, and done and over almost as soon as they began to be. If to-day he cut down a tree, or relieved the famishing, or visited the sick, or taught the ignorant, or transcribed a page of Scripture, this

[1] *Vid.* Daniel, Etudes Classiques, p. 100, etc.; Launoy, de Scholis, Opp. t. iv., 1.

was a good in itself, though nothing was added to it to-morrow. He cared little for knowledge, even theological, or for success, even though it was religious. It is the character of such a man to be contented, resigned, patient, and incurious; to create or originate nothing; to live by tradition. He does not analyze, he marvels; his intellect attempts no comprehension of this multiform world, but on the contrary, it is hemmed in, and shut up within it. It recognizes but one cause in nature and in human affairs, and that is the First and Supreme; and why things happen day by day in this way, and not in that, it refers immediately to His will.[1] It loves the country, because it is His work; but "man made the town," and he and his works are evil. This is what may be called the Benedictine idea, viewed in the abstract; and, as being such, I gave it, in my former Essay, the title of "poetical," when contrasted with that of other religious orders; and I did so, because I considered I saw in it a congeniality, *mutatis mutandis*, with the spirit of a great Roman Poet, who has perhaps a better title to that high name than any one else, at least in this respect, as having received a wider homage than others, and that among nations in time, place, and character, further removed from each other.[2]

[1] Quoties videtur contra naturam aliquid evenire, quodammodo non contra naturam est, quia rerum natura hoc habet eximium, ut à quo est, semper ejus obtemperet jussis. Paschas. p. 155, Opp. ed. 1618.

[2] This analogy between the monastic institute and Virgil is recognized by Cassiodorus, who, after impressing on his monks, in the first place, the study of Holy Scripture and the Fathers, continues, "However, the most holy Fathers have passed no decree, binding us to repudiate secular literature; for in fact such reading prepares the mind in no slight measure for understanding the sacred writings." Presently, "In some cases indeed, Frigidus obstiterit circum præcordia sanguis," so as to hinder a man's perfect mastery whether of human or divine letters; but even with but a poor measure of knowledge, *he may be able to choose the life which follows in the next verse*, "Rura mihi et rigui placeant in vallibus amnes;" for "*it is even congenial to monks to have the care of a garden, to till the land, and to take interest in a good crop of apples.*"—De Inst. div. litt. 28. Here, by the bye, is in fact the same contrast between the "Felix qui"

Now, supposing the historical portrait of the Benedictine to be such as this, and that we were further told, that he was concerned with study and with teaching, and then were asked, keeping in mind the notion of his poetry of character, to guess what books he studied and what sort of pupils he taught, we should without much difficulty conclude that Scripture would be his literature, and that children would be the members of his school.[1] And, if we were further asked what was likely to be, after Scripture, the subject-matter of the schooling imparted to these boys, probably we should not be able to make any guess at all; but we surely should not be very much surprised to be told that the same spirit which led him to prefer the old basilicas for worship instead of any new architecture of his own inventing, and to honour his emperor or king with spontaneous loyalty more than by theological definitions, had also induced him, in the matter of education, to take up with the old books and subjects which he found ready to his hand in the pagan schools, as far as he could religiously do so, rather than to venture on any experiments or system of his own.[2] This, as I have already intimated, was the case. He adopted the Roman curriculum, professed the Seven Sciences, began with Grammar, that is, the Latin classics, and, if he sometimes finished with them, it was because his boys left him ere he had time to teach them more. The subjects he chose were his fit recompense for choosing them. He adopted the Latin writers from his love of prescription, because he found them in possession. But there were in fact no writings, after Scripture,

---

and the "Fortunatus et ille," which I have suggested to the reader in my former article (*Supra.* p. 254, note). Mr. Keble, in a passage of his beautiful Prelections, p. 648, considers Virgil to allude to Lucretius in the "Felix," and to ascribe to himself the "Fortunatus."

1 "Mos in Benedictino ordine usatissimus scholas instituere, et pueros cùm pietate tum litteris imbuere." Dachery in Lanfranc. Opp. p. 28. Brower. Antiqu. Fuld., pp. 35-38.

2 On the monastic schools taking up the imperial, *vid.* Guizot, Civil. vol. ii., p. 100, etc. *Vid.* also Ampère, Hist. Lit., t. ii., p. 277.

more congenial, from their fresh and natural beauty, and their freedom from intellectualism, to the monastic temperament. Such were his schoolbooks; and as "the boy is father of the man," the little monks, who had heard them read or pored over them, when they grew up filled the atmosphere of the monastery with the tasks and studies with which they had thus been imbued in their childhood.

For so it was, strange as it seems to our ideas, these boys were monks [1]—monks as truly as those of riper years. About St. Benedict's time the Latin Church innovated upon the discipline of former centuries, and allowed parents not only to dedicate their infants to a religious life, but to do so without any power on the part of those infants, when they came to years of reason, to annul the dedication. This discipline continued for five or six centuries, beginning with the stern Spaniards, nor ending till shortly before the pontificate of Innocent the Third. Divines argued in behalf of it from the case of infant baptism, in which the sleeping soul without being asked, is committed to the most solemn of engagements; from that of Isaac on the Mount, and of Samuel, and from the sanction of the Mosaic Law; and they would be confirmed in their course by the instances of compulsion, not uncommon in the early centuries, when high magistrates or wealthy heads of families were suddenly seized on by the populace or by synods, and, against their remonstrances, tonsured, ordained, and consecrated, before they could well take breath and realize to themselves their change of station. Nor must we forget the old Roman law, the spirit of which they had inherited, and which gave to the father the power even of life and death over his refractory offspring.

However, childhood is not the age at which the severity of the law would be felt, which bound a man by his parent's act to the service of the cloister. While these oblates were but children, they were pretty much like other children; they threw a grace over the stern features of monastic asceticism, and

[1] Thomass., Disc. Eccles., t. i., 821.

peopled the silent haunts of penance with a crowd of bright innocent faces. "Silence was pleased," to use the poet's language, when it was broken by the cheerful, and sometimes, it must be confessed, unruly voices of a set of school-boys. These would sometimes, certainly, be inconveniently loud, especially as St. Benedict did not exclude from his care lay-boys, destined for the world. It was more than the devotion of some good monks could bear; and they preferred some strict Reform, which, among its new provisions, prohibited the presence of these uncongenial associates. But, after all, it was no great evil to place before the eyes of austere manhood and unlovely age a sight so calculated to soften and to cheer. It was not adolescence, with its curiosity, its pride of knowledge and its sensitiveness, with its disputes and emulations, with its exciting prizes and its impetuous breathless efforts, which St. Benedict undertook to teach; he was no professor in a University. His convent was an infant school, a grammar school, and a seminary; it was not an academy. Indeed, the higher education in that day scarcely can be said to exist. It was a day of bloodshed and of revolution; before the time of life came when the University succeeds the School, the student had to choose his profession. He became a clerk or a monk, or else he became a soldier.

The fierce northern warriors, who had won for themselves the lands of Christendom with their red hands, rejoiced to commit their innocent offspring to the custody of religion and of peace. Nay, sometimes with the despotic will, of which I have just now spoken, they dedicated them, from or before their birth, to the service of Heaven. They determined that some at least of their lawless race should be rescued from the contamination of blood and licence, and should be set apart in sacred places to pray for their kindred. The little beings,[1] of three or four or five years old, were brought in the

[1] Calmet, Reg. Bened., t. ii., pp. 2, 4, 116, 278, 325-6, 380, 385. *Vid.* also Thomassin. Disc. Eccl., t. i., p. 821, and Magagnotti's Dissert. in Fleury's Disc. Pop. Dei.

arms of those who gave them life to accept at their bidding the course in which that life was to run. They were brought into the sanctuary, spoke by the mouth of their parents, as at the font, put out their tiny hand for the sacred corporal to be wrapped round it, received the cowl, and took their place as monks in the monastic community. In the first ages of the Benedictine Order, these children were placed on a level with their oldest brethren. They took precedence according to their date of admission, and the grey head gave way to them in choir and refectory, if junior to them in monastic standing. They even voted in the election of abbot, being considered to speak by divine instinct, as the child who cried out, "Ambrose is Bishop." [1] If they showed waywardness in community meetings, inattention at choir, ill behaviour at table, which certainly was not an impossible occurrence, they were corrected by the nods, the words, or the blows of the grave brother who happened to be next them: it was not till an after time that they had a prefect of their own, except in school hours.

That harm came from this remarkable discipline is only the suggestion of our modern habits and ideas; that it was not expedient for all times, follows from the fact that at a certain date it ceased to be permitted. However, that, in those centuries in which it was in force, its result was good, is seen in the history of the heroic men whom it nurtured, and might have been anticipated from the principle which it embodied. The monastery was intended to be the paternal home, not the mere refuge of the monk: it was an orphanage, not a reformatory; father and mother had abandoned him, and he grew up from infancy in the new family which had adopted him. He was a child of the house; there were stored up all the associations of his wondering boyhood, and there would lie the hopes and interests of his maturer years. He was to seek for sympathy in his brethren, and to give them his own sym-

[1] Calmet, t. ii., p. 324. This early dedication of the monk might tend to suggest or defend the abuse of boy priests. *Vid.* St. Bernard, de Off. Ep. 7.

pathy in return. He lived and died in their presence. They prayed for his soul, cherished his memory, were proud of his name, and treasured his works. A pleasing illustration of this brotherly affection meets us in the life of Walafrid Strabo, Abbot of Richenau, whose poems, written by him when a boy of fifteen and eighteen, were preserved by his faithful friends, and thus remain to us at this day. Walafrid is but one out of many, whose names are known in history, dedicated from the earliest years to the cloister. St. Boniface, Apostle of Germany, was a monk at the age of five; St. Bede came to Wiremouth at the age of seven; St. Paul of Verdun is said by an old writer to have left his cradle for the cloister; St. Robert entered it as soon as he was weaned; Pope Paschal the Second was taken to Cluni, Ernof to Bec, the Abbot Suger to St. Denis, from their "most tender infancy."

4

INFANTS CAN BUT GAZE ABOUT at what surrounds them, and their learning comes to them through their eyes. In the instances I have been considering, their minds would receive the passive impressions which were made on them by the monastic scene, and would be moulded by the composed countenances and solemn services which surrounded them. Such was the education of these little ones, till perhaps the age of seven; when, under the title of *pueri,*[1] they commenced their formal school-time, and committed to memory their first lesson. That lesson was the Psalter—that wonderful manual of prayer and praise, which, from the time when its various portions were first composed down to the last few centuries, has been the most precious *viaticum* of the Christian mind in its journey through the wilderness. In early times St. Basil speaks of it as the popular devotion in Egypt, Africa, and Syria; and St. Jerome had urged its use upon the Roman ladies whom he directed. All monks were enjoined to know it by heart; the

[1] Calmet, t. i., p. 495.

young ecclesiastics learned it by heart; no bishop could be ordained without knowing it by heart; and in the parish schools it was learned by heart. The Psalter, with the Lord's Prayer and Creed, constituted the *sine quâ non* condition of discipleship. At home pious mothers, as the Lady Helvidia, the mother of St. Leo the Ninth, taught their children the Psalter. It was only, then, in observance of a universal law [1] that the Benedictine children were taught it;—they mastered it, and then they passed into the secular schoolroom, and were introduced to the study of grammar.[2]

By Grammar, it is hardly necessary to say, was not meant, as now, the mere analysis or rules of language, as denoted by the words etymology, syntax, prosody; but rather it stood for scholarship, that is, such an acquaintance with the literature of a language as is implied in the power of original composition and the *vivâ voce* use of it. Thus Cassiodorus defines it to be "skill in speaking elegantly, gained from the best poets and orators;" St. Isidore, "the science of speaking well;" and Raban, "the science of interpreting poets and historians, and the rule of speaking and writing well." In the monastic school, the language of course was Latin; and in Latin literature first came Virgil; next Lucan and Statius; Terence, Sallust, Cicero; Horace, Persius, Juvenal; and of Christian poets, Prudentius, Sedulius, Juvencus, Aratus. Thus we find that the monks of St. Alban's, near Mayence, had standing lectures in Cicero, Virgil, and other authors. In the school of Paderborne there were lectures in Horace, Virgil, Statius, and Sallust. Theodulf speaks of his juvenile studies in the Christian authors, Sedulius

[1] Thomass. Disc., t. ii., p. 280, etc.

[2] The following sketch is drawn up from the works of the Benedictines, in Bibl. Max. Patr., tomm. 14, 15, 17, 18, 21; Mabillon's Acta SS. Bened.; Ceillier's Auteurs, tomm. 18-20; Neander's Hist., vol. vi., (Bohn); Guizot, Hist. Civil., vol. ii., (Bohn); Ampère, Hist. Lit. t. iii., and two recent works, Mgr. Landriot's Ecoles Littéraires, and P. Daniel's Etudes Classiques, to which I am much indebted for many points of detail. *Vid.* also M. l'Abbé Lalanne's Influence des Pères, and P. Cahour's Etudes Classiques.

and Paulinus, Aratus, Fortunatus, Juvencus, and Prudentius, and in the classical Virgil and Ovid. Gerbert, afterwards Sylvester the Second, after lecturing his class in logic, brought it back again to Virgil, Statius, Terence, Juvenal, Persius, Horace, and Lucan. A work is extant of St. Hildebert's, supposed to be a school exercise; it is scarcely more than a cento of Cicero, Seneca, Horace, Juvenal, Persius, Terence, and other writers. Horace he must have almost known by heart.

Considering the number of authors which have to be studied in order to possess a thorough knowledge of the Latin tongue, and the length to which those in particular run which are set down in the above lists, we may reasonably infer, that with the science of Grammar the Benedictine teaching began and ended, excepting of course such religious instruction as is rather the condition of Christian life than the acquisition of knowledge. At fourteen, when the term of boyhood was completed,[1] the school-time commonly ended too, the lay youths left for their secular career, and the monks commenced the studies appropriate to their sacred calling. The more promising youths, however, of the latter class were suffered or directed first to proceed to further secular studies; and, in order to accompany them, we must take some more detailed view of the curriculum, of which Grammar was the introductory study.

This curriculum,[2] derived from the earlier ages of heathen philosophy, was transferred to the use of the Church on the authority of St. Augustine, who in his *de Ordine* considers it to be the fitting and sufficient preparation for theological learning. It is hardly necessary to refer to the history of its formation; we are told how Pythagoras prescribed the study of arithmetic, music, and geometry; how Plato and Aristotle insisted on grammar and music, which, with gymnastics, were the substance of Greek education; how Seneca speaks, though not as approving, of grammar, music, geometry, and astronomy

[1] Calmet, Reg., t. i., p. 495.

[2] Brucker, Phil. t. iii., p. 594, etc. Appul. Florid. iv. 20.

as the matter of education in his own day; and how Philo, in addition to these, has named logic and rhetoric. Augustine, in his enumeration of them, begins with arithmetic and grammar, including under the latter history; then he speaks of logic and rhetoric; then of music, under which comes poetry, as equally addressing the ear; lastly, of geometry and astronomy, which address the eye. The Alexandrians, whom he followed, arranged them differently; viz., grammar, rhetoric, and logic or philosophy,[1] which branched off into the four mathematical sciences of arithmetic, music, geometry, and astronomy. And this order was adopted in Christian education, the first three sciences being called the Trivium, the last four the Quadrivium.

Grammar was taught in all these schools; but for those who wished to proceed further than the studies of their boyhood, seats of higher education had been founded by Charlemagne in the principal cities of his Empire, under the name of public schools,[2] which may be considered the shadow, and even the nucleus of the Universities which arose in a subsequent age. Such were the schools of Paris, Tours, Rheims, and Lyons in France; Fulda in Germany; Bologna in Italy Nor did they confine themselves to the Seven Sciences above mentioned, though it is scarcely to be supposed that, in any science whatever, except Grammar, they professed to impart more than the elements. Thus we read of St. Bruno of Segni (A.D. 1080), after being grounded in the *litteræ humaniores*, as a boy, by the monks of St. Perpetuus near Aste, seeking the rising school of Bologna for the *altiores scientiæ*.[3] St. Abbo of Fleury (A.D. 990), after mastering, in the monastery of that place, grammar, arithmetic, logic, and music, went to Paris and Rheims for philosophy and astronomy; and afterwards taught himself

[1] The Quadrivium was called "philosophy." Ampère, t. iii., p. 267.

[2] Charlemagne's schools taught Grammar, Rhetoric, Leges, Canones, Theology biblical and patristical. *Vid.* Thomass. Disc. t. iii., pp. 271-294; Ampère, Hist., t. iii., p. 267.

[3] Vit. ap. Brun. Opp. ed. 1759.

rhetoric and geometry. Raban (A.D. 822) left the school of Fulda for a while for Alcuin's lectures, and learned Greek of a native of Ephesus. Walafrid (A.D. 840) passed from Richenau to Fulda. St. William (A.D. 908), dedicated by his parents to St. Benedict at St. Michael's near Vercellæ, proceeded to study at Pavia. Gerbert (A.D. 990), one of the few cultivators of physics, after Fleury and Orleans, went to Spain.[1] St. Wolfgang (A.D. 994), after private instruction, went to Richenau. Lupus (A.D. 840), after Ferrières, was sent for a time to Fulda. Fulbert too of Chartres (A.D. 1000), though not a monk, may be mentioned as sending his pupils in like manner to finish their studies at schools of more celebrity than his own.[2]

History furnishes us with specimens of the subjects taught in this higher education. We read of Gerbert lecturing in Aristotle's Categories and the Isagogæ of Porphyry; St. Theodore taught the Anglo-Saxon youths Greek and mathematics; Alcuin, all seven sciences at York; and at some German monasteries there were lectures in Greek,[3] Hebrew, and Arabic. The monks of St. Benignus at Dijon gave lectures in medicine; the abbey of St. Gall had a school of painting and engraving; the blessed Tubilo of that abbey was mathematician, painter, and musician.[4] We read of another monk of the same monastery, who was ever at his carpentry when he was not at the altar; and of another, who worked in stone. Hence

[1] Brucker, t. iii., p. 646.

[2] Thomass. Disc. t. ii., pp. 296-8.

[3] Fredegodus of Canterbury (A.D. 960) wrote in Greek. *Vid.* Cave's Hist. Litt. in nom. In the Life of St. Odo of Canterbury we read that his patron Athelm "Græcâ et Latinâ linguâ magistris edocendum eum tradidit, quarum linguarum *plerisque* tunc temporis in gente Anglorum usus erat, à discipulis beatæ memoriæ Theodori archiepiscopi profectus. Factusque est in utrâque linguâ valdè gnarus, ita ut posset poemata fingere, continuare prosam, et omnia, quicquid ei animo sederet, luculentissimo sermone proferre." Mabillon, Act. Sæc. v., p. 289.

[4] I quoted in my former article a passage from Brower on the arts cultivated at Fulda. For a parallel in the East, *vid.* the account of the monks of Theodore Studita, Vit. p. 29, Sismond.

Vitruvius was in repute with them. Another accomplishment was that of copying manuscripts, which they did with a perfection unknown to the scholastic age which followed them.[1]

These manual arts, far more than the severer sciences, were the true complement of the Benedictine ideal of education, which, intellectually considered, was, after all, little more than a fair or a sufficient acquaintance with Latin literature. Such is the testimony of the ablest men of the time. "To pass from Grammar to Rhetoric, and then in course to the other liberal sciences," says Lupus, speaking of France, is *fabula tantum.*[2] "It has ever been the custom in Italy," says Glaber Radulphus, writing of the year 1000, "to neglect all arts but Grammar."[3] Grammar, moreover, in the sense in which we have defined it, is no superficial study, nor insignificant instrument of mental cultivation, and the school-task of the boy became the life-long recreation of the man. Amid the serious duties of their sacred vocation the monks did not forget the books which had arrested and refined their young imagination. Let us turn to the familiar correspondence of some of these more famous Benedictines, and we shall see what were the pursuits of their leisure, and the indulgences of their relaxation. Alcuin, in his letters to his friends, quotes Virgil again and again; he also quotes Horace, Terence, Pliny, besides frequent allusions to the heathen philosophers. Lupus quotes Horace, Cicero, Suetonius, Virgil, and Martial. Gerbert quotes Virgil, Cicero, Horace, Terence, and Sallust. Petrus Cellensis quotes Horace, Seneca, and Terence. Hildebert quotes Virgil and Cicero, and refers to Diogenes, Epictetus, Crœsus, Themistocles, and other personages of ancient history. Hincmar of Rheims quotes Horace. Paschasius Radbert's favourite authors were Cicero and Terence. Abbo of Fleury was especially familiar with Terence, Sallust, Virgil, and Horace; Peter the Venerable, with

[1] Guizot, Civil., t. ii., p. 236; Hallam, Lit., i., 1, 87.

[2] Ep. 1.

[3] Muratori, Dissert. xliii., p. 831.

Virgil and Horace; Hepidann of St. Gall took Sallust as a model of style.[1]

Nor is their anxiety less to enlarge the range of their classical reading. Lupus asks Abbot Hatto through a friend for leave to copy Suetonius's *Lives of the Cæsars,* which is in the monastery of St. Boniface in two small *codices.* He sends to another friend to bring with him the Catilinarian and Jugurthan Wars of Sallust, the *Verrines* of Cicero, and any other volumes which his friend happens to know either that he has not, or possesses only in faulty copies, bidding him withal beware of the robbers on his journey. Of another friend he asks the loan of Cicero's *de Rhetoricâ,* his own copy of which is incomplete, and of Aulus Gellius. In another letter he asks the Pope for Cicero's *de Oratore,* the *Institutions* of Quintilian, and the commentary of Donatus upon Terence. In like manner Gerbert tells Abbot Gisilbert that he has the beginning of the *Ophthalmicus* of the philosopher Demosthenes, and the end of Cicero's *Pro rege Deiotaro;* and he wants to know if he can assist in completing them for him. He asks a friend at Rome to send him by Count Guido the copies of Suetonius and Aurelius, which belong to his archbishop and himself; he requests Constantine, the lecturer (scholasticus) at Fleury, to bring him Cicero's *Verrines* and *de Republicâ,* and he thanks Remigius, a monk of Treves, for having begun to transcribe for him the *Achilleid* of Statius, though he had been unable to proceed with it for want of a copy. To other friends he speaks of Pliny, Cæsar, and Victorinus. Alcuin's Library contained Pliny, Aristotle, Cicero, Virgil, Statius, and Lucan; and he transcribed Terence with his own hand.

Not only the memory of their own youth, but the necessity of transmitting to the next generation what during it they had learned themselves, kept them loyal to their classical acquirements. They were, in this aspect of their history, not unlike the fellows in our modern English universities, who first learn

[1] The School of Ouen produced 500 writers in 50 years. Landriot, p. 138. *Vid.* the curious Letter of Gunzo, Marten., Ampl. Coll. t. i., col. 294.

and then teach. It is impossible, indeed, to overlook their resemblance generally to the elegant scholar of a day which is now waning, especially at Oxford, such as Lowth or Elmsley, Copleston or Keble, Howley or Parr, who thought little of science or philosophy by the side of the authors of Greece and Rome. Nor is it too much to say that the Colleges in the English Universities may be considered in matter of fact to be the lineal descendants or heirs of the Benedictine schools of Charlemagne. The modern of course has vastly the advantage in the comparison; for he is familiar with Greek, has an exacter criticism and purer taste, and a more refined cultivation of mind. He writes, verse at least, far better than the Benedictine, who had commonly little idea of it; and he has the accumulated aids of centuries in the shape of dictionaries and commentaries. I am not writing a panegyric on the classical learning of the dark age, but describing what it was; and, with this object before me, I observe that, whatever the monks had not, a familiar knowledge and a real love they had of the great Latin writers, and I assert, moreover, that that knowledge and love were but in keeping with the genius and character of their institute. For they instinctively recognized in the graceful simplicity of Virgil or of Horace, in his dislike of the great world, of political contests and of ostentatious splendour, in his unambitious temper and his love of the country, an analogous gift to that religious repose, that distaste for controversy, and that innocent cheerfulness which were the special legacy of St. Benedict to his children. This attachment to the classic is well expressed by a monk of Paderborn,[1] who, when he would describe the studies of the place, suffers his prose almost to dissolve into verse, as he names his beloved authors.

Viguit Horatius, magnus et Virgilius,
Crispus et Sallustius, et urbanus Statius.

Ludusque fuit omnibus, insudare versibus,
Et dictaminibus jucundisque cantibus.

[1] *Vid.* Daniel, p. 115. Landriot, p. 139.

The latter of these stanzas, as they may be called, illustrates what we have wished to express, in speaking of the classical temperament of the Benedictines. As far as they allowed themselves in any recreation, which was not of a sacred nature, they found it in these beautiful authors, who might be considered as the prophets of the human race in its natural condition. How strongly they contrast in this respect with the scholastic age which swallowed them up! Amid the religious or ecclesiastical matters which were the subject of their correspondence, questions of grammar and criticism are mooted, and a loving curiosity about the nicety of languages is temperately indulged. Whether *rubus* is masculine or feminine is argued from analogy and by induction; Ambrose makes it feminine, and the names of trees, which have no plurals, are feminine, as *populus, fraxinus;* on the other hand Virgil makes it masculine, and Priscian allows it to be an exception to the rule. Again, is it *dispexeris* or *despexeris*? Priscian says *despicio,* and makes *de* answer to the Greek κατὰ, *down;* but the Greek in the Psalm is, not κατίδῃς, but ὑπερίδῃς, *above.* Again, is the penultima of *voluerimus* long or short? long, says Servius on Virgil.[1] They carry their fidelity to the Classics into their own poetical compositions; far from resigning themselves to that merely rhythmical versification, which is ever grateful to the popular ear, which had been in use from the Augustan age, and which afterwards developed into *rhyme,*[2] they rather affect the archaisms and the licences of the classical times. "*Contraria rerum,*" "*genus omne animantum,*" "*retundier,*" "*formarier,*" "*benedicier,*" "*scribier,*" "*indupediret,*" "*indunt,*" savour of Ennius or Lucretius rather than of Virgil. They keep to the Augustan metres, and they are never unwilling to use them. Their theological treatises begin, their epistles to kings end, with hexameters and pentameters. They moralize, they protest, they soothe their sorrows, they ask favours, they compile chronicles, they record their journeys in heroics, elegiacs, and epigrams. They are versifiers, one and all, or at least those

[1] Alcuin, Ep. 23; Lupus, Ep. pp. 5, 8, 20, 34.

[2] *Vid.* Muratori Dissert. 40.

whose names or works are best known in history, or in our libraries. The habit was formed at school, and it endured through life. Some indeed, as Lupus or Gerbert, had too many occupations to indulge in it; but others, as Theodulf, bishop of Orleans, return to it in the evening of life, after the manner of Gregory Nazianzen in patristic times, or Lord Wellesley in our own. Bede, Alcuin, Aldhelm, Raban, Theodulf, Hildebert, Notgar, Adelhard, Walafrid, Agobard, Florus, Modoin, Heiric, Gerbert, Angilbert, Herman, Abbo, Odo, Hucbald, Lupus, Fridouard, Paschasius, with many others, all wrote verse. I am not insinuating that they wrote it so happily as the Patriarch of Constantinople or the Governor-General of India; on the contrary, it was not their *forte;* but Florus, for instance, is eloquent, and Walafrid Virgilian.[1] Their subjects, when most sacred, are such as the great phenomena of nature, the country, woods, mountains, flocks, and herds, plants, flowers, and others which I have called Benedictine. I have no space for extracts; but here is one, as a specimen of what I mean, when I speak of the alliance of St. Benedict and Virgil. It is the conclusion of the *Hortulus* of Walafrid, and presents us with a very pretty picture of an old monk amid children and fruit trees:—

> Hæc tibi servitii munuscula vilia parvi
> Strabo tuus, Grimalde pater! . . . . . .
> Ut, cùm conseptu viridis consederis horti,
> Inter apricatas frondenti germine malos,
> Persicus imparibus crines ubi dividit umbris,
> Dum tibi cana legunt tenerâ lanugine poma
> Ludentes pueri, schola lætabunda tuorum,
> Atque volis ingentia mala capacibus indunt,
> Grandia conantes includere corpora palmis,
> Quo moneare habeas nostri, pater alme, laboris,
> Dum relegis quæ dedo volens, interque legendum
> Et vitiosa secas bonus, et meliora reformas.

[1] Du Pin, however, says, "Theodulf's poems are very fine." Cent. viii., p. 126, ed. 1699. "Tolerable poetry," says Dr. Murdock, on Mosheim, vol. ii., p. 151.

I have taken a liberty with the last line, which any how is somewhat feeble.

Their prose is superior to their verse; it has little claim indeed to the purity of taste and of vocabulary, which we call classical; but it is good Latin both in structure and in idiom. At any rate the change is wonderful, when we pass from the Benedictine centuries to the Dominican which followed.

In so speaking I have no disrespectful meaning as regards those great authors whose Latinity happens not to be equal to their sanctity or their intellectual power. Their merit, in respect to language, is of a different kind; it consists in their success in making the majestic and beautiful Latin tongue minister to scientific uses, for which it was never intended. But, because they have this merit of their own, that is no reason why we should deny to the writers who preceded them the praise of being familiar with the ancient language itself, a praise which is justly theirs, though seldom allowed to them. The writers of the Benedictine centuries are supposed to have the barbarism, without the science, of the Dominican period; and modern critics, who wish to be fair, seem to consider it a great concession, if they grant that an age must at least have some smattering in classical literature, which, as the foregoing pages show, is ever quoting it and referring to it. Thus Mr. Hallam, in the opening chapter of his *Literature of Europe*, can but say, "Alcuin's own poems *could at least not* have been written by one *unacquainted* with Virgil." Again: "From this time, though *quotations* from the Latin poets, especially Ovid and Virgil, and *sometimes* from Cicero, are *not very* frequent, they occur sufficiently to show that manuscripts had been brought to *this* side of the Alps."—p. 7. Some pages lower he says, quoting some of St. Adelhard's verses, "the quotation from Virgil in the ninth century *perhaps deserves remark, though* in one of Charlemagne's monasteries it is not by any means *astonishing;*" as if Virgil were not the text-book in the northern schools, as my foregoing quotations make clear, and ignorance, in that day, when it was to be found, had not its special seat in the southern side of the Alps, rather than in France and Germany. Passages such as these in men of wide research are simply perplexing. I ask myself whether I have rightly understood their words, or whether I read wrongly the historical facts which they profess to be generalizing. Perhaps it is that I assume without warrant that the quotations of Alcuin and the rest are *bonâ fide* such, and not derived, as some have said, from catenas of passages, commonplace books, or traditionary use; [1] but such an account of them is absolutely inconsistent, first, with the testimonies which I have above cited, as to the actual studies of the young, and next, with the literary habits which those studies actually formed in the persons who were exercised in them. Can it be that critics of the nineteenth century, possessing the fine appreciation of classical poetry, imparted in the public schools of England, glance their eyes over the rude versification of Theodulf or Alcuin, and consider it the measure of the secular learning which gave it birth? M. Guizot, Protestant as he is, is a fairer and kinder judge of the cloister literature than Mr. Hallam or Dean Milman.

5

AND NOW, TO PREVENT misapprehension of my meaning in this review of the Benedictine Schools, I have two remarks to make before I bring it to an end, one on each side of the description to which that review has led me.

On the one hand, the classical studies and tastes which I have been illustrating, even though foreign to the monastic

[1] "Bede . . . had some familiarity with Virgil, Ovid, Lucan, Statius, and even Lucretius. . . . It may be questioned, however, whether many of the citations from ancient authors, often adduced from medieval writers, as indicating their knowledge of such authors, are more than traditionary, almost proverbial, insulated passages, brilliant fragments, broken off from antiquity, and reset again and again by writers borrowing them from each other, but who had never read another word of the lost poet, orator, or philosopher."—Milman, Latin Christ. vol. ii., p. 39.

masses, as they may be called,—even though historically traceable to the mission of St. Theodore from the Holy See to England,—must still be regarded a true offspring of the Benedictine discipline, and in no sense the result of seasons or places, of relaxation and degeneracy. At first sight, indeed, there is some plausibility in saying that with the change of times a real change came over a portion of the great family of monks, and that however usefully employed, Cassiodorus or Theodore, Alcuin or Walafrid, did certainly fall from their proper vocation, and did really leave it to Romuald and others like him, to be, not only the most faithful imitators, but the only true children of the ancient monachism. And, in confirmation of this view, it might be added that the same circumstances which led the monks to literary pursuits, led them to political entanglements also, and that in the same persons, as Theodulf, Lupus, and Gerbert, learning and secular engagements were combined; and that, as no one would say that the cares of office were proper to a monk's vocation, as little could be fairly included in it classical attainments. Whatever be the best mode of treating this difficulty, which of course demands a candid and equitable consideration, here, in addition to what I have said by the way, I shall make one answer of a different kind, which seems to me conclusive, and there leave the question. When, then, I am asked whether these studies are but the accidents and the signs of a time of religious declension, I reply that they are found in those very persons, on the contrary, who were pre-eminent in devotional and ascetic habits, and who were so intimately partakers in the spirit of mortification, whether of St. Benedict or St. Romuald, that they have come down to us with the reputation of saints,—nay, have actually received canonization or beatification. Theodore himself is a saint; Alcuin and Raban are styled *beati;* Hildebert is "venerable;" Bede and Aldhelm are saints; and we can say the same of St. Angilbert, St. Abbo, St. Bertharius, St. Adelhard, St. Odo, and St. Paschasius Radbert. At least Catholics must feel the full force of this argument; for they cannot permit themselves to attribute any dereliction of vocation to those, whom the Church holds up as choice specimens of divine power, and, as being such, sealed by miracle for eternal bliss.

This is my remark on one side the question; on the other, it must not of course be supposed,—indeed my last remark negatives the idea,—that critical scholarship or classical erudition was the business of life, even in the case of this minority of the monastic family, who took so prominent a part in the education of their time. I have distinctly said that, after their school years, the monks were as little taken up with the classics, *exceptis excipiendis,* as members of parliament or country gentlemen at the present day. They had their serious engagements, as statesmen have now, though of a different kind, and to these they gave themselves. Theology was their one study; to theology secular literature ministered, first as an aid and an ornament, then as a relaxation, amid the mental exertion which it involved. Nor was this literature cultivated without some holy jealousy on the part of the cultivators; *nuces pueris;*—there was a time of life when it ought to be put aside; there was even danger of its seductiveness. Alcuin himself, if we may trust the account, reproved on one occasion the study, at least of the poets; and in one of his extant letters he complains of a former pupil, then raised to the episcopate, for preferring Virgil to his old master Flaccus, that is, to himself, and prays that "the four Gospels, not the twelve Æneids, may fill his breast."—*Ep.* 129. St. Paschasius, too, in spite of his love for Terence and Cicero, expresses a judgment, in one passage of his comment upon Ezekiel (*Bibl. Max. P.* t. xiv., p. 788), against the elder monks being occupied with the heathen poets and philosophers. Lanfranc, when an Irish Bishop asked him some literary question, made answer, *Episcopale propositum non decet operam dare hujusmodi studiis;* we passed in these our time of youth, but, when we took on ourselves the pastoral care, we bade them farewell."—*Ep.* 33. The instance of Pope Gregory is well known: when the Bishop of Vienne had been led to lecture in the classics, he wrote, "A fact has come to our ears, which we cannot name without a blush, that you, my brother, lecture on literature" (*grammatica*).—*Ep.* xi. 54. Such occupations, indeed, were in those centuries generally and reasonably held to be inconsistent with the calling of a Bishop.[1] St. Jerome speaks as strongly in an earlier age.

What was true of the Bishop was on the whole true of the monk also; he might perhaps have special duties as the *scholasticus* of his monastery, but ordinarily, while his manual labour was either in the field or in the *scriptorium,* so his intellectual exercises were for the most part combined with his devotional, and consisted in the study of the sacred volume. This was mainly what at that time was meant by theology. *Theologia, hoc est, Scripturarum meditatio,* says Thomassin.—*Disc. Eccl.* t. ii., p. 288. Their theology was a loving study and exposition of Holy Scripture, according to the teaching of the Fathers, who had studied and expounded it before them. It was a loyal adherence to the teaching of the past, a faithful inculcation of it, an anxious transmission of it to the next generation. In this respect it differed from the theology of the times before and after them. Patristic and scholastic theology each involved a creative action of the intellect; that this is the case as regards the Schoolmen need not be proved here; nor is it less true, though in a different way, of the theology of the Fathers. Origen, Tertullian, Athanasius, Chrysostom, Augustine, Jerome, Leo, are authors of powerful, original minds, and engaged in the production of original works. There is no greater mistake, surely, than to suppose that a revealed truth precludes originality in the treatment of it. The contrary is acknowledged in the case of secular subjects, in which it is the very triumph of originality, not to invent or discover what is not already known, but to make old things read as if they were new, from the novelty of aspect in which they are placed. This faculty of investing with associations, of applying to particular purposes, of deducing consequences, of impressing

[1] *Vid.* Thomass. Disc. Eccl., t. ii., pp. 268-286.

upon the imagination, is creative; and though false associations, applications, deductions, and impressions are often made, and were made by some theologians of the early Church, such as Origen and Tertullian, this does but prove that originality is not co-extensive with truth. And so in like manner as to Scripture; to enter into the mind of the sacred author, to follow his train of thought, to bring together to one focus the lights which various parts of Scripture throw upon his text, and to give adequate expression to the thoughts thus evolved, in other words, the breadth of view, the depth, or the richness, which we recognize in certain early expositions, is a creation. Nor is it an inferior faculty to discriminate, rescue, and adjust the truth, which a fierce controversy threatens to tear in pieces, at a time when the ecclesiastical atmosphere is thick with the dust of the conflict, when all parties are more or less in the wrong, and the public mind has become so bewildered as not to be able to say what it does or what it does not hold, or even what it held before the strife of ideas began. In such circumstances, to speak the word evoking order and peace, and to restore the multitude of men to themselves and to each other, by a reassertion of what is old with a luminousness of explanation which is new, is a gift inferior only to that of revelation itself.

This gift is not the characteristic of the history, nor is it akin to the spirit or the object, as I have described them, of the Benedictine Order. At the time of which I am writing, the Christian athlete, after running one length of the stadium, was taking breath before commencing a second course: the Christian combatant was securing his conquests in the wide field of thought by a careful review and catalogue of them, before going forth to make new ones. He was fitly represented, therefore, at such a season, by the Benedictine, faithful, conscientious, affectionate, and obedient, like the good steward who keeps an eye on all his master's goods, and preserves them from waste or decay. First, then, he compared, emendated, and transcribed the text of Scripture; next he transcribed the Fathers who directly or indirectly commented on it; then he attached to its successive portions such passages from the Fathers as illustrated them; then he fused those catenated passages into one homogeneous comment of his own: and there he stopped. He seldom added anything original. In such a task the skill would lie in the happy management and condensation of materials brought together from very various quarters, and here he would find the advantage of the literary habits gained in his early education. A taste for criticism would be another result of it, which we see in Bede, and which would result in so much of leaning to the literal interpretation of Scripture as was consistent with the profession of editing and republishing, as it may be called, the comments of the Fathers. We see this tendency in Alcuin, Paschasius, and especially in Druthmar. Indeed, Alcuin's greatest work was the revision of the Scripture text.[1] Other commentators were Ansbert, Smaragdus, Haymo, Remi, and the Irish Sedulius, if he was a Benedictine. The most widely celebrated, however, of these works was the *Glossa Ordinaria* of Walafrid, which was in great measure an abridgement of Raban's *Catena*, and became a standard authority in the centuries which followed.

6

BUT TIMES WERE APPROACHING when such peaceful labours were not sufficient for the Church's needs, and when theology required to be something more than the rehearsal of what her champions had achieved and her sages had established in ages passed away. As the new Christian society, which Charlemagne inaugurated, grew, its intellect grew with it, and at last began to ask questions and propose difficulties, which *catenæ* and commentaries could not solve. Hard-headed objectors were not to be subdued by the reverence for an-

[1] "Codex, Alcuini labor, in Vallicellensi Bibliothecâ asservatur." Baron. an. 778.

tiquity and the amenities of polite literature; and, when controversies arose, the Benedictines found themselves, from the necessity of the times, called to duties which were as uncongenial to the spirit of their founder as the political engagements of St. Dunstan or St. Bernard. Nor must it be supposed that the other parts of Christendom did not furnish matters demanding their theological acumen, even though none had arisen in the Frankish Churches themselves. And here, I conceive, we have this remarkable confirmation of the identity of the Benedictine character, that, in proportion as these matters were in substance already decided by the Fathers, they acquitted themselves well in the controversy, and in proportion as these matters demanded some original explanations, the monastic disputants were less successful. And in speaking of them, I speak of course of their age itself, of which they were the leading teachers, and which they represent. And I speak, not of individual monks, who would have the natural talents, the intellectual acuteness and subtlety of other men, but of the action of the monasteries, considered as bodies and historically, which is the true measure of the mental discipline to which their Rule subjected them. I speak of those whose direct duty lay, by virtue of their vocation, not in confronting doubts but in suppressing them, and who were not likely on the whole to succeed in exercises of reason in which they had no practice.

One of the countries to which I allude, as being at the era of Charlemagne the seat of theological error, was Spain, then under the power of the Saracens. The victorious infidels, in spite of their general toleration of Catholicism, of course could not avoid inflicting on it the most serious injuries. One of these was the decay or destruction of its schools,[1] and the want of education in its priesthood, which was the consequence. Another injury lay in the circumstance that Mahometanism, being a misbelief or heresy, more than a direct denial of the faith,

[1] "The Spanish Latin of that period was unquestionably extremely corrupt." Neander, Hist., vol. vi., p. 118.

might think it had a right to interfere with it, and had a tendency to corrupt it by the insinuation of its own opinions and traditions about Christian facts and doctrines. Mahomet is said to have been indebted to the teaching of a Nestorian monk, and the demolition of images was one of the watchwords of his armies. Now, from Spain at this time proceeded the heresy of the Adoptionists, which is of a Nestorian character; and it was in Spain that Claudius of Turin matured those uncatholic opinions, especially on the subject of images, which have given him a place in ecclesiastical history.

The conflict with Nestorianism had been completed long before the time of Charlemagne; accordingly the theologians of the age, in refuting it, had but to repeat the arguments which they found ready for them in the pages of the Fathers. Alcuin was one of those who undertook the controversy, and proved himself abundantly prepared for the work. "Paulinus and Alcuin," says Professor Döllinger, "proved their point with a degree of theological acumen, and with a knowledge of the Fathers, which in that age may surprise us." [1]

Such was their success, when the doctrine in question had already been defined; but, on the other hand, the question with which Claudius's name is connected, the honour due to images, was still *sub judice,* and when the ecumenical decision came from Nicæa, from whatever cause, the Franks misunderstood and disputed it. The same great council of Frankfort, which condemned the Adoptionists, acted as a protection to the Iconoclasts of Constantinople. I am far indeed from insinuating that the Fathers of the Frankish churches really differed from the definition which came to them from the East; but even for a century afterwards those churches regarded it, to say the least, with dissatisfaction.

Meanwhile the spirit of inquiry was alive and operative even within the hearts of these peaceful monastic communities themselves. We find it, as it would seem, in one of the immediate friends and pupils of Alcuin. Fredegis, of the school of

[1] Cox's Translation, vol. iii., p. 60.

York, to whom he addressed various of his letters and works, and whom he made his successor at Tours, has left behind him an argumentative fragment of so strange a nature that it has been thought a mere exercise in disputation and not a portion of a serious work.[1] He starts, moreover, with a proposition in favour of the supremacy of reason as contrasted with authority, which, though admitting of a Catholic explanation, is capable also of being made the basis of a philosophy to which I shall immediately have occasion to allude.[2] Soon after, Gotteschalc, a monk of Orbais, taught that the decree of divine predestination has direct reference to the lost as well as the saved; and about the same time Ratramn of the monastery of Corbie, opposed the Catholic doctrine of the Holy Eucharist. But these intellectual movements within the Benedictine territory were eclipsed by a manifestation of the sceptical spirit which came from a country, where from its prevalent religious temperament such a phenomenon was little to have been expected.

There was a portion of the Western Church which had never been included in the Roman Empire, and but partially, if át all, included within the range of the Benedictine discipline. While that discipline made its way northward, became the instrument of Anglo-Saxon conversion, and even supplanted the rule of Columban in the French monasteries, the countrymen of Columban remained faithful to their old monachism, descended southwards a second time, and retaliated on the convents of the continent by a fresh introduction of themselves and their traditions. At this period, whatever may have been their literary attainments, they were most remarkable for a bold independence of mind, a curiosity, activity, and vigour of thought, which contrasted strongly with the genius of Bede and Raban. Their strength lay in those exercises of pure reason which go by the name of "philosophy," or of "wisdom." Thus in an ancient writer the Irish Scots are

[1] *Vid.* Ittig. Biblioth., p. 313.

[2] *Vid.* Neander, vol. vi., p. 161; Baluz. Miscell., t. ii., p. 56.

spoken of as *sophiâ clari.*[1] By Heric of Auxerre, in the passage so often quoted, they are described as *philosophorum greges,* venturing across the stormy sea to the wide continent of Europe. And so in the legendary account, by a monk of St. Gall, of the Irish scholars who accosted the Frankish Emperor, they are represented as crying out, "Who wants *wisdom*? who will buy *wisdom*?" Dunstan, again, is said to have learned "*philosophy*" in Ireland; and Benedict of Aniane, the second founder of the Benedictines, is expressly described as looking with suspicion on their syllogistic method, which was so hostile to the habits of mind which his own Order cultivated. These Irish scholars, indeed, were too sincere Catholics, viewing them in the mass, to warrant this jealousy; but it was not without foundation, as we shall see, as regards individuals, and at least would be amply justified in the judgments of those who differed so much from them in mental characteristics as did the Benedictines. On the other hand, there was much in the Anglo-Saxon temper intimately congenial with the latter: then, as now, the occupants of the British soil seem to have been practical rather than speculative, fond of hard work rather than of hard thought, tenacious of what they had received, jealous of novelty, the champions of law and order. Thus the English and Irish may be said so far to represent respectively the two great Orders which came in succession on the stage of ecclesiastical history; and, as they were not without their collisions at home, so we detect some instances, and may conjecture others, of their rivalry as missionaries and teachers in central Europe. We read, for instance, in the history of St. Boniface, that one of his antagonists, in his organization of the Churches, which he had founded in Germany, was an Irish priest of the name of Clement. Boniface relates, if his account is to be received to the letter, that this priest neither allowed the authority of Jerome, Augustine, or Gregory, nor of the sacred canons; that he maintained the marriage of bishops; argued from Scripture in defence of marriage with a

[1] Brucker, Philos., t. iii., p. 574.

sister-in-law, and taught a sort of universalism. Also he had to report to Pope Zacharias the false teaching of another Scottish or Irish priest, named Samson, in relation to the Sacraments.[1] Another Irishman, with whom Boniface had a quarrel, was Virgil, afterwards Bishop of Salzburgh, who has been acknowledged, as well as Boniface, for a saint. He offended Boniface by maintaining what seems like a doctrine of the existence of *antipodes.*

The antagonism between the two schools extended into the next century. Of course John Scotus Erigena, whom Charles the Bald placed in the chair of Alcuin in the School of the Palace, is the palmary specimen of the philosophical party among the Irish monks. This remarkable man, while acknowledging the authority of Revelation, propounded it as a first principle of his speculations, as Fridegis had done before him, that reason must come first, and authority second. Such a proposition indeed was faulty only in its application; for St. Austin himself had laid it down in his treatise *de Ordine.* It is self-evident, that we should not know what was revelation and what was not, unless we used our reason to decide the point. Whatever we are obliged in the event to learn from external sources, our process of inquiry must begin from within. The ancient Father to whom I have referred propounds both the principle and the sense in which it is true. "We learn things necessarily in two ways," he says, "by authority and by reason. *Tempore auctoritas, re autem ratio prior est;*" but Erigena, as is generally agreed, accounted reason, not only as the ultimate basis of religious truth, but the direct and proper warrant for it; and, armed with this principle, he proceeded to take part in the two controversies which I have already had occasion to mention, the Predestinarian and the Eucharistic. "The writings have come to us," says the church of Lyons, speaking of his tendencies, like Clement's, to universalism, "the writings have come to us, *vaniloqui et garruli hominis,* who, disputing on divine prescience and predestina-

[1] Boniface, Epp. 82, p. 237.

tion with human, or, as he boasts, philosophical reasonings, without any deference to Scripture, or regard to the authority of the Holy Fathers, has dared to define by his own independent assertion what is to be held and followed." Thus Erigena adopted Clement's argumentative basis as well as his doctrine. His views upon reason and authority are distinctly avowed in the first book of his work, *De divisione naturæ*. "You are not ignorant," he argues, "that what is *prius naturâ* ranks higher than what is *prius tempore*. We have been taught," referring apparently to St. Austin, "that reason is prior in nature, authority in time; now, whereas nature was created together with time, authority did not begin with the beginning of time and nature; on the other hand, reason had its origin with nature and time in the first beginning of things." The Scholar replies to him, "Reason itself teaches this; for authority has proceeded from right reason, reason by no means from authority. For all authority which is not approved by right reason is weak; whereas right reason, when it is fortified in its own strength, settled and immovable, need not be corroborated by the concurrence of any authority."—*Lib.* 1. *n.* 71. In like manner, in the commencement of his work on Predestination, while appealing to St. Austin, he makes philosophy and religion convertible terms.[1]

Erigena was succeeded in the Schola Palatii by Mannon, who inherited his master's philosophy. He himself had called Plato the greatest of philosophers, and Aristotle the most subtle of investigators; and, according to the testimony of Friar Bacon, he was a successful interpreter of the latter writer; and Mannon, in like manner, has left commentaries on Plato's *de Legibus* and *de Republicâ* and on Aristotle's *Ethics*. About the same time flourished in France another Irishman, named Macarius; and he too showed the same leaning towards pantheism which has been imputed to Erigena.[2] From him this error was introduced into the monastery of Corbie. At a latter

[1] Guizot, Civil., t. ii., p. 375.

[2] Lanigan. Hist., vol. iii., p. 320.

date we hear of one Patrick, who from his name may be considered as an Irishman, holding the same heterodox opinion about the Eucharist which Ratramn and Erigena advanced.[1]

As to the two controversies, which have been mentioned more than once, while they exemplify to us the *scholasticismus ante scholasticos* then in action, they afford fresh illustrations also of the insufficiency of such instruments as the Church at that time had in her service to meet this formidable antagonist of her religious supremacy. No mind equal to Erigena appeared on the side of traditionary teaching; and the vigour with which the Adoptionists were condemned and the *Filioque* inserted in the Creed did not manifest itself in the dealing of the Frankish Synods with the bold doctrine of Gotteschalc and Ratramn. Gotteschalc, as I have said, was a monk of Orbais. We suddenly find him asserting categorically that the reprobate have been predestined to damnation from eternity. Raban and the Synod of Mentz condemned this doctrine. Hincmar and the Synod of Quiercy condemn it also; and Pardulus, bishop of Laon, writes against it. Then Lupus writes, if not in defence of Gotteschalc, at least not in accordance with Hincmar, who, in distress for a champion, has recourse to no other than Erigena, and Erigena, as might be expected from what has been said above, proceeds to commit himself to an extreme doctrine of universalism, as Gotteschalc had to an extreme predestinarianism. Upon this, Florus and Prudentius write against Erigena; and Remigius, explaining or espousing the thesis of Gotteschalc, writes against the three Epistles of Raban, Hincmar, and Pardulus. Hincmar replies in a second Synod of Quiercy; and the Bishops of Lorraine rejoin in the Synod of Valence. The controversy ceases rather than terminates at the Synod of Savonnières, in which all parties were represented, and in which four important articles were received, bearing indirectly on the subject of dispute, but leaving without distinct notice the original position of Gotteschalc.

[1] *Vid.* Rather. Ep. apud Dach. Spic., t. i., p. 375.

In the Eucharistic controversy, which lasted through several centuries, the Benedictine Paschasius, supported by Haimo, Hincmar, and Ratherius, expounded the traditionary doctrine afterwards defined: but his statements were met by the dissent, or the hesitation, as it would appear, of men of his own schools, Raban, Ratramn, Amalarius, Heribald, Heriger, Druthmar, and Florus. At the end of two centuries indeed appeared the great Benedictines Lanfranc and Anselm, who dealt successfully with this as well as other controversies. But it must be recollected that, though their school of Bec is confessedly the historical fountain-head of the new theology which was making its way into Christendom, it is as far from a specimen of the Benedictine character in matters of teaching, as imperial minds such as their brother-monk and contemporary, Hildebrand, can be considered in ecclesiastical politics.

7

AND THUS THE PERIOD, properly Benedictine, ended; this honour being shown by Providence to the great Order from which it is named, in reward for its long and patient services to religion, that, though its monks were not to be immediately employed by the Church in the special sense in which they had been her ministers for some hundreds of years, still they should be the first to point out, and that they should hansel, those new weapons, which Orders of a different genius were destined to wield against a new description of opponents.

Nor is it without significancy that the Anglo-Saxon Church, itself the creation of the Benedictines, and the seat from which their influence went out for the education or conversion of Europe, from the Baltic to the Bay of Biscay, should have its share in this honour; and that, as Theodore was brought all the way from Tarsus to Canterbury, so Lanfranc from Lombardy and Anselm from Piedmont should successively fill the archiepiscopal throne of Theodore.

IV

AN INTERNAL ARGUMENT FOR CHRISTIANITY

AN INTERNAL ARGUMENT FOR CHRISTIANITY

THE WORD "REMARKABLE" has been so hacked of late in theological criticism—nearly as much so as "earnest" and "thoughtful"—that we do not like to apply it without an apology to the instance of a recent work, called *Ecce Homo*, which we propose now to bring before the reader. In truth, it presents itself as a very convenient epithet, whenever we do not like to commit ourselves to any definite judgment on any subject before us, and prefer to spread over it a broad neutral tint to painting it distinctly white, red, or black. A man, or his work, or his deed, is "remarkable" when he produces an effect; be he effective for good or for evil, for truth or for falsehood—a point which, as far as that expression goes, we by adopting it, leave it for others or for the future to determine. Accordingly it is just the word to use in the instance of a Volume in which what is trite and what is novel, what is striking and what is startling, what is sound and what is untrustworthy, what is deep and what is shallow, are so mixed up together, or at least so vaguely suggested, or so perplexingly confessed,—which has so much of occasional force and circumambient glitter, of pretence and of seriousness,—as to make it impossible either with a good conscience to praise it, or without harshness and unfairness to condemn. Such a book is at least likely to be effective, whatever else it is or is not; it may be safely called remarkable; and therefore we apply the epithet "remarkable" to this *Ecce Homo*.

It is remarkable, then, on account of the sensation which it has made in religious circles. In the course of a few months it has reached a third edition, though it is a fair-sized octavo, and not an over-cheap one. And it has received the praise of critics and reviewers of very distinct shades of opinion. Such a reception must be owing either to the book itself, or to the circumstances of the day in which it has appeared, or to both of these causes together. Or, as seems to be the case, the needs of the day have become a call for some such work; and the work, on its appearance, has been thankfully welcomed, on account of its professed object, by those whose needs called for it. The author includes himself in the number of these; and while providing for his own wants he has ministered to theirs. This is what we especially mean by calling his book "remarkable." It deserves remark, because it has excited it.

I

Disputants may maintain, if they please, that religious doubt is our appropriate, our normal state; that to cherish doubts is our duty; that to complain of them is impatience; that to dread them is cowardice; that to overcome them is inveracity; that it is even a happy state, a state of calm philosophic enjoyment, to be conscious of them;—but after all, unavoidable or not, such a state is not natural, and not happy, if the voice of mankind is to decide the question. English minds, in particular, have too much of a religious temper in them, as a natural gift, to acquiesce for any long time in positive, active doubt. For doubt and devotion are incompatible with each other; every doubt, be it greater or less, stronger or weaker, involuntary as well as voluntary, acts upon devotion, so far forth, as water sprinkled, or dashed, or poured out upon a flame. Real and proper doubt kills faith, and devotion with it; and even involuntary or half-deliberate doubt, though it does not actually kill faith, goes far to kill devotion; and religion without devotion is little better than a burden, and soon becomes a superstition. Since, then, this is a day of objection and of doubt about the intellectual basis of Revealed Truth, it follows that there is a great deal of secret discomfort and distress in the religious portion of the community, the result of that general curiosity in speculation and inquiry which has been the growth among us of the last twenty or thirty years.

The people of this country, being Protestants, appeal to Scripture, when a religious question arises, as their ultimate informant and decisive authority in all such matters; but who is to decide for them the previous question, that Scripture is really such an authority? When, then, as at this time, its divine authority is the very point to be determined, that is, the character and extent of its inspiration and its component parts, then they find themselves at sea, without the means of directing their course. Doubting about the authority of Scripture, they doubt about its substantial truth; doubting about its truth, they have doubts concerning the Object which it sets before their faith, about the historical accuracy and objective reality of the picture which it presents to us of our Lord. We are not speaking of wilful doubting, but of those painful misgivings, greater or less, to which we have already referred. Religious Protestants, when they think calmly on the subject, can hardly conceal from themselves that they have a house without logical foundations, which contrives indeed for the present to stand, but which may go any day,—and where are they then?

Of course Catholics will bid them receive the canon of Scripture on the authority of the Church, in the spirit of St. Augustine's well-known words: "I should not believe the Gospel, were I not moved by the authority of the Catholic Church." But who, they ask, is to be voucher in turn for the Church, and for St. Augustine?—is it not as difficult to prove the authority of the Church and her doctors as the authority of the Scriptures? We Catholics answer, and with reason, in the negative; but, since they cannot be brought to agree with us here, what argumentative ground is open to them? Thus they seem drifting, slowly perhaps, but surely, in the direction of scepticism.

2

IT IS UNDER THESE CIRCUMSTANCES that they are invited, in the Volume of which we have spoken, to betake themselves to the contemplation of our Lord's character, as it is recorded by the Evangelists, as carrying with it its own evidence, dispensing with extrinsic proof, and claiming authoritatively by itself the faith and devotion of all to whom it is presented. Such an argument, of course, is as old as Christianity itself; the young man in the Gospel calls our Lord "Good Master," and St. Peter introduces Him to the first Gentile converts as one who "went about doing good;" and in these last times we can refer to the testimony even of unbelievers in behalf of an argument which is as simple as it is constraining. *"Si la vie et la mort de Socrate sont d'un sage,"* says Rousseau, *"la vie et la mort de Jésus sont d'un Dieu."* And he clenches the argument by observing, that were the picture a mere conception of the sacred writers, *"l'inventeur en serait plus étonnant que le héros."* The force of this argument lies in its directness; it comes to the point at once, and concentrates in itself evidence, doctrine, and devotion. In theological language, it is the *motivum credibilitatis,* the *objectum materiale,* and the *formale,* all in one; it unites human reason and supernatural faith in one complex act; and it comes home to all men, educated and ignorant, young and old. And it is the point to which, after all and in fact, all religious minds tend, and in which they ultimately rest, even if they do not start from it. Without an intimate apprehension of the personal character of our Saviour, what professes to be faith is little more than an act of ratiocination. If faith is to live, it must love; it must lovingly live in the Author of faith as a true and living Being, *in Deo vivo et vero;* according to the saying of the Samaritans to their townswoman: "We now believe, not for thy saying, for we ourselves have heard Him." Many doctrines may be held implicitly; but to see Him as if intuitively is the very promise and gift of Him who is the object of the intuition. We are constrained to believe when it is He that speaks to us about Himself.

Such undeniably is the characteristic of divine faith viewed in itself: but here we are concerned, not simply with faith, but with its logical antecedents; and the question returns on which we have already touched, as a difficulty with Protestants,—how can our Lord's Life, as recorded in the Gospels, be a logical ground of faith, unless we set out with assuming the truth of those Gospels; that is, without assuming, as proved, the original matter of doubt? And Protestant apologists, it may be urged—Paley, for instance—show their sense of this difficulty when they place the argument drawn from our Lord's character only among the auxiliary Evidences of Christianity. Now the following answer may fairly be made to this objection; nor need we grudge Protestants the use of it, for, as will appear in the sequel, it proves too much for their purpose, as being an argument for the divinity not only of Christ's mission, but of that of His Church also. However, we say this by the way.

It may be maintained then, that, making as large an allowance as the most sceptical mind, when pressed to state its demands in full, would desire, we are at least safe in asserting that the books of the New Testament, taken as a whole, were existing about the middle of the second century, and were then received by Christians, or were in the way of being received, and nothing else but they were received, as the authoritative record of the origin and rise of their Religion. In that first age they were the only account of the mode in which Christianity was introduced to the world. Internal as well as external evidence sanctions us in so speaking. Four Gospels, the book of the Acts of the Apostles, various Apostolic writings, made up then, as now, our sacred books. Whether there was a book more or less, say even an important book, does not affect the general character of the Religion as those books set it forth. Omit one or other of the Gospels, and three or four Epistles, and the outline and nature of its objects and its teaching remain what they were before the omission. The moral peculiarities, in particular, of its Founder are, on the whole, identical, whether we learn them from St. Matthew, St. John, St. Peter, or St. Paul. He is not in one book a Socrates, in another a Zeno, and in a third an Epicurus. Much less is the religion changed or obscured by the loss of particular chapters or verses, or even by inaccuracy in fact, or by error in opinion, (supposing *per impossibile* such a charge could be made good,) in particular portions of a book. For argument's sake, suppose that the three first Gospels are an accidental collection of traditions or legends, for which no one is responsible, and in which Christians had faith because there was nothing else to put faith in. This is the limit to which extreme scepticism can proceed, and we are willing to commence our argument by granting it. Still, starting at this disadvantage, we should be prepared to argue, that if, in spite of this, and after all, there be shadowed out in these anonymous and fortuitous documents a Teacher *sui generis*, distinct, consistent, and original, then does that picture, thus accidentally resulting, for the very reason of its accidental composition, only become more marvellous; then is He an historical fact, and again a supernatural or divine fact;—historical from the consistency of the representation, and because the time cannot be assigned when it was not received as a reality; and supernatural, in proportion as the qualities with which He is invested in those writings are incompatible with what it is reasonable or possible to ascribe to human nature viewed simply in itself. Let these writings be as open to criticism, whether as to their origin or their text, as sceptics can maintain; nevertheless the representation in question is there, and forces upon the mind a conviction that it records a fact, and a superhuman fact, just as the reflection of an object in a stream remains in its general form, however rapid the current, and however many the ripples, and is a sure warrant to us of the presence of the object on the bank, though that object be out of sight.

3

SUCH, WE CONCEIVE, though stated in our own words, is the argument drawn out in the pages before us, or rather such is the ground on which the argument is raised; and the interest which it has excited lies, not in its novelty, but in the particular mode in which it is brought before the reader, in the originality and precision of certain strokes by which is traced out for us the outline of the Divine Teacher. These strokes are not always correct; they are sometimes gratuitous, sometimes derogatory to their object; but they are always determinate; and, being such, they present an old argument before us with a certain freshness, which, because it is old, is necessary for its being effective.

We do not wonder at all, then, at the sensation which the Volume is said to have caused at Oxford, and among Anglicans of the Oxford school, after the wearisome doubt and disquiet of the last ten years; for it has opened the prospect of a successful issue of inquiries in an all-important province of thought, where there seemed to be no thoroughfare. Distinct as are the liberal and Catholicizing parties in the Anglican Church both in their principles and their policy, it must not be supposed that they are also as distinct in the members that compose them. No line of demarcation can be drawn between the one collection of men and the other, in fact; for no two minds are altogether alike; and individually, Anglicans have each his own shade of opinion, and belong partly to this school, partly to that. Or rather, there is a large body of men who are neither the one nor the other; they cannot be called an intermediate party, for they have no discriminating watchwords; they range from those who are almost Catholic to those who are almost Liberals. They are not Liberals, because they do not glory in a state of doubt; they cannot profess to be

"Anglo-Catholics," because they are not prepared to give an internal assent to all that is put forth by the Church as truth of revelation. These are the men who, if they could, would unite old ideas with new; who cannot give up tradition, yet are loth to shut the door to progress; who look for a more exact adjustment of faith with reason than has hitherto been attained; who love the conclusions of Catholic theology better than the proofs, and the methods of modern thought better than its results; and who, in the present wide unsettlement of religious opinion, believe indeed, or wish to believe, Scripture and orthodox doctrine, taken as a whole, and cannot get themselves to avow any deliberate dissent from any part of either, but still, not knowing how to defend their belief with logical exactness, or at least feeling that there are large unsatisfied objections lying against parts of it, or having misgivings lest there should be such, acquiesce in what is called a practical belief, that is, accept revealed truths, only because such acceptance of them is the safest course, because they are probable, and because to hold them in consequence is a duty, not as if they felt absolutely certain, though they will not allow themselves to be actually in doubt. Such is about the description to be given of them as a class; though, as we have said, they so materially differ from each other, that no general account of them will apply strictly to any individual in their body.

Now, it is to this large class which we have been describing that such a work as that before us, in spite of the serious errors which they will not be slow to recognize in it, comes as a friend in need. They do not stumble at the author's inconsistencies or shortcomings; they are arrested by his professed purpose, and are profoundly moved by his successful hits (as they may be called) towards fulfilling it. Remarks on the Gospel history, such as Paley's, they feel to be casual and superficial; such as Rousseau's to be vague and declamatory; they wish to justify with their intellect all that they believe with their heart; they cannot separate their ideas of religion from its revealed Object; but they have an aching dissatisfaction within them, that they should be apprehending Him so feebly, when they should fain (as it were) see and touch Him as well as hear. When, then, they have logical grounds presented to them for holding that the recorded picture of our Lord is its own evidence, that it carries with it its own reality and authority, that His *revelatio* is *revelata* in the very act of being a *revelatio,* it is as if He Himself said to them, as He once said to His disciples, "It is I, be not afraid"; and the clouds at once clear off, and the waters subside, and the land is gained for which they are looking out.

The author before us, then, has the merit of promising what, if he could fulfil it, would entitle him to the gratitude of thousands. We do not say, we are very far from thinking that he has actually accomplished so high an enterprise, though he seems to be ambitious enough to hope that he has not come far short of it. He somewhere calls his book a treatise; he would have done better to call it an essay; nor need he have been ashamed of a word which Locke has used in his work on the Human Understanding. Before concluding, we shall take occasion to express our serious sense, how very much his execution falls below his purpose; but certainly it is a great purpose which he sets before him, and for that he is to be praised. And there is at least this singular merit in his performance, as he has given it to the public, that he is clear-sighted and fair enough to view our Lord's work in its true light, as including in it the establishment of a visible Kingdom or Church. In proportion, then, as we shall presently find it our duty to pass some severe remarks upon his Volume, as it comes before us, so do we feel bound, before doing so, to give some specimens of it in that point of view in which we consider it really to subserve the cause of Revealed Truth. And in the sketch which we are now about to give of the first steps of his investigation, we must not be understood to make him responsible for the language in which we shall exhibit them to our readers, and which will unavoidably involve our own corrections of his argument, and our own colouring.

4

AMONG A PEOPLE, THEN, accustomed by the most sacred traditions of their Religion to a belief in the appearance, from time to time, of divine messengers for their instruction and reformation, and to the expectation of One such messenger still to come, the last and greatest of all, who should also be their king and deliverer as well as their teacher, suddenly is found, after a long break in the succession, and a period of national degradation, a prophet of the old stamp, in one of the deserts of the country—John, the son af Zachary. He announces the promised kingdom as close at hand, calls his countrymen to repentance, and institutes a rite symbolical of it. The people seem disposed to take him for the destined Saviour; but, instead, he points out to them a private person in the crowd which is flocking about him; and henceforth the interest which his own preaching has excited centres in that Other. Thus our Lord is introduced to the notice of His countrymen.

Thus brought before the world, He opens His mission. What is the first impression it makes upon us? Admiration of its singular simplicity and directness, both as to object and work. Such of course ought to be its character, if it was to be the fulfilment of the ancient, long-expected promise; and such it was, as our Lord proclaimed it. Other men, who do a work, do not at once set about it as their object; they make several failures; they are led on to it by circumstances; they miscalculate their powers; or they are drifted from the first in a different direction from that which they had chosen; they do most where they are expected to do least. But our Lord said and did. "He formed one plan and executed it" (p. 18).

In the next place, what was that plan? Let us consider the force of the words in which, as the Baptist before Him, He introduced His ministry: "The kingdom of God is at hand." What was meant by the kingdom of God? "The conception was no new one, but familiar to every Jew" (p. 19). At the first formation of the nation and state of the Israelites, the Almighty had been their King; when a line of earthly kings was introduced, then God spoke by the prophets. The existence of the theocracy was the very constitution and boast of Israel, as limited monarchy, liberty, and equality are the boast respectively of certain modern nations. Moreover, the Gospel proclamation ran, "*Pœnitentiam agite;* for the kingdom of heaven is at hand:" here again was another and recognized token of a theophany; for the mission of a prophet, as we have said above, was commonly a call to reformation and expiation of sin.

A divine mission, then, was a falling back upon the original covenant between God and His people; but again, while it was an event of old and familiar occurrence, it ever had carried with it in its past instances something new in connexion with the circumstances under which it took place. The prophets were accustomed to give interpretations, or to introduce modifications of the letter of the Law, to add to its conditions and to enlarge its application. It was to be expected, then, that now, when the new Prophet to whom the Baptist pointed, opened His Commission, He too, in like manner, would be found to be engaged in a restoration, but in a restoration which should be a religious advance; and that the more, if He really was the special, final Prophet of the theocracy, to whom all former prophets had looked forward, and in whom their long and august line was to be summed up and perfected. In proportion as His work was to be more signal, so would His new revelations be wider and more wonderful.

Did our Lord fulfil these expectations? Yes; there was this peculiarity in His mission, that He came, not only as one of the prophets in the kingdom of God, but as the King Himself of that kingdom. Thus His mission involves the most exact return to the original polity of Israel, which the appoinment of Saul had disarranged, while it recognizes also the line of Prophets, and infuses a new spirit into the Law. Throughout His ministry our Lord claimed and received the title of King, which no prophet ever had done before. On His birth, the wise men came to worship "the King of the Jews." "Thou art the Son of God, Thou art the King of Israel," cried Nathaniel after His baptism; and on His cross the charge recorded against Him was that He professed to be "King of the Jews." "During His whole public life," says the author, "He is distinguished from the other prominent characters of Jewish history by His unbounded personal pretensions. He claims expressly the character of that Divine Messiah for which the ancient prophets had directed the nation to look."—P. 25.

He is, then, a King, as well as a Prophet; but is He as one of the old heroic kings, David or Solomon? Had such been His pretension, He had not, in His own words, "discerned the signs of the times." It would have been a false step in Him, into which other would-be champions of Israel, before and after Him, actually fell, and in consequence failed. But here this young Prophet is from the first distinct, decided, and original. His contemporaries, indeed, the wisest, the most experienced, were wedded to the notion of a revival of the barbaric kingdom. "Their heads were full of the languid dreams of commentators, the unpracticable pedantries of men who live in the past" (p. 27). But He gave to the old prophetic promises an interpretation which they could undeniably bear, but which they did not immediately suggest; which we can maintain to be true, while we can deny it to be imperative. He had His own prompt, definite conception of the restored theocracy; it was His own, and not another's; it was suited to the new age; it was triumphantly carried out in the event.

5

IN WHAT, THEN, did He consider His royalty to consist? First, what was it not? It did not consist in the ordinary functions of royalty; it did not prevent His payment of tribute to Cæsar; it did not make Him a judge in questions of criminal or of civil law, in a question of adultery, or in the adjudication of an inheritance; nor did it give Him the command of armies. Then perhaps, after all, it was but a figurative royalty, as when the Eridanus is called "*fluviorum rex*," or Aristotle "the prince of philosophers." No; it was not a figurative royalty either. To call oneself a king, without being one, is playing with edged tools—as in the story of the innkeeper's son, who was put to death for calling himself "heir to the crown." Christ certainly knew what He was saying. "He had provoked the accusation of rebellion against the Roman government: He must have known that the language He used would be interpreted so. Was there then nothing substantial in the royalty He claimed? Did He die for a metaphor?" (p. 28). He meant what He said, and therefore His kingdom was literal and real; it was visible; but what were its visible prerogatives, if they were not those in which earthly royalty commonly consists? In truth, He passed by the lesser powers of royalty to claim the higher. He claimed certain divine and transcendent functions of the original theocracy, which had been in abeyance since that theocracy had been infringed, which even to David had not been delegated, which had never been exercised except by the Almighty. God had created, first the people, next the state, which He deigned to govern. "The origin of other nations is lost in antiquity" (p. 33); but "this people," runs the sacred word, "have I formed for Myself." And "He who first called the nation did for it the second work of a king: He gave it a law" (p. 34). Now it is very striking to observe that these two incommunicable attributes of divine royalty, as exemplified in the history of the Israelites, are the very two which our Lord assumed. He was the Maker and the Law-giver of His subjects. He said in the commencement of His ministry, "*Follow* Me;" and He added, "and I will make you" —you in turn—"fishers of men." And the next we read of Him is, that His disciples came to Him on the Mount, and He opened His mouth and *taught* them. And so again, at the end of it, "Go ye, make *disciples* of all nations, *teaching* them." "Thus the very works for which the [Jewish] nation chiefly hymned their Jehovah, He undertook in His name to do. He undertook to be the Father of an everlasting state, and the Legislator of a world-wide society" (p. 36); that is, showing Himself, according to the prophetic announcement, to be *Admirabilis, consiliarius, pater futuri sæculi, princeps pacis.*

To these two claims He added a third: first, He chooses the subjects of His kingdom; next, He gives them a law; but thirdly, He judges them—judges them in a far truer and fuller sense than in the old kingdom even the Almighty judged His people. The God of Israel ordained national rewards and punishments for national obedience or transgression; He did not judge His subjects one by one; but our Lord takes upon Himself the supreme and final judgment of every one of His subjects, not to speak of the whole human race (though, from the nature of the case, this function cannot belong to His present visible kingdom). "He considered, in short, heaven and hell to be in His hand" (p. 40).

We shall mention one further function of the new King and His new kingdom: its benefits are even bound up with the maintenance of this law of political unity. "To organize a society, and to bind the members of it together by the closest ties, were the business of His life. For this reason it was that He called men away from their homes, imposed upon some a wandering life, upon others the sacrifice of their property, and endeavoured by all means to divorce them from their former connexions, in order that they might find a new home in the Church. For this reason He instituted a solemn initiation, and for this reason He refused absolutely to any one a dispensation from it. For this reason, too . . . He established a common feast, which was through all ages to remind Christians of their indissoluble union" (p. 92). But *cui bono* is a visible kingdom, when the great end of our Lord's ministry is moral advancement and preparation for a future state? It is easy to understand, for instance, how a sermon may benefit, or personal example, or religious friends, or household piety. We can learn to imitate a saint or a martyr, we can cherish a lesson, we can study a treatise, we can obey a rule; but what is the definite advantage to a preacher or a moralist of an external organization, of a visible kingdom? Yet Christ says, "Seek ye *first* the kingdom of God," as well as "His justice." Socrates wished to improve man, but he laid no stress on their acting in concert in order to secure that improvement; on the contrary, the Christian law is political, as certainly as it is moral.

Why is this? It arises out of the intimate relation between Him and His subjects, which, in bringing them all to Him as their common Father, necessarily brings them to each other. Our Lord says, "Where two or three are gathered together in My name, I am in the midst of them." Fellowship between His followers is made a distinct object and duty, because it is a means, according to the provisions of His system, by which in some special way they are brought near to Him. This is declared, still more strikingly than in the text we have just quoted, in the parable of the Vine and its Branches, and in that (if it is to be called a parable) of the Bread of Life. The almighty King of Israel was ever, indeed, invisibly present in the glory above the Ark, but He did not manifest Himself there or anywhere else as a present cause of spiritual strength to His people; but the new King is not only ever present, but to every one of His subjects individually is He a first element and perennial source of life. He is not only the head of His kingdom, but also its animating principle and its centre of power. The author whom we are reviewing does not quite reach the great doctrine here suggested, but he goes near it in the following passage: "Some men have appeared who have been 'as levers to uplift the earth and roll it in another course.' Homer by creating literature, Socrates by creating science, Cæsar by carrying civilization inland from the shores of the Mediterranean, Newton by starting science upon a career of steady progress, may be said to have attained this eminence. But these men gave a single impact like that which is conceived to have first set the planets in motion. Christ claims to be a perpetual attractive power, like the sun, which determines their orbit. They contributed to men some discovery, and passed away; Christ's discovery is Himself. To humanity struggling with its passions and its destiny He says, Cling to Me;—cling ever closer to Me. If we believe St. John, He represented Himself as the Light of the world, as the Shepherd of the souls of men, as the Way to immortality, as the Vine or Life-tree of humanity" (p. 177). He ends this beautiful passage, of which we have quoted as much as our limits allow, by saying that "He instructed His followers to hope for life from feeding on His Body and Blood."

6

O SI SIC OMNIA! Is it not hard, that, after following with pleasure a train of thought so calculated to warm all Christian hearts, and to create in them both admiration and sympathy for the writer, we must end our notice of him in a different tone, and express as much dissent from him and as serious blame of him as we have hitherto been showing satisfaction with his object, his intention, and the general outline of his argument? But so it is. In what remains to be said we are obliged to speak of his work in terms so sharp that they may seem to be out of keeping with what has gone before. With whatever abruptness, we must suddenly shift the scene, and manifest our disapprobation of portions of his book as plainly as we have shown an interest in it. We have praised it in various points of view. It has stirred the hearts of many; it has recognized a need, and gone in the right direction for supplying it. It serves as a token, and a hopeful token, of what is going on in the minds of numbers of men external to the Church. It is so far a good book, and, we trust, will work for good. Especially as we have seen, is it interesting to the Catholic, as acknowledging the visible Church to be our Lord's own creation, as the direct fruit of His teaching, and the destined instrument of His purposes. We do not know how to speak in an unfriendly tone of an author who has done so much as this; but at the same time, when we come to examine his argument in its details, and study his chapters one by one, we find, in spite of, and mixed up with, what is true and original, and even putting aside his patent theological errors, so much bad logic, so much of rash and gratuitous assumption, so much of half-digested thought, that we are obliged to conclude that it would have been much wiser in him, instead of publishing what he seems to confess, or rather to proclaim, to be the jottings of his first researches upon sacred territory, to have waited till he had carefully traversed and surveyed and mapped the whole of it. We now proceed to give a few instances of the faults of which we complain.

His opening remarks will serve as an illustration. In p. 41 he says, "We have not rested upon *single* passages, nor drawn from the *fourth Gospel*." This, we suppose, must be his reason for ignoring the passage in Luke ii. 49: "Did you not know that I must be about My Father's business?" for he directly contradicts it, by gratuitously imagining that our Lord came for St. John's baptism with the same intention as the penitents around Him; and that, in spite of His own words, which we suppose are to be taken as another "single passage," "So it becometh us to fulfil all justice" (Matt. iii. 15). It must be on this principle of ignoring single passages such as these, even though they admit of combination, that he goes on to say of our Lord, that "in the agitation of mind caused by His baptism, and by the Baptist's designation of Him as the future Prophet, He retired into the wilderness," and there "He matured the plan of action which we see Him executing from the moment of His return into society" (p. 9); and that not till then was He "conscious of miraculous power" (p. 12). This neglect of the sacred text, we repeat, must be allowed him, we suppose, under cover of his acting out his rule of abstaining from single passages and from the fourth Gospel. Let us allow it; but at least he ought to adduce passages, single or many, for what he actually does assert. He must not be allowed arbitrarily to add to the history, as well as cautiously to take from it. Where, then, we ask, did he learn that our Lord's baptism caused Him "agitation of mind," that He "matured His plan of action in the wilderness," and that He then first was "conscious of miraculous power"?

But again: it seems he is not to refer to "single passages or the fourth Gospel"; yet, wonderful to say, he actually does open his formal discussion of the sacred history by referring to a passage from that very Gospel,—nay, to a particular text, which is not to be called "single," only because it is not so much as a single text, but an unfair half text, and half a text such, that, had he taken the whole of it, he would have been obliged to admit that the part which he puts aside just runs counter to his interpretation of the part which he recognizes. The words are these, as they stand in the Protestant version: "Behold the Lamb of God, which taketh away the sin of the world." Now, it is impossible to deny that "which taketh away," etc., fixes and limits the sense of "the Lamb of God"; but our author notices the latter half of the sentence, only in order to put aside the light which it throws upon the former half; and instead of the Baptist's own interpretation of the title which he gives to our Lord, he substitutes another, radically different, which he selects for himself out of one of the Psalms. He explains "the Lamb" by the well-known image, which represents the Almighty as a shepherd and His earthly servants as sheep—innocent, safe, and happy under His protection. "The Baptist's opinion of Christ's character, then," he says, "is summed up for us in the title he gives Him—the Lamb of God, taking away the sins of the world. There *seems* to be, in the last part of this description, an allusion to the usages of the Jewish sacrificial system; and, in order to explain it fully, it would be necessary to anticipate much which will come more conveniently later in this treatise. *But* when we remember that the Baptist's mind was *doubtless* full of imagery drawn from the Old Testament, and that the conception of a lamb of God makes the subject of one of the most striking of the Psalms, *we shall perceive what he meant to convey by this phrase*" (pp. 5, 6). This is like saying, to take a parallel instance, "Isaiah declares, 'Mine eyes have seen the King, the Lord of hosts;' *but,* considering that doubtless the prophet was well acquainted with the first and second books of Samuel, and that Saul, David, and Solomon are the three great kings there represented, we shall easily perceive that, by 'seeing the King,' he meant to say that he saw Uzziah, King of Judah, in the last year of whose reign he had the vision. As to the phrase 'the Lord of hosts,' which seems to refer to the Almighty, we will consider its meaning by-and-by";—but, in truth, it is difficult to invent a paralogism, in its gratuitous inconsecutiveness parallel to his own.

7

WE MUST OWN THAT, with every wish to be fair to this author, we never recovered from the perplexity of mind which this passage, in the very threshold of his book, inflicted on us. It needed not the various passages, constructed on the same argumentative model, which follow it in his work, to prove to us that he was not only an *incognito,* but an enigma. "Ergo," is the symbol of the logician:—what is the scientific method of a writer whose symbols, profusely scattered through his pages are "probably," "it must be," "doubtless," "on this hypothesis," "we may suppose," and "it is natural to think," and that at the very time that he pointedly discards the comments of school theologians? Is it possible that he can mean us to set aside, in his own favour, the glosses of all that went before him, and to exchange our old lamps for his new ones? Men have been at fault, when trying to determine whether he was an orthodox believer on his road to liberalism, or a liberal on his road to orthodoxy: this doubtless may be to some a perplexity; but our own difficulty is, whether he comes to us as an investigator or rather as a prophet, as one unequal or superior to the art of reasoning. Undoubtedly he is an able man; but what can he possibly mean by startling us with such eccentricities of argumentation as are quite familiar with him? Addison somewhere bids his readers bear in mind, that if he is ever especially dull, he always has a special reason for being so; and it is difficult to reconcile one's imagination to the supposition that this anonymous writer, with so much religious thought as he certainly evidences, is without some recondite reason for seeming so inconsequent, and does not move by some deep subterraneous process of investigation, which, if once brought to light, would clear him of the imputation of castle-building.

There is always a danger of misconceiving an author who has no antecedents by which we may measure him. Taking his work as it lies, we can but wish that he had kept his imagination under control; and that he had more of the hard head of a lawyer, and the patience of a philosopher. He writes like a man who cannot keep from telling the world his first thoughts, especially if they are clever or graceful; he has come for the first time upon a strange world, and his remarks upon it are too often obvious rather than striking, and crude rather than fresh. What can be more paradoxical than to interpret our Lord's words to Nicodemus, "Unless a man be born again," etc., as the necessity of external religion, and as a lesson to him to profess his faith openly and not to visit Him in secret? (p. 86). What can be more pretentious, not to say vulgar, than his paraphrase of St. John's passage about the woman taken in adultery? "In His burning embarrassment and confusion," he says, "He stooped down so as to hide His face. . . . They had a glimpse perhaps of the glowing blush upon His face," etc. (p. 104).

We should be very sorry to use a severe word concerning an honest inquirer after truth, as we believe this anonymous writer to be; but we will confess that Catholics, kindly as they may wish to feel towards him, are scarcely even able, from their very position, to give his work the enthusiastic reception which it has received from some other critics. The reason is plain; those alone can speak of it from a full heart, who feel a need, and recognize in it a supply of that need. We are not in the number of such; for they who have found, have no need to seek. Far be it from us to use language savouring of the leaven of the Pharisees. We are not assuming a high place, because we thus speak, or boasting of our security. Catholics are both deeper and shallower than Protestants; but in neither case have they any call for a treatise such as this *Ecce Homo.* If they live to the world and the flesh, then the faith which they profess, though it is true and distinct, is dead; and their certainty about religious truth, however firm and unclouded, is but shallow in its character, and flippant in its manifestations. And in proportion as they are worldly and sensual, will they be flippant and shallow.[1] But their faith is as indelible as the pigment which colours the skin, even though it is skin-deep. This class of Catholics is not likely to take interest in a pictorial *Ecce Homo.* On the other hand, where the heart is alive with divine love, faith is as deep as it is vigorous and joyous; and, as far as Catholics are in this condition, they will feel no drawing towards a work which is after all but an arbitrary and unsatisfactory dissection of the Object of their devotion. Faith, be it deep or shallow, does not need Evidences. That individual Catholics may be harassed with doubts, particularly in a day like this, we are not denying; but, viewed as a body, Catholics, from their religious condition, are either too deep or too shallow to suffer from those elementary difficulties, or that distress of mind, and need of argument, which serious Protestants so often experience.

[1] On this whole subject, *vide* "Difficulties felt by Anglicans," etc., Lecture IX.

We confess, then, as Catholics, to some unavoidable absence of cordial feeling in following the remarks of this author, though not to any want of real sympathy; and we seem to be justified in our indisposition by his manifest want of sympathy with us. If we feel distant towards him, his own language about Catholicity, and (what may be called) old Christianity, seems to show that that distance is one of fact, one of mental position, not any fault in ourselves. Is it not undeniable, that the very life of personal religion among Catholics lies in a knowledge of the Gospels? It is the character and conduct of our Lord, His words, His deeds, His sufferings, His work, which are the very food of our devotion and rule of our life. "Behold the Man," which this author feels to be an object novel enough to write a book about, has been the contemplation of Catholics from the first age when St. Paul said, "The life that I now live in the flesh, I live in the faith of the Son of God, who loved me, and delivered Himself for me." As the Psalms have ever been the manual of our prayer, so have the Gospels been the subject-matter of our meditation. In these latter times especially, since St. Ignatius, they have been divided into portions, and arranged in a scientific order, not unlike that which the Psalms have received in the Breviary. To contemplate our Lord in His person and His history is with us the exercise of every retreat, and the devotion of every morning. All this is certainly simple matter of fact; but the writer we are reviewing lives and thinks at so great a distance from us, as not to be cognizant of what is so patent and so notorious a truth. He seems to imagine that the faith of a Catholic is the mere profession of a formula. He deems it important to disclaim, in the outset of his work, all reference to the theology of the Church. He eschews with much precision, as something almost profane, the dogmatism of former ages. He wishes "to trace" our Lord's "biography from point to point, and accept those conclusions—not which Church doctors or even Apostles have sealed with their authority—but which the facts themselves critically weighed, appear to warrant."—(Preface.) Now, what Catholics, what Church doctors, as well as Apostles, have ever lived on, is not any number of theological canons or decrees, but, we repeat, the Christ Himself, as He is represented in concrete existence in the Gospels.[1] Theological determinations about our Lord are far more of the nature of landmarks or buoys to guide a discursive mind in its reasonings, than to assist a devotional mind in its worship. Common sense, for instance, tells us what is meant by the words, "My Lord and my God;" and a religious man, upon his knees, requires no commentator; but against irreligious speculators, Arius or Nestorius, a denunciation has been passed, in Ecumenical Council, when "science falsely so-called" encroached upon devotion. Has not this been insisted on by all dogmatic Christians over and over again? Is it not a representation as absolutely true as it is trite? We had fancied that Protestants generally allowed the touching beauty of Catholic hymns and meditations; and after all is there not That in all Catholic churches which goes beyond any written devotion, whatever its force or its pathos? Do we not believe in a Presence in the sacred Tabernacle, not as a form of words, or as a notion, but as an Object as real as we are real? And if before that Presence we need neither profession of faith nor even manual of devotion, what appetite can we have for the teaching of a writer who not only exalts his first thoughts about our Lord into professional lectures, but implies that the Catholic Church has never known how to point Him out to her children?

8

IT MAY BE OBJECTED, that we are making too much of so accidental a slight as is contained in his allusion to "Church doctors," especially as he mentions Apostles in connexion with them; but it would be affectation not to recognize in other places of his book an undercurrent of antagonism to us, of which the passage already quoted is but a first indication.

[1] *Vide* "Essay on Assent," ch. iv. and v.

Of course he has quite as much right as another to take up an anti-Catholic position, if he will; but we understand him to be putting forth an investigation, not a polemical argument: and if, instead of keeping his eyes directed towards his own proper subject, he looks to the right or left, hitting at those who view things differently from himself, he is damaging the ethical force of a composition which claims to be, and mainly is, a serious and manly search after religious truth. Why cannot he let us alone? Of course he cannot avoid seeing that the lines of his own investigation diverge from those drawn by others; but he will have enough to do in defending himself, without making others the object of his attack. He is virtually opposing Voltaire, Strauss, Renan, Calvin, Wesley, Chalmers, Erskine, and a host of other writers, but he does not denounce *them;* why then does he single out, misrepresent, and anathematize a main principle of Catholic orthodoxy. It is as if he could not keep his hand off us, when we crossed his path. We are alluding to the following magisterial passage:

"If He (our Lord) meant anything by His constant denunciation of hypocrites, there is nothing which He could have visited with sterner censure than that *short cut to belief* which many persons take, when, overwhelmed with difficulties which beset their minds, and afraid of damnation, they *suddenly* resolve to strive no longer, but, giving their minds a holiday, to rest content with *saying* that they believe, and acting *as if* they did. A melancholy end of Christianity indeed! Can there be such a disfranchised pauper class among the citizens of the New Jerusalem?" (p. 79).

He adds shortly afterwards:

"Assuredly, those who represent Christ as presenting to man an abstruse theology, and saying to them peremptorily, 'Believe or be damned,' have the coarsest conception of the Saviour of the world" (p. 80).

Thus he delivers himself: Believe or be damned is so detestable a doctrine, that if any man denies that it *is* detestable,

I pronounce him to be a hypocrite; to be without any true knowledge of the Saviour of the world; to be the object of His sternest censure; and to have no part or place in the Holy City, the New Jerusalem, the eternal Heaven above.—Pretty well for a virtuous hater of dogmatism! We hope we shall show less dictatorial arrogance than his in the answer which we proceed to make to him.

Whether or not there are persons such as he describes, Catholics, or, Protestant converts to Catholicism,—men who profess a faith which they do not believe, under the notion that they shall be eternally damned if they do not profess it without believing,—we really do not know—we never met with such; but since facts do not concern us here so much as principles, let us, for argument's sake, grant that there are such men. Our author believes they are not only "many," but enough to form a "class;" and he considers that they act in this preposterous manner under the sanction, and in accordance with the teaching, of the religious bodies to which they belong. Especially there is a marked allusion in his words to the Athanasian Creed and the Catholic Church. Now we answer him thus:

It is his charge against the teachers of dogma that they impose on men as a duty, instead of believing, to "act as if they did" believe:—now in fact this is the very kind of profession which, if it is all that a candidate has to offer, absolutely shuts him out from admission into Catholic communion. We suppose, that by belief of a thing this writer understands an inward conviction of its truth;—this being supposed, we plainly say that no priest is at liberty to receive a man into the Church who has not a real internal belief, and cannot say from his heart, that the things taught by the Church are true. On the other hand, as we have said above, it is the very characteristic of the profession of faith made by numbers of educated Protestants, and it is the utmost extent to which they are able to go in believing, to hold, not that Christian doctrine is certainly true, but that it has such a semblance of truth, it has such considerable marks of probability upon it, that it is their duty to accept and act upon it as if it were true beyond all question or doubt: and they justify themselves, and with much reason, by the authority of Bishop Butler. Undoubtedly, a religious man will be led to go as far as this, if he cannot go farther; but unless he can go farther, he is no catechumen of the Catholic Church. We wish all men to believe that her creed is true; but till they do so believe, we do not wish, we have no permission, to make them her members. Such a faith as this author speaks of to condemn—(our books call it "*practical* certitude")—does not rise to the level of the *sine qua non*, which is the condition prescribed for becoming a Catholic. Unless a convert so believes that he can sincerely say, "After all, in spite of all difficulties, objections, obscurities, mysteries, the creed of the Church undoubtedly comes from God, and is true, because He who gave it is the Truth," such a man, though he be outwardly received into her fold, will receive no grace from the sacraments, no sanctification in baptism, no pardon in penance, no life in communion. We are more consistently dogmatic than this author imagines; we do not enforce a principle by halves; if our doctrine is true, it must be received as such; if a man cannot so receive it, he must wait till he can. It would be better, indeed, if he now believed; but since he does not as yet, to wait is the best he can do under the circumstances. If we said anything else than this, certainly we should be, as the author thinks we are, encouraging hypocrisy. Nor let him turn round on us and say that by thus proceeding we are laying a burden on souls, and blocking up the entrance into that fold which was intended for all men, by imposing hard conditions on candidates for admission; for, as we shall now show, we have already implied a great principle, which is an answer to this objection, and which the Gospels exhibit and sanction, but which he absolutely ignores.

9

LET US AVAIL OURSELVES of his own quotation. The Baptist said, "Behold the Lamb of God." Again he says, "This is the Son of God." 'Two of his disciples heard him speak, and they followed Jesus." They believed John to be "a man sent from God" to teach them, and therefore they believed his word to be true. We suppose it was not hypocrisy in them to believe in John's word; rather they would have been guilty of gross inconsistency or hypocrisy, had they professed to believe that he was a divine messenger, and yet had refused to take his word concerning the Stranger whom he pointed out to their veneration. It would have been "saying that they believed," and *not* "acting as if they did;" which at least is not better than saying and acting. Now was not the announcement which John made to them "a short cut to belief"? and what the harm of it? They believed that our Lord was the promised Prophet, without making direct inquiry about Him, without a new inquiry, on the ground of a previous inquiry into the claims of John himself to be accounted a messenger from God. They had already accepted it as truth that John was a prophet; but again, what a prophet said must be true; else he would not be a prophet; now, John said that our Lord was the Lamb of God; this, then, certainly was a sacred truth.

Now it might happen, that they knew exactly and for certain what the Baptist meant in calling our Lord "a Lamb;" in that case they would believe Him to be that which they knew the figurative word meant, as used by the Baptist. But, as our author reminds us, the word has different senses; and though the Baptist explained his own sense of it on the first occasion of using it, by adding "that taketh away the sin of the world," yet when he spoke to the two disciples he did not thus explain it. Now let us suppose that they went off, taking the word each in his own sense, the one understanding by it a sacrificial lamb, the other a lamb of the fold; and let us suppose that, as they were on their way to our Lord's home, they became aware of this difference between their several impressions, and disputed with each other which was the right interpretation. It is clear that they would agree so far as this, viz., that, in saying that the proposition was true, they meant that it was true in that sense in which the Baptist spoke it, whatever that was; moreover, if it be worth noticing, they did after all even agree, in some vague way, about the meaning of the word, understanding that it denoted some high characteristic, or office, or ministry. Anyhow, it was absolutely true, they would say, that our Lord was a Lamb, whatever it meant; the word conveyed a great and momentous fact, and if they did not know what that fact was, the Baptist did, and they would accept it in its one right sense, as soon as he or our Lord told them what that was.

Again, as to that other title which the Baptist gave our Lord, "the Son of God," it admitted of half a dozen meanings. Wisdom was "the only begotten;" the Angels were the sons of God; Adam was a son of God; the descendants of Seth were sons of God; Solomon was a son of God; and so is "the just man." In which of these senses, or in what sense, was our Lord the Son of God? St. Peter, as the after-history shows us, knew, but there were those who did not know; the centurion who attended the crucifixion did not know, and yet he confessed that our Lord was the Son of God. He knew that our Lord had been condemned by the Jews for calling Himself the Son of God, and therefore he cried out, on seeing the miracles which attended his death, "Indeed this *was* the Son of God." His words evidently imply, "I do not know precisely what He meant by so calling Himself; but this I do know,–what He said He was, that He is; whatever He meant, I believe Him; I believe that His word about Himself is true, though I cannot prove it to be so, though I do not even understand it; I believe His word, for I believe *Him.*"

Now to return to the accusation which has led to these remarks. Our author says that certain persons are hypocrites, because they "take a short cut to belief, suddenly resolving to strive no longer, but to rest content with saying they believe." Does he mean by "a short cut," believing on the word of another? As far as we see, he can mean nothing else; yet how *can* he really mean this and mean to blame this, with the Gospels before him? He cannot mean it, if he pays any deference to the Gospels, because the very staple of the sacred narrative, from beginning to end, is a call on all men to believe what is not proved, not plain, to them, on the warrant of divine messengers; because the very form of our Lord's teaching is to substitute authority for argument; because the very principle of His grave earnestness, the very key to His regenerative mission, is the intimate connexion of faith with salvation. Faith is not simply trust in His legislation, as the writer says; it is definitely trust in His word, whether that word be about heavenly things or earthly; whether it is spoken by His own mouth, or through His ministers. The Angel who announced the Baptist's birth, said, "Thou shalt be dumb, because thou believest not my words." The Baptist's mother said of Mary, "Blessed is she that believed." The Baptist himself said, "He that believeth on the Son hath everlasting life; and he that believeth not the Son shall not see life, but the wrath of God abideth on him." Our Lord, in turn said to Nicodemus, "We speak that we do know, and ye receive not our witness; he that believeth not is condemned already, because he hath not believed in the Name of the Only-begotten Son of God." To the Jews, "He that heareth My word, and believeth on Him that sent Me, shall not come into condemnation." To the Capharnaites, "He that believeth on Me hath everlasting life." To St. Thomas, "Blessed are they that have not seen, and yet have believed." And to the Apostles, "Preach the Gospel to every creature; he that believeth not shall be damned."

How is it possible to deny that our Lord, both in the text and in the context of these and other passages, made faith in a message, on the warrant of the messenger, to be a condition of salvation, and enforced it by the great grant of power which He emphatically conferred on His representatives? "Whosoever shall not receive you," He says, "nor hear your words, when ye depart, shake off the dust of your feet." "It is not ye that speak, but the Spirit of your Father." "He that heareth you, heareth Me; he that despiseth you, despiseth Me; and he that despiseth Me, despiseth Him that sent me." "I pray for them that shall believe on Me through their word." "Whose sins ye remit, they are remitted unto them; and whose sins ye retain, they are retained." "Whatsoever ye shall bind on earth shall be bound in heaven." "I will give unto thee the keys of the kingdom of heaven; and whatsoever thou shalt bind on earth shall be bound in heaven, and whatsoever thou shalt loose on earth shall be loosed in heaven." These characteristic and critical announcements have no place in this author's gospel; and let it be understood, that we are not asking why he does not determine the exact doctrines contained in them—for that is a question which he has reserved (if we understand him) for a future Volume—but why he does not recognize the principle they involve—for that is a matter which falls within his present subject.

10

It is not well to exhibit some sides of Christianity, and not others; this we think is the main fault of the author we have been reviewing. It does not pay to be eclectic in so serious a matter of fact. He does not overlook, he boldly confesses, that a visible organized Church was a main part of our Lord's plan for the regeneration of mankind. "As with Socrates," he says, "argument is everything, and personal authority nothing; so with Christ, personal authority is all in all, and argument altogether unemployed" (p. 94). Our Lord rested His teaching, not on the concurrence and testimony of His hearers, but on His own authority. He imposed upon them the declarations of a Divine Voice. Why does this author stop short in the delineation of principles which he has so admirably begun? Why does he denounce "short cuts," as a mental disfranchisement, when no cut can be shorter than to "believe and be saved"? Why does he denounce religious fear as hypocritical, when it is written, "He that believeth not shall be damned"? Why does he call it dishonest in a man to sacrifice his own judgment to the word of God, when, unless he did so, he would be avowing that the Creator knew less than the creature? Let him recollect that no two thinkers, philosophers, writers, ever did, ever will agree, in all things with each other. No system of opinions, ever given to the world, approved itself in all its parts to the reason of any one individual by whom it was mastered. No revelation then is conceivable, which does not involve, almost in its very idea as being something new, a collision with the human intellect, and demands accordingly, if it is to be accepted, a sacrifice of private judgment on the part of those to whom it is addressed. If a revelation be necessary, then also in consequence is that sacrifice necessary. One man will have to make a sacrifice in one respect, another in another, all men in some.

We say, then, to men of the day, Take Christianity, or leave it; do not practise upon it; to do so is as unphilosophical as it is dangerous. Do not attempt to halve a spiritual unit. You are apt to call it a dishonesty in us to refuse to follow out our reasonings, when faith stands in the way; is there no intellectual dishonesty in your self-trust? First, your very accusation of us is dishonest; for you keep in the background the circumstance, of which you are well aware, that such a refusal on our part to back Reason against Faith, is the necessary consequence of our accepting an authoritative Revelation; and next you profess to accept that Revelation yourselves, whilst you dishonestly pick and choose, and take as much or as little of it as you please. You either accept Christianity, or you do not: if you do, do not garble and patch it; if you do not, suffer others to submit to it ungarbled.

June, 1866.

INDEX